WE ALL MUST PRAISE GODZILLA!

Yikes! This new issue boasts loads of mouth-wateringly marvellous Godzilla-related contents, plus a massive celebration of the bloody cult classic *Shogun Assassin*, and other goodies too, including reviews of such entertaining movies as *The Last Sacrifice*, *River of Blood*, and the gill-man picture *Monster Island*.

Some of these articles originally appeared in issue 2 of *Film Frenzy*, a magazine I edited and co-published through *Eastern Heroes*. Now that I'm running my own publication, I wanted to share some of those contents, notably the *Shogun Assassin* features, because, well, I really love them, especially the interviews with two key figures connected to the making of the movie: Jim Evans and Gibran Evans. Hopefully more folks will now get the chance to read and enjoy this material.

The most fun I've had with this issue is getting a whole bunch of creative people - writers, directors, actors and so on - to choose their favourite Godzilla movie and write something about it. As *Godzilla Minus One* is such a classic of its kind, that particular film was chosen a few times, which is no surprise because it is a stonkingly marvellous Big G film, but rest assured that a wonderful selection of other Godzilla productions have also been picked and praised by the likes of director Hans Kaufmann and writer Diallo Jackson. This is your chance to discover which Godzilla film inspired a young Joe Castro to become a special FX artist, which kaiju movie gem is loved by *The Dark Side* editor Allan Bryce, and what memories were triggered when director Mark Duffield reminisced about his visit to the cinema as a kid to watch the Showa era Godzilla film *Monsters from an Unknown Planet*.

All in all, there are 51 pages devoted to Godzilla, and another 40 pages are given over to honouring *Shogun Assassin* and the *Lone Wolf and Cub* films & comics that came before it! Also look out for the 4-page piece on the work of comic book artist Russell Fox. His illustrations have adorned the pages of *Imaginator* before and I'm sure they will again!

Oh, and thanks must go out to Johnny Burnett, the YouTube reviewer known as the Fanatical Dragon, for penning his article looking at Godzilla films on 4K and Blu-ray. Johnny's feature on *Lone Wolf and Cub* Blu-rays and DVDs is lurking in this issue too! Niiiiiiice!

Okay, I must be off now. See you all again soon.

Ken Miller *K. Miller*
Editor

Design and Layout
Ken Miller

Contributors
Ramsey Campbell, William Martell, Russell Fox, Simon Pritchard, Joe Castro, Jörg Buttgereit, Allan Bryce, Hans Kaufmann, David Fitzgerald, Ricky Baker, Diallo Jackson, Raimund Huber, Johnny Burnett, Russell Shaw, Mark Duffield, Dan Nicks, Noah Kneal, Zilla Man (illustrations)

Special Thanks
Ken Barthelmey, Howard J. Ford, Toby Russell, Nicole Mikuzis, Katie Hamilton, David Gregory, Rupert Russell, Gibran Evans, Jim Evans

Printing
IngramSpark

CONTENTS

A TRIBUTE TO GODZILLA

PART 1

Sometimes he's the villain!
Sometimes he's the hero!
He's a gigantic, roaring, atomic force of nature!

He is Godzilla!

Join us now for a dive into the glorious world of the greatest monster ever to stomp across the silver screen!

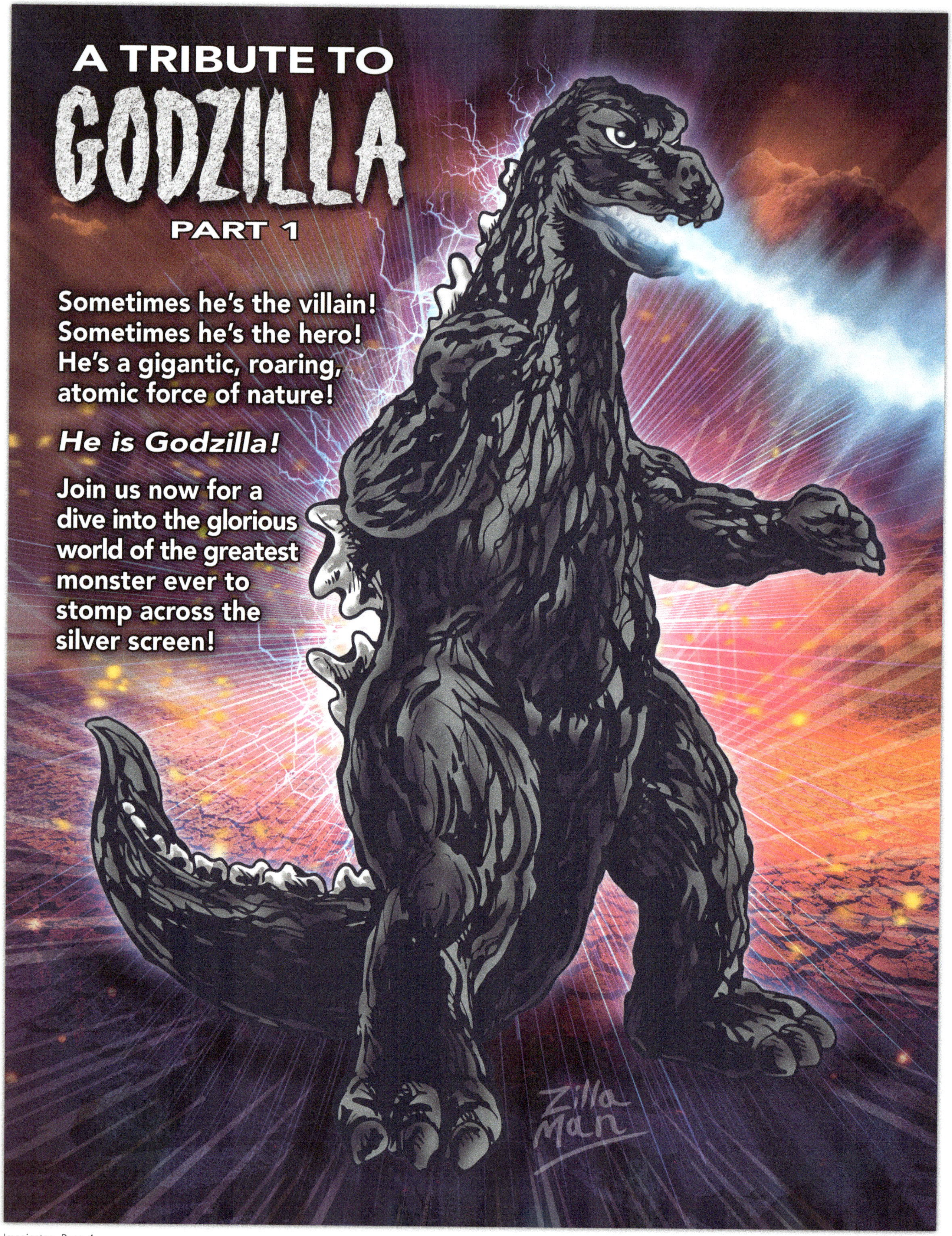

JÖRG'S TOP FIVE GODZILLA MOVIES

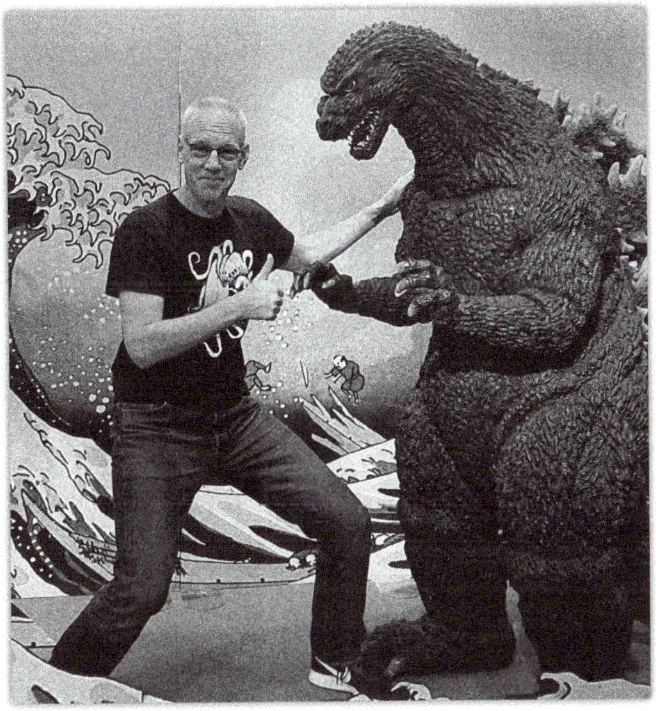

Jörg Buttgereit is a German filmmaker famed for his transgressive arthouse-horror movies *Nekromatik* (1988), *Der Todesking* (1990), *Nekromatik 2* (1991) and *Schramm* (1993). Jörg has directed for the stage, he has helmed radio plays, and he's written issues of the comic book *Captain Berlin*, a character Jörg himself created.

Jörg is also a fan of Japanese creature features: his book, *Japan - Die Monsterinsel* (Japan the Monster Island), is a guide to kaiju movies, covering in detail all the Japanese monster movies that were released in Germany. For his book Jörg visited film studios in Japan and he interviewed monster actors, directors, and special effects experts. *Japan - Die Monsterinsel* also looks at US Godzilla films, as well as kaiju movies that didn't get a release in Germany but are important for the genre.

Imaginator asked Jörg to share with us his top five favourite Godzilla films...

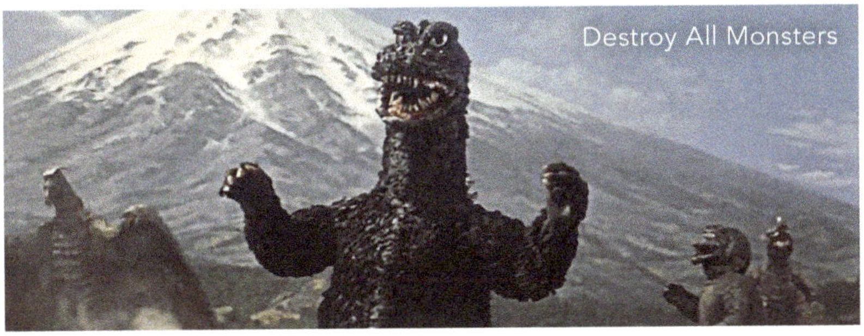

Destroy All Monsters

DESTROY ALL MONSTERS (1968)

All my beloved monsters in one movie. Plus the best soundtrack by Akira Ifukube.

GODZILLA VS. THE SMOG MONSTER (1971)

In the early 70s, when the world was going down because of pollution, this movie freaked me out and taught me awareness to save the planet.

GODZILLA VS. KING GHIDORAH (1991)

The best of the Heisei Era. Composer Akira Ifukube was back with an incredible score!

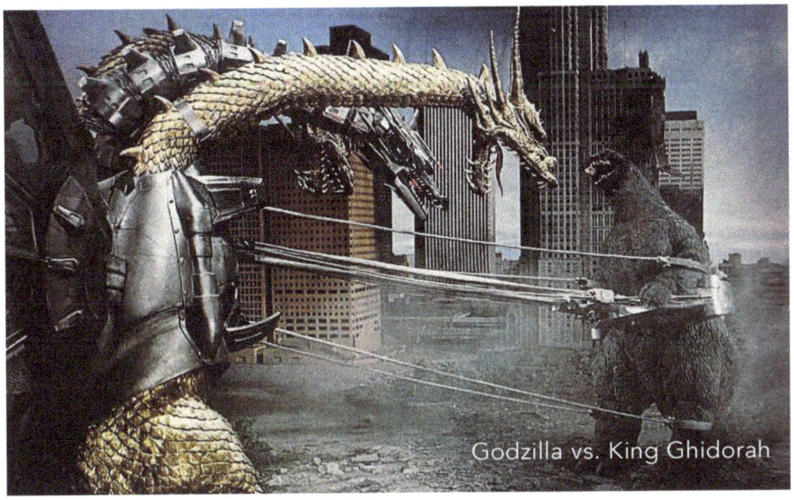

Godzilla vs. King Ghidorah

SHIN GODZILLA (2016)

Godzilla as a metaphor for Fukushima.

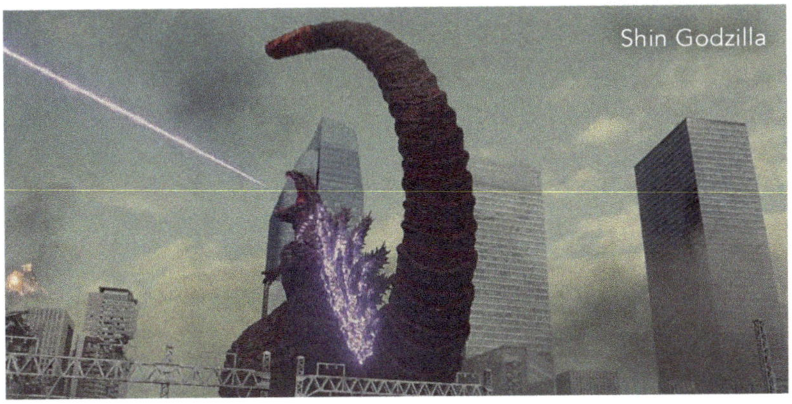

Shin Godzilla

GODZILLA MINUS ONE (2023)

This is a touching reinvention and homage to the original Godzilla.

RUSSELL FOX PRAISES...

GODZILLA

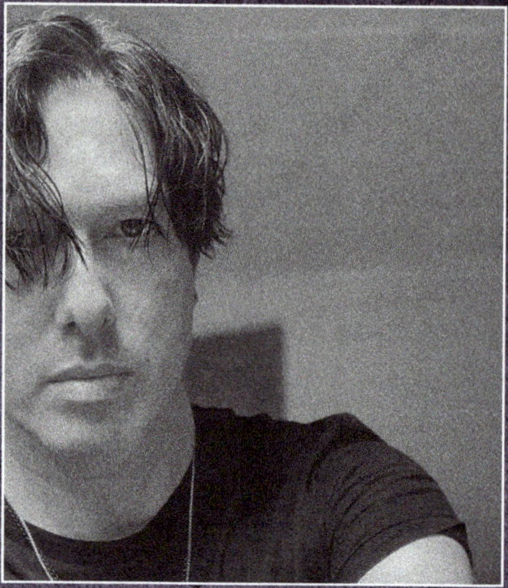

Russell Fox is a comic book artist with credits that include work for *2000AD* and cover art for Dynamite Entertainment's *Vampirella* and *Purgatori* comics.

Russell is an ardent fan of the original ***Godzilla*** (1954). And now he tells us why...

The original *Godzilla* (*Gojira*) movie is still my favourite. Its serious tone and sombre visuals really sell this unstoppable force wreaking destruction upon Japan.

Rewatching it recently, I realised how well the film was lit: it has definitely had an influence on my own approach to creating light and shadow in my art.

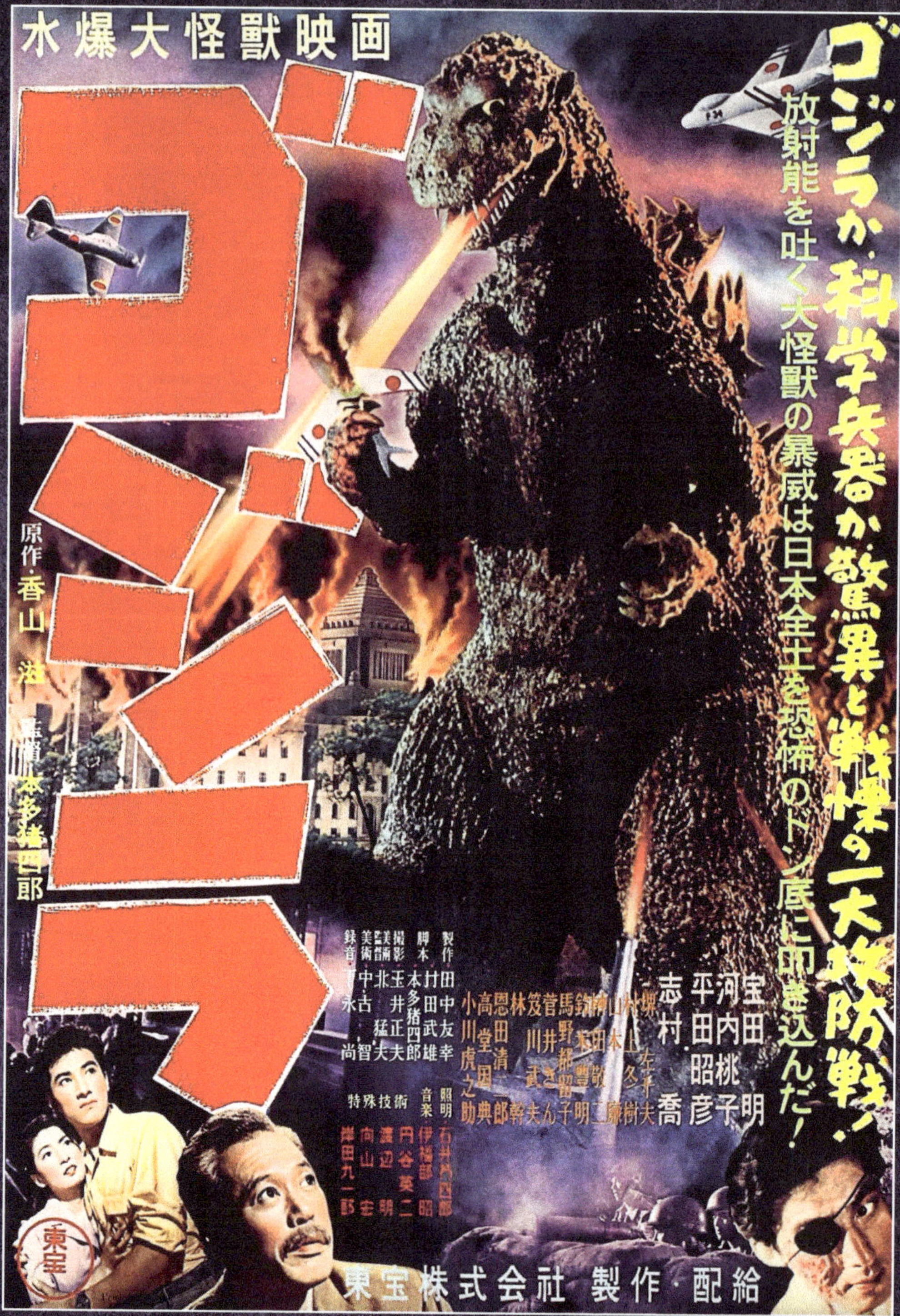

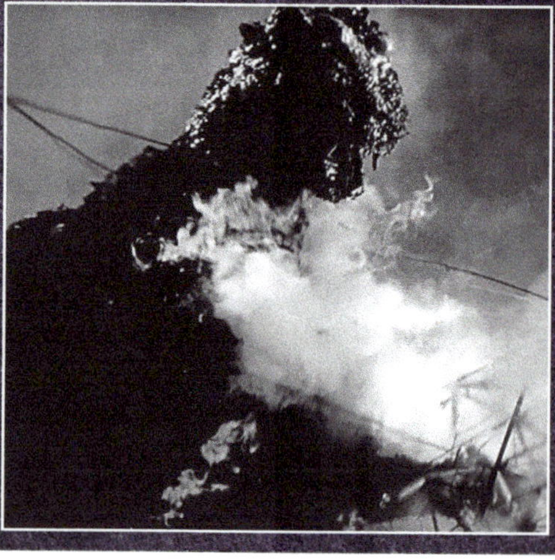

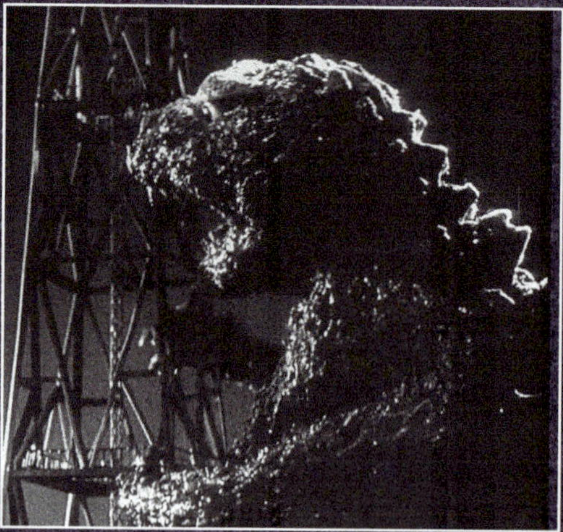

As Godzilla stomps his way through Tokyo in this film you get a real sense of his size, his mass - though not through a man-in-suit kicking over doll's houses, but via the use of heavy black shadows and nightmarish grey skies thundering above.

The music's also great, although I do prefer the theme from *Mothra vs. Godzilla*.

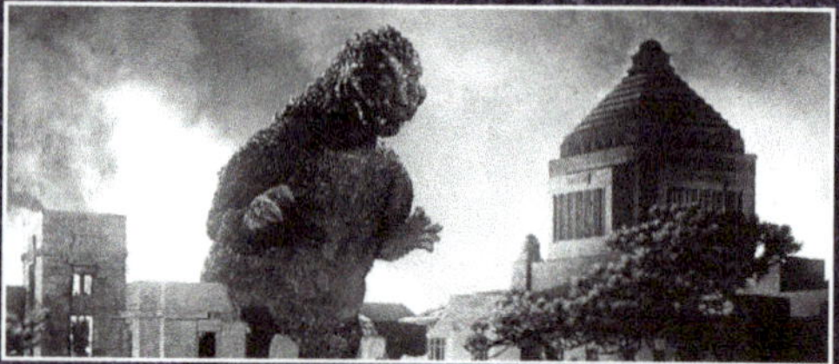

ALLAN BRYCE PRAISES...

MOTHRA VS. GODZILLA

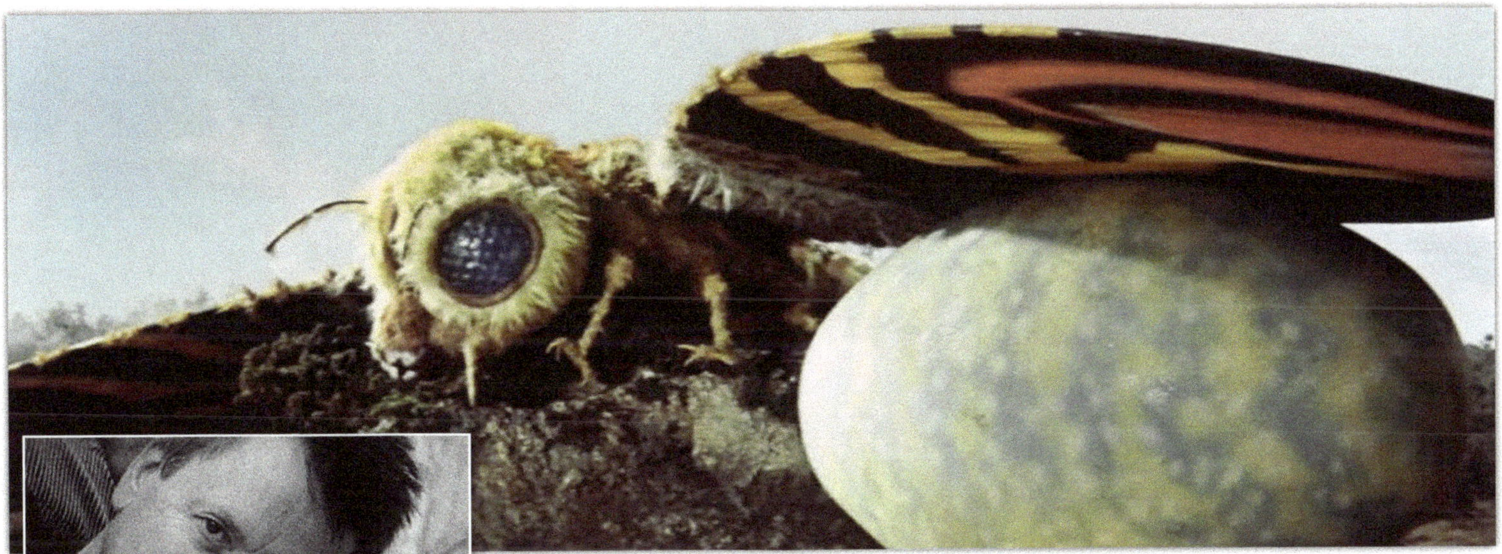

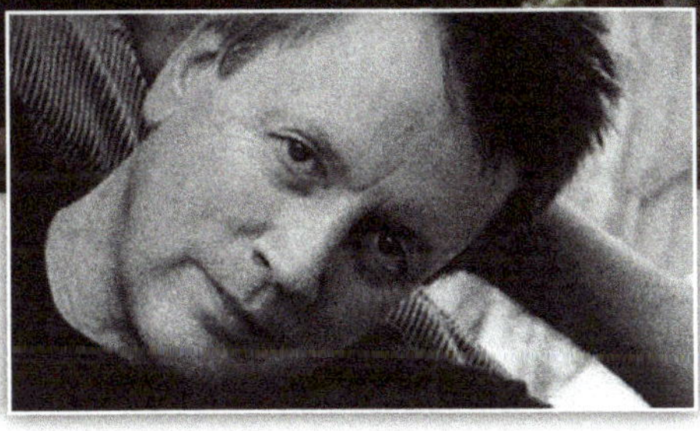

Allan Bryce is the convivial editor of the very popular magazines *The Dark Side* and *Infinity*. Some of the many colourful, entertaining books he has authored include *Italian Horrors, Classic Screen Monsters, Die Laughing: the Dark Side Guide to Comedy Horror* and *Amicus, the Studio That Dripped Blood*.

Allan is an admirer of Godzilla movies from the Shōwa era, and he's here to reveal why ***Mothra vs. Godzilla*** (1964) is the release that tickles his fancy the most...

We all know that the original 1954 *Godzilla* remains the gold standard of classic Kaiju, though of course *Godzilla Minus One* is now to be added to that pantheon.

However, we all have our own favourites and in my case it's 1964's *Mothra vs. Godzilla*, aka *Godzilla vs. the Thing*. As I'm sure you all know, *Mothra* (1961) was a huge hit for Toho and therefore after pitting Godzilla against King Kong the previous year, they quickly set up a grudge match between the Big G and the divine Moth.

Godzilla vs. the Thing, directed by Ishiro Honda, natch, is one of the bigger budgeted and best of the series, featuring fine special effects accompanying an intriguing storyline in which one of Mothra's eggs is taken and exploited by carnival promoters. Eventually, it hatches into twin junior Mothras who avenge their parent in a battle against fire-breathing Godzilla. The wild narrative also features the cute, miniaturised "Peanut Sisters."

I always wondered why the US version was called *Godzilla vs. the Thing*. 13 years on from release of *The Thing from Another World*, surely it was a bit too late to cash in on the Howard Hawks hit?

It's also interesting to note that this was the final film in the Showa Era where Godzilla was actually a bit of a baddie. He turned over a new leaf after this and became almost heroic.

Anyway, I saw this on the relatively big screen of the Kingston Kinema back in the late 1960s and really enjoyed it. On my return, and suitably enlivened by devouring 350 calories of Vesta Prawn Curry, I scribbled in my Letts Schoolboys Diary... "Much more fun than you could hope for in a film about men in rubber suits punching each other."

So there we have it, and all I need add is my considered opinion that *Godzilla vs. the Thing* may be the best of all of the Toho monster rallies. If you don't agree then, like Mothra, you need to see the light.

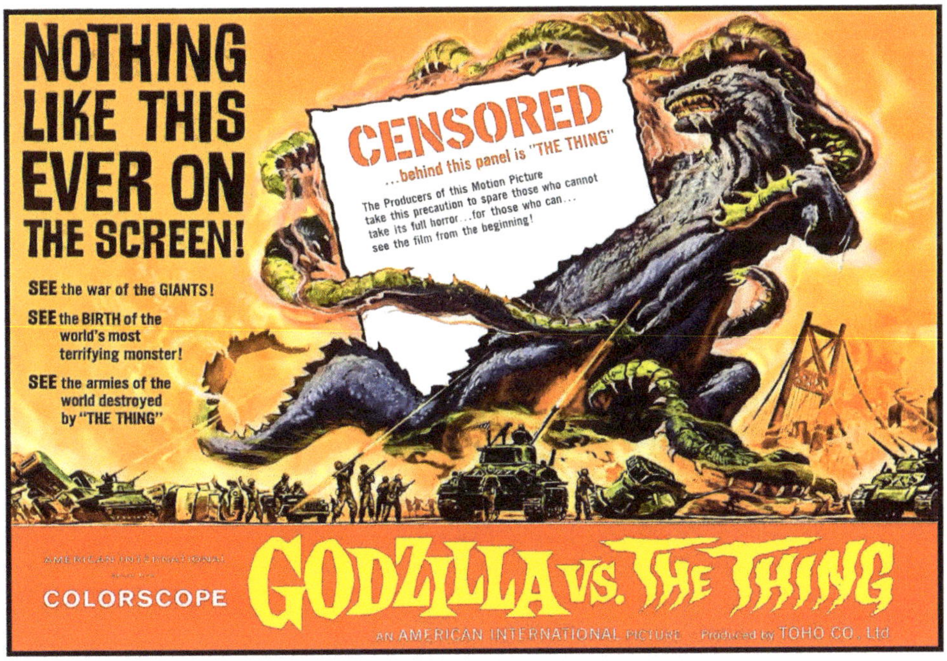

WILLIAM MARTELL PRAISES...

GODZILLA MINUS ONE

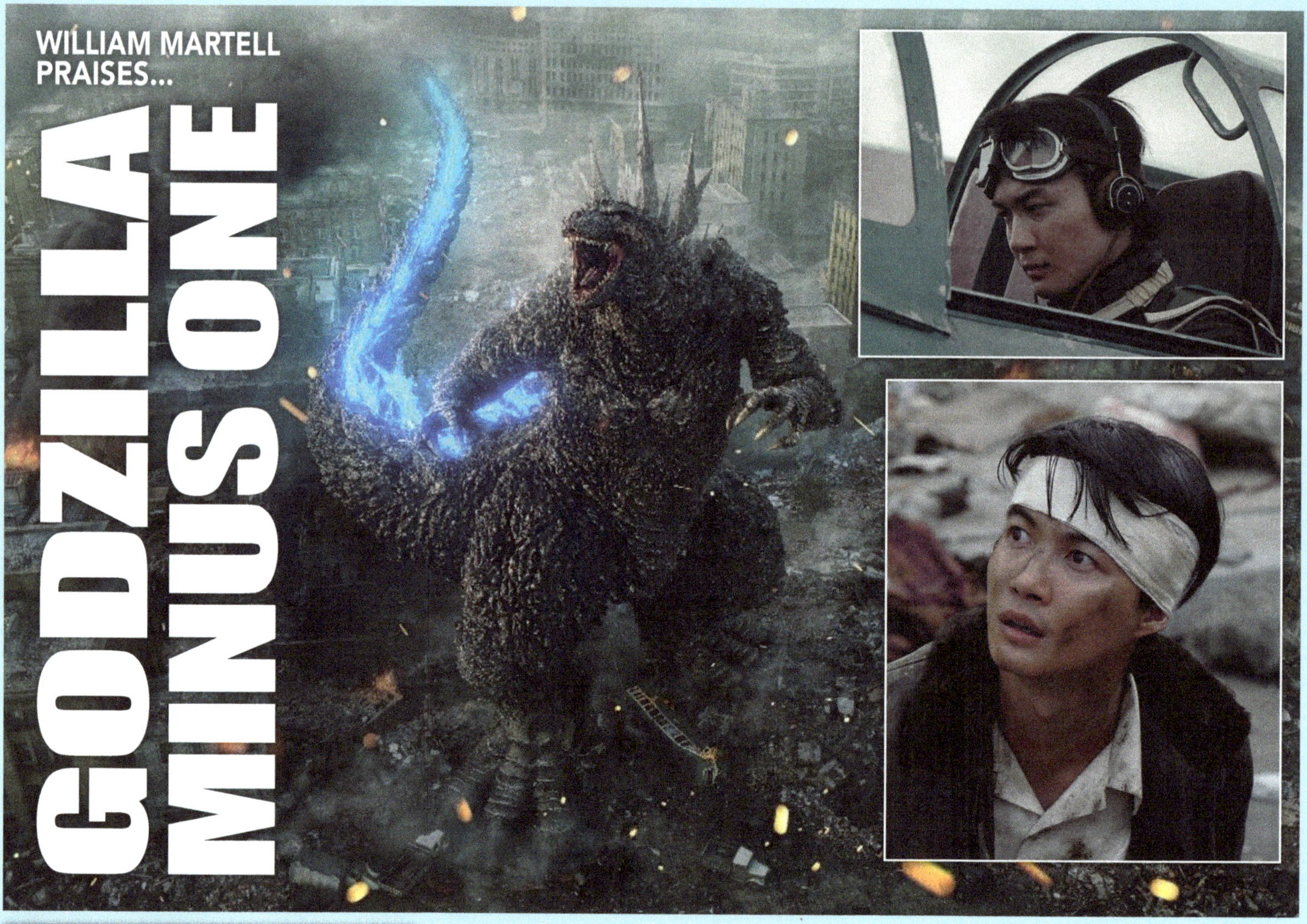

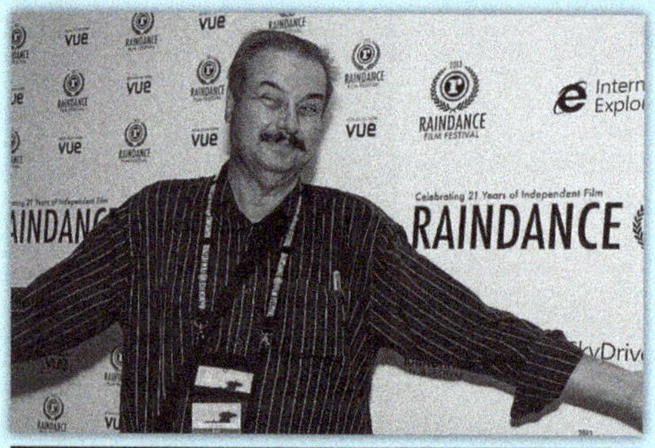

William Martell has written the screenplays for films including *Ninja Busters* (1984), *Droid Gunner* (1995), *Hard Evidence* (1995), *Steel Sharks* (1997), *Black Thunder* (1998) and *Dante's Hotel* (2023) - and he's the author of the incredibly helpful how-to book on writing for the movies: *The Secrets of Action Screenwriting*.

William, who knows a well-constructed plot when he sees one, was impressed with ***Godzilla Minus One* (2023)**...

Godzilla Minus One proves that you can make a serious movie with big emotional moments... that also works as popcorn entertainment. Yes, this is a Godzilla movie. But it's also about the trauma of war, feelings of failure and responsibility for he deaths of others, how people and families are displaced after war, and living with the horrors of war haunting every moment of your life. And Godzilla.

It's also an exciting film, and the director has obviously seen *Jaws* (1975) because we get several scenes that were inspired by that film - including barrels sinking below the surface and the fin chasing the ship. All of this might not be obvious to the casual viewer, however, because it's used in different ways.

This film makes you care deeply about characters... and then Godzilla attacks. Some characters may not survive...

One of the great things about this film is how well it sets up all of the twists and turns of the plot. Also, how it gives us information visually that ramps up the suspense. When Godzilla is present under the water, the fish die and float to the surface. That happens in one of the first scenes... so that later on, on a boat when the dead fish start popping to the surface in the background, we know what this means.

Another nice set up involves Godzilla using his nuclear option: his "fins" grow and glow. So, when that happens, you really know that you're screwed. Godzilla can destroy anything!

This is exciting and emotional and probably the first Godzilla movie where I really cared about the characters, and you probably could have removed Godzilla and it could have still worked well as a drama film. But with Godzilla? More dramatic, more emotional, more exciting.

Hollywood - this is how it's done.

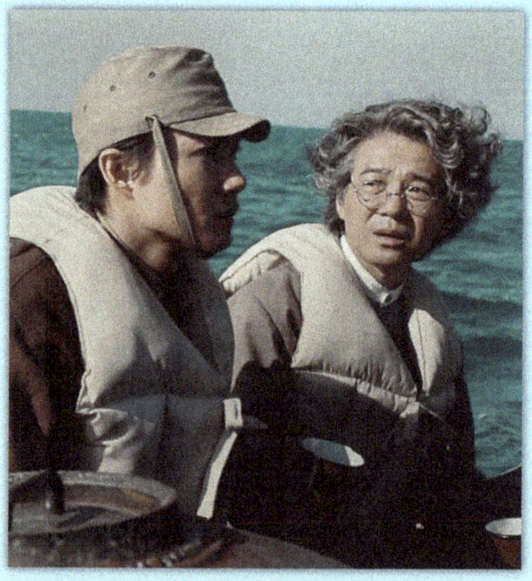

KEN MILLER PRAISES...

DESTROY ALL MONSTERS

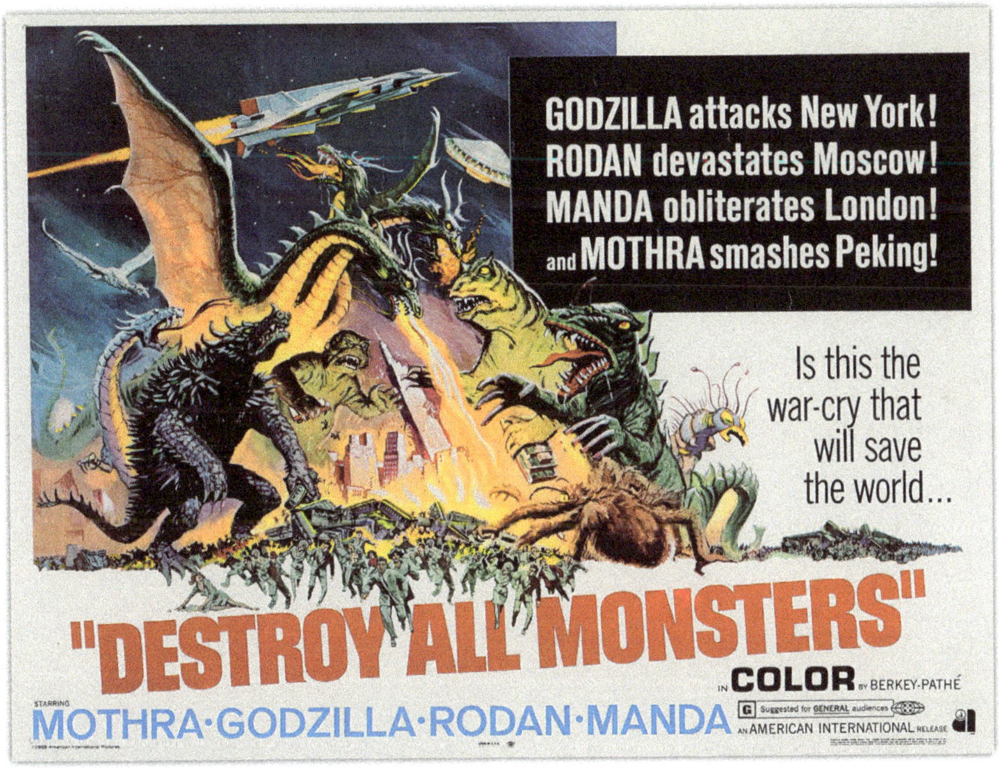

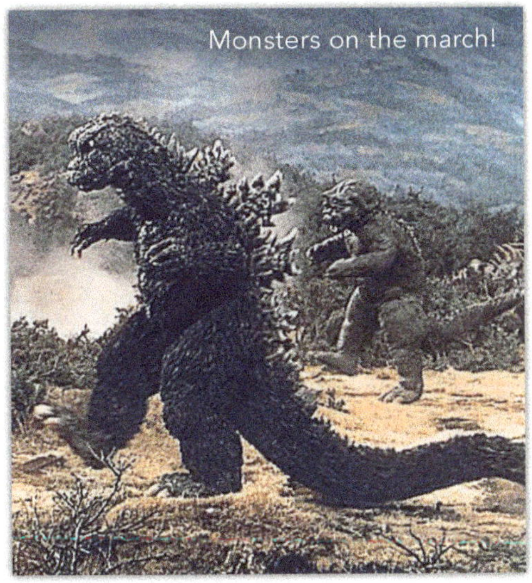
Monsters on the march!

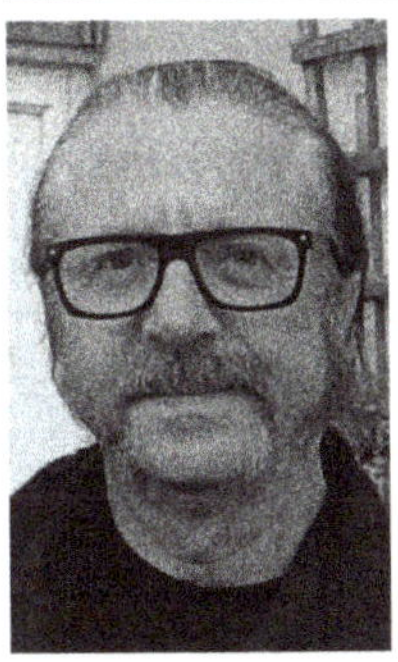

Ken Miller, the editor of Imaginator Magazine, is here to rave about the extremely fun and entertaining Showa era monster-fest: **Destroy All Monsters (1968)...**

I adore this movie.

Destroy All Monsters was actually intended at the time to be the final film in the Godzilla series, but, obviously, that didn't happen and production of Big G movies continued - but maybe the fact Toho was considering ending the franchise here is why they decided to really push the boat out with this film and cram in SO MANY MONSTERS! Only the much later Millennium era Toho release *Godzilla: Final Wars* (2004) boasts more kaiju.

Set at the end of the 20th century (English-language versions specifically cite the year as being 1999), *Destroy All Monsters* takes place in a world where travelling to the moon is commonplace, and all of Earth's kaiju now reside in Monsterland: an isle that's part of the Bonin Islands archipelago. Here we're shown Godzilla, Rodan, Anguirus, larval-stage Mothra, Kumonga and Minilla hanging out with monsters who'd never previously appeared in a Godzilla film: Manda, Varan, Gorosaurus and Baragon. Varan and Baragon don't actually feature much in the film, but it's still cool seeing them getting some screen time.

The plot concerns a race of silver-clad lady-aliens (that actually resemble slug-like living metal organisms) called Kilaaks, who are able to mind-control the monsters, sending them off on city-wrecking sprees around the globe. It's left up to the heroic space rocket captain Katsuo Yamabe to attempt to thwart the Kilaaks' plans by flying to Cassini Crater on the moon and destroying a device that's been sending the aliens' brainwashing signal to Earth.

Katsuo succeeds in his mission, puts the signal out of action, and the monsters, now free of Kilaak control, all decide to march on the aliens' main base situated on the side of Mount Fuji... but the Kilaaks have a way to fight back... they summon King Ghidorah! OMG!

I've already told you that I adore this film, right? There's so much to love about it: cool miniature landscapes, model rockets blasting off to the moon, a great theme tune, the fine use of a primary colour palette that fills scenes with lots of greens, reds, yellows and oranges, and, obviously, an abundance of suitmation property damage! Rodan attacks Moscow! Gorosaurus (I love that mega-dino!) smashes the Arc de Triomphe in Paris! Godzilla fries the UN Building in New York! Mothra totals a train near Beijing! And, at one point, Rodan, Godzilla, Manda *and* Mothra all assault Tokyo at the same time! Tokyo, you'll not be surprised to learn, gets utterly trashed!

Seeing model vehicles getting stomped on, missile-tanks unleashing their ordnance, and lots of explosions going off is a lot of fun, of course, but the real enjoyment comes when the monsters finally team-up and take-on three-headed King Ghidorah! It's great to see an eager news reporter name-checking each kaiju as it arrives on the scene, ready to rumble! Though Rodan, Mothra and Kumonga do their bit, it's Godzilla, Gorosaurus and Anguirus who are the main combatants in the fight against Ghidorah, biting and stomping the gold space-dragon into the ground! I've always liked the drop-kick Gorosaurus uses during this showdown! Ace stuff!

A flaming 'monster' arrives next, ultimately revealed to be a Kilaak drone-UFO, but it's definitely the extended sequence showing the monsters battling as a group that lodges itself in the memory.

Destroy All Monsters finishes on a happy note, showing all the monsters back on their island, at peace. Niiiiiiice.

Sheer fun.
Sheer escapism.
Sheer awesomeness.

HANS KAUFMANN PRAISES...

GODZILLA

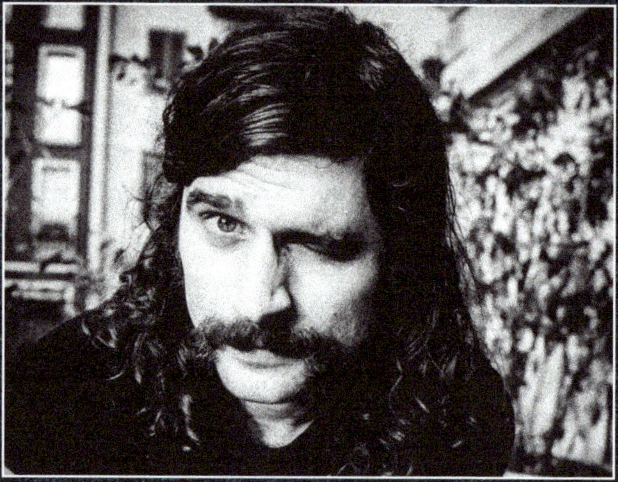

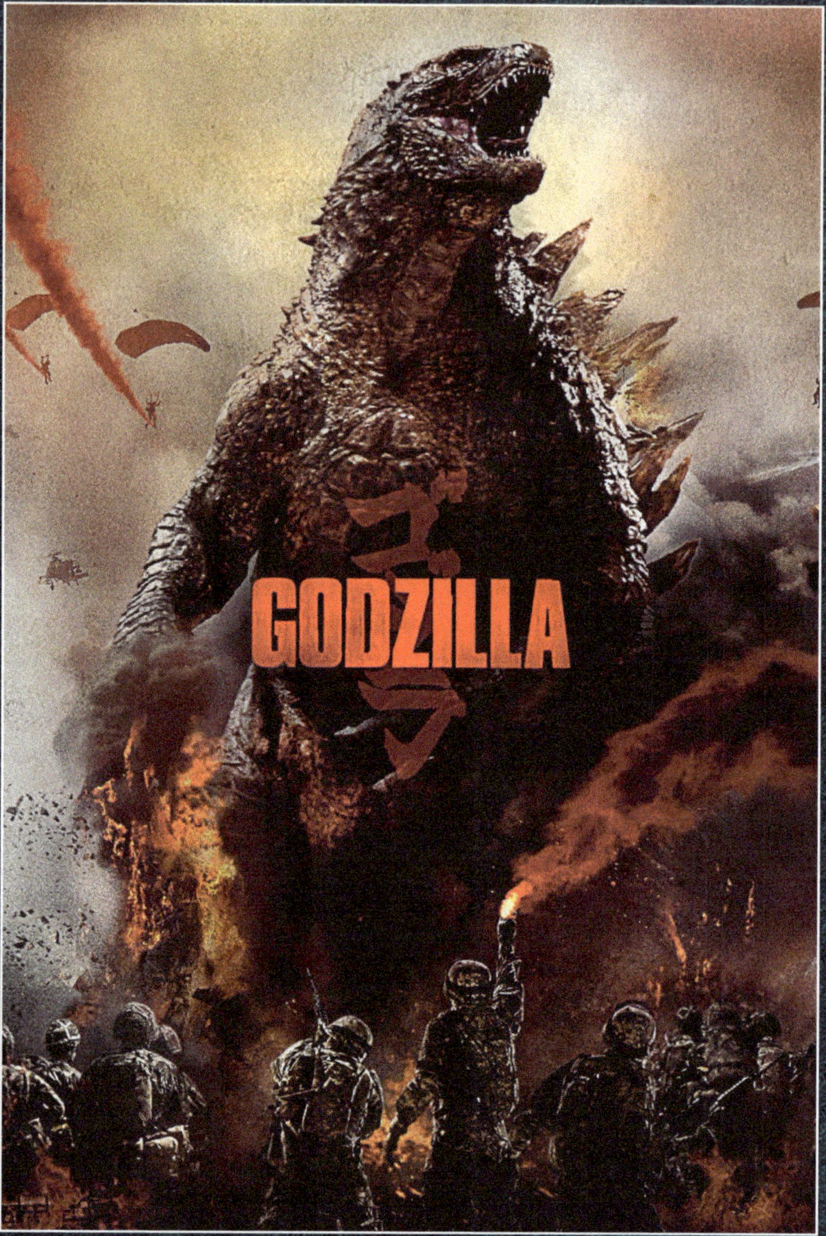

Hans Kaufmann is the director, writer, editor and producer of the compelling social-drama-meets-*Taxi-Driver* movie *The Working Man* (2019).

Hans loves Legendary Entertainment's ***Godzilla* (2014)** and he's eager to share his enthusiasm for it with us...

What I've always loved about *Godzilla* (2014) is the sheer patience Gareth Edwards shows in bringing the King of the Monsters to the screen. In an age where blockbusters often reveal their creatures in the first 10 minutes, Edwards makes us wait almost an hour before we truly see Godzilla. By the time the Hawaii sequence arrives, the anticipation is electric - teased through shadows, dorsal fins, and distant rumbles, but also in small, human-scale details: a little girl noticing the sea pulling back, a dog barking and bolting, crowds suddenly running for higher ground. Our imagination builds the monster long before we lay eyes on him.

The reveal itself is masterfully staged. The city goes dark after a tsunami crashes through the streets, the chaos giving way to a tense silence. Then, soldiers fire red illumination flares into the pitch-black sky, and for fleeting moments we catch partial glimpses - a head, an arm, the curve of his back. It's a painterly, almost mythic presentation, as if the creature is too vast to fit into a single frame. By holding back, Edwards makes Godzilla feel monumental, a force of nature rather than just another CG spectacle.

This slow-burn approach doesn't just honour the spirit of the 1954 original; it makes Godzilla's eventual full appearance in the finale feel earned. When he finally unleashes his roar in all his glory, it's not just a visual reveal — it's the payoff to nearly an hour of mounting dread and awe. ●

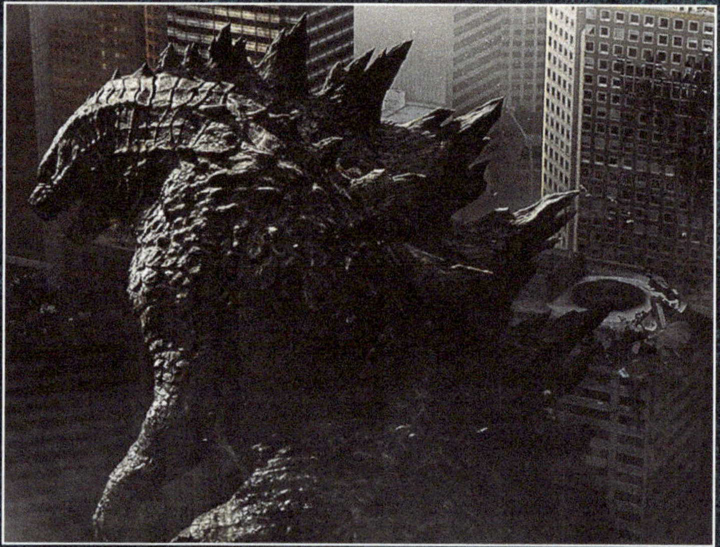

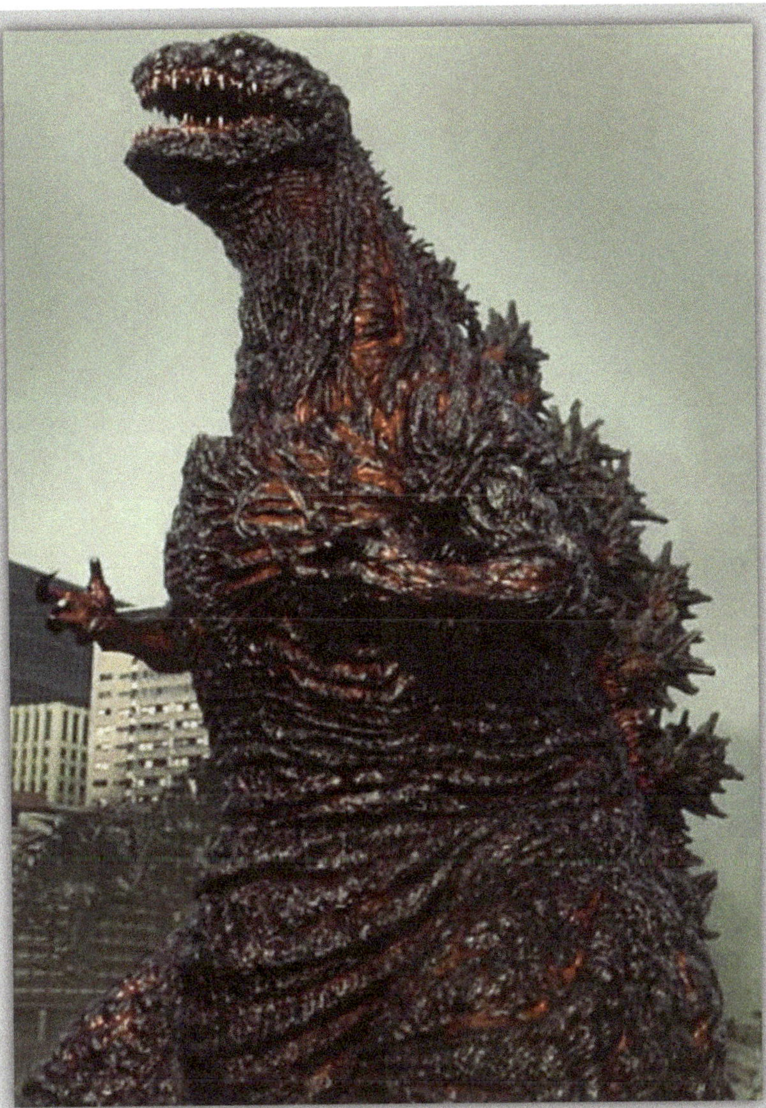

DAVID FITZGERALD PRAISES...

SHIN GODZILLA

David Fitzgerald constructed the ghostly demon-dog seen in the M.R. James parody film *Squeak and I'll Run to You*, he helped create the barbaric outfit worn by the god-monster in *Rawhead Rex* (1986), he provided the vocal work for animator Brett Piper's short film *H.G. Wells' First Men in the Moon* (2017), and he also played the lead role of Rex Shepherd in *Squeak and I'll Run to You* (2021).

David holds the 2016 Toho film ***Shin Godzilla*** in high regard. He explains to **Ken Miller** why he appreciates the film so much...

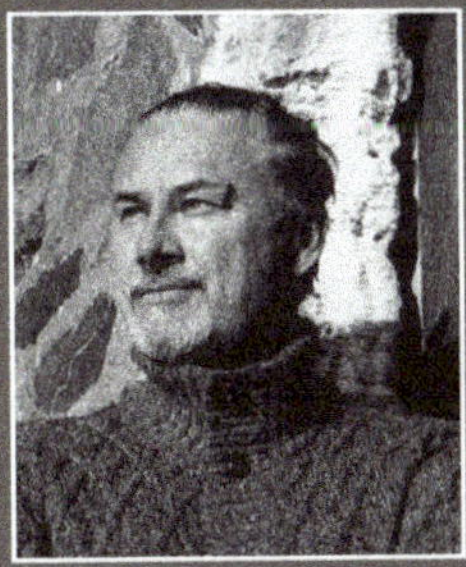

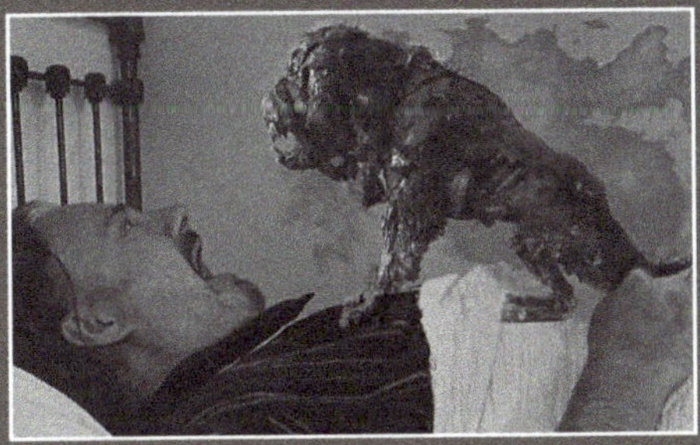

I know you love the look of the early-stage Godzilla in this film, when he has gills, walks on all four limbs, and has weird fish-eyes: what was it about this design you particularly liked?

I loved how clumsy and destructive it was. Then it starts to take form as the upright Godzilla. I think it was a brilliant idea.

The later Godzilla form is very, very distinctive-looking, isn't it?

Yes - that's when we get the mouth-splitting before the spraying of his atomic breath, which I think is awesome. Shin Godzilla is by far the meanest-looking Godzilla.

Shin Godzilla not only has atomic breath, he is also able to discharge devastating photon beams. Did you enjoy seeing this upgrade of Godzilla's powers?

Yes, the photon beams are a superb upgrade.

Shin Godzilla is definitely a dark, harmful force in this movie. Do you prefer Godzilla when he's cast in a more antagonistic, destructive role?

I really love Godzilla as an all-powerful catastrophic force. He's like a living element of Earth showing its destructive power as a warning to us.

As a creature designer yourself, what is it you like most about the look of the final-stage design of Shin Godzilla?

As already mentioned, I love the photon upgrade - but what I like most about Shin Godzilla is the fact, for me, he has the best teeth arrangement ever.

Finally, would you like to see a sequel to *Shin Godzilla*?

A sequel? You bet!

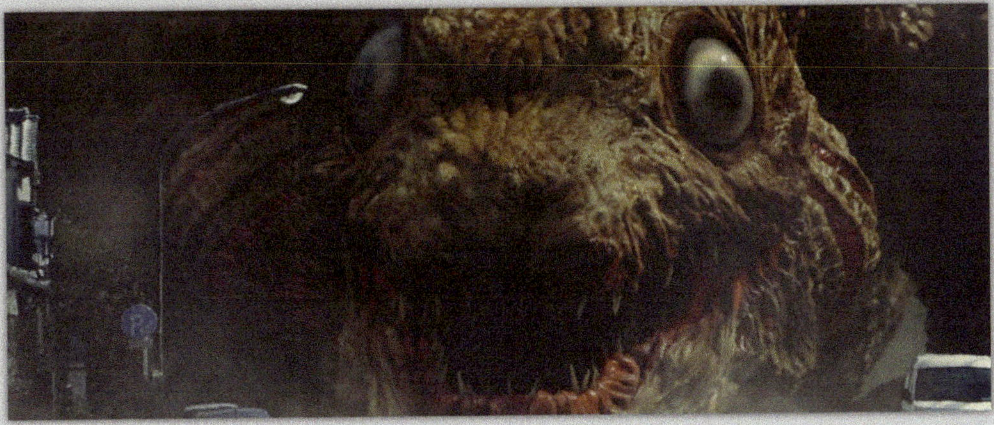

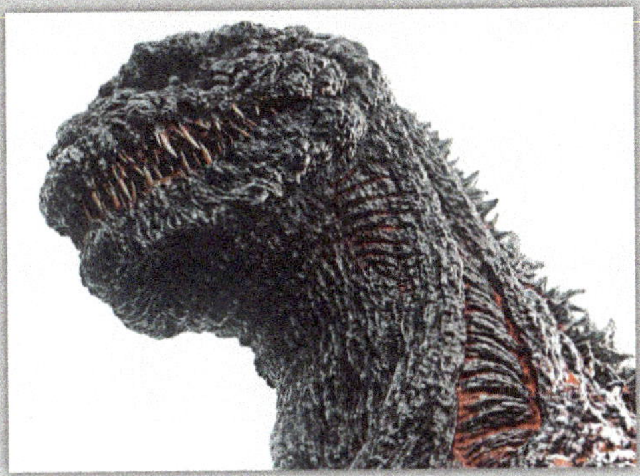

RICKY BAKER PRAISES...

GODZILLA MINUS ONE

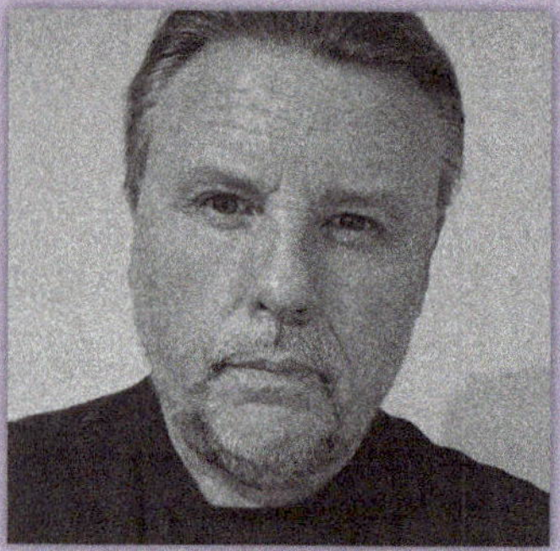

Ricky Baker is the editor of the kung-tastic magazine *Eastern Heroes*, the co-author of *The New Essential Guide to Hong Kong Movies*, and he has published such entertaining, photo-crammed books as *The Essential Guide to Deadly China Dolls* and *The Essential Guide to the Best of Eastern Heroes*.

Ricky is here to tell **Ken Miller** why he is so fond of *Godzilla Minus One*...

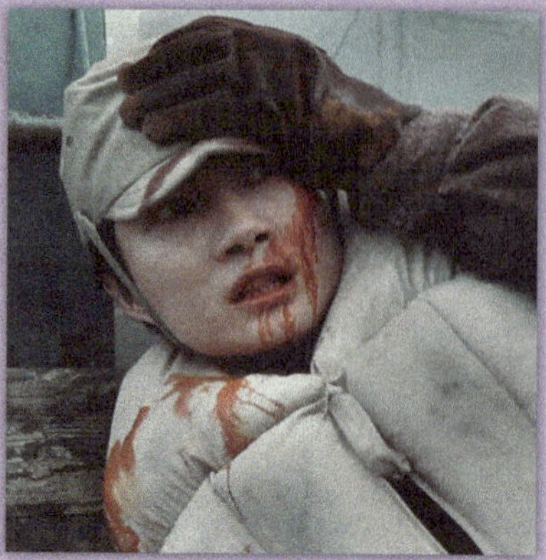

You're a fan of Toho's 2023 modern kaiju classic *Godzilla Minus One*. Do you think Big G works best when he's shown as a building-crushing, unstoppable atomic force, rather than as a world-saving heroic creature?

Ah, the eternal Godzilla dilemma - is he the city's worst nightmare or its scaly saviour? When I was younger, watching him stomp Tokyo into matchsticks was like a kaiju version of knocking over Lego towers - pure, glorious chaos. But as I've grown older (and maybe slightly more responsible), I've come to appreciate Hero Godzilla. These days, I like the idea that, if a giant radioactive lizard must exist, he might as well be on our side.

That said, *Godzilla Minus One* shows that the Big G's true power lies in unpredictability. Whether he's saving humanity or vaporising it depends entirely on his mood... and maybe how much coffee he's had that morning.

So I am going to say that Godzilla works best when he's both: an unstoppable atomic force who occasionally decides, "Fine, I'll save you tiny humans... but I'm still stepping on your train station on the way home."

Were you surprised at how accomplished and touching the human drama elements were in this film?

I can't say I've seen a huge number of the early Godzilla films. My viewing has tended more towards the later, more polished productions. Those are the ones that really caught my attention. In the more recent films, Godzilla often comes across as a more thoughtful, almost measured presence... at least until he's provoked. Then the red mist rises, and suddenly you've got that unstoppable, fire-breathing force of nature showing no mercy: a truly pissed-off Godzilla. But yes, I was pleasantly surprised at how accomplished and touching the human drama was here, but also how well it balanced with that raw, untamed side of the monster we all know.

What's your favourite moment in the movie?

I really enjoyed *Godzilla Minus One* from start to finish, but there were a few moments that stood out as truly unforgettable. One of the most tense sequences was when Kōichi, desperate to support his new-found family, takes a job as a minesweeper. On one fateful day, he notices telltale signs that Godzilla is about to emerge from the ocean. With only a small boat and limited resources, Kōichi and his crew have to improvise a way to keep the kaiju at bay. The suspense in that scene was incredible.

Another highlight was when the plan to take Godzilla down starts falling apart, only for a fleet of tugboats to arrive as reinforcements in spectacular fashion. As great as that was, though, Kōichi completely steals the show in the final confrontation. Knowing Godzilla is vulnerable to internal attacks, he flies straight toward the monster's open mouth just as it is about to unleash a fatal blast. For a moment, it seems like he has sacrificed himself... until the brilliant twist reveals that the former Navy Air Service mechanic Tachibana had prepared an ejection seat in advance.

That ending wasn't just about defeating Godzilla! It was about Kōichi conquering his own personal demons. It was the perfect cap to an emotional, beautifully executed, and thrilling story.

Godzilla is brought to the screen via computer graphics in *Godzilla Minus One*. Do you have a soft spot for man-in-suit portrayals of Godzilla in earlier movies, or do you prefer CGI?

I can appreciate the fondness many fans have for the man-in-suit Godzilla: it's what they grew up with, and for them, those films hold a lot of special memories. Personally though, I have to admit that the man in the suit always made it feel a bit silly for me. Maybe as a young child I would have been more impressed, but as we get older, we tend to see things differently.

I think the newer CGI versions bring so much more realism to the screen. *Godzilla Minus One* was a perfect example - the effects were incredible, especially considering the modest $15 million budget. The CGI really brought the creature to life in a way that made it feel believable and truly threatening, and I think that level of realism is a big part of why the newer films perform so well at the worldwide box office.

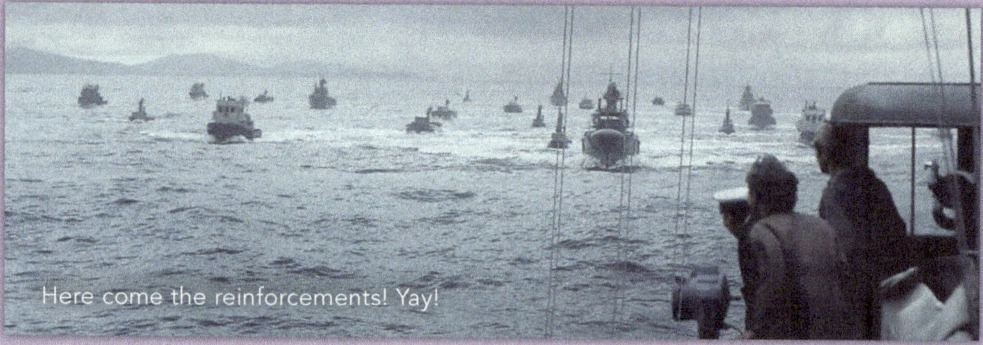

Here come the reinforcements! Yay!

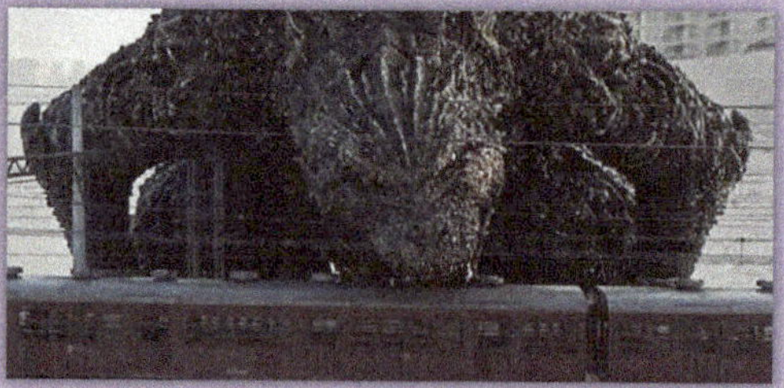

DIALLO JACKSON PRAISES...

KING KONG VS. GODZILLA

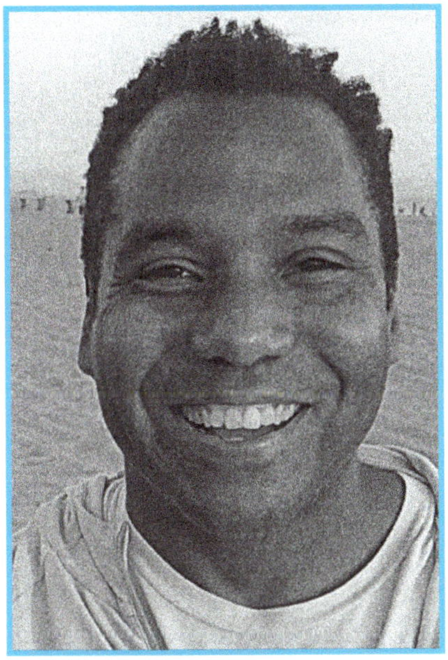

Diallo Jackson is a writer/creator whose work includes short stories and novels, the motion comic *Angela and the Dark: Volume Zero*, and the comic book *The Paranormals*.

Diallo is obviously a man of very good taste as he has chosen Toho's ***King Kong vs. Godzilla*** (1963) as his fave Big G film. Let's find out why...

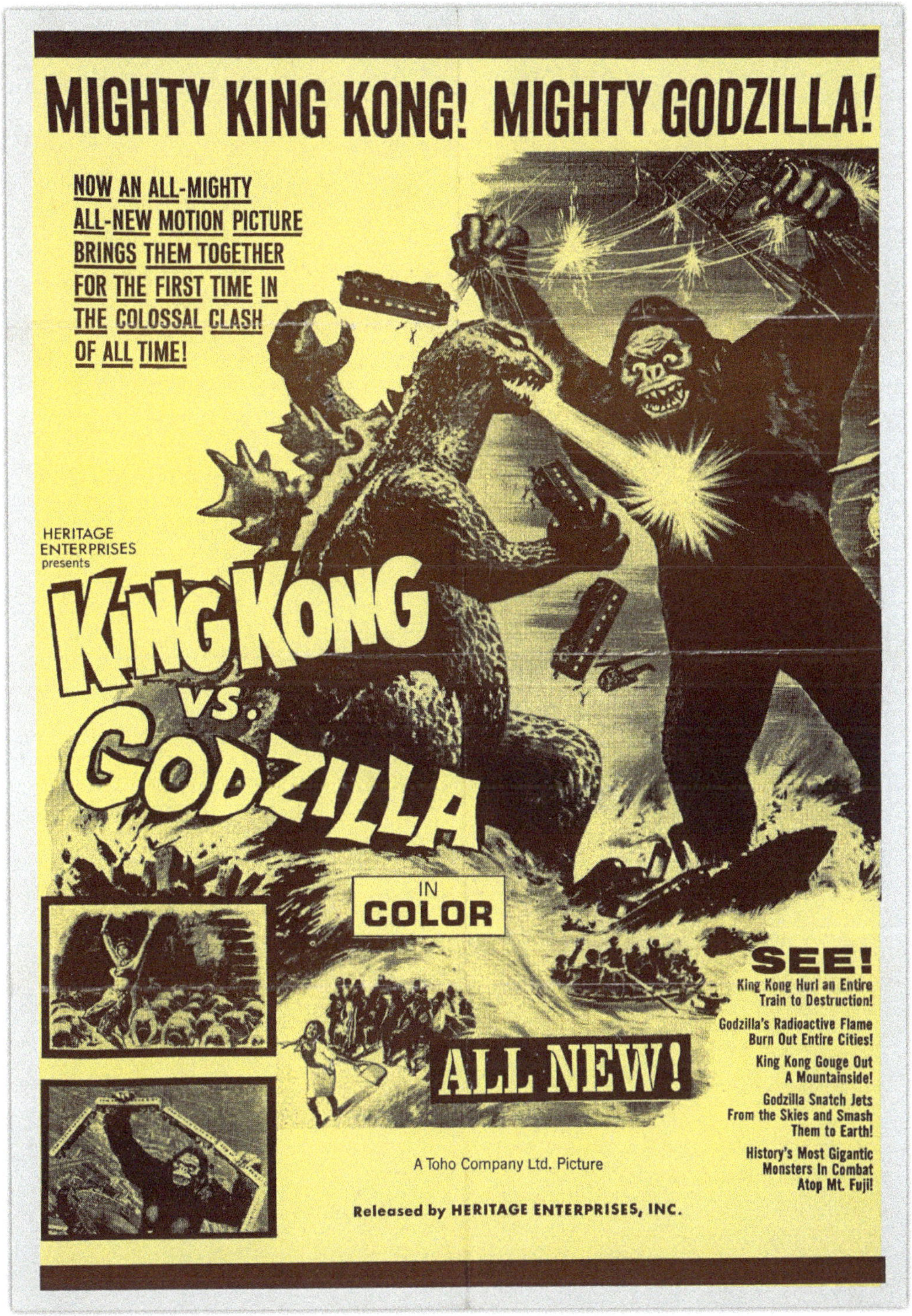

My favourite Godzilla movie is *King Kong vs. Godzilla*, which was appointment viewing for me every single time I came across it on TV.

Back in the late '70s and early '80s, before *Avengers*, *X-Men*, and *Infinity War* were somewhat commonplace, this movie was the literal titan capturing my imagination of what could be. It took a big idea and made it even bigger. That idea? These two iconic monsters together on the same screen: it blew my mind.

There's nothing... nothing... more satisfying than two monsters fighting and punching each other!

And the East vs. West subtext? I even caught that before my frontal cortex was fully formed.

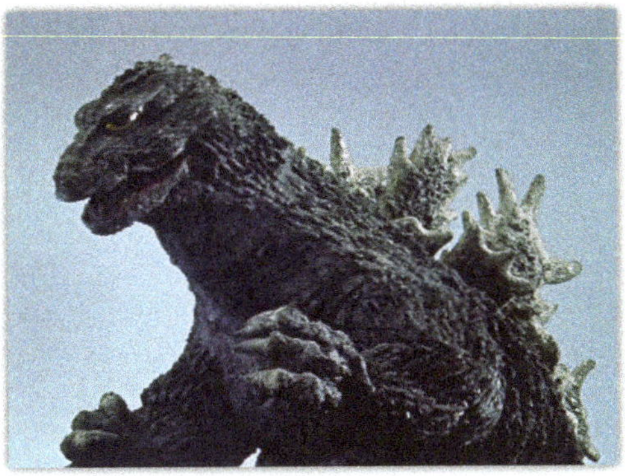

I also love the way they effectively wrapped an actual plot around it. And the song the native people of the island sing still bounces around in my head to this day...

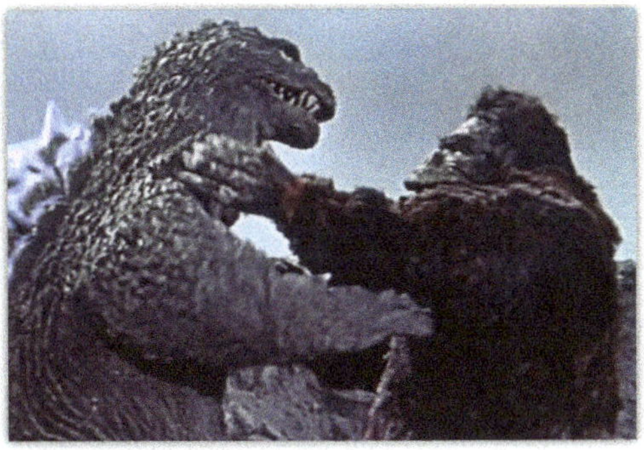

RAIMUND HUBER PRAISES...

GODZILLA MINUS ONE

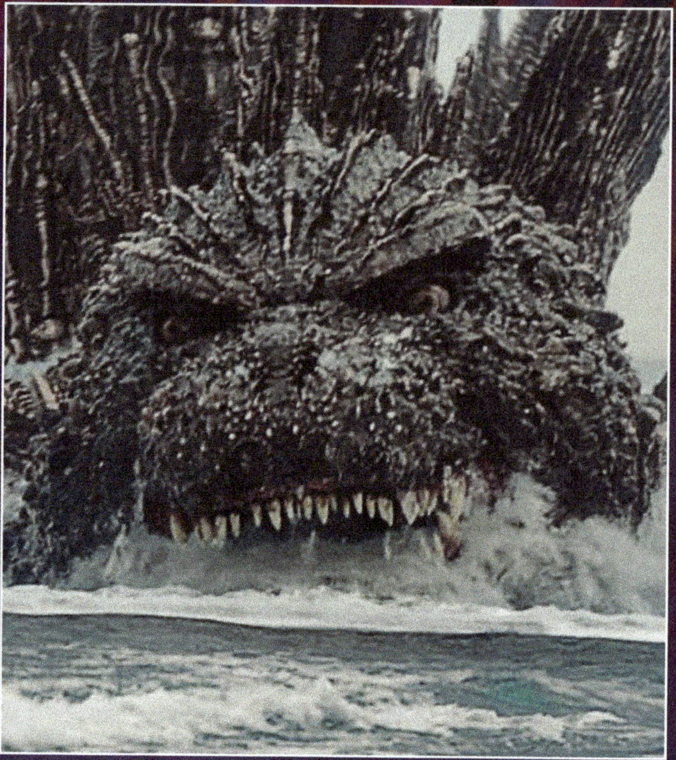

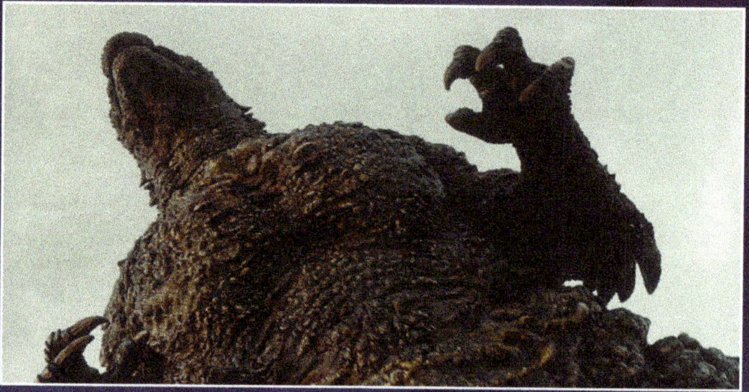

Raimund Huber is a film director, writer and producer. His films include the thrilling, kinetic, adrenaline-fuelled martial arts actioners *Bangkok Adrenaline* (2009) and *Kill 'Em All* (2012).

He was very impressed by **Godzilla Minus One**: here are his thoughts concerning Takashi Yamazaki's fabulous flick...

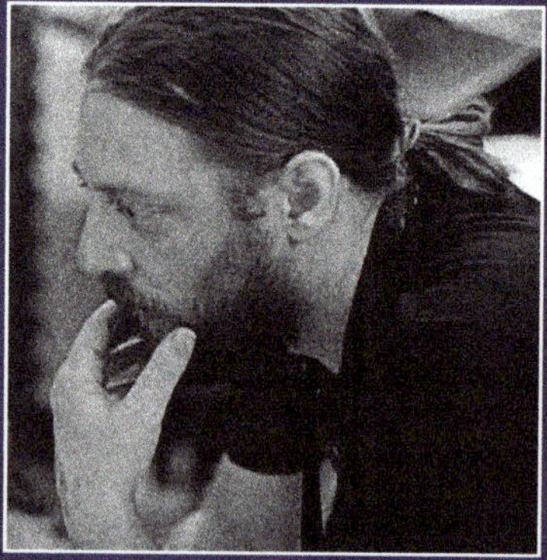

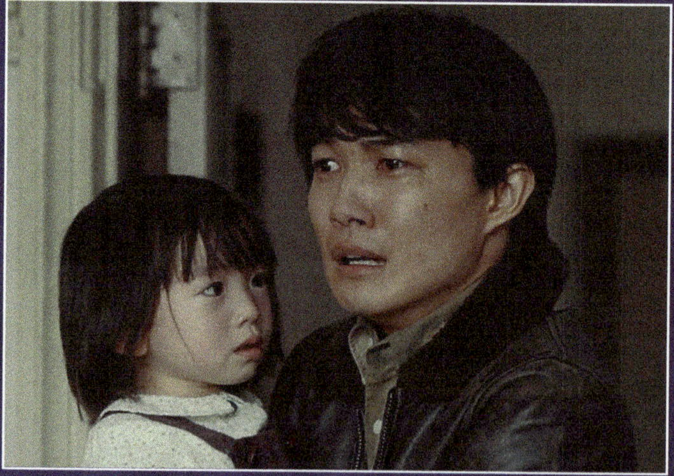

For me, *Godzilla Minus One* stands out as the best because director Takashi Yamazaki brought back the sense of genuine terror. Instead of the semi-heroic Godzilla we've seen in some recent films, here he's pure horror, unstoppable, and unpredictable. The tension isn't just in the battles, but in the dread of what happens if Godzilla appears at all, reminding me of Spielberg's *Jaws*.

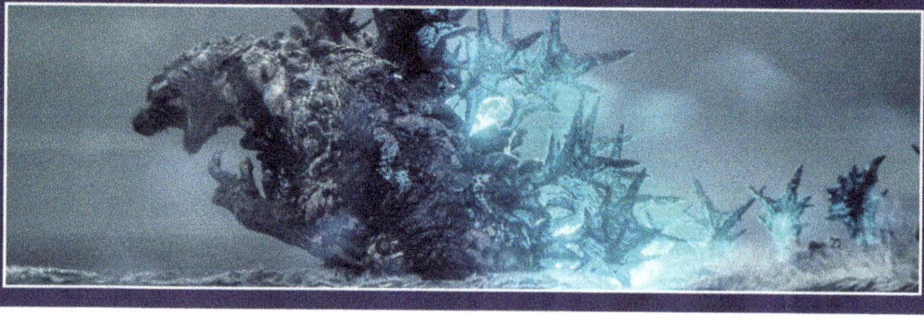

The film is built on a gripping post-war human drama, following a kamikaze pilot struggling with survivor's guilt after World War II. There are no giant monster "royal rumble" distractions, just one monster, one nation, one struggle.

And as a filmmaker, I was blown away by the fact they did all this for under $15 million. Oh, and Godzilla's atomic breath? Absolutely unforgettable.

GODZILLA ゴジラ VS MARVEL

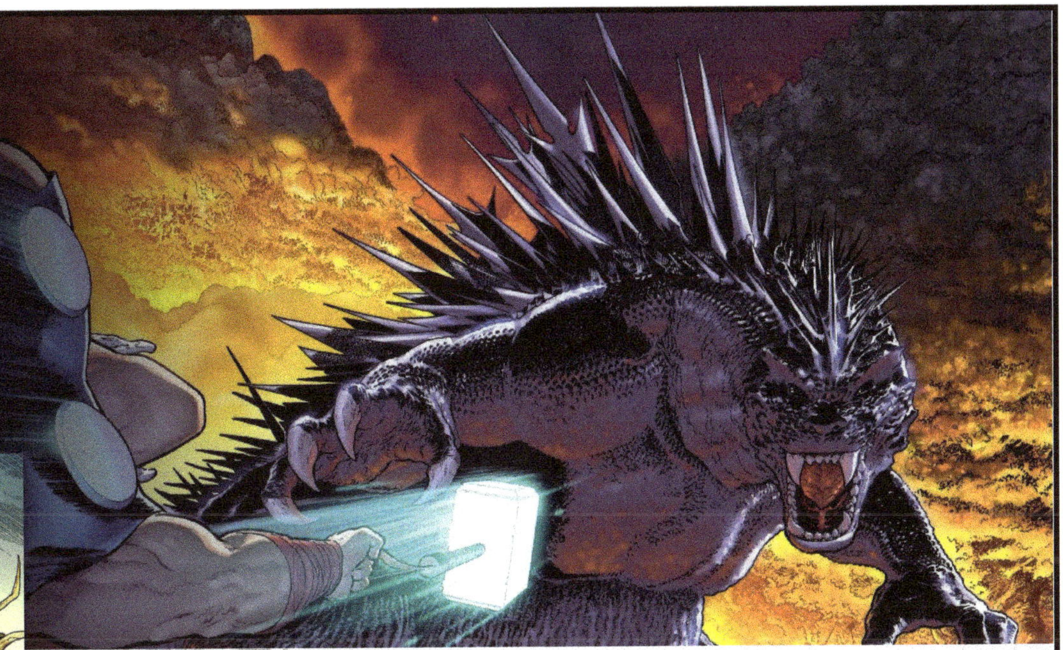

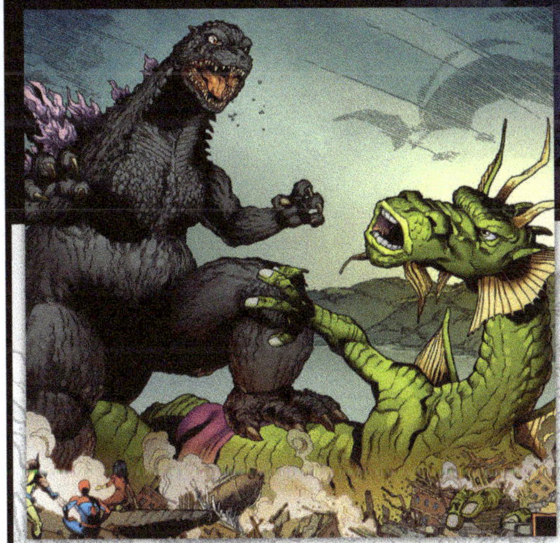

Godzilla vs. Marvel is a terrific series of six one-shot comic books from good ol' Marvel Comics. Each of the issues were done by different creative teams, and they feature Godzilla crossing paths with Marvel's high-profile superheroes, including Spider-Man, the Hulk, the Fantastic Four, the X-Men, the Avengers, and Thor. These one-off action throwdowns were Marvel's first new Godzilla comic books since *Godzilla* #24 was published back in July of 1979.

Dan Nicks thoroughly enjoyed reading *Godzilla vs. Avengers* and *Godzilla vs. Thor*. Over to you, Dan...

GODZILLA VS. AVENGERS

Written by David F. Walker, drawn by Georges Jeanty, inked by Karl Story, colours by Frank D'Armata.

This issue's story is told as a series of flashbacks during a debriefing, as the New Avengers answer questions fired at them by S.H.I.E.L.D. Deputy Director Maria Hill, who is grilling them about their skirmish with Godzilla, Fin Fang Foom (and a certain mega-robot) in Astoria, Oregon.

The tone of the issue is a tad too humorous, but it looks great. For starters, there's a gorgeous two-page illo of Godzilla fighting Marvel's very own kaiju: Fin Fang Foom! There's also a cool full-page panel that's just as good, showing (a new) Jet Jaguar flying above Godzilla and (a surprised-looking) Fin Fang Foom!

In one of the flashbacks Iron Man name-checks Goro Ibuki, the inventor of the first Jet Jaguar. Goro was a character featured in *Godzilla vs. Megalon* (1973), and it's a nice touch having Tony Stark, another inventor, knowing all about this guy!

The reason as to why the monsters were having a face-off is as light-hearted and jokey as the rest of the issue: a grumpy Fin Fang Foom (he can talk, remember?) admits to Hill and the Avengers that he took on Godzilla because he wanted to prove he was the King of Monsters, not Godzilla, but Godzilla just dismissively knocked Fin Fang Foom away with a slap of his tail!

It's an amusing, throwaway tale, and I'm quite fond of Fin Fang Foom: a long-faced, green-skinned dragon who wears purple pants! "But why is he wearing underwear?" Luke Cage asks at one point in the comic. Well, I don't know for sure, but I definitely think those pants are hiding something...

GODZILLA VS. THOR

Written by Jason Aaron, art by Aaron Kuder, colours by Jesus Aburtov.

The Archpriestess of The Hand (the occult, kill-happy ninja clan that has menaced many Marvel heroes over the years) uses the freshly spilled blood of murdered murderers to resurrect Godzilla... so that the great beast can become The Hand's messiah: King of All Killers!!!

The Archpriestess is able to do this because she's in possession of Godzilla's gigantic, still-beating heart, thus making *Godzilla vs. Thor* a direct sequel to the story told in the Toho movie *Godzilla, Mothra and King Ghidorah: Giant Monsters All-Out Attack* (2001). That film ended with Godzilla's disembodied heart continuing to beat as it lies on the ocean floor, and in this comic book we're shown that same enormous heart being doused with the blood of a group of convicted killers. To make sure we're fully aware of the link to the 2001 film, Aaron gives his story the subheading: "*Ragnarok All-Out Attack*".

The revived Godzilla rampages through Tokyo, much to the bloodthirsty delight of the Archpriestess, who believes no force can stand against the beast... but then... the Mighty Thor arrives - and from now on the scale of the conflict escalates until its scope goes beyond human comprehension!

Jason Aaron is such a great writer! He tells an epic tale, where Thor at first bests the atomic beast but, after the Archpriestess fuses Godzilla with a sliver of Gorr the God Butcher's Necrosword, the kaiju becomes a super-powerful bringer of destruction, capable of wrecking Asgard itself: Big G has become Godzilla the God Butcher!!! Godzilla is now a kaiju equipped with necrobreath capable of obliterating worlds! But Thor does not back down - he calls upon every tempest from every world across creation, he uses the energy of every solar squall and cosmic cyclone... he utilises every storm that has blustered from anywhere throughout infinity! Thor wields a cosmic hurricane the size of a galaxy! But Godzilla still stands tall! So, even though it might lead to his own destruction, Thor focuses the entirety of the superstorm through himself, and he plunges at Godzilla, yelling: "See you in Hel!" And, indeed, this comes to pass: both Thor and Godzilla now reside in Hel, on the shores of Gjoll - the land of the restless fallen. And they continue to fight! Every dawn in the land of the dead sees the battle renewed... combat beyond compare, raging until the end of time.

Damn this comic is good. The art is top class and, more importantly, Aaron delivers a story that evolves into a cosmic-scale Norse saga, with Thor and Godzilla playing the roles of ultimate hero vs. ultimate dragon in a cycle of furious battles that transcends death. Simply awe-inspiring.

GODZILLA

KING OF THE KAIJU

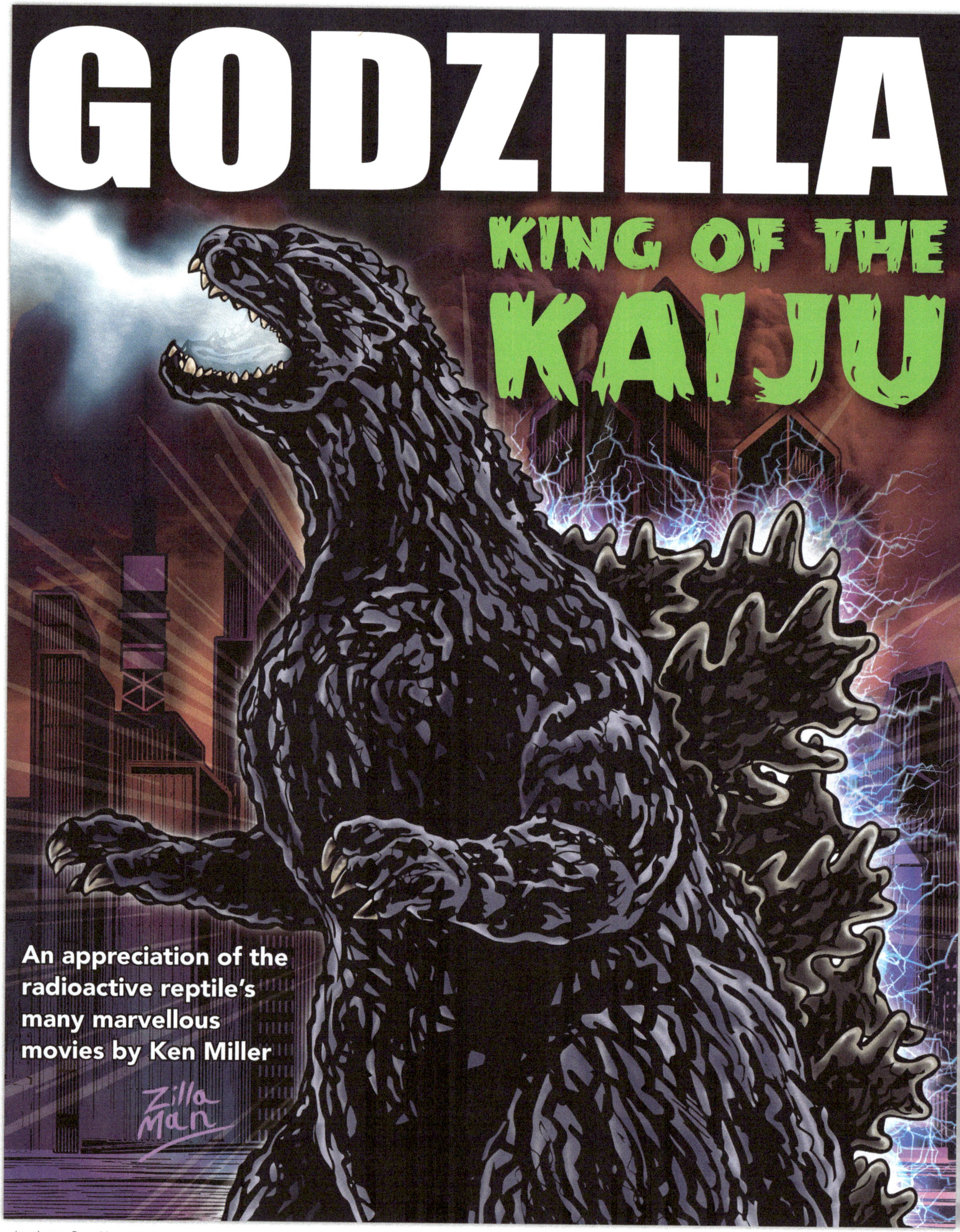

An appreciation of the radioactive reptile's many marvellous movies by Ken Miller

Godzilla, the big, roaring, reptilian star of so many giant monster movies, has repeatedly evolved over the decades. This gigantic super-beast has been depicted as a foe, as an anti-hero, and as a force of nature, in films that have fluctuated in their views of the kaiju king, treating Godzilla sometimes with deadly seriousness, then shifting tone to depict the uber-lizard in a far more lightweight, even humorous fashion.

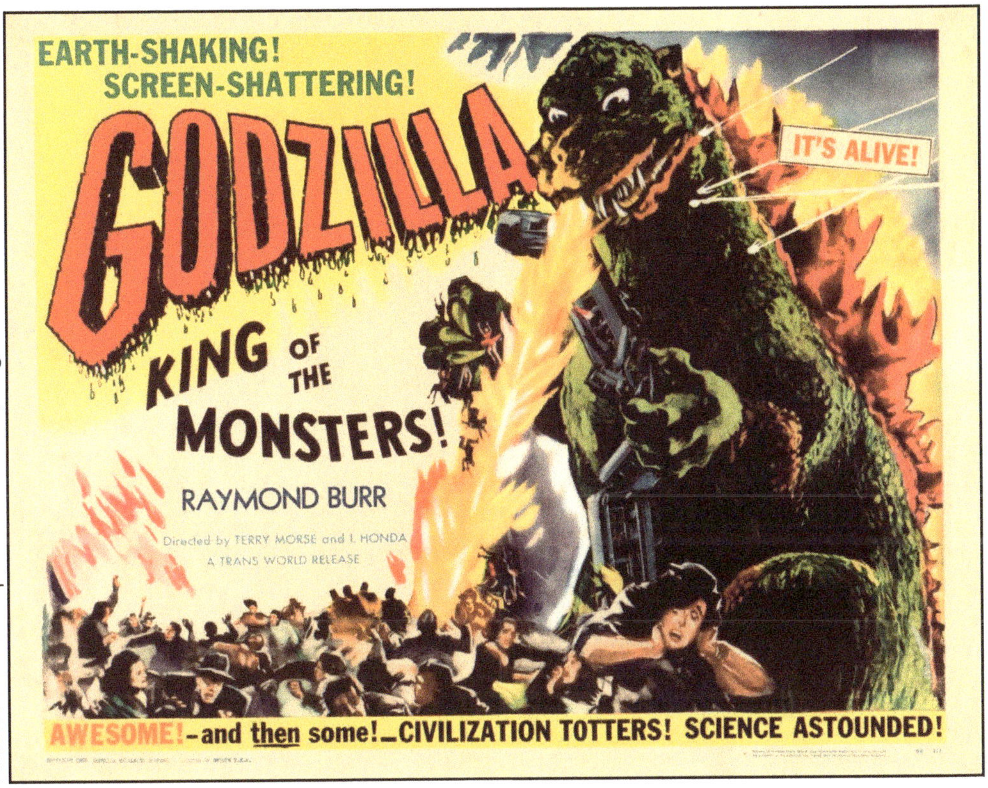

American half sheet poster for Godzilla, King of the Monsters!

The 70th anniversary of the release of the first Godzilla film was celebrated in 2024, garnering lots of media attention. The most recent Japanese Godzilla film, *Godzilla Minus One* (2023), continues to get loads of praise, and Godzilla's success in a string of smash hit, big budget US movies (plus live action TV series *Monarch: Legacy of Monsters*) is ongoing. So now is the time to have a look back at this cool, characterful creature, who is an international icon and one of the most famous and recognisable symbols of Japanese popular culture...

Japanese film company Toho was motivated to make the original *Godzilla* movie following the box office successes of *The Beast from 20,000 Fathoms* (1953) and the re-release of 1933's *King Kong* in 1952. *The Beast from 20,000 Fathoms*, with stop-motion special effects by Ray Harryhausen, was the first film to feature a gigantic creature awakened by an atomic bomb explosion, and *Godzilla* (1954) would use a similar concept. The name Godzilla is a romanisation of the Japanese name Gojira, which is a combination of two Japanese words meaning 'gorilla' and 'whale'. The raging, radioactive reptile obviously doesn't resemble a whale or a gorilla, but the name was intended to imply something truly huge, powerful, animalistic and aquatic.

Ishirō Honda directed and co-wrote *Godzilla*, the music was by Akira Ifukube, who composed the famous Godzilla theme, and special effects were supplied by Eiji Tsuburaya, who helped to pioneer the various tokusatsu (special effects) techniques that would be used in subsequent kaiju productions, including the use of scale model buildings and men in monster suits (suitmation).

But what gave *Godzilla* much more gravitas compared to *The Beast from 20,000 Fathoms* was the fact that the Toho movie was produced by a nation that had actually suffered from and lived through two atomic bomb attacks on its cities during World War 2. The titular beast was not just an enormous monster on the loose, he could be viewed as an ominous, living personification of Japan's fears of the threat of radioactivity in this new atomic age.

The look of Godzilla in the first film was that of a bipedal, humongous, dinosaur-like reptile that had jagged Stegosaurus-style plates running along his back and tail. With stout, pillar-like legs, the ability to emit radioactive heat-blasts from his mouth, and a distinctive roar, Godzilla's features have stayed pretty much the same (until *Shin Godzilla*), but with slight (and not so slight) differences from movie to movie, including alterations in Godzilla's facial expressions, a reduction in the amount of toes, the removal and then reincorporation of larger fangs, and overall size fluctuations (Godzilla's size can change from scene to scene in a film sometimes).

The 1954 film was a hit, launching the kaiju eiga (monster movies) genre in Japan. An extensively re-edited version (titled *Godzilla, King of the Monsters!*) was

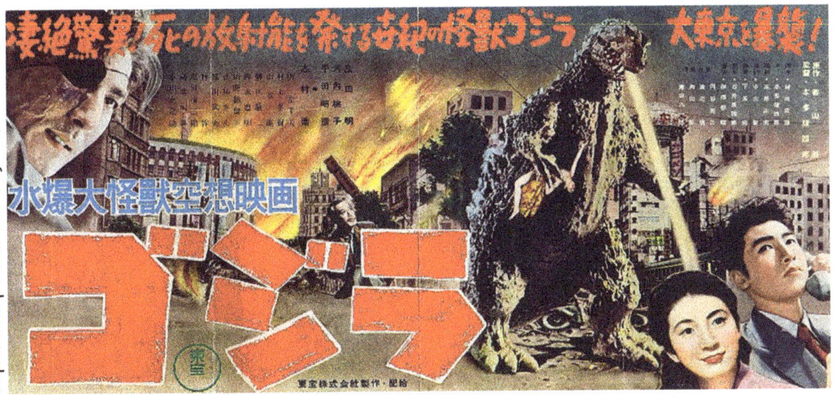

Japanese poster for *Gojira* (*Godzilla*)

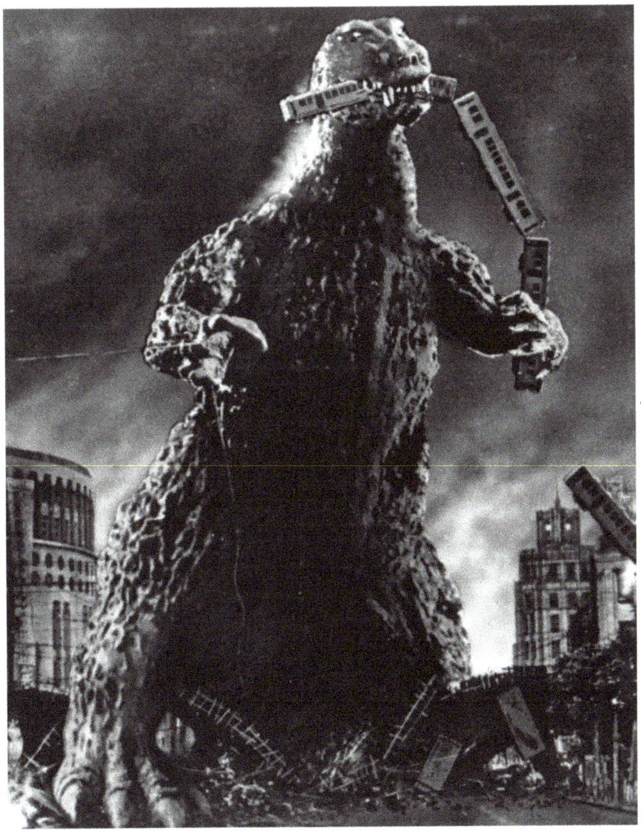

Nom, nom, nom... train carriages taste good!

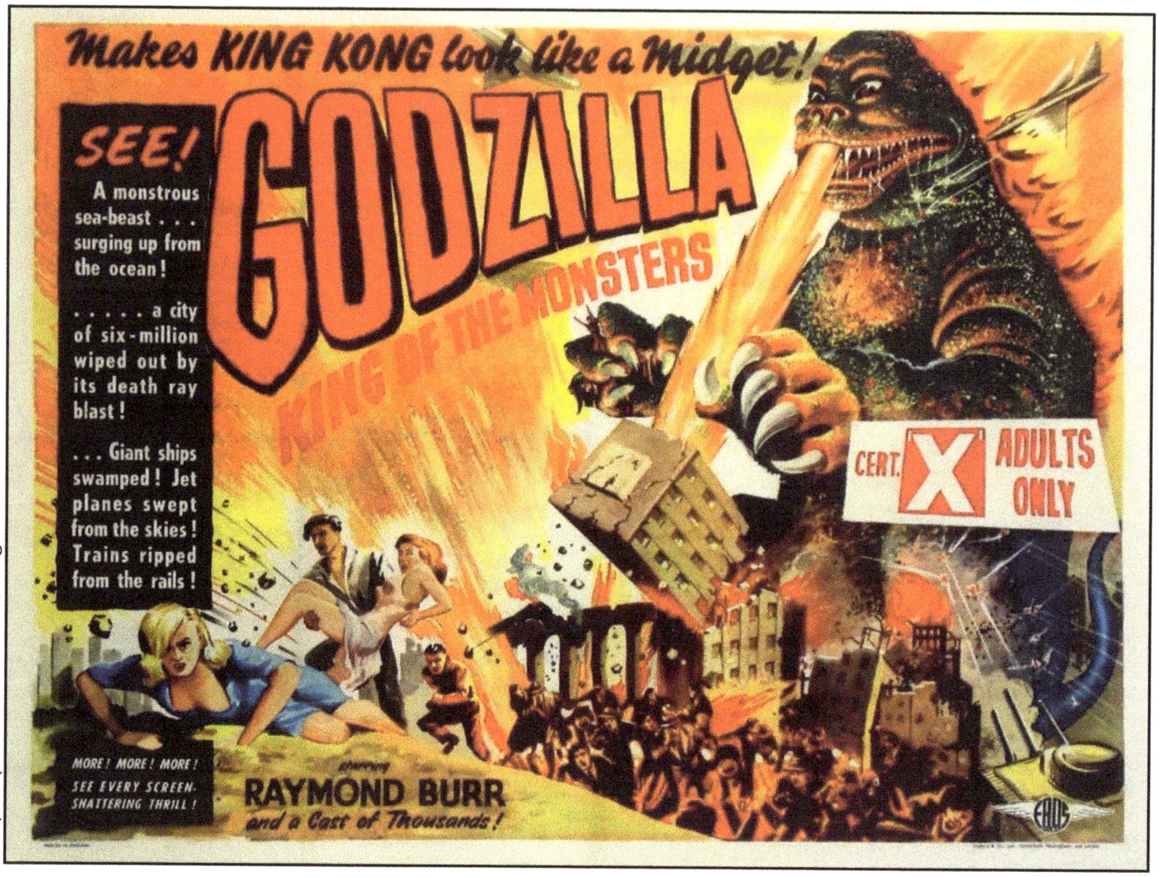

UK quad poster for *Godzilla, King of the Monsters!*

released in America in 1956. This featured over 20 minutes of new footage, starring Raymond Burr playing journalist Steve Martin, which was edited into the original Japanese movie. (The habit of incorporating a Western actor became fairly routine in subsequent tokusatsu kaiju films, such as with the US releases of *Half Human*, *Gamera the Giant Monster* and *King Kong vs. Godzilla*).

Whatever you think about *Godzilla, King of the Monsters!*, this was the version of the film that was responsible for introducing Godzilla to an international audience. In Great Britain the movie was slapped with an 'X' certificate, for adults only.

The Godzilla franchise would go from strength to strength, with the popularity of the movies leading to Godzilla appearing in other types of media, including cartoons, music, books, magazines, comics, toys, model kits and video games.

The Godzilla film series is broken down into four different 'eras'. The first, second, and fourth eras are named after the Japanese emperor who was reigning during production: the Shōwa era (Emperor Shōwa is known as Emperor Hirohito in English), the Heisei era (the period corresponding to the reign of Emperor Emeritus Akihito), and the Reiwa era (when the then-crown prince Naruhito ascended to the throne). The third era is called the Millennium era, because the Emperor (Heisei) was the same, but these Godzilla movies are considered to have a different style and they feature storylines that differ a lot from the Heisei era flicks.

Shōwa era (1954 - 1975)

The first series of movies started with 1954's *Godzilla* and ended with 1975's *Terror of Mechagodzilla*.

After 1955's sequel *Godzilla Raids Again* (re-edited and released as *Gigantis, the Fire Monster* in the US), which first featured the staple of having Godzilla battling it out with another massive monster (in this case the ankylosaur-like Anguirus), the Godzilla films from then on would be shot in colour, starting with the hugely profitable *King Kong vs. Godzilla* (1962).

The genesis of *King Kong vs. Godzilla* is interesting, in that it was originally a project conceived by stop-motion effects master Willis O'Brien as a sequel to *King Kong* (1933), with the big ape coming face to face with an equally enormous Frankenstein Monster. The film would've been titled *King Kong vs. Prometheus*. O'Brien's story idea was stolen by producer John Beck, who sold it to Toho, who ultimately made *King Kong vs. Godzilla* instead. O'Brien did contemplate suing Beck for intent to defraud, but he did not have enough money for a protracted legal battle. *King Kong vs. Godzilla* was released theatrically in Japan on August 11th, 1962, and O'Brien died of a heart attack in his home on November 10th, 1962. His widow, Darlyne, would later cite "the frustration of the King Kong Vs. Frankenstein deal" as a contributing factor to his death.

In this movie Godzilla was still depicted as the villain, breaking free of an iceberg to cause havoc. The film was colourful and a lot of fun, though King Kong purists will no doubt continue to frown and wince when looking at the rather inexpressive mask used for the heroic ape, which only showed any movement in a handful of close-ups, where a separate head was utilised to show Kong doing such things as eating berries.

With shots of Kong being floated to his showdown with Godzilla by balloons (an updated version of this Kong airlift occurs in 2021's US MonsterVerse flick *Godzilla vs. Kong*), and a fight with a big octopus, the movie's real highpoint is the super-fight on Mount Fuji. This finale has a lot of oomph to it, as Kong gets trashed, knocked to the ground, covered in boulders, and smacked about the cranium by Godzilla's tail. Then... an electrical storm appears, lightning strikes Kong, he absorbs its power, his face glows blue, and he really lays into the radioactive reptile, his every touch giving

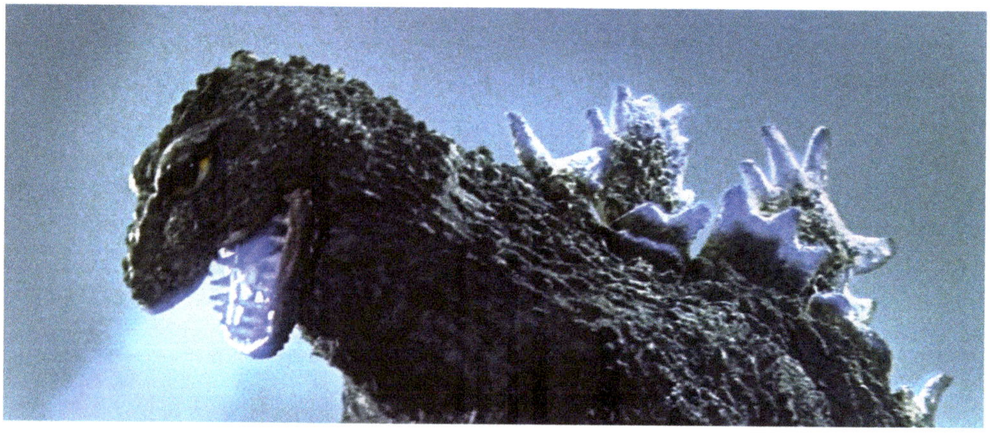
King Kong vs. Godzilla (1962)

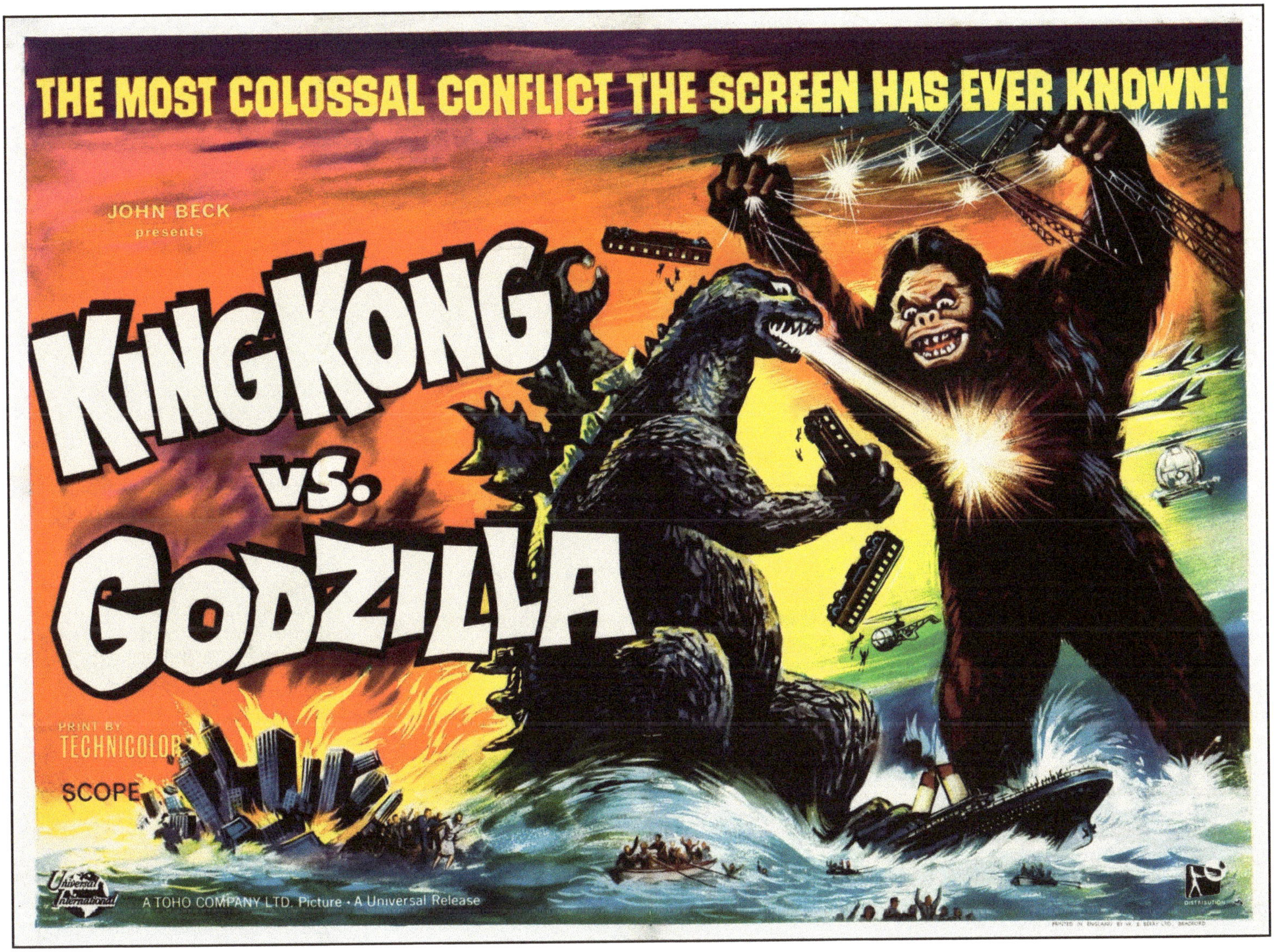

off bolts of electricity, whilst trees burn about the beasts thanks to Godzilla's bad breath. Fun, fun, fun!

1964's *Mothra vs. Godzilla* (also known as *Godzilla vs. The Thing)*, dealing with issues like corporate greed, nuclear testing, themes of unity and mysticism, is considered to be one of Ishiro Honda's best Godzilla entries. Huge insect-deity Mothra, seen previously in her own movie *Mothra* (1961), battles Godzilla, and then, after her demise, her two newborn larvae take over, entrapping Godzilla in their silk. Godzilla was still clearly a menacing, destructive monster at this point of the series, but things would change with the next release...

Beginning with *Ghidorah, the Three-Headed Monster* (1964), Godzilla started to change into a more positive, anti-hero-type critter. The large, golden-skinned, winged space-dragon King Ghidorah would become one of Godzilla's key enemies, returning again and again to face-off against Godzilla. Producing hurricane-force winds by flapping its wings, the massive, twin-tailed Ghidorah is usually such a handful that Godzilla often teams-up with other monsters to battle his nemesis, as happens here when the new Mothra and titanic pterosaur Rodan both join up to aid Godzilla.

Invasion of Astro-Monster (1965), also known as *Monster Zero*, *Invasion of the Astro-Monsters*, *Invasion of Planet X* and *Battle of the Astros*, saw Ghidorah return, referred to here as Monster Zero, in a film boasting some good UFO miniature work and nice cartoon laser/sound-wave FX. A high point involves a three-way monster fight between Godzilla, Rodan and King Ghidorah on Planet X's rocky surface, with Godzilla doing a preposterous victory dance after seeing off King Ghidorah! With devious, shades-wearing aliens using the monsters to attack Earth, *Invasion of Astro-Monster* ends with King Ghidorah being given a good beating-up by Godzilla and Rodan. Great stuff!

Ebirah, Horror of the Deep (1966), aka *Godzilla vs. the Sea Monster*, was an entertaining yarn (originally planned to star King Kong before the ape was replaced with Godzilla) that featured a villainous group called the Red Bamboo, based on an island guarded by a giant lobster! Not to be taken seriously, the film's best moment for me was the confrontation between Godzilla and his shrimpy adversary, where they take turns smacking a huge boulder at

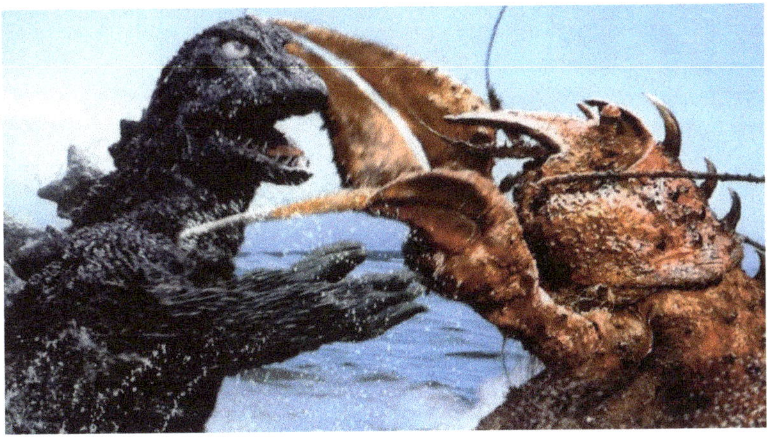
Godzilla fights Ebirah!

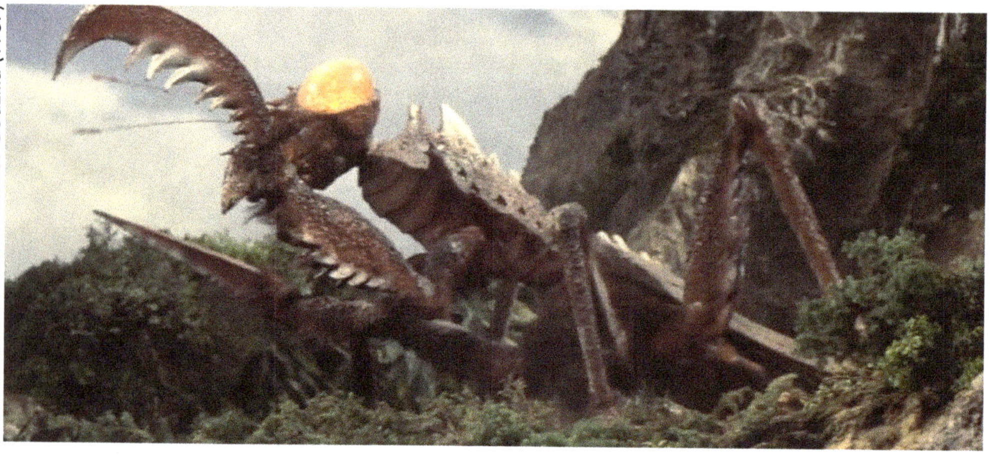

A cool Kamacuras from *Son of Godzilla* (1967)

each other, as if they're playing volleyball! This bright, tightly-budgeted, lightweight production also had a brief fight between Godzilla and a giant condor, a nuclear power plant getting smashed, and a cameo from Mothra.

Son of Godzilla (1967) came next, and it was another colourful, island-set story. This time we got some wonderfully entertaining monsters brought to life as marionettes, rather than men in suits. The Kamacuras were three mutated giant praying mantises, and Kumonga was an eight-legged, massive, web-spitting spider. These puppet beasts are great fun to watch, especially the mantises. The other new creature that appeared in this Godzilla flick, which I definitely found less appealing to watch, was Minilla... Godzilla's son! Obviously intended to appeal to younger audiences, this pug-faced lil' bugger blew smoke rings, made babyish noises and was meant to be cuddly and cute, but I've always found the critter (also referred to in some dubs as Minya) to be rather annoying... and it doesn't even resemble Godzilla! Talking of which, the Godzilla suit used in this entry has a goofy, toad-like face. But, hey, the big bug monsters are the main reasons for watching this playful flick.

All Monsters Attack (1969), also known as *Godzilla's Revenge*, was another release to really aim at the kiddie audience, and is disliked by many for cutting costs and just regurgitating footage from previous Toho films (*Ebirah, Horror of the Deep, King Kong Escapes*, *Son of Godzilla*, etc). Focusing on a childish tale of a young boy dreaming that he can visit Monster Island and become pals with Minilla, who can shrink down to human size and chat with him, the film's new monster footage involved a bullying beast called Gabara, a somewhat foolish-looking creature who fights Minilla and Godzilla. With a message about standing up to bullies, *All Monsters Attack*, though much maligned, was a sweet flick that probably doesn't quite deserve all the vitriol it received.

Released the previous year was *Destroy All Monsters* (1968), a very entertaining example of Toho's Shōwa era kaiju flicks: a universe where monsters are an everyday occurrence, the suits worn by astronauts are bright yellow, cities are regularly wiped-out (but always reconstitute themselves for the next film), and the various armed forces are always on standby with numerous rocket launchers, jets and tanks (which pretty much never have the proper firepower to really hurt the monsters!) In *Destroy All Monsters* we see Godzilla, Rodan, Mothra (larval stage), Anguirus, Gorosaurus, Manda and other kaiju denizens of Monsterland (also known as Monster Island) becoming the pawns of an alien race, called the Kilaaks, who use mind-control devices to turn the (now quite benign) creatures into aggressive, city-wrecking weapons of mass destruction.

Destroy All Monsters was a staggeringly fun production filled with cell-animated laser effects, UFOs, moon bases, some sweet model work, a satisfyingly large quota of monsters, and a knockabout final fight near Mount Fuji, where the re-grouped Earth super-critters kicked and bit Ghidorah the three-headed space dragon until he was well and truly mullered!

Two of the best portions of the film, for me, were the opening scenes, where we get a helicopter tour of Monsterland that shows us all the great beasties chilling out on their island home, and, of course, the other highlight is the aforementioned no holds barred multi-monster battle

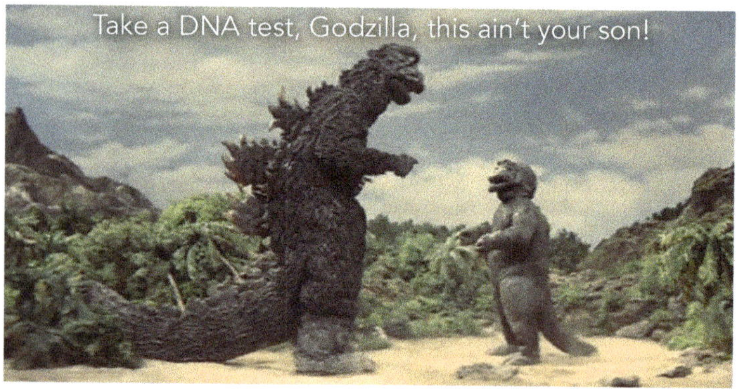

Take a DNA test, Godzilla, this ain't your son!

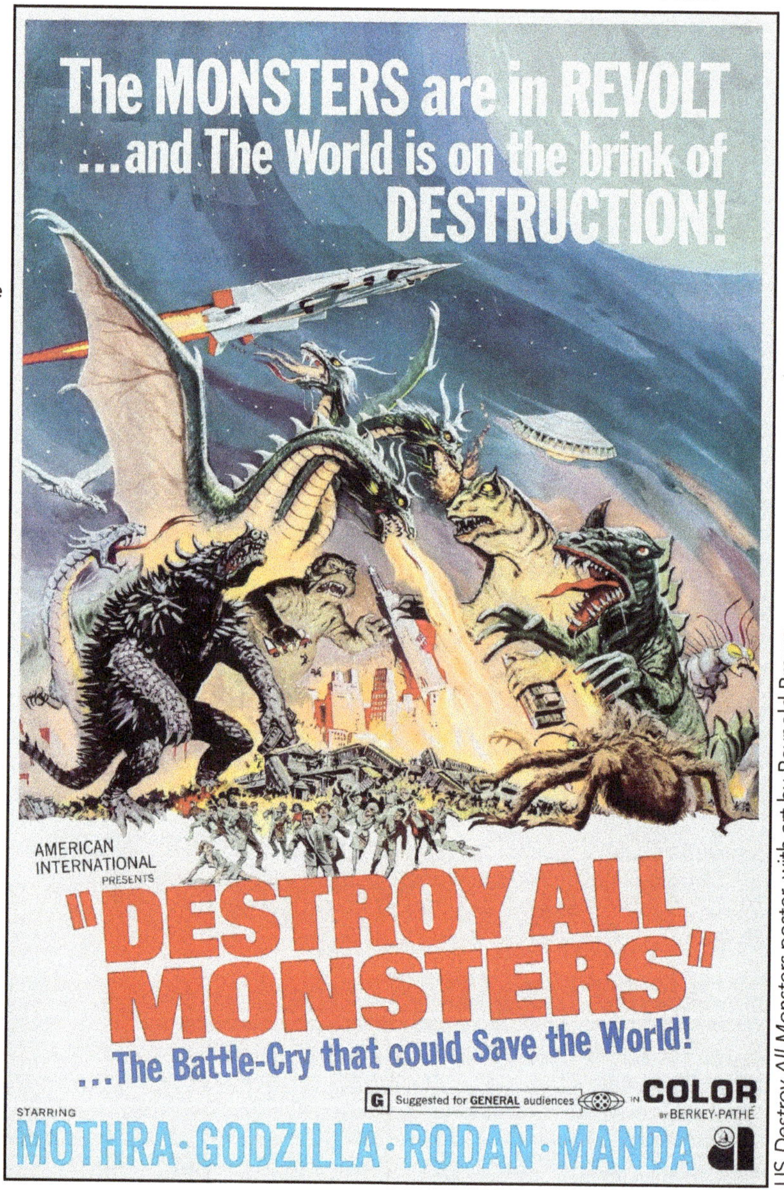

US *Destroy All Monsters* poster, with art by Reynold Brown

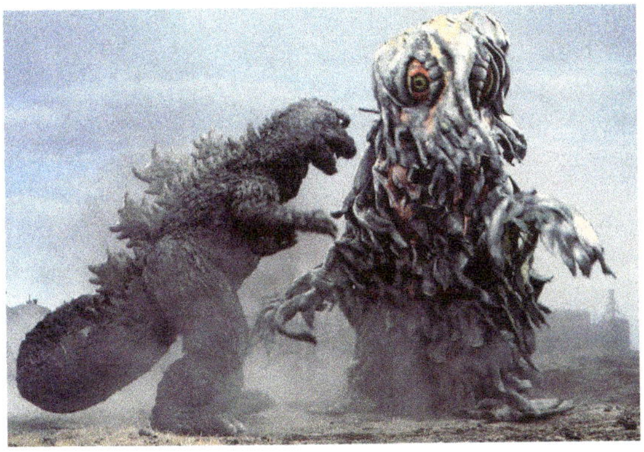

Godzilla confronts Hedorah!

sequence at the end. Stonkingly amazing entertainment!

1971's *Godzilla vs. Hedorah*, also known as *Godzilla vs. the Smog Monster*, was another shift of tone, telling the story of an ever-changing alien creature that arrived on Earth to devour the world's pollution. It then begins to expel toxic killer mists and sludge-globs! Psychedelic, hippyish, trippy moments, animated interludes, a worthy environmental message backed up by numerous shots of muddy, pollution-ravaged Tokyo bay, a monstrous adversary that sometimes resembles a flying lump of muck with eyes, and scenes of victims getting turned into skeletons, were all mixed together to make this into a quite bizarre, nightmarishly fun/cheesy outing for Godzilla, who even gets to 'fly' in an embarrassing scene that shows the heroic reptile using his atomic breath as a kind of jet propulsion! Oh, the madness of it all!

Godzilla vs. Gigan (aka *War of the Monsters* and *Godzilla on Monster Island*), from 1972, was a far less grim entry and is a real hoot. The film saw Godzilla, with best beast pal Anguirus, take on King Ghidorah and Gigan, who have been sent to attack Japan by alien cockroaches. The space monster Gigan, a bio-mechanical critter with buzzsaw-like gut-spikes, a beak, metal mandibles, a large back-fin, curved prongs for hands, and a kind of glowing visor instead of eyes, is a truly ludicrous-looking design... and I love it!

The best bit comes when Godzilla does the 'Ali Shuffle' as he 'boxes' with King Ghidorah. The silliest thing in *Godzilla vs. Gigan*, however, is the scene where Godzilla and Anguirus have a chat together! Word balloons were used in the Japanese version, but the US release uses actual English-dubbed voices. There was an over-use of stock footage in this film again, that's for sure, but you do get to see Godzilla bleed from wounds and, of course, you also get to see silly ol' Gigan! And, hooray, Gigan returned in the next movie, *Godzilla vs. Megalon* (1973)! This flick, which was guilty of reusing stock footage too, has a story that revolves around the denizens of the undersea kingdom of Seatopia, who are hopping mad about the repeated nuclear tests on Earth that have disturbed their tranquillity... so they decide to unleash a monster named Megalon topside to wreck lots of stuff.

Megalon is another unhinged Toho monster design: it has a bug-like face, beetle-wings on its back, and a central

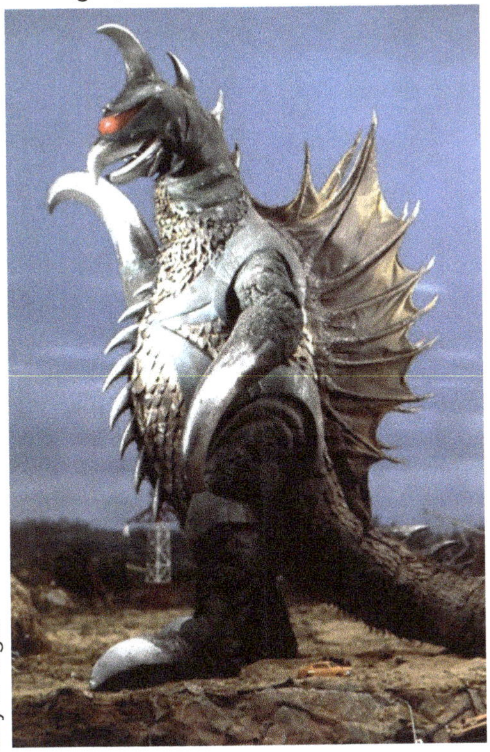

Silly ol' Gigan

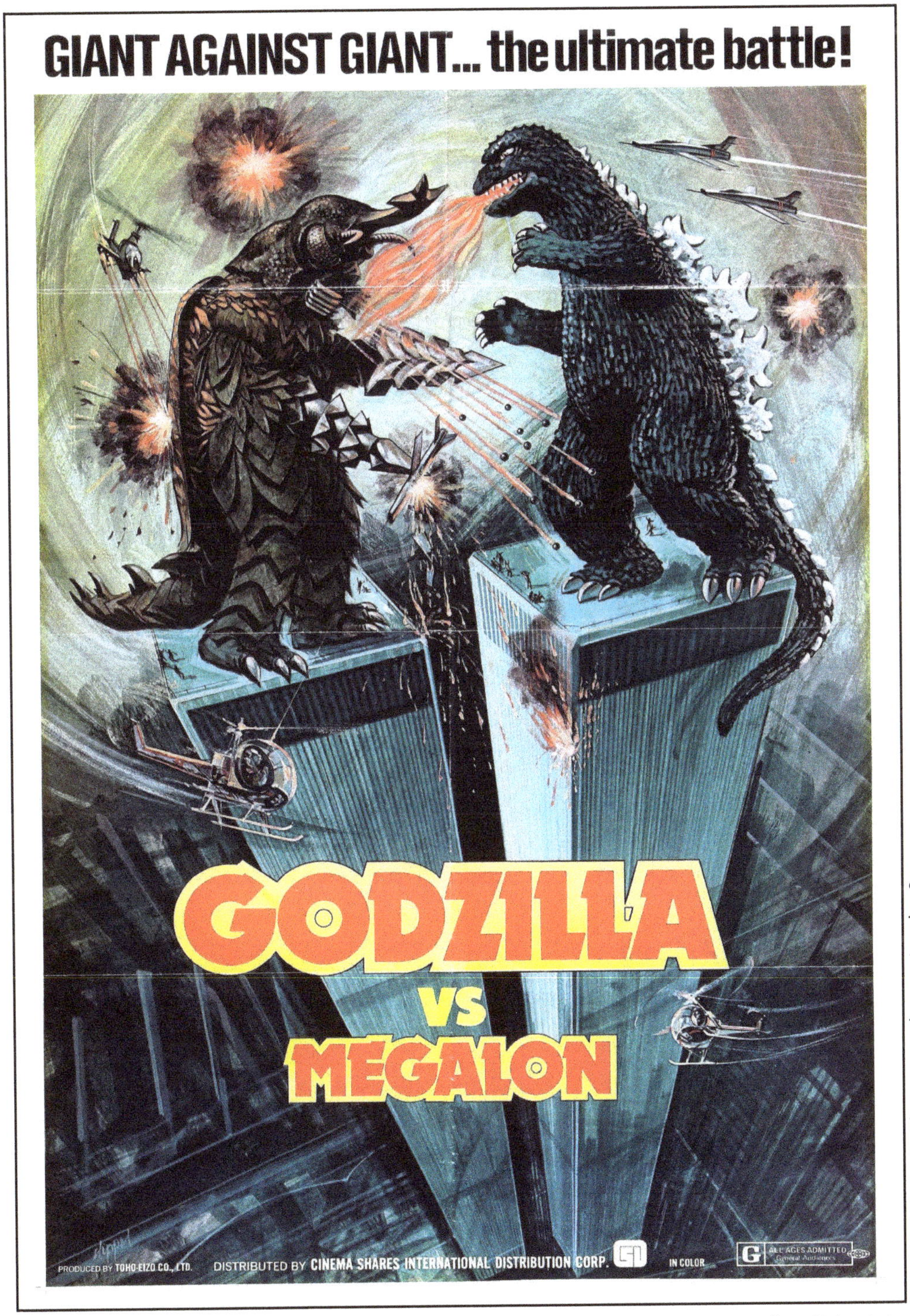

This doesn't actually happen in the movie, okay?

projection sticking from the top of its head (inspired by the long cephalic horn of the Japanese rhinoceros beetle), from which it can fire yellow lightning bolts. The mad-lookin' monster also has metallic forearm appendages, which can be combined to form a single rotating drill, allowing the beastie to speedily burrow underground!

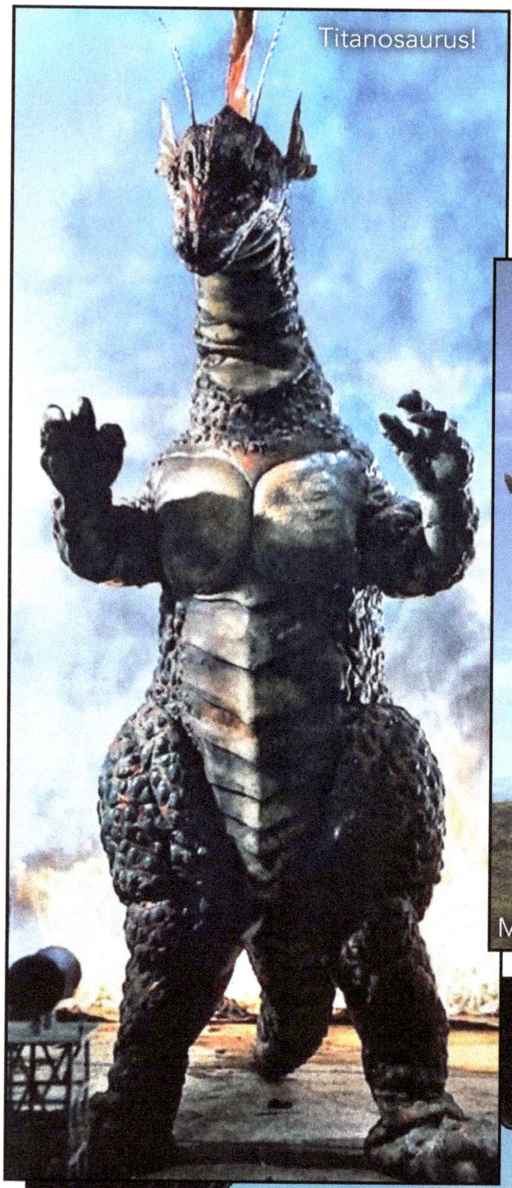

Titanosaurus!

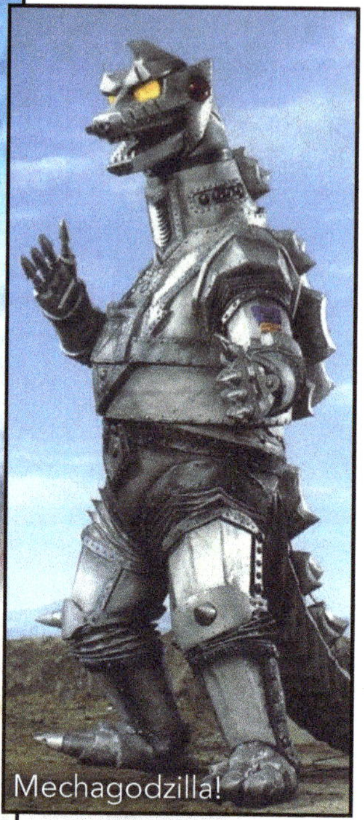

Mechagodzilla!

The oddball, absurd, bio-mechanical look of Megalon's design certainly put the bug-eyed beast in the same category as the cyborg-kaiju Gigan, which is cool as Gigan arrives to team-up with Megalon in this film, to do battle with Godzilla, who joins forces with Jet Jaguar, a humanoid (Ultraman knock-off) robot that can grow from human size to kaiju dimensions! Big G and Jet Jaguar are ultimately victorious, of course, forcing Megalon and Gigan to retreat, after which Godzilla and Jet Jaguar shake each other's hands and go their separate ways! They're mates! Was this movie silly, ludicrous and cheap? You bet! But it is all kinds of fun too, with a splendidly cheesy, loopy, mad suitmation-tastic third act WWE-style fight, where Godzilla (with a face like a giant, cheeky gecko) performs two jaw-droppingly exaggerated, gravity-defying drop kicks!

The final two Godzilla films to be released as part of the Shōwa era both featured the fan-favourite robo-kaiju... Mechagodzilla!

Godzilla vs. Mechagodzilla (1974), also known as *Godzilla vs. Bionic Monster* and *Godzilla vs. Cosmic Monster*, which came out to celebrate Godzilla's 20th anniversary, presented us with the massive reptilian hero tackling his mechanical doppelgänger, controlled by alien apes! Failing to beat his robo-twin in combat on his own, Godzilla is assisted by dog-faced Okinawan god-monster King Caesar (aka King Seeser). Godzilla's beastly buddy Angiurus returns, and is shown to be capable of leaping at his foes now, leading to a very physical skirmish with Mechagodzilla. Mecha-G is definitely the stand-out element in this film, firing rockets from its fingers, discharging lightning bolts from its chest, emitting colourful beams from its eyes, and creating whirling forcefields with its spinning metal head! The fights are really enjoyable, full of multiple explosions and animated power beams. Even Mechagodzilla's knees are lethal, as they fire projectiles at Godzilla and King Caesar!

Terror of Mechagodzilla (1975), also known as *Monsters from an Unknown Planet*, has Godzilla combating a new

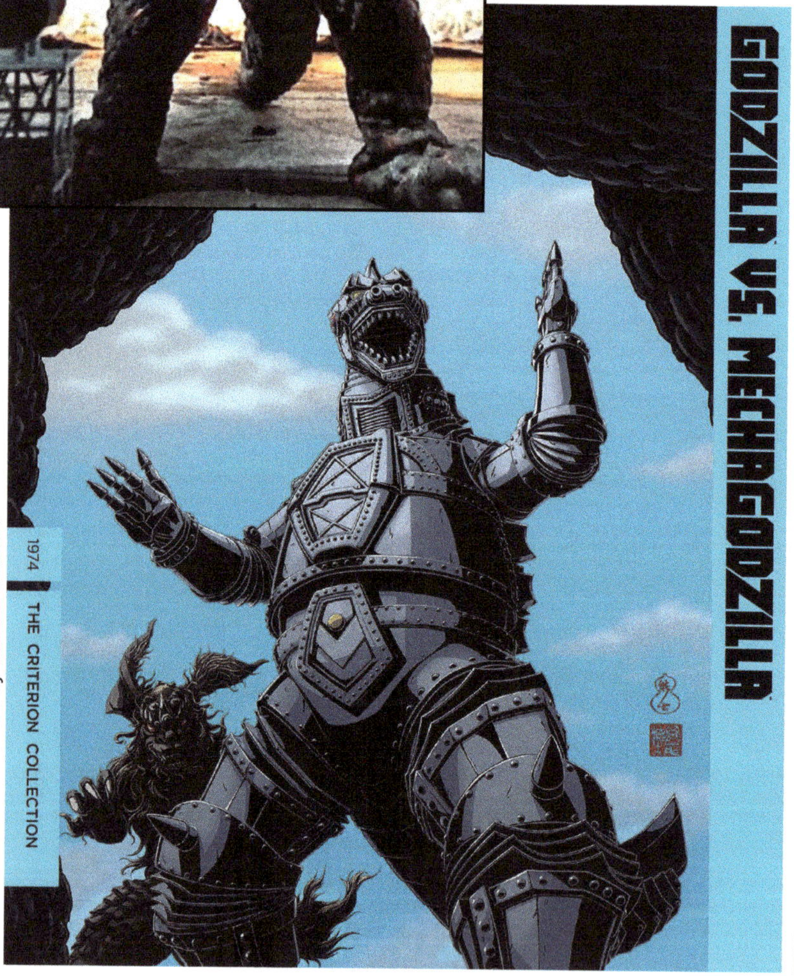

Criterion Collection artwork by Takashi Okazaki

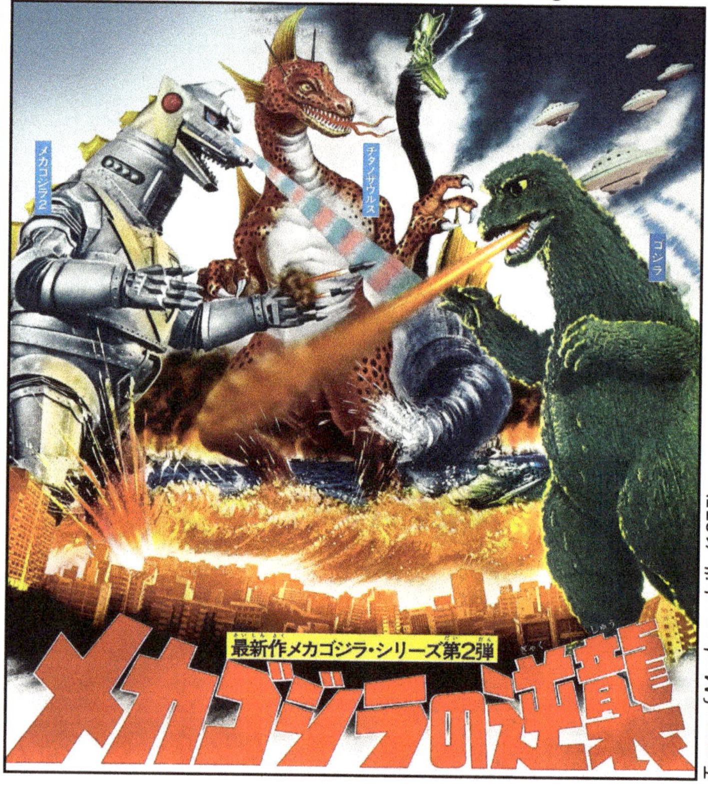

Terror of Mechagodzilla (1975)

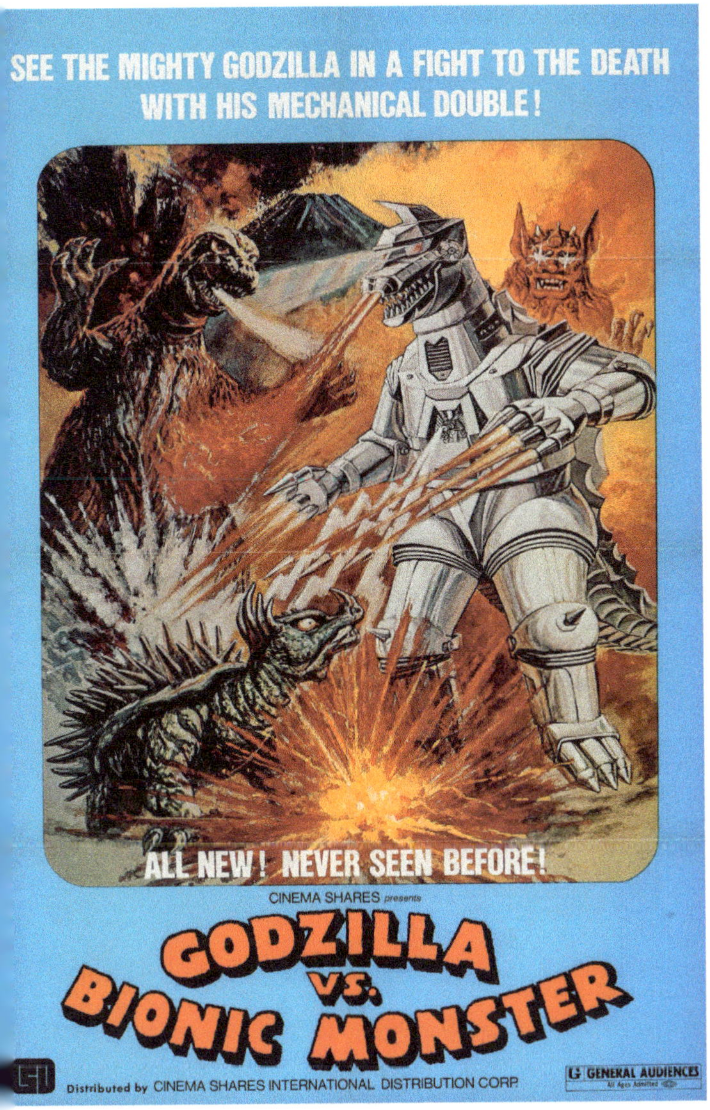

Mechagodzilla (controlled again by the extraterrestrial ape-beings), with the mecha-monster this time helped by a long-necked kaiju-dinosaur called Titanosaurus, an aquatic behemoth capable of creating powerful winds with its webbed tail! Titanosaurus could often look pretty goofy in its scenes, but I still like the beast!

Even though Toho brought back Ishirô Honda to direct and Akira Ifukube to compose the great score, *Terror of Mechagodzilla* performed poorly at the box office, leading to an almost decade-long hiatus in the series.

Heisei era (1984 - 1995)

The series was rebooted with *The Return of Godzilla* in 1984, which ignored every movie after the 1954 original, taking on a darker and more serious tone.

The film's dialogue often deals with musings concerning whether or not the great reptile is somehow a terrible offspring of man's pride and carelessness, here to remind us of just how puny we are. All these deep meditations were a far cry from the 70s-era Godzilla flicks, where a valiant, do-gooder Godzilla fought cockroach aliens and Minilla taught children how to deal with bullies, so, in the context of *The Return of Godzilla*, it made a lot of sense to ignore all the films that came after the original.

Godzilla is still obviously a suitmation creation here, but the sets are more spectacular, and there is a pretty respectable fight with fighter jets. Scenes of the main actors attempting to escape a wrecked skyscraper work well, imbuing the enterprise with a disaster movie feel.

New World Pictures produced an edited English-language version titled *Godzilla 1985*, which added Raymond Burr, reprising his role of Steve Martin from *Godzilla, King of the Monsters!* Burr's scenes look tacked-on, though, and really could've been done without.

Godzilla vs. Biollante (1989) featured a plant monster created by a scientist who spliced cells from his dead daughter and some Godzilla cells into a rose. Bad idea! This genetically altered plant-animal hybrid kaiju appears in different forms, at first resembling a giant rose with long, prehensile vines and a set of jaws inside a large, red flower. Its second

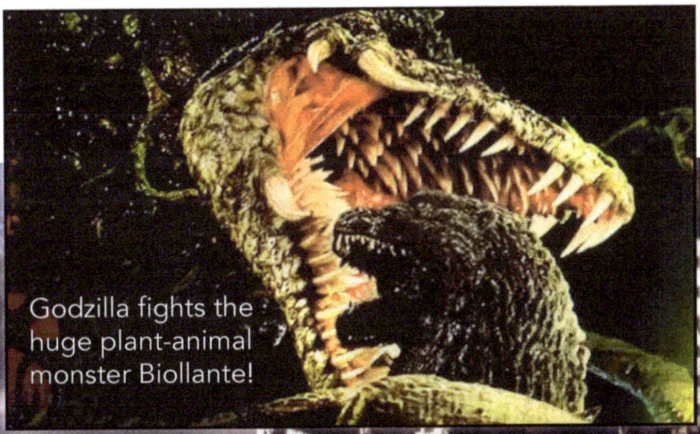
Godzilla fights the huge plant-animal monster Biollante!

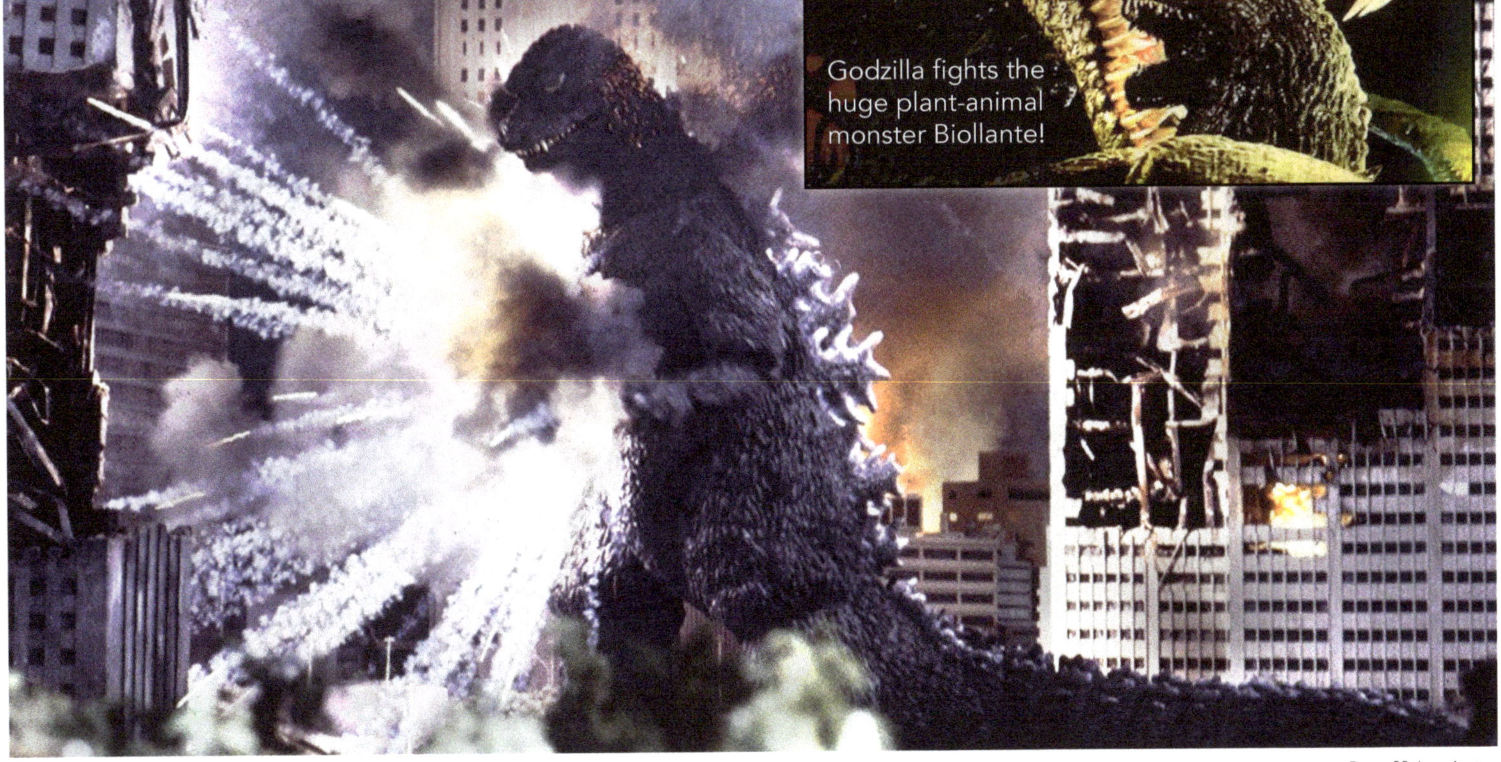
It's all kicking off in *The Return of Godzilla!*

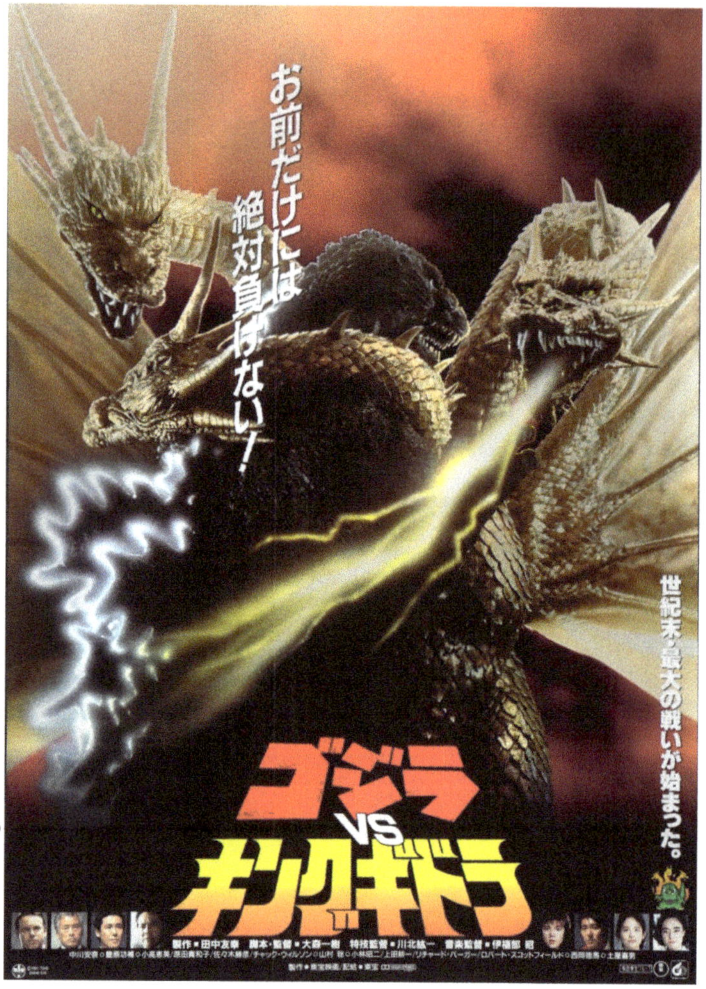

Godzilla vs. King Ghidorah (1991)

form develops more reptilian attributes: a long-snouted, tooth-filled, crocodilian head, lots of tendrils and vines, some of which have dangerously-sharp ends and others that terminate in small, toothy mouths! This massive kaiju only appeared in this one live action Godzilla movie, but it remains a fan favourite.

1991's *Godzilla vs. King Ghidorah* saw the return of Big G's three-headed nemesis! The story involves time travellers from the future arriving in Japan to say that they are going to save the country from Godzilla by heading back to 1944 to remove a carnivorous dinosaur (Godzillasaurus) from an island before it could be mutated into Godzilla by the Castle Bravo H-bomb test conducted at the nearby Bikini Atoll in 1954. The future folk turn out to actually have ulterior motives, however, and their real plan results in the creation of King Ghidorah!

The triple-necked, winged menace really looks good in this film! King Ghidorah battles Godzilla, but loses its middle head and its wings get wrecked, leaving the beast in a comatose state.... but its remains are salvaged and the critter is revived as... Mecha-King Ghidorah! This cyborg iteration of the great dragon-monster sports a robot middle head, plus mechanical neck, chest, wings, knees and tail-tips! Mecha-King Ghidorah's cybernetic central head can fire a triple laser beam from the cannon housed in its mouth, the cyborg-beast can also deploy four electrified capture-cables, and even possesses a big mechanical hand with which it can grab onto Godzilla!

The success of *Godzilla vs. King Ghidorah* at the box office inspired Toho to start reintroducing classic monsters from the Shōwa series into these Heisei Godzilla movies. And so it was time for a certain Lepidopterous kaiju to be reintroduced...

Godzilla vs. Mothra (1992), also known as *Godzilla and Mothra: The Battle for Earth,* showcased the return of everybody's favourite divine moth: Mothra! Also appearing in this film, for Godzilla to battle, was a more destructive dark deity moth-monster called Battra! This critter had yellow horns on its head and wings that were more ragged and evil-looking. As this film involved Mothra, we got some preachy save-the-environment messages, a chance to see the new micro-sized twin priestesses of Mothra (called the 'Cosmos'), and scenes of both Mothra and Battra in their larval forms. Lots of fighting and colourful special effects abound in this film (and the popular Mothra would go on to star in her own trilogy of 90s movies).

Godzilla vs. Mechagodzilla II (1993) saw Toho bring back their good ol' robo-zilla character, though I have to admit I preferred the meaner-faced look of the 70s version of Mechagodzilla. The reason the filmmakers made Mechagodzilla (who has been reverse-engineered from the remains of Mecha-King Ghidorah in this story) look less evil now is probably down to the fact that this cyber-critter is actually a good guy in the movie. Godzilla gets to skirmish with famed pterosaur-kaiju Rodan in this flick too, plus there is also the return of... BabyGodzilla! No!!! Ah, but wait, this BabyGodzilla monster suit is infinitely better-looking than the pug-faced costume used for the mewling, annoying Minilla back in the 70s. In the following two films BabyGodzilla would grow up to be first LittleGodzilla and then a sub-adult, named Godzilla Junior, but I digress, let's get back to *Godzilla vs. Mechagodzilla II*... This entry features the international joint military organization known as G-Force, there's lots of chaos and destruction, the seemingly

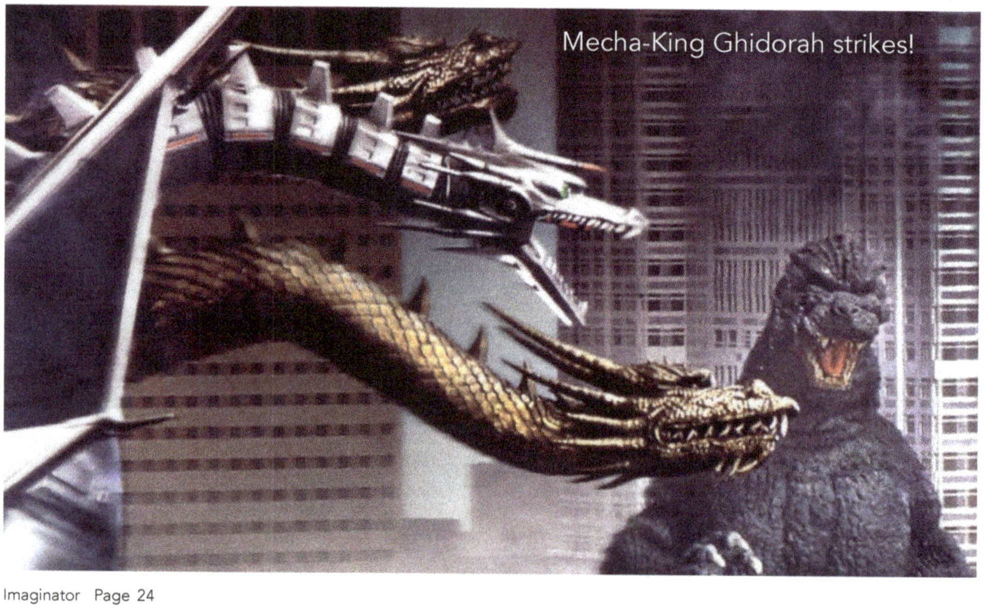

Mecha-King Ghidorah strikes!

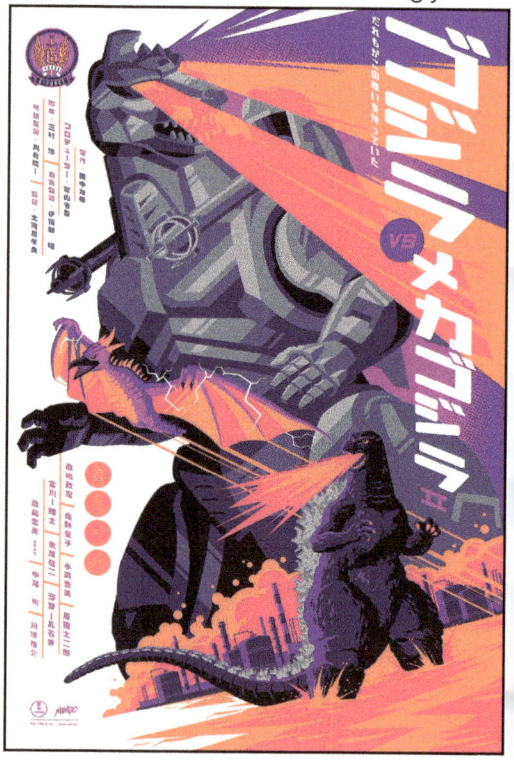

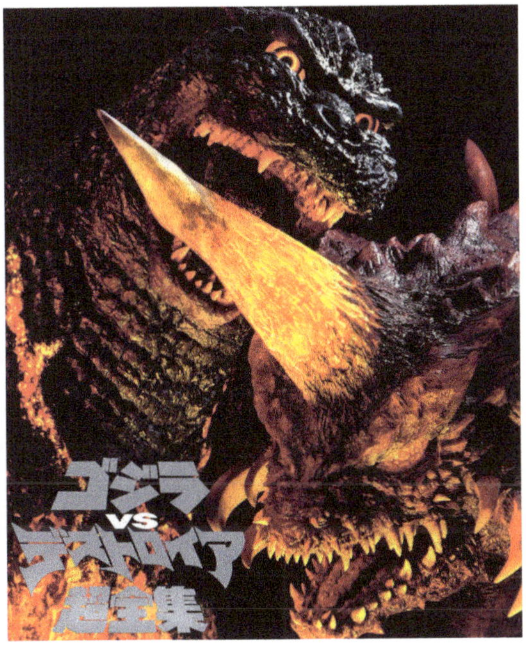

dead Rodan is resurrected as the red-skinned Fire Rodan, and we get to witness the damaged Mechagodzilla being modified to become Super MechaGodzilla!

G-Force would build yet another anti-Godzilla machine in 1994's *Godzilla vs. SpaceGodzilla*, this time calling it MOGUERA (an acronym for Mobile Operations Godzilla Universal Expert Robot Aero-type). This drill-nosed robotic machine, which was actually a reimagining of the robo-monster seen in Toho's 1957 sci-fi flick *The Mysterians*, actually ends up fighting with Godzilla, rather than against him, to combat the bigger threat posed by SpaceGodzilla.

SpaceGodzilla is an interesting creation, closely resembling Godzilla (it was spawned when some of Big G's cells ended up in space), but with massive, glowing crystals thrusting from its back. This extraterrestrial beastie, with its energy attacks, psychic powers, and its ability to create and use crystals in varying ways, was a very resilient, tough opponent for Godzilla.

This entertaining film marked Godzilla's 40th anniversary and also featured LittleGodzilla (blech!), Fairy Mothra and Mothra (plus stock footage of Battra and Biollante).

The final Heisei era Godzilla movie was *Godzilla vs. Destoroyah* (1995), which I like a lot. Directed by Takao Okawara, with a script written by Kazuki Omori and special effects by Koichi Kawakita, this film saw Godzilla, coated in hot, glowing, lava-like rashes, going on a wrecking spree in Hong Kong. It is revealed that Godzilla's internal nuclear fission processes have gone haywire, threatening to explode and destroy the world. If this wasn't bad enough, another monster has appeared: a creature that is a conglomeration of masses of crustaceans that were mutated by the Oxygen Destroyer weapon used to kill the very first Godzilla back in 1954.

Destoroyah is a novel, nasty kaiju, becoming a massive beast with a large, central head-horn, glowing orange eyes, big tusks projecting from its face, huge shoulder horns and massive wings. Godzilla bests this beast, which had killed Big G's son, Godzilla Junior, but Destoroyah returns to fight, as a swarm of multiple-legged mini-Destoroyahs! Even after Godzilla wipes out these things, Destoroyah returns yet again in winged form. But Destoroyah is eventually killed and the terminally overheating Godzilla stands alone, dying... so the Japanese Self Defence Force desperately shoot cryo-lasers and fire coolant-projectiles to prevent a full-on meltdown. As an Akira Ifukube theme, reworked with choral voices, plays on the soundtrack, Godzilla roars while his flesh falls off him and he decays... and the human characters watch on as radiation levels rapidly reduce... and the camera moves through the smoke and steam and there, backlit, is Godzilla Junior, who has been brought back to life by his dying father's energies, and has rapidly matured, ready to take on the role of king of the monsters. This is truly the most emotional moment in Godzilla history! I'm welling-up as I write about it!

This was an awesome way to end the Heisei era Godzilla series, with a very memorable-looking Godzilla, who was in pain much of the time, glowing with uncontrollable inner-heat, emitting steam, bleeding lava, his great back-plates uncontrollably flickering.

Millennium era (1999 - 2004)

Toho put the Godzilla series on a temporary pause, to make space for TriStar Pictures' big budget US *Godzilla* movie, which was eventually released in 1998. The widespread fan backlash against Dean Devlin and Roland Emmerich's take on the property, plus new-found demand for a Japanese-made Godzilla film, persuaded Toho to release a new live action entry in the series, titled *Godzilla 2000: Millennium*, in 1999, which started the third era of Godzilla films, known as the Millennium series. The Millennium era Godzilla films can be viewed as an anthology series, because most of these films were standalone stories, with the 1954 film acting as the only previous point of reference. Just *Godzilla Against Mechagodzilla* and *Godzilla: Tokyo S.O.S.* share continuity with each other.

In *Godzilla 2000: Millennium*, aka *Godzilla 2000*, we got to see the new-look Godzilla suit, which boasted large, sharp back-plates, a head with a toothy, big mouth, a somewhat flattened cranium, and eyes positioned further towards the front of the very reptilian-looking face.

Here Godzilla is like a living force of nature, forever being tracked by a Japanese organisation called the Godzilla

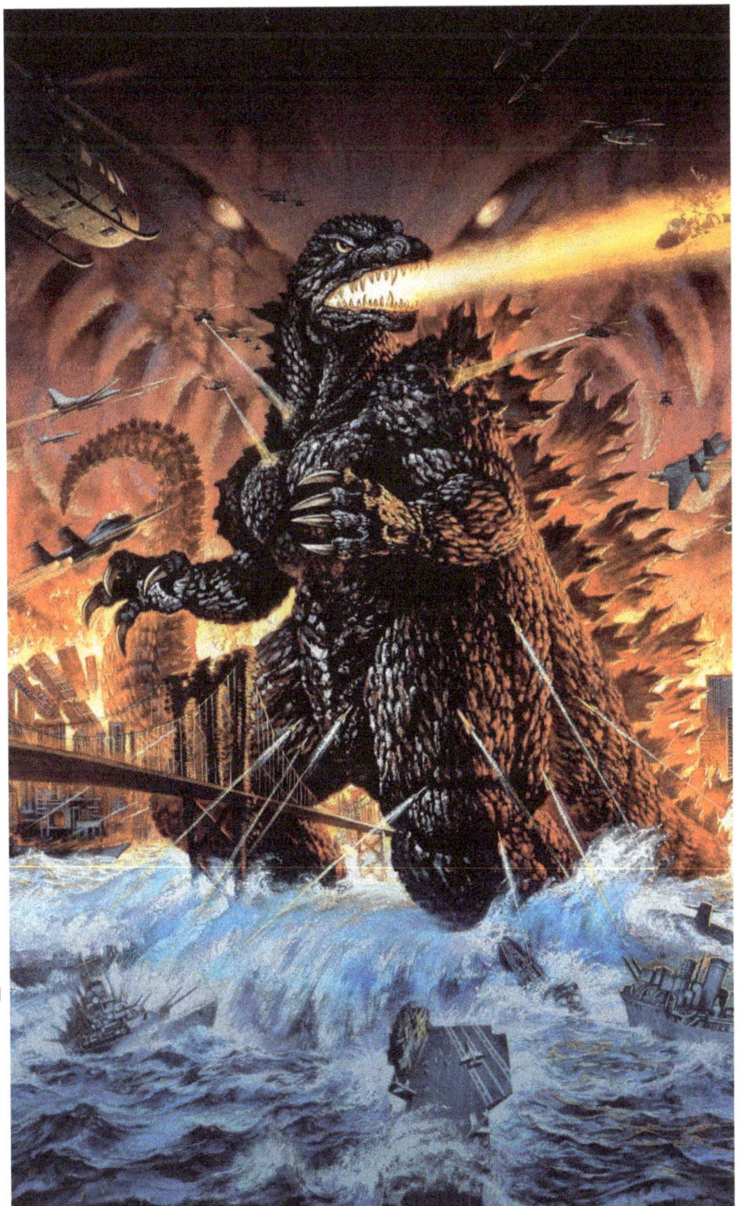

Stunning artwork for the US *Godzilla 2000* poster

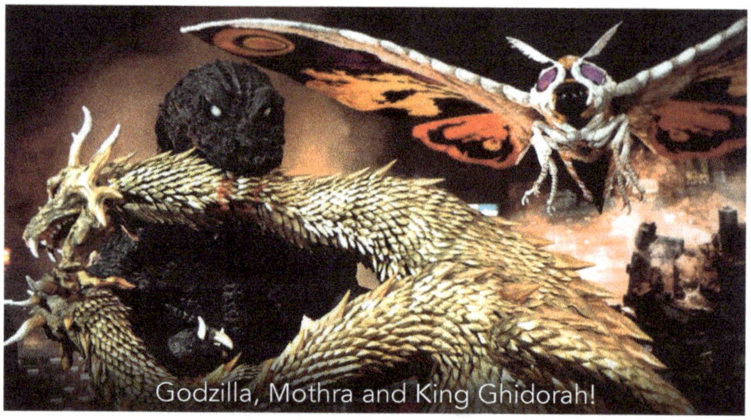
Godzilla, Mothra and King Ghidorah!

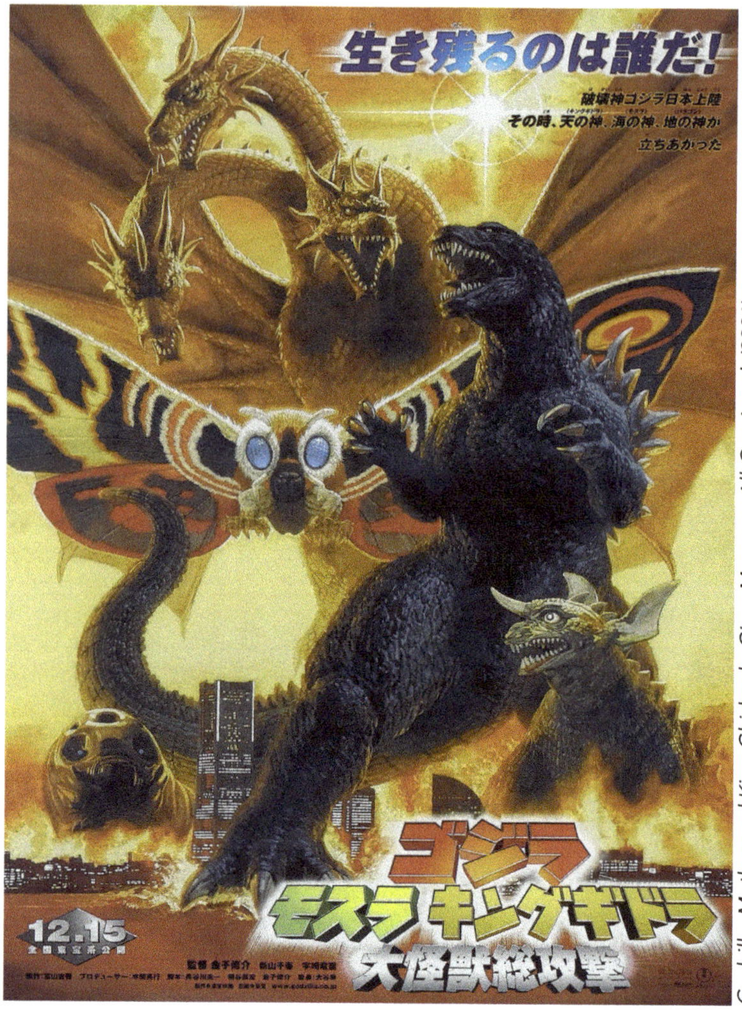

Godzilla, Mothra and King Ghidorah: Giant Monsters All-Out Attack (2001)

Prediction Network. Meanwhile, an ancient UFO, discovered within a big rock, is eventually revealed to have occupants who crave the regenerative substance contained in Godzilla's cells. The UFO finally absorbs Godzilla's DNA, which is transferred to its occupants, who transform into a single tentacled life form that exits the UFO. The octo-alien, rendered via some just-about-acceptable CGI effects, starts to mutate due to the volatile effects of Godzilla's DNA, and it transforms into an enormous kaiju with gigantic, clawed hands. This beast, known as Orga, looks pretty damn good, because it is a practical suitmation creation augmented with digital effects. Orga continues to mutate, finally developing dorsal-plates and an extendable maw that starts to swallow Godzilla whole, but Godzilla releases pent-up energy and destroys the massive monster!

A memorable moment early in this movie has characters rapidly reversing their vehicle along a road tunnel, with Godzilla's huge foot repeatedly smashing through the tunnel ceiling as Big G pursues them. The film, all in all, was a solid start to the new series.

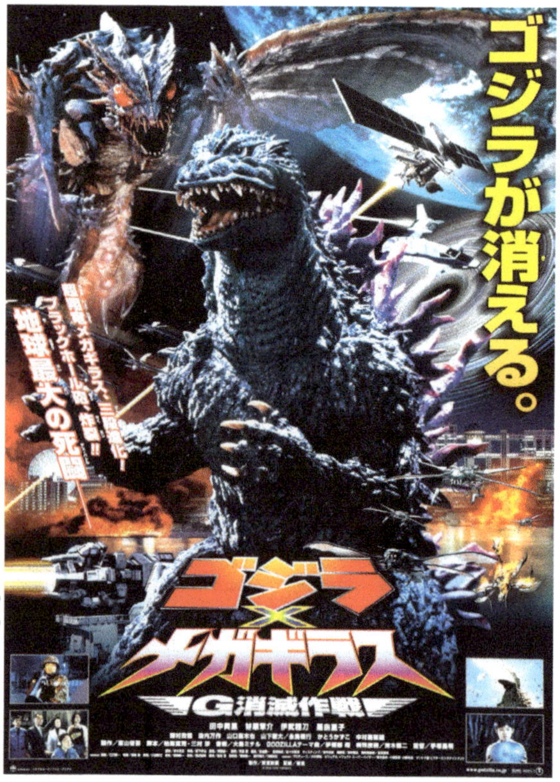

Godzilla vs. Megaguirus (2000)

Meanwhile, in the story continuity of *Godzilla vs. Megaguirus* (2000), Japan has been attacked repeatedly by Godzilla since 1954. The new Japanese capital is in Osaka, where the government forms a special unit that creates a weapon called the Dimension Tide, a miniature black hole gun designed to trap Godzilla within another dimension. The weapon is test-fired, a wormhole is created, which allows a Meganula (a big, prehistoric dragonfly) to reach present day Tokyo via a time distortion, where it lays an egg, from which swarms of Meganulon (monster dragonfly nymphs) hatch and begin to attack people in the city. These insectoid beasts moult their skins and transform into Meganula dragonflies, which steal energy from Godzilla and transfer it to their queen, transforming her into the gigantic Megaguirus. I hope you followed all that!

Suffice to say, Godzilla must fight the fast-flying, stinger-wielding Megaguirus and contend with the human forces who are eager to blast him with their black hole weapon.

2001's *Godzilla, Mothra and King Ghidorah: Giant Monsters All-Out Attack* (now there's a mouthful), also known as *Godzilla, Mothra and King Ghidorah: Attack of the Giant Monsters* (now there's another mouthful), gave us yet another continuity reboot to the series. This movie was directed by Shusuke Kaneko, the man behind the wonderful, acclaimed Gamera (Heisei) Trilogy of movies (yes, Kaneko made Daiei Film's giant flying turtle hero into a really cool kaiju!)

In this entry, Godzilla faces-off against three guardian monsters: Baragon (the burrowing, horned kaiju last seen in *Destroy All Monsters*), Mothra, and King Ghidorah. The creature fights are pretty violent here, and the special effects are good. The film received a lot of praise, although some fans weren't happy that King Ghidorah was a good kaiju in this story and Godzilla was portrayed as the full-on badass villain. Nevertheless, *Godzilla, Mothra and King Ghidorah: Giant Monsters All-Out Attack* ended up being the most successful Godzilla film of the Millennium era.

Godzilla Against Mechagodzilla (2002) was, you guessed it, yet another reboot to the Godzilla continuity. The movie reintroduced everyone's favourite robo-zilla into the Millennium series, but this time the cyborg was created using the skeleton and DNA of the first, dead Godzilla (from 1954). Codenamed Kiryu, this bio-mechanical beast turned on its human controllers when Godzilla's roar awakened the first Godzilla's soul residing within the mecha-monster, enabling it to possess the machine!

Kiryu is repaired, eventually being guided by human pilot First Lieutenant Akane Yashiro in a battle with Godzilla, using a powerful Absolute Zero Cannon to fight

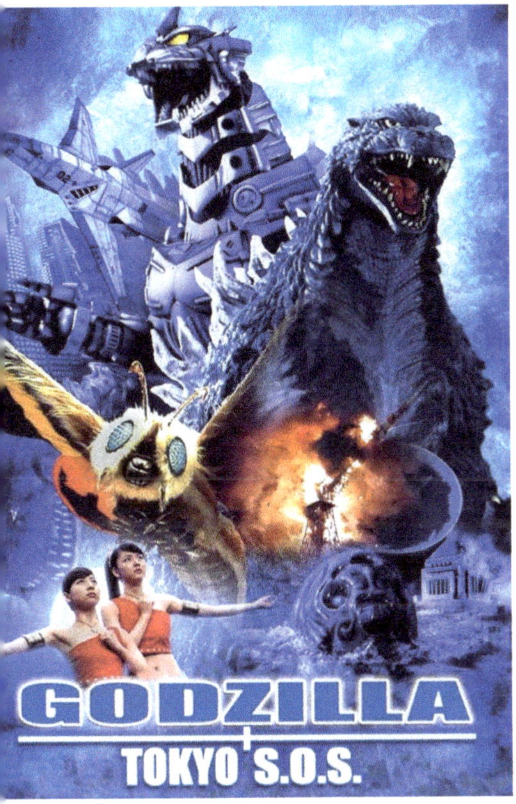

Godzilla to a draw... meaning that the next film, *Godzilla: Tokyo S.O.S.* (2003), is a direct sequel and not another story reboot!

This follow-up flick involves fights between Godzilla, Kiryu, Mothra and two of her larvae. The itsy-bitsy Shobijin (the priestesses of Mothra) show up to say that the first Godzilla's bones (used to build the cyborg-beast Kiryu, remember?) must be returned to the sea, because kaiju-deity Mothra considers the use of these bones in a machine to be sacrilegious and against the natural order of things. After various battles and the death of momma Mothra, Yashiro flies an injured Godzilla across the ocean and plunges the cyborg-zilla beneath the waves, thus returning the original Godzilla's bones to their watery grave. *Godzilla: Tokyo S.O.S.* features another monster, albeit just a carcass washed up on a beach: a Kamoebas giant turtle, which is the same species of creature also seen in Toho's kaiju film *Space Amoeba* (1970).

The sixth and final instalment in the Millennium series was *Godzilla: Final Wars* (2004). Directed by Ryuhei Kitamura, the man behind such entertaining, stylised genre flicks as *Versus*, *Azumi* and *Sky High*, the film commemorates the 50th anniversary of the Godzilla franchise by featuring LOADS of kaiju! It is a fast-paced production that reaches levels of near-lunacy that some Godzilla purists may frown upon, but I love this immensely enjoyable monster mash!

Here's just some of the outlandish stuff that happens in this film...

Godzilla is confronted with Zilla, the iteration of Godzilla seen in Roland

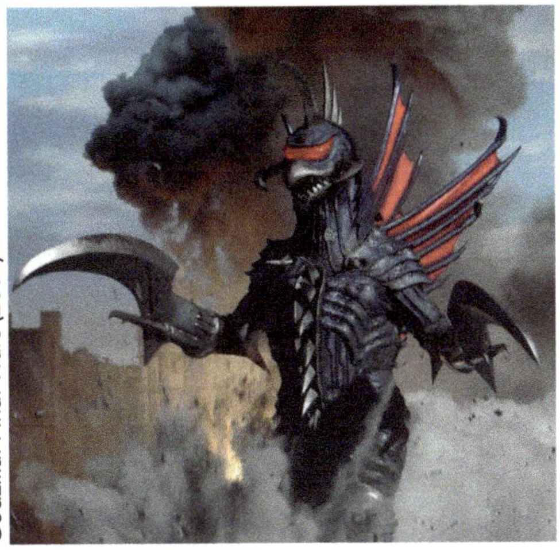
Godzilla: Final Wars (2004)

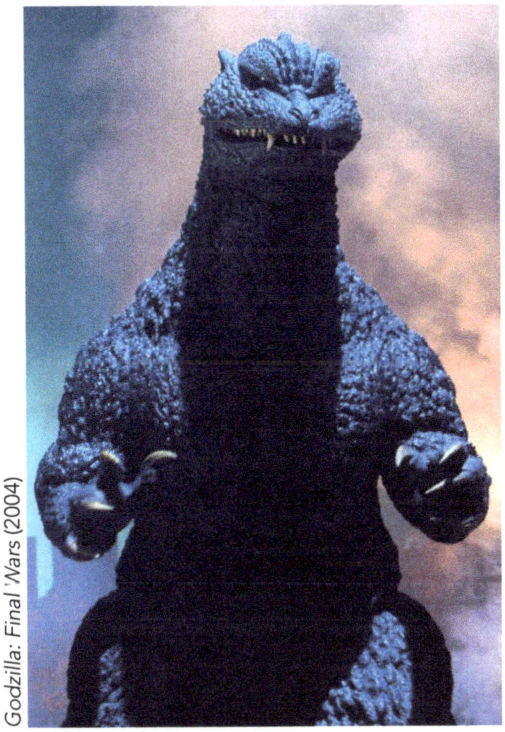
Godzilla: Final Wars (2004)

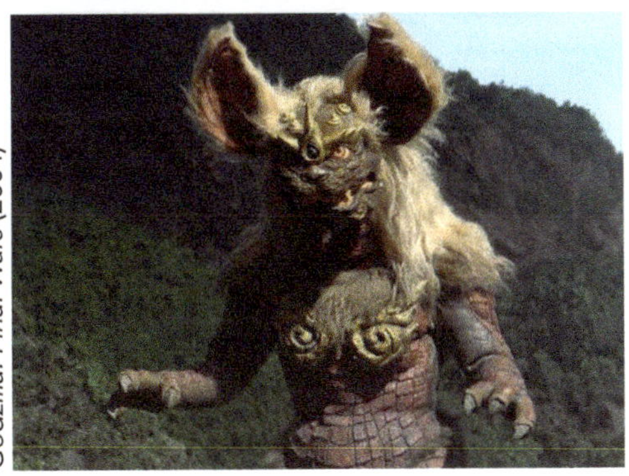
Godzilla: Final Wars (2004)

Emmerich's much-derided 1998 US *Godzilla* movie, has a super-brief skirmish with this CGI critter, then hurls Zilla into an exploding Sydney Opera House: boom! Gigan, looking trimmer, sharper and cooler, faces-off against Godzilla with new cable-firing abilities, but he soon loses his head! The flying, drill-nosed warship Gotengo (first seen in 1963's *Atragon*) is commanded by Captain Douglas Gordon (Don Frye), who is the spitting image of Joseph Stalin! In New Guinea, Godzilla swings spider-kaiju Kumonga around and around on its own web, then hurls it over the horizon! Monster X, the most powerful kaiju controlled by the evil Xilien aliens, mutates into Keizer Ghidorah, which gives Big G a sound beating with the gravity beams it spews from its mouths, but Godzilla soon mauls, decapitates and blows-up the beast! And, best of all, Godzilla battles Rodan, Anguirus and dog-eared King Caesar, resulting in hilariously over-the-top hijinks as Anguirus rolls-up into a spiky ball and propels himself at Godzilla, who whacks him away with his tail, and King Caesar retaliates by kicking the spike-ball like a pro-footballer, booting curled-up Anguirus straight at Godzilla, who attempts to grab hold of him like a goalkeeper!

Other kaiju featured in the flick include Manda, Hedorah, Minilla (gawd) and Kamacuras.

Ryuhei Kitamura manages to make *Godzilla: Final Wars* slick, cheesy, fun, exciting and silly, all at once. Some of his characters have the same kind of glam, hip vibe as the protagonists and antagonists seen in his other movies, such as *Versus*, and he somehow succeeds in being both respectful and disrespectful to the Godzilla franchise: the movie is an absolutely ridiculous, outlandish, don't-give-a-f*ck joy!

Reiwa era (2016 - present)

Toho put the Godzilla series on hold after the release of *Godzilla: Final Wars*, though director Yoshimitsu (*Godzilla vs. Hedorah*) Banno attempted to raise money to make a short IMAX Godzilla film called *Godzilla 3-D*. This project never came to fruition, but Banno's attempts to secure funding, together with producers Kenji Okuhira and Brian Rogers, led to US company Legendary Entertainment acquiring the rights to the Godzilla character in 2010, resulting in the creation of the American MonsterVerse movie series, beginning with *Godzilla* (2014). The American film was an international success, and Toho finally decided to make a new Godzilla movie of their own, called *Shin Godzilla* (2016), which was the first Japanese Godzilla movie of the Reiwa era.

Shin Godzilla was a huge critical and financial smash in Japan. Some western fans, however, bemoaned the amount of time the film spent with the politicians and bureaucrats, but I think that watching how all the many viewpoints, red tape and opinions swamped the decision makers contributed lots of realism to the story.

The movie adds new twists to Godzilla's life cycle, with the creature evolving through different forms, which I personally liked: you can't just keep doing the same old schtick every time. In this iteration of the Big G

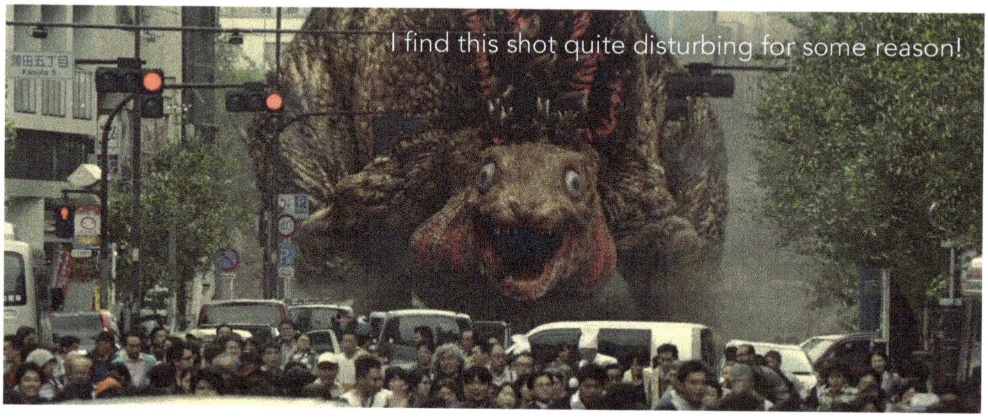

I find this shot quite disturbing for some reason!

Shin Godzilla (2016)

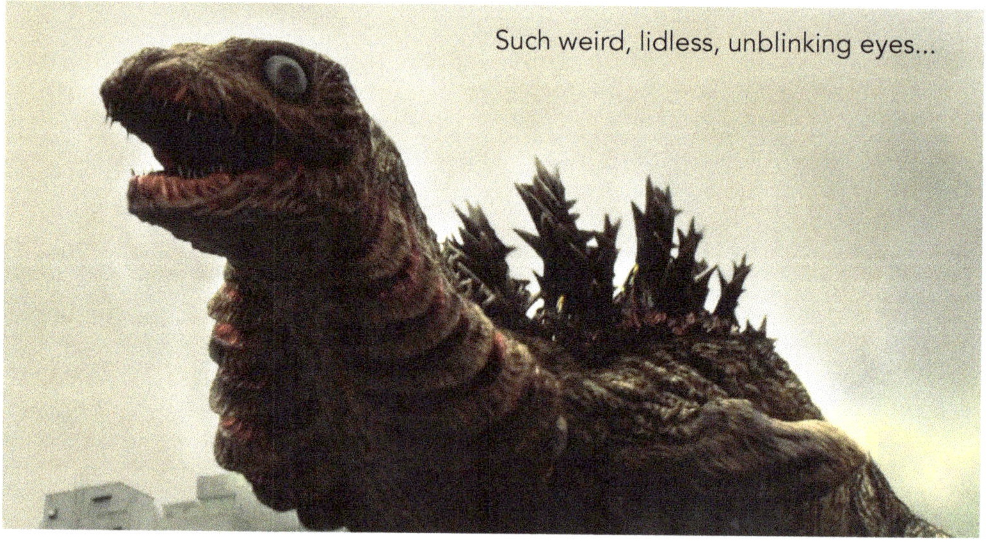

Such weird, lidless, unblinking eyes...

Shin Godzilla (2016)

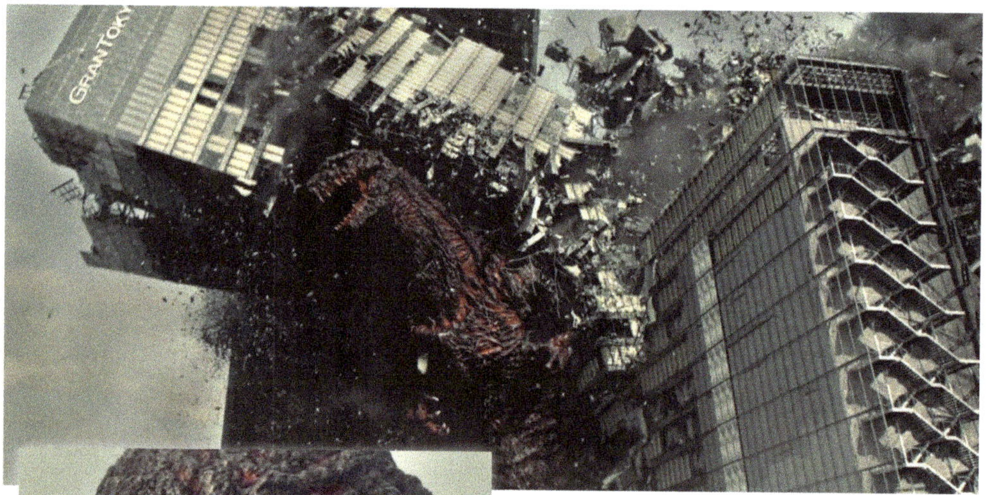

Shin Godzilla (2016)

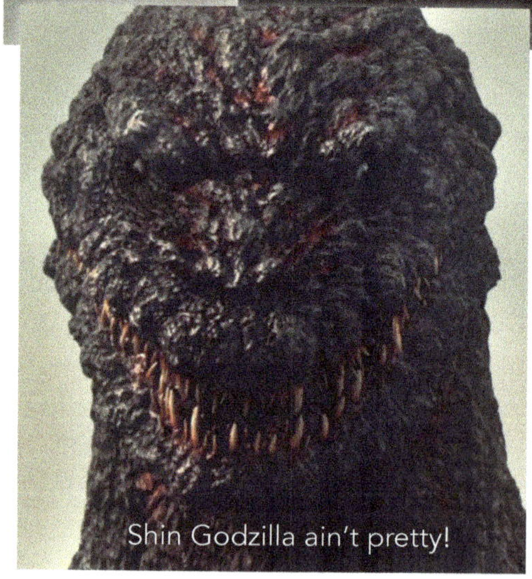

Shin Godzilla ain't pretty!

we see him transform from a low-sprawling aquatic beast to upright god-reptile. We watch him continually adapt, utilising atomic breath and then photon beams. Maybe old school Godzilla fans might not like this updating of his abilities, but I thought the ever-evolving powers and adaptations kept the story intriguing (such as that last shot of the tail hinting that an even weirder evolutionary step was underway within the great beast).

The devastation shots of boats & debris being pushed down the river effectively replicated real disaster imagery seen during the 2011 Japanese tsunami, and I liked the many scenes of Godzilla stomping through the city seen in extreme long shot, giving us an expansive view of the creature's progress through Tokyo.

And I loved the way the Japanese forces not only use tanks, helicopters and jets against Godzilla... they also utilised 'train bombs' - cool!

There were some odd design choices, I agree, like the early-stage googly fish eyes, for instance, but, as already stated, I think there was a lot to enjoy with this version of Godzilla, who, once in adult form, looks quite different to his typical body shape, with very tiny eyes and a longer neck. Shin Godzilla was the first Japanese Godzilla to be rendered primarily through CGI, though he somehow retains a slight suitmation vibe, maybe because actor Mansai Nomura portrayed Godzilla through motion capture.

As the Reiwa era continued we got a trilogy of anime Godzilla movies, with Netflix distributing the films worldwide. The cartoon films, which had cinema releases in Japan, were *Godzilla: Planet of the Monsters* (2017), *Godzilla: City on the Edge of Battle* (2018) and *Godzilla: The Planet Eater* (2018).

For me, the plotting in these films is needlessly convoluted. For instance, in the first story, the monsters menace Earth just as aliens turn up and then everyone leaves, then come back thousands of years later. It doesn't help that Godzilla moves around so very slowly: he sucks all the vitality from many of the scenes in this trilogy. Having said all that, *Godzilla: The Planet Eater*, despite suffering from far, far too much chat in the earlier part of the movie, does become extremely interesting once King Ghidorah arrives. This version of Ghidorah is from another dimension and it functions in ways that confound the laws of our dimension's physics. Only seen as three glowing heads on very long necks that sinuously extrude from singularities hovering amongst the clouds, Ghidorah is only able to manifest itself here because

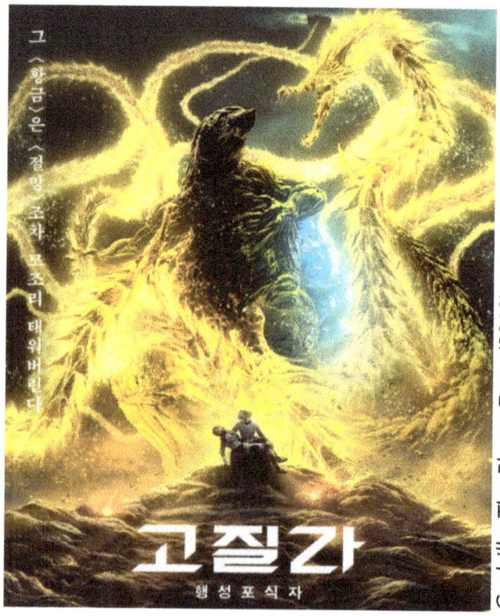

Godzilla: The Planet Eater (2018)

ACTORS WITHIN THE BEAST

Here are some of the hard-working guys who have donned the heavy, iconic costumes to play Godzilla...

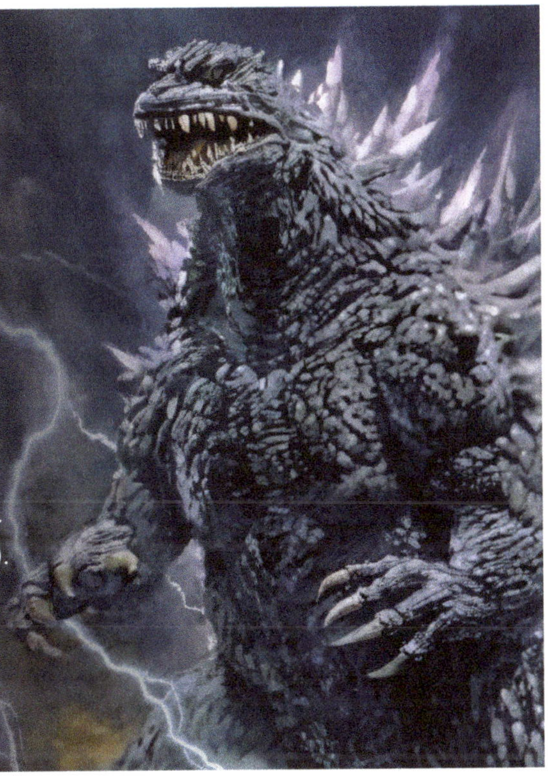

Haruo Nakajima - An actor and stuntman who played Godzilla in the first 12 films, from 1954 to 1972.

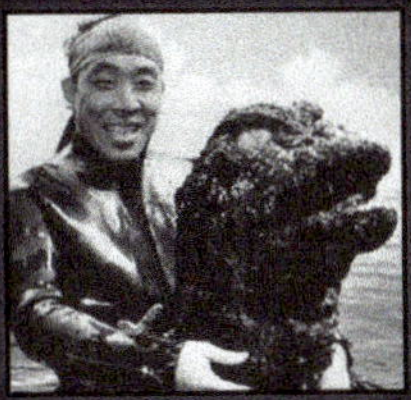

Tsutomu Kitagawa - Wore the huge, scaly suit for five of the Millennium series of Godzilla films.

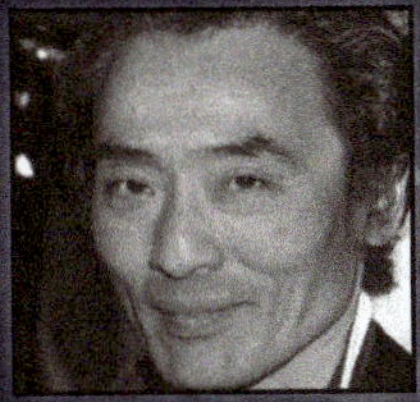

Kenpachiro Satsuma - Played Godzilla in *The Return of Godzilla* (1984) and in all of the Heisei films.

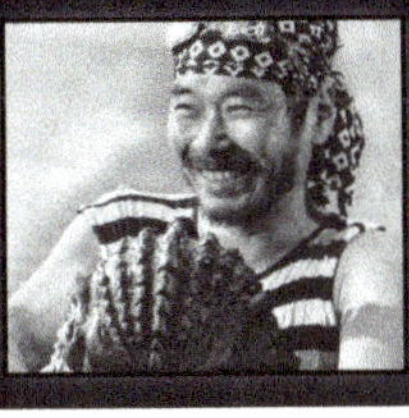

Satsuma passed away recently, on December 16th, 2023. RIP

Mizuho Yoshida - Was Big G in *Godzilla, Mothra and King Ghidorah: Giant Monsters All-Out Attack* (2001).

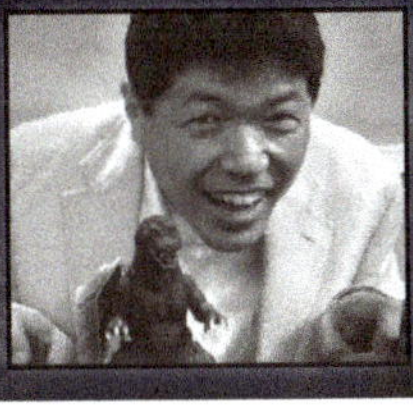

the triple-headed world-destroyer is being observed by a specific character, which is an explanation that leans quite heavily into quantum physics concepts. The finale becomes a tour de force of metaphysical mutterings, flashbacks, and great shots of Ghidorah's other-dimensional heads as they entangle and bite Godzilla, siphoning away all of his energies!

These three anime films all certainly looked good and involved some cool future-tech contraptions, but what I was far more interested in was seeing what Toho did next with its newest live action film... *Godzilla Minus One* (2023)! Wow! What a revelation this movie was!

Godzilla Minus One, written and directed by Takashi Yamazaki, really ramps up the melodramatic aspects of the plot, showing the events from the point of view of the everyday people, rather than via the actions of the government leaders or Big G himself. The film expertly pulls you into the lives of these ordinary protagonists, making you really care for them, which adds extra impact to the scenes when Godzilla attacks. And, boy, when Godzilla lets loose with his atomic breath in this movie it is truly a devastating apocalypse to behold! Stunning stuff!

Takashi Yamazaki has really invigorated the Japanese Godzilla franchise and I await his Godzilla sequel with bated breath.

The eras...

There are films that I like from all four eras, but I guess I have a real soft spot for the Shōwa era, no doubt because it spans a lot more films, with big shifts in tone and themes. From the dark, serious, symbolism-heavy, doom-laden *Godzilla* (1954), to the colourful, more juvenile releases like *Godzilla vs. Gigan* and *All Monsters Attack*, there's such a mind-bogglingly vast difference in style between them that it adds to the overall enjoyment of this era's releases. Godzilla himself morphs from an unstoppable force of nature, to anti-hero, to caring parent!

Godzilla movies can be enjoyed for all sorts of reasons. The stories can sometimes have political themes, whilst others go to town with backstories featuring quite in-depth internal mythologies, and others, of course, are simply no-nonsense action-sci-fi movies that include everything from ape-aliens, space-cockroaches, hi-tech military gizmos and a menagerie of massive monsters. Maybe the human characters in these films are often bland or forgettable,

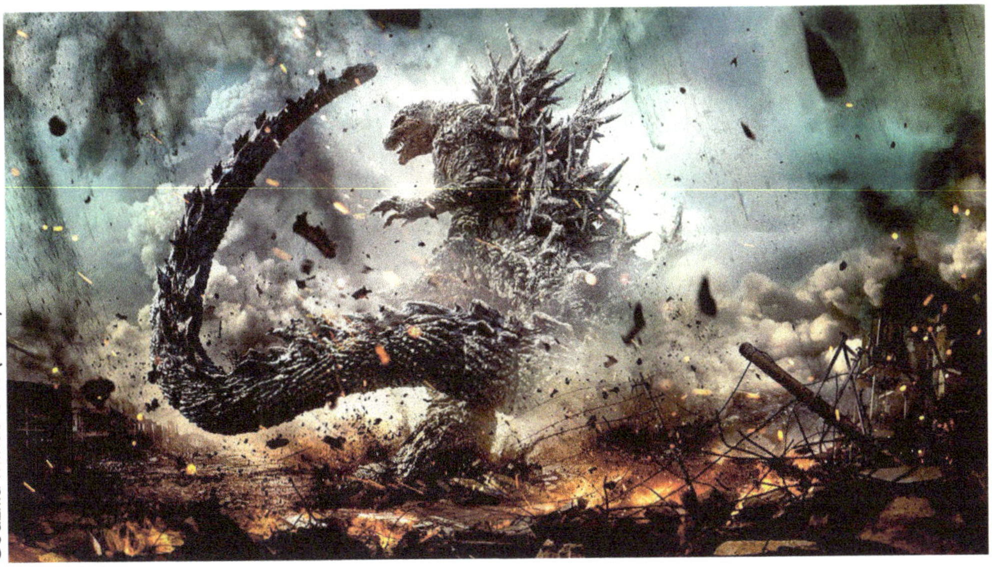

Godzilla Minus One (2023)

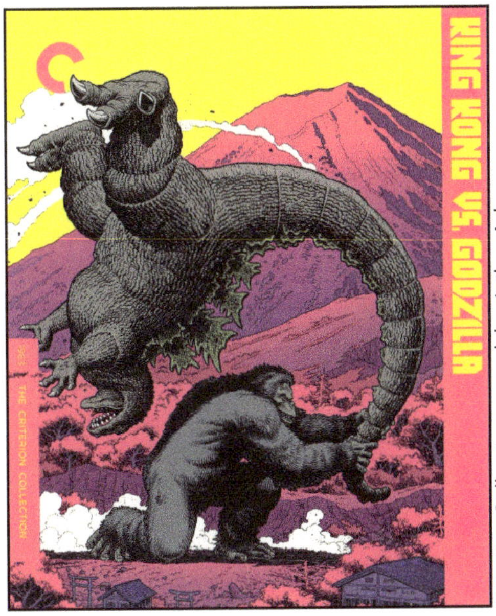

Criterion Collection artwork by Arthur Adams

and there will be some viewers who'll never take seriously the way the Toho creatures are brought to life via suitmation techniques. Some Godzilla suits have been far more complex, well-designed and better made than others, that's for sure, but, hey, I like 'em all!

Even at the most basic man-in-rubber-suit-stomping-on-model-houses level, there's lots to enjoy: it's a sort of cinematic representation of the kind of enjoyably juvenile joy that one used to have, as a child, when, after building your Lego houses... you wrecked them! This toy-trashing bliss is enhanced by the fact the planes and tanks in some of these flicks actually do look very much like toys, adding to the fun of seeing them get smashed by often absurd-looking creatures: wouldn't you just love to run around a scale model city and do the same thing?! *Godzilla Minus One* is obviously far removed from this lo-fi aspect of the Godzilla franchise. It still boasts scenes of cathartic, large-scale property damage and ship-wrecking, though, which is definitely capable of pleasing your inner destructive child!

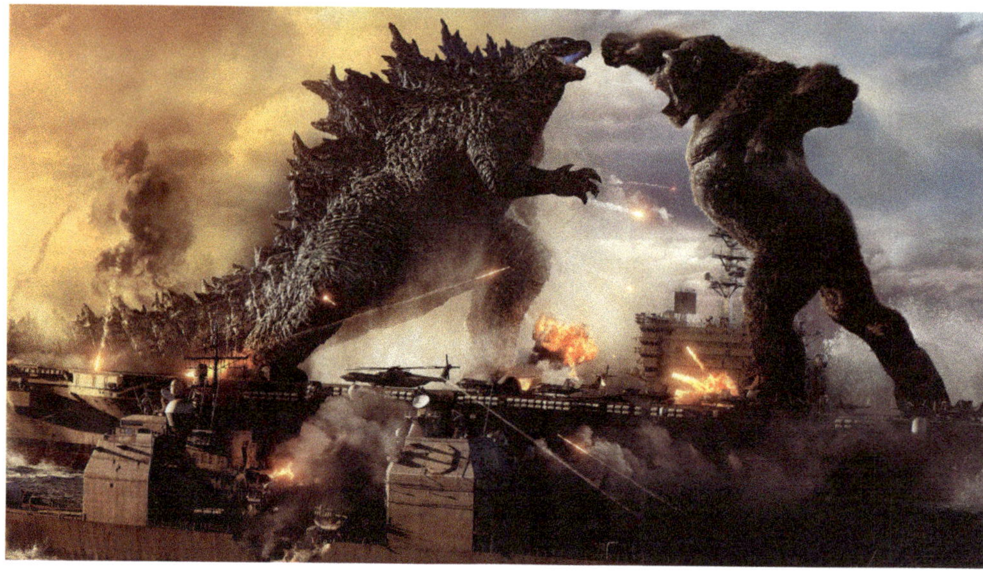

Godzilla vs. Kong (2021)

The American Godzilla movies...

There can be a distinct divide between fans of the Toho Godzilla movies and lovers of the US MonsterVerse flicks. One group of adherents tend to reflexively dismiss the films liked by the others. But what's the point of that? Isn't it wonderful to be a Godzilla movie enthusiast today, with all this Godzilla content to choose from?!

Anyway, here are my thoughts regarding the American Godzilla films...

Godzilla (1998) failed due to the arrogance of Roland Emmerich and Dean Devlin, who came on board the TriStar Godzilla project (which had initially been developed by writers Ted Elliott and Terry Rossio, with Jan De Bont attached to direct) and said that they were only willing to take on the film if they were allowed to totally reinvent Godzilla into something wholly their own. So they ditched the way Elliott and Rossio portrayed Godzilla as a guardian of world ecosystems in a story that would see Godzilla do battle with an evil monster called the Gryphon. Instead, Devlin and Emmerich turned Godzilla into a plain and simple giant creature, like a T-Rex with a jutting chin! They also got rid of all of the other monsters in the screenplay.

The finished film did have some decent model effects on show and some of the creature stuff was okay, but so many bad choices were made: Godzilla doesn't look like Godzilla, Godzilla is not big enough, Godzilla RUNS AWAY from the military, Godzilla doesn't have radioactive breath, Godzilla just wants to munch on piles of fish, and Godzilla seems to be just a mutated (French) iguana. Plus, the military are such idiots in this film: they blow up the Flatiron Building, they shoot the top off the Chrysler Building with missiles and they torpedo their own subs. If the film had been called something else, and wasn't linked to Godzilla, it would've been better received, I am sure.

The Gareth Edwards-directed *Godzilla* (2014), the first of Legendary Entertainment's MonsterVerse movies, is much, much better than the '98 version. It can be seen as a movie of many good images & moments, rather than a perfect whole, but the scenes and imagery are really good, such as the view of the inside of a 'cave' that is actually a fossil Godzilla, the heartbreaking scene where Juliette Binoche is locked inside the radioactive steam-filled corridor, the halo dive, the first time we see Godzilla's blue flame breath, and so on. Awesome stuff!

There are some really nice touches, as when Godzilla inadvertently causes a tsunami when he comes ashore because he's so damn big. The finale, when Godzilla is revealed to be alive after killing the MUTOs and everyone cheers the big critter like he's a heroic king of monsters, is also brilliant!

The makers of *Godzilla: King of the Monsters* (2019) certainly set out to create their version of a Japanese kaiju movie writ large: we get gigantic monsters kicking each other's butts, jet attacks, cities flattened, fire and fury.

There are lots of cool elements in this film: using the original Godzilla theme tune (and Mothra's theme plays during the end credits), introducing the Oxygen Destroyer weapon, referencing the Infant Island twins, and much more.

The movie is full of striking images: Ghidorah powering up with electricity zapping out from its wingtips! Godzilla going into action with the backup of military jets! Ghidorah raising its wings atop a mountain like a giant demon (with a crucifix in the foreground)! The remaining monsters bowing in deference to the victorious Godzilla! Yes, there was definitely lots of stuff to like! *Godzilla: King of the Monsters* certainly delivered in the monster department: seeing Godzilla, Mothra, Ghidorah and Rodan in action in a big Hollywood picture was a great experience, plus we got to see several other monsters too, including Behemoth, a bizarre tusked Titan!

Godzilla vs. Kong (2021), directed by Adam Wingard, was definitely a big punch 'em up production, crammed with

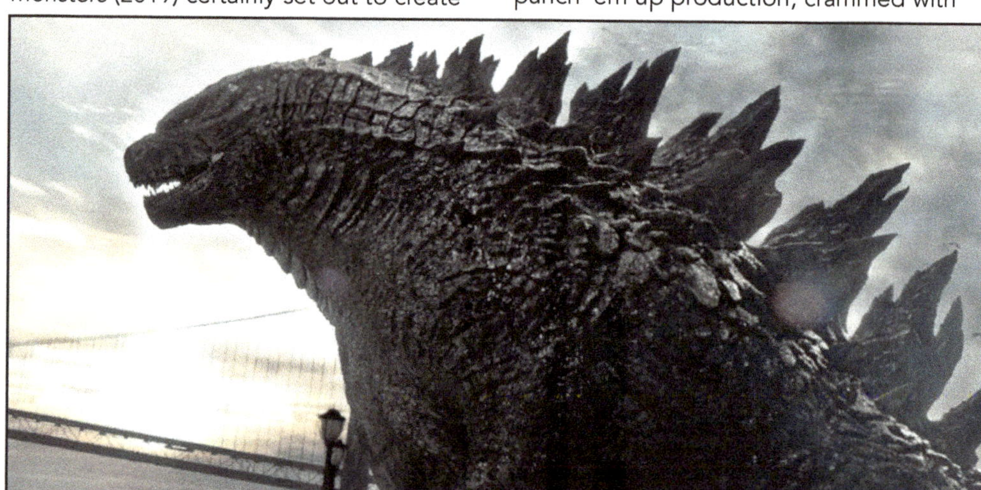

Godzilla (2014)

a neon-lit deluge of eye candy monster effects, including the introduction of the US Mechagodzilla! It delivered on the promise of its title, with the titular creatures duking it out with themselves and others. From a plot perspective it certainly didn't attempt to inject the serious tone of 2014's *Godzilla* and was much more aligned with *Godzilla: King of the Monsters*, where the focus was on creating set-ups to allow for a series of kaiju battles. That said, the 2019 film still attempted to balance the human drama with the scenes of spectacle more evenly than *Godzilla vs. Kong*, which definitely put the emphasis on the grand FX moments. The fantastical elements, like the trip to the Hollow Earth and Kong utilising a powered-up giant axe, were dealt with pretty briskly in this film, and perhaps this was the best way to handle such things – so viewers weren't given too much time to ponder the logic of it all!

The final smackdown battle, taking place in Hong Kong, allowed for gorgeous looking neon vistas that made the night time action easy to follow and see. I have to say I do wonder what the body count must have been for this fight as a LOT of skyscrapers get demolished! Maybe aware of this, the film doesn't feature any characters commenting on casualties.

Ultimately, if you go into this just for the spectacle there's lots to like, but there are quite a few things you can pick apart with *Godzilla vs. Kong*. It would've been preferable if the film had developed a more pleasing mix of pulp action, interesting characterisations and monster madness, as seen in the non-Godzilla MonsterVerse release *Kong: Skull Island* (2017).

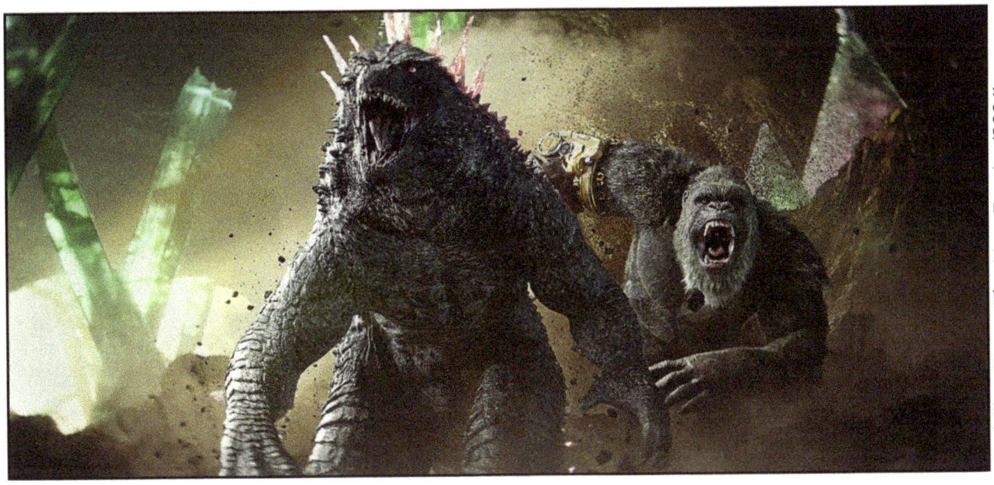

Godzilla x Kong: The New Empire (2024)

Godzilla x Kong: The New Empire (2024), with Adam Wingard in the director's chair once more, is so cartoony and outlandish it manages to make *Godzilla vs. Kong* look like a serious, realistic drama by comparison! But I enjoyed the hell out of it anyway! The film sets out to be an over-the-top visual treat, with Kong brandishing a bionic arm and Godzilla showing off pink-glowing back-plates!

Dan Stevens, in the role of Trapper, portrays his character almost like a live action version of the animated weasel Buck from the *Ice Age* movies - and this performance fits the tone of the movie so well! We know we're not meant to take this film too seriously when we're presented with shots of Godzilla curling up in Rome's Colosseum to sleep, using the building like a giant dog bed!

There are loads of monsters in *Godzilla x Kong: The New Empire*, including the quadrupedal ice-beast Shimo, the serpentine sea critter Tiamat, and a tribe of giant apes led by the simian titan Skar King. With Skar King resembling a huge, gangly Orangutan, the film does lack an impactful central antagonist, but if you're in a mood to see Godzilla leaping off the Rock of Gibraltar, and a finale involving zero-gravity kaiju battles in the Hollow Earth, then this silly, lightweight, action-fest flick is for you!

Godzilla heaven!

For fans of the king of monsters there's never been a better time, with both Japanese and American Godzilla movies regularly stomping our way. The follow-up to *Godzilla Minus One*, of course, is the Big G film that everyone will be most eager to see. Bring it on!

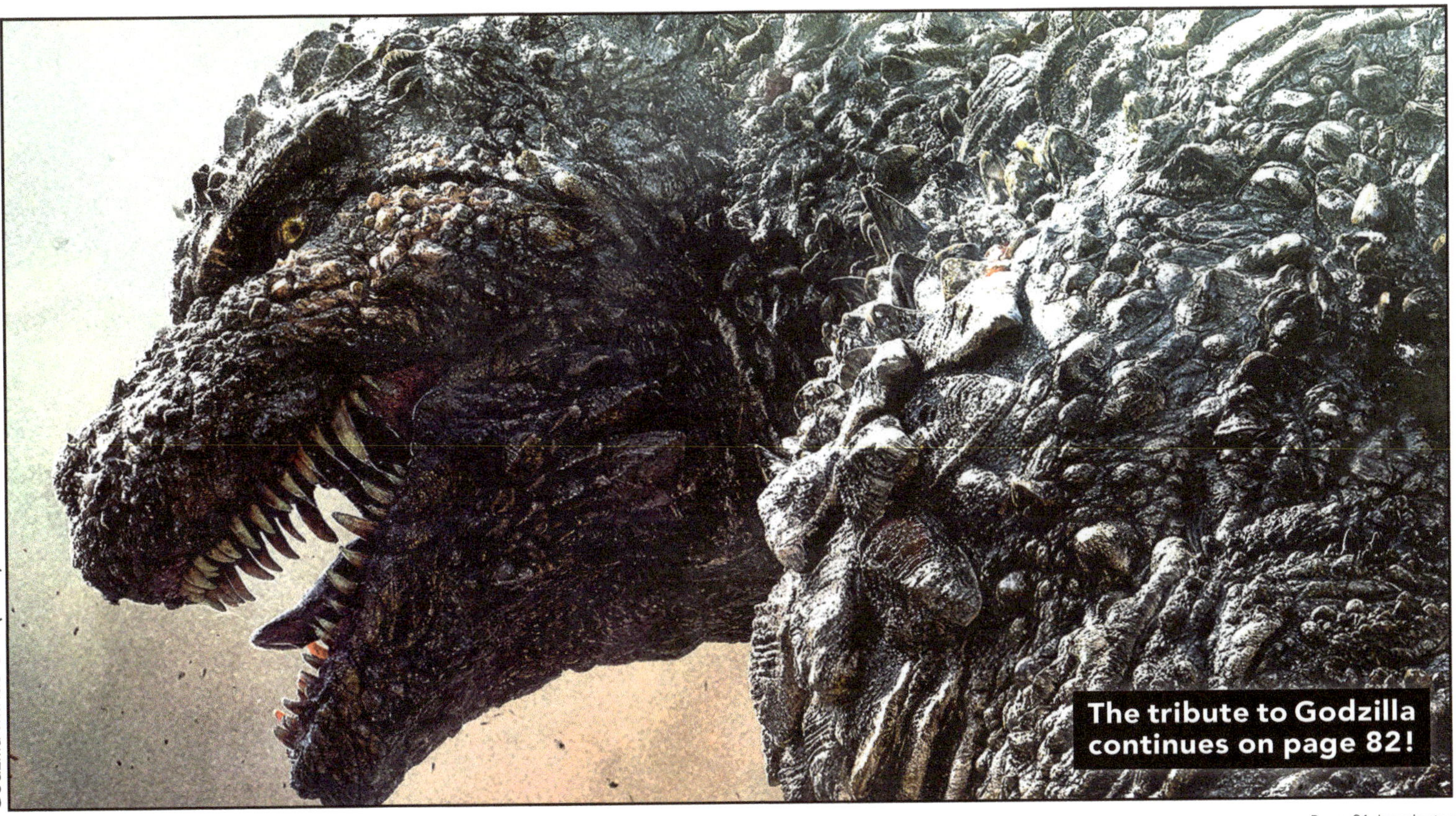

The tribute to Godzilla continues on page 82!

Godzilla Minus One (2023)

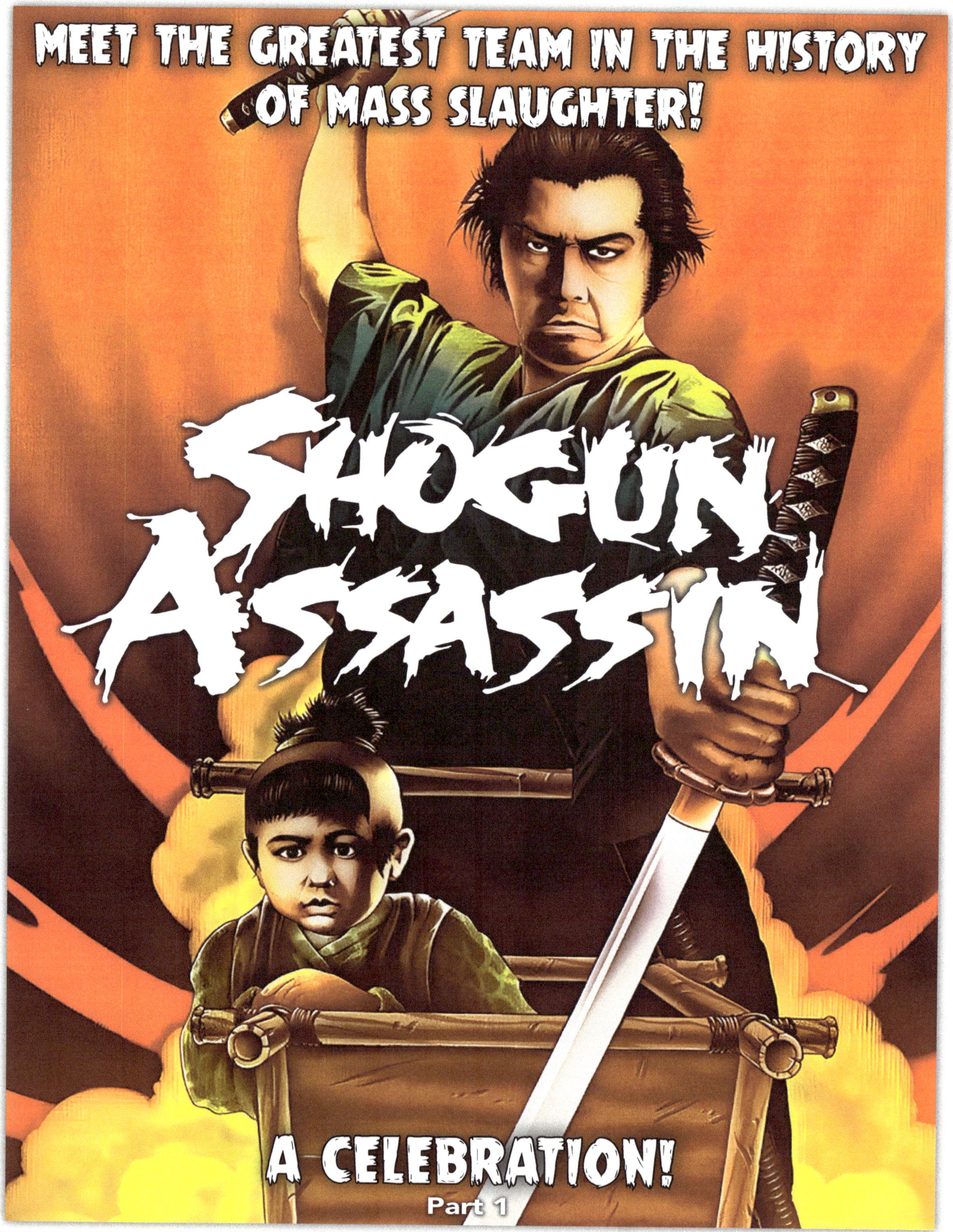
MEET THE GREATEST TEAM IN THE HISTORY OF MASS SLAUGHTER!
SHOGUN ASSASSIN
A CELEBRATION!
Part 1

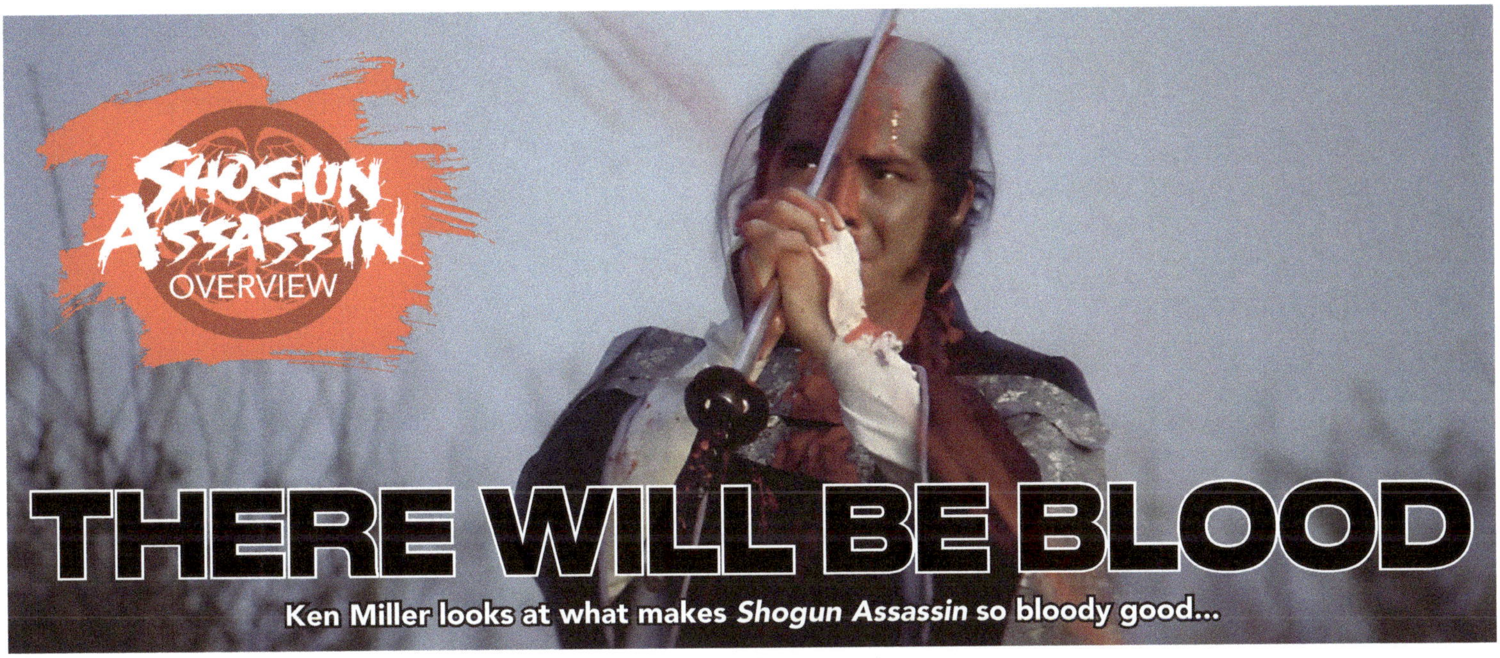

THERE WILL BE BLOOD

Ken Miller looks at what makes *Shogun Assassin* so bloody good...

Vivid, blood-spraying carnage, impeccable use of voice-overs, gorgeous cinematography, a fascinating feudal Japanese setting, a lethal wooden perambulator, and a thrilling electronic score written by Mark Lindsay (formerly of the band Paul Revere & the Raiders) and W. Michael Lewis (one-time keyboard player with the band Quicksilver Messenger Service), ensured that *Shogun Assassin* became a cult favourite after its grindhouse movie circuit release in the US (by New World Pictures), and then later when it was unleashed as a video cassette by Vipco in the UK and MCA/Universal Home Video in America.

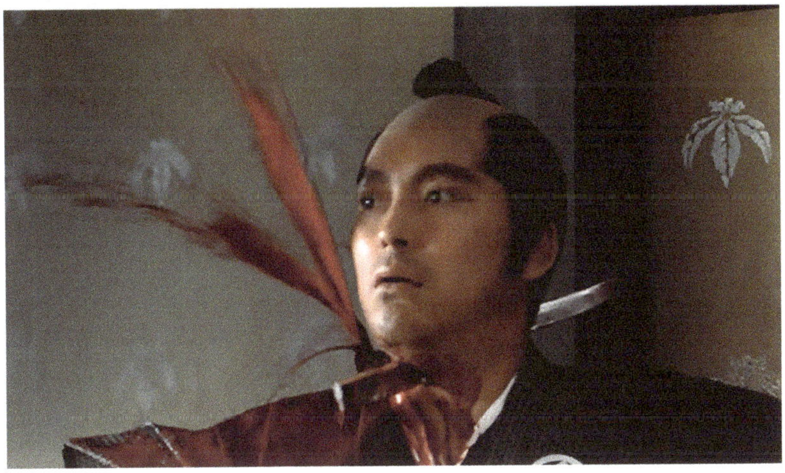

Shogun Assassin would end up being included on the BBFC's banned list of films (the infamous 'Video Nasties' list) and the movie was prosecuted for obscenity, but the prosecution failed.

Like so many fans of *Shogun Assassin*, when I first viewed this movie during its initial video release I didn't know that it was, in fact, an Americanised concoction created by splicing footage from two different Japanese films together. These movies, *Lone Wolf and Cub: Sword of Vengeance* (1972) and *Lone Wolf and Cub: Baby Cart at the River Styx* (1972), were the first two of six films based on the popular manga series *Lone Wolf and Cub*, which told the story of the Shogun's lethal executioner, Ogami Ittō, becoming a ronin after the murder of his wife. Would I have thought differently about *Shogun Assassin* had I seen the original films first? Perhaps I would have, but I don't think so, as this production somehow manages to go way beyond its potentially trashy cut-and-paste origins to become a unique, bloody cool and memorable movie thanks to its own very special qualities, namely the effective use of dubbing, the reworked, tight plot, and the damn catchy, driving synth soundtrack.

Robert Houston, who'd acted in *The Hills Have Eyes* (1977) and *1941* (1979), became a first-time director, producer and writer with *Shogun Assassin*, a project that came into being with the help of co-writer and co-producer David Weisman, who'd been a movie poster designer, an assistant to Otto Preminger, and had co-written, co-produced and co-directed cult flick *Ciao Manhattan* (1972). Weisman would go on to be instrumental in the financing and making

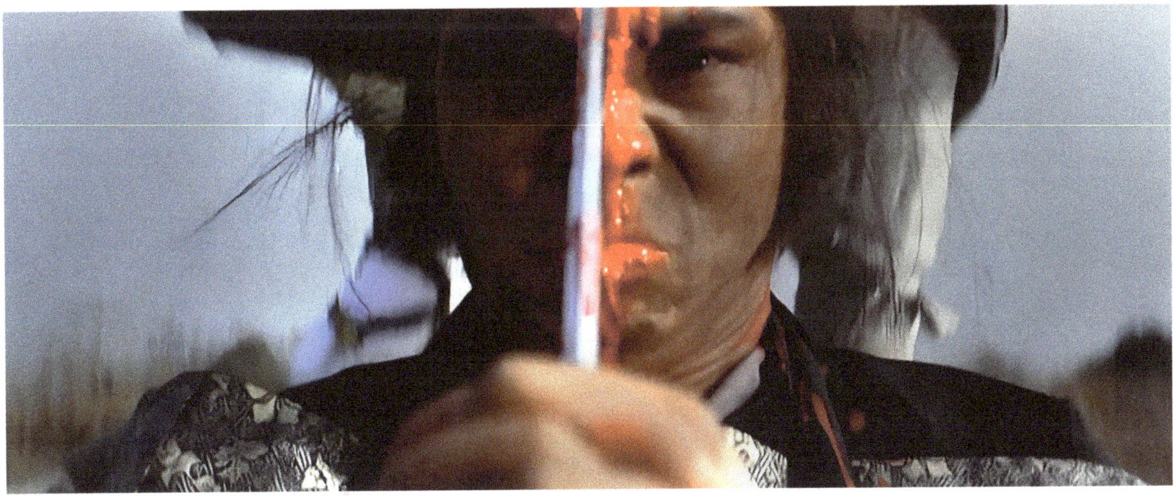

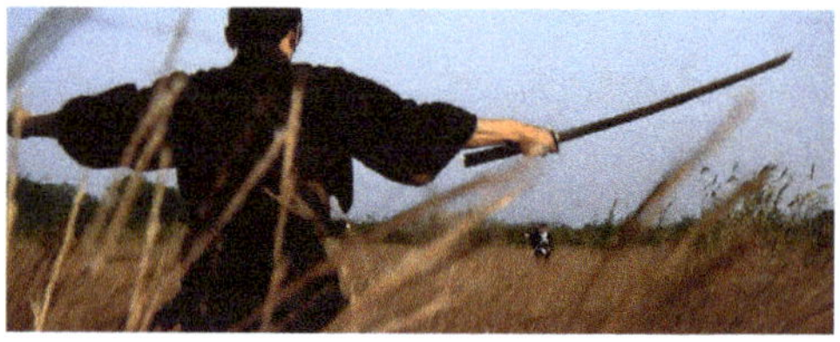

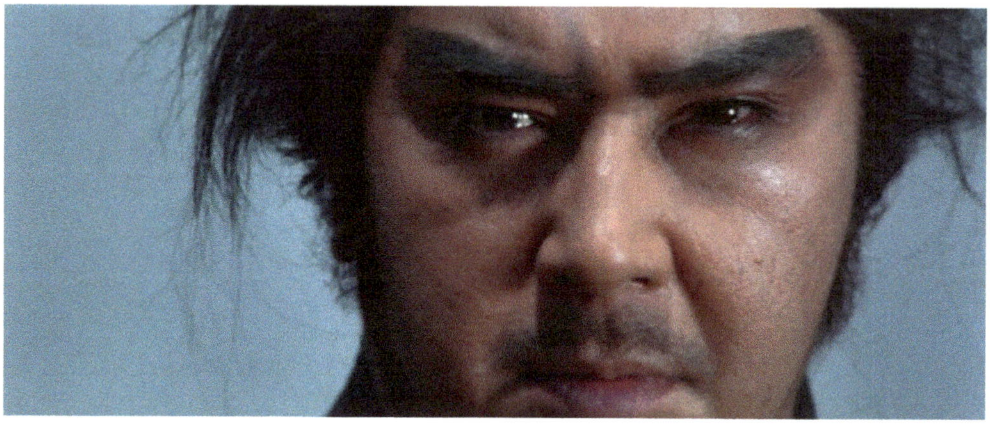

of the Oscar-winning *Kiss of the Spider Woman* (1985), and was the art director and title designer for the nihilistic, mondo-style cult doc *The Killing of America* (1981). Another collaborator was movie & rock poster artist/designer Jim Evans, who not only was the person who urged the late David Weisman to buy the rights to the *Lone Wolf and Cub* movies, he also created the legendary *Shogun Assassin* poster *and* he's the father of Gibran Evans, the boy who provides the voice of Ogami Ittō's son Daigorō!

I'm pretty sure even Robert Houston himself, who made Academy award-winning documentary *Mighty Times: The Children's March* (2004), would be the first to acknowledge that being referred to as the 'director' of Shogun Assassin is quite a stretch! All the wonderful direction is obviously courtesy of Kenji Misumi, the Japanese director of the two source movies. Misumi directed two of the other Lone Wolf and Cub movies as well: 1972's *Lone Wolf and Cub: Baby Cart to Hades* and 1973's *Lone Wolf and Cub: Baby Cart in the Land of Demons* (1972's *Lone Wolf and Cub: Baby Cart in Peril* was directed by Buichi Saitō and 1974's *Lone Wolf and Cub: White Heaven in Hell* was directed by Yoshiyuki Kuroda).

Suffice to say, Kenji Misumi (who also directed 1972's *Hanzo the Razor: Sword of Justice*, which was another film based on a manga written by Kazuo Koike, the writer of the *Lone Wolf and Cub* manga) deserves all of the praise when it comes to *Shogun Assassin*'s visual panache. Widescreen wonderfulness abounds throughout!

Beautiful cinematography and brutality rub shoulders, most strikingly when slo-mo jets of blood spurt from the neck of a decapitated adversary standing in a gorgeous-looking, sun-bathed field!

The gory aspects of *Shogun Assassin* certainly stick in the memory. Some of the vicious, bloodstained moments include: a sword getting wedged in an attacker's forehead, a ninja losing ears, fingers and other body parts as he attempts to escape from a room full of female assassins, a head being hacked completely in two by Ittō's blade, and throats and chests erupting with super-charged geysers of blood!

These action scenes can border on the outlandish, as assailants disguised a peasant women hurl vegetables with knives

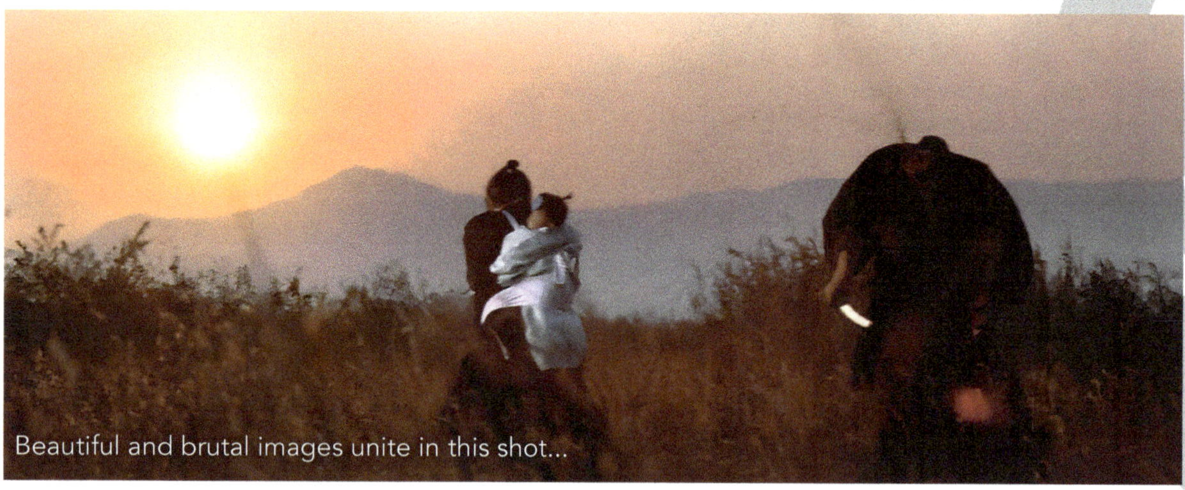

Beautiful and brutal images unite in this shot...

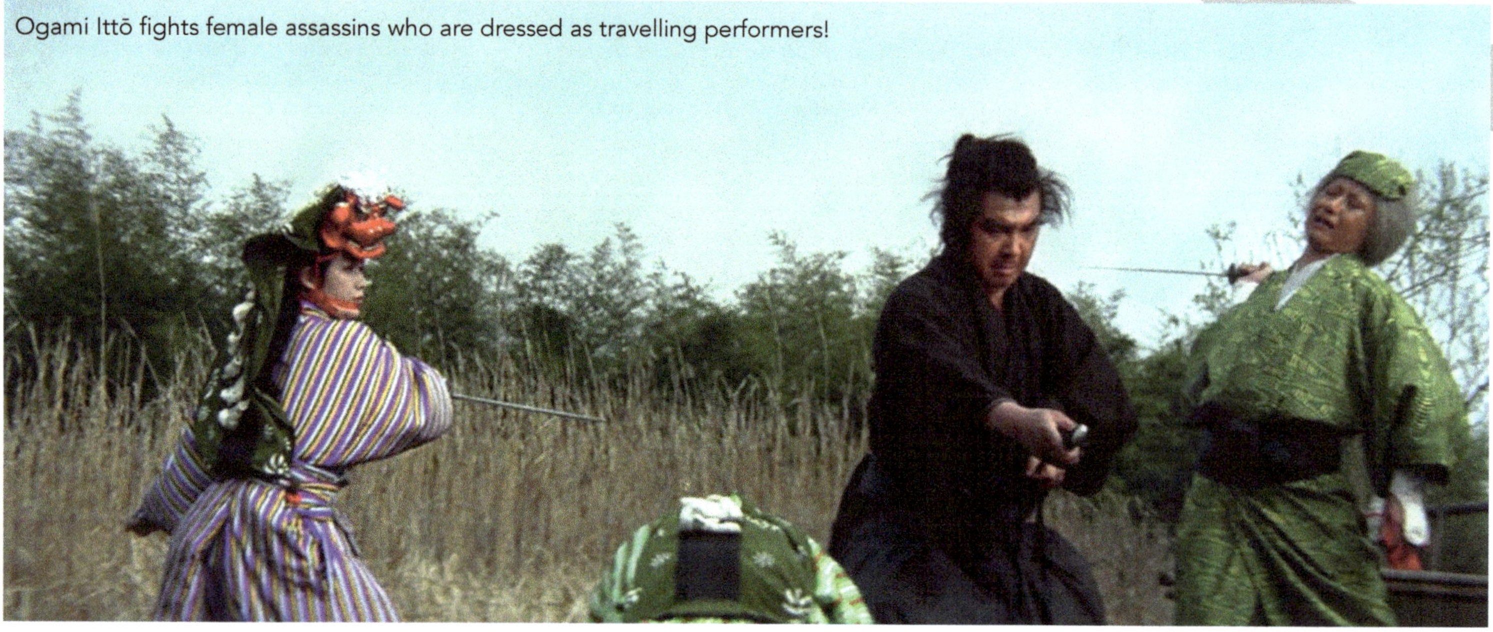

Ogami Ittō fights female assassins who are dressed as travelling performers!

hidden inside them, the wooden baby cart sprouts shin-slicing blades from its wheels, and Ogami Ittō carries his son on his back, then bends over so that sunlight glints off a mirror attached to Daigorō's head to dazzle an opponent during a duel.

Other sequences are just a joy to watch, whether it's Ittō sitting in a bath, checking the room for danger, as the camera does a slow, wary 360-degree circle of the place, or the shots of little Daigorō doing his best to bring water from a river to give to his injured father, finally resorting to carrying the water to Ittō in his mouth.

An early scene, showing Ogami Ittō putting a sword and a ball in front of his very young son, in a test to see whether Daigorō chooses the toy (and hence will soon be joining his dead mother in heaven) or the blade (and will be accompanying his father on his road to vengeance), perfectly encapsulates the dour lead character's uncompromising mindset. As played by Tomisaburo Wakayama, Ittō is a stoic, imperturbable character who never backs down and always kills his enemies, with the exception of a senior female assassin whom Ittō shows mercy to after she hesitates in a face-off in which his son's life hangs in the balance. Wakayama, brother of actor Shintaro Katsu (the star of the *Zatoichi* blind swordsman movie series), is not your typical leading man. Unlike the more handsome, prime physical specimen depicted in the manga, Tomisaburo Wakayama is a stern, somewhat plain dude with, let's face it, a dad bod! Yet this somehow enhances Lone Wolf's scowling on-screen presence, as we watch this character, who is definitely no ripped, powerful-looking badass, overcome all the obstacles and adversaries in his path, simply because he's an implacable dude who is really, really good at what he does: fighting and killing!

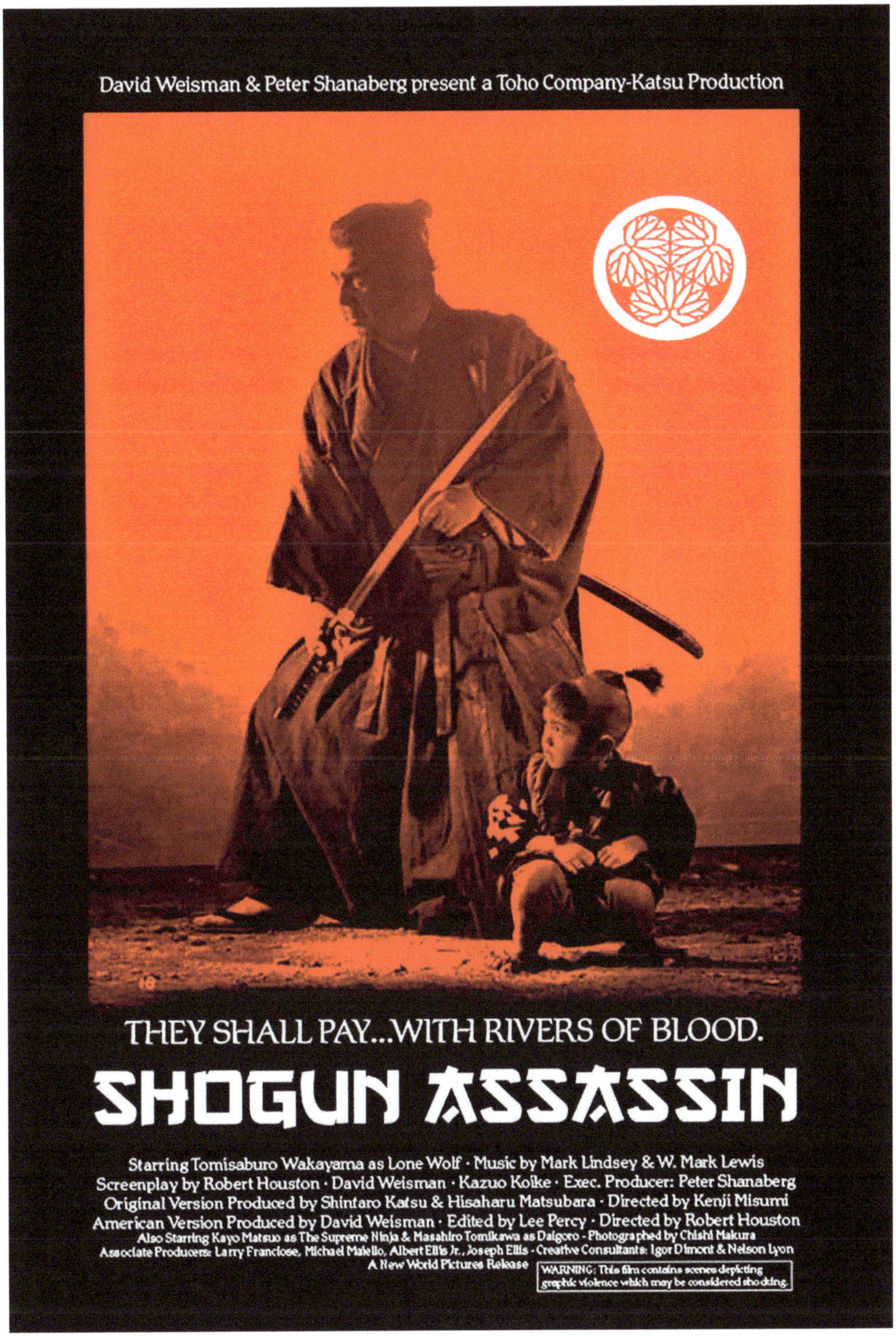

Arresting images abound in *Shogun Assassin*, many relating to the Masters of Death, super-fighter bodyguards who wear roningasa hats (made from bamboo palms) and are armed with weapons specific to each character: a club, iron claws, spiked gloves. At one point, as the Masters of Death cross a desert landscape, we see the lead Master plunge his iron claws into the sand... and blood begins to seep to the surface. A very memorable visual! It's revealed that rebels are hiding beneath the desert sands and the Masters of Death soon begin bloodily dealing with them, but Ogami Ittō is also waiting in the dunes... and the Masters of Death finally get a violent taste of their own medicine.

All of this impressive imagery is courtesy of the source material, of course. Around

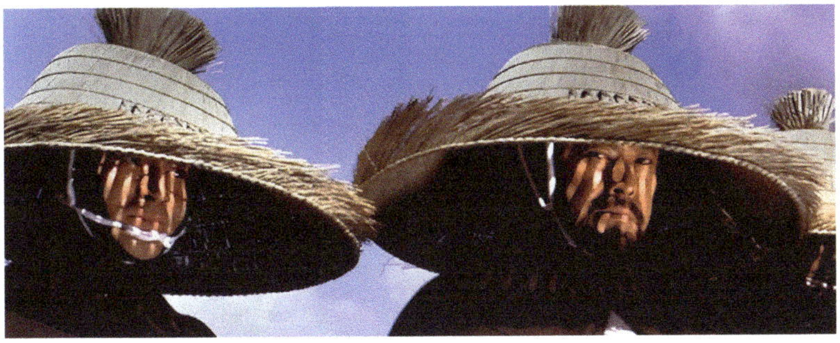

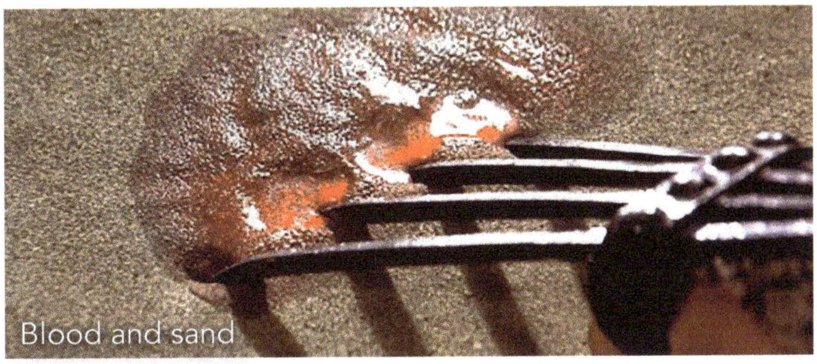
Blood and sand

12 minutes from the first *Lone Wolf and Cub* movie and the rest of the footage taken from the second in the series. But it's how it's all mixed into this newly edited and dubbed brew that imbues *Shogun Assassin* with its own individual flavour.

First and foremost, the new English dub works wonderfully, especially the matter-of-fact/innocent tones of Daigorō, delightfully voiced by Gibran Evans, who, sounding like a genuine young boy (which he was at the time), acts as the narrator of the story. This use of voice-over allows Houston and Weisman to alter the narrative, streamlining the tale, discarding the story thread (from the manga and original films) involving the Yagyū clan, turning the clan's leader, Retsudo, into the crazed Shogun in this self-contained plot. In the reworked script Daigorō tells us that the Shogun has gone mad, "People said his brain was infected by devils." The child's voice goes on to explain why Ogami Ittō becomes a ronin, "Then, one night, the Shogun sent his ninja spies to our house. They were supposed to kill my father, but they didn't. That was the night everything changed, forever. That was when my father left his samurai life and became a demon. He became an assassin who walks the road of vengeance. And he took me with him." Wonderful stuff!

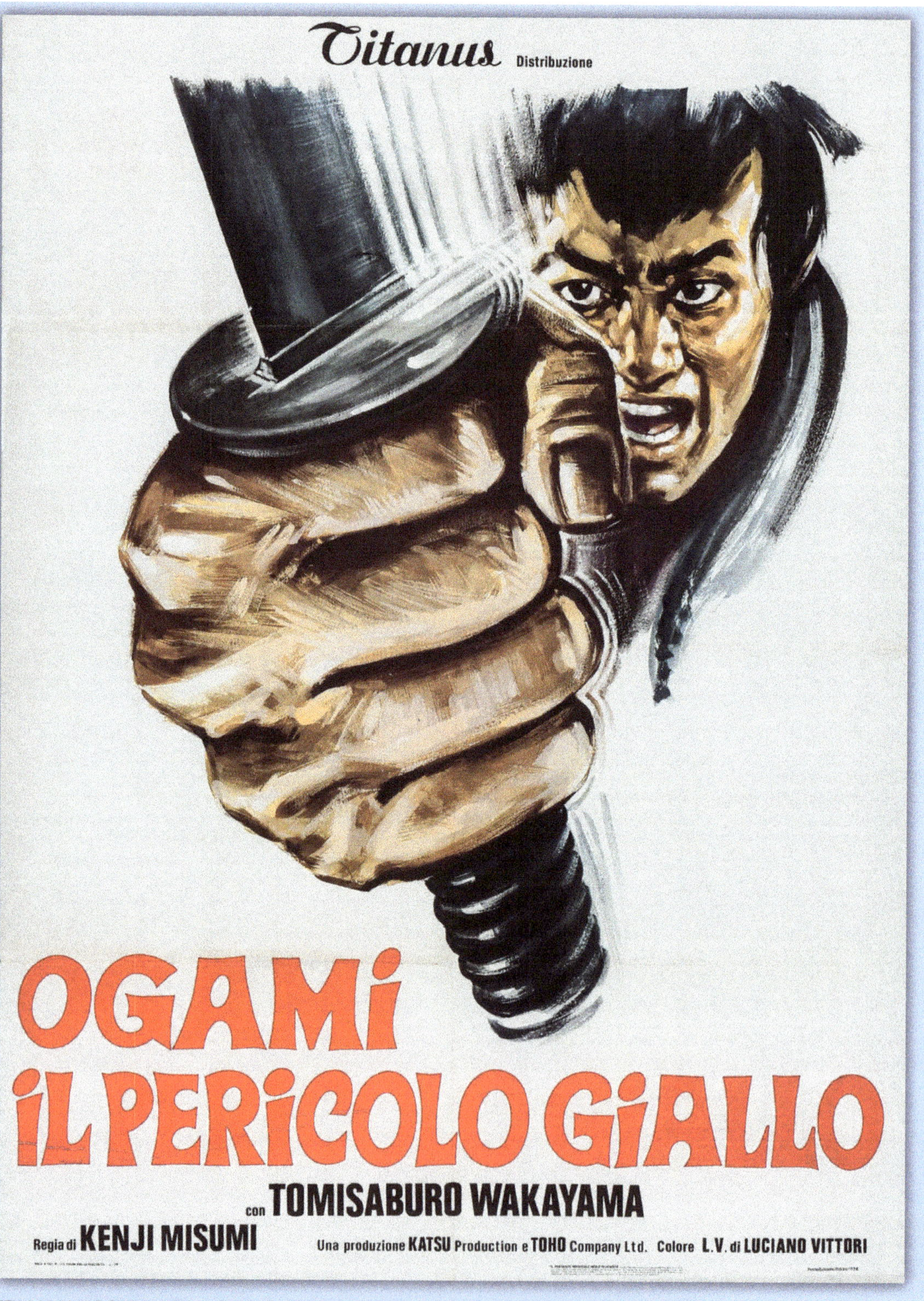

ITALIAN POSTER FOR *LONE WOLF AND CUB: BABY CART AT THE RIVER STYX*

Footage from 1972's *Lone Wolf and Cub: Baby Cart at the River Styx* formed a large part of what became *Shogun Assassin*...

Quotable dialogue abounds in the film, such as when the Masters of Death leader, with a fine spray of blood spritzing from his severed jugular vein, waxes lyrical about the nature of the wound Ittō has inflicted on him: "Your technique is magnificent. When cut across the neck, a sound like wailing winter winds is heard, they say. I'd always hoped to cut someone like that someday, to hear that sound. But to have it happen to my own neck is... ridiculous." Wow!

The reworking of the story condenses the plot, so that the fights, the face-offs, the confrontations and story beats occur in quick succession, really adding to the movie's pace.

The other key new element is, obviously, the cool, propulsive soundtrack, most of it performed on a Prophet-5 synthesizer. This score, recorded by Mark Lindsay and W. Michael Lewis over at Lindsay's Wonderland Avenue studio in the Los Angeles Hills, is definitely one of the big points of difference between *Shogun Assassin* and the Japanese *Lone Wolf and Cub* films.

The sound effects, as the weapons are zinged about, etc, were created at the Wonderland Avenue studio

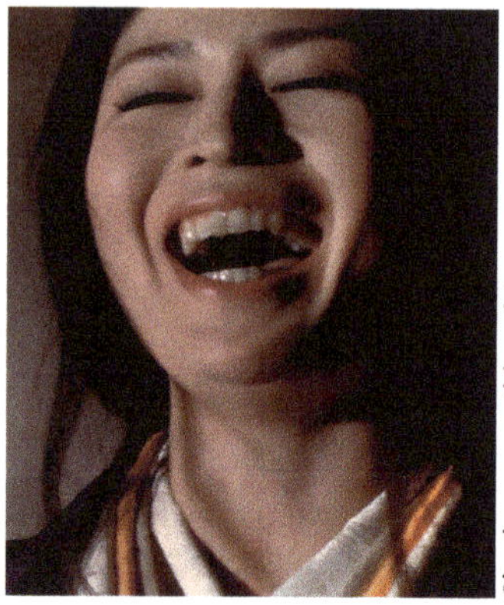

She has an evil laugh!

too, produced on an E-mu Modular System (a large, wall-sized synth) and recorded on a Trident Fleximix console.

Somehow a special alchemy occurred within all these elements, as the original footage was merged with the new dub, gelling together well, resulting in such a unique vibe that *Shogun Assassin* remains a very memorable chanbara (samurai film) that definitely continues to generate a nostalgic frisson for those viewers, including myself, who first saw this furiously good 'n' gory flick in their formative years.

Look, the movie is awesome, okay? Really awesome!

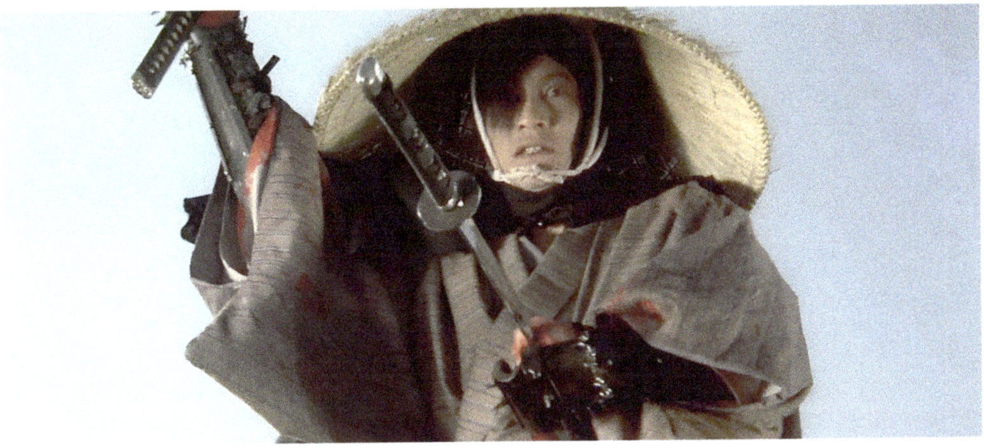

One of the Masters of Death gets skewered!

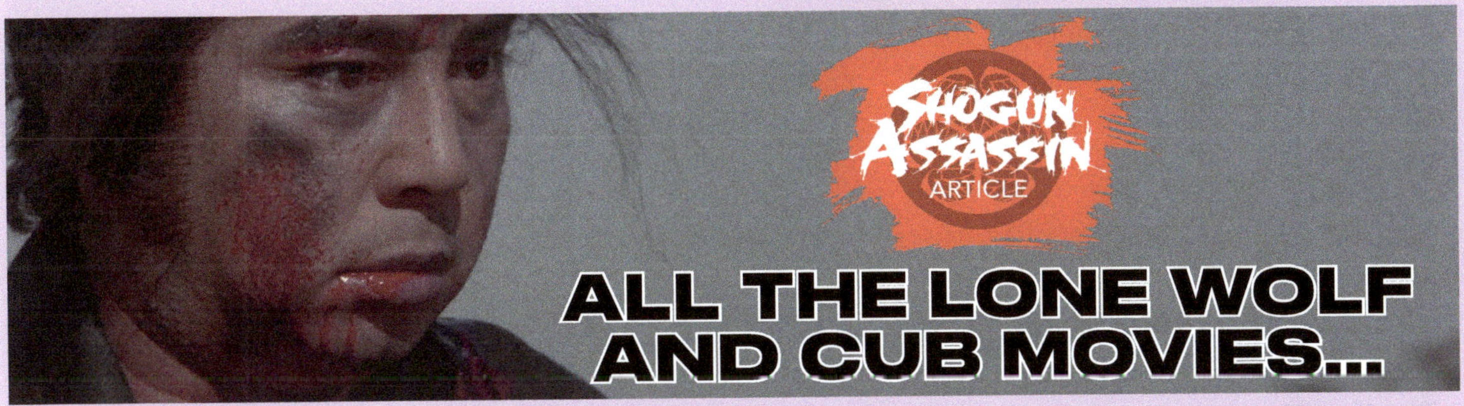

ALL THE LONE WOLF AND CUB MOVIES...

Ken Miller provides a quick lowdown on every *Lone Wolf and Cub* movie that has been produced so far, including, of course, *Shogun Assassin*, plus the television shows...

LONE WOLF AND CUB: SWORD OF VENGEANCE (1972)
Six *Lone Wolf and Cub* films starring Tomisaburo Wakayama as Ogami Ittō and Tomikawa Akihiro as Daigorō were made. The first movie focuses on Lone Wolf and Cub's origin, when Ogami Ittō, the Shogun's decapitator, is framed for treason by the Yagyū clan, resulting in Ittō hitting the vengeance trail with his son.

LONE WOLF AND CUB: BABY CART AT THE RIVER STYX (1972)
Ogami Ittō takes-on a group of female assassins in the employ of the Yagyū clan and must assassinate a traitor planning to sell his clan's secrets to the Shogunate, but this man is guarded by three lethal brothers... the Gods of Death.

LONE WOLF AND CUB: BABY CART TO HADES (1972)
The third film features a ronin who wants a duel with Ittō, a prostitute whom Ittō comes to the aid of, even allowing himself to be tortured, plus more assassins sent by the Yagyū clan and a battle with an army of adversaries.

LONE WOLF AND CUB: BABY CART IN PERIL (1972)
Here Ittō deals with a grudge-bearing swordsman called Gunbei and a topless, tattooed female killer called Oyuki, he vanquishes an entire army, and gets to cross swords with Yagyū leader Retsudo.

LONE WOLF AND CUB: BABY CART IN THE LAND OF DEMONS (1973)
Ittō duels with five different warriors of the Kuroda clan, each of whom delivers a portion of the information Itto requires to take on his latest contract. Meanwhile, Daigorō is caught up in a subplot involving a female pickpocket.

LONE WOLF AND CUB: WHITE HEAVEN IN HELL (1974)
Ittō faces off against hordes of clansmen led by the one-eyed Lord Retsudo. Horror elements are mixed into the narrative with the introduction of zombie warriors who can burrow through the ground. An icy encounter sees Ittō battle hordes of skiing enemies!

SHOGUN ASSASSIN (1980)
The cool, fun, rejigged, dubbed American release that uses footage from the first two Japanese *Lone Wolf and Cub* movies and retools the plot, turning the Retsudo character into the Shogun. The Gods of Death brothers from *Baby Cart at the River Styx* are renamed the Masters of Death here.

LONE WOLF AND CUB: FINAL CONFLICT (1993)
A revisionist reboot that changes Ogami Ittō's character (here played by Masakazu Tamura), turning him into a sensitive father who cries... which is far removed from the stoic Ogami Ittō seen in all previous movies. The story concentrates on Ittō's mission of revenge against the Yagyū clan, ignoring the assassin-for-hire subplots. Yushi Shoda plays Daigorō.

LONE WOLF AND CUB TV SERIES (1973-1976)
This show ran for three seasons. The episodes were 45 minutes long. It was originally aired on Nippon TV in Japan, and was broadcast in the US titled *The Fugitive Samurai*. Starring Kinnosuke Nakamura as Ogami Ittō and Kazutaka Nishikawa as Daigorō in the first two seasons, replaced by Takumi Satō as the son in the third season.

TV movies were aired in Japan in connection with the 70's television series. KOZURE ÔKAMI: OSANAGO NO ME (1985) and KOZURE ÔKAMI: NAMIDA ITO (1986) both starred the TV series actor Kinnosuke Nakamura as Ittō.

LONE WOLF AND CHILD: ASSASSIN ON THE ROAD TO HELL (1989)
A standalone 140 minute TV movie covering much of the Lone Wolf and Cub saga, starring Hideki Takahashi as Ittō. This has TV production values and the gore is toned-down.
Directed by Tokuzô Tanaka, with Tomisaburo Wakayama playing the villainous archenemy Yagyu Retsudo!

LONE WOLF AND CUB TV SERIES (2002-2004)
Kin'ya Kitaôji plays Ogami Ittō in this series, with Tsubasa Kobayashi in the role of Daigorō, and Isao Natsuyagi playing Retsudo, in a show produced by TV Asahi and Toei Company.

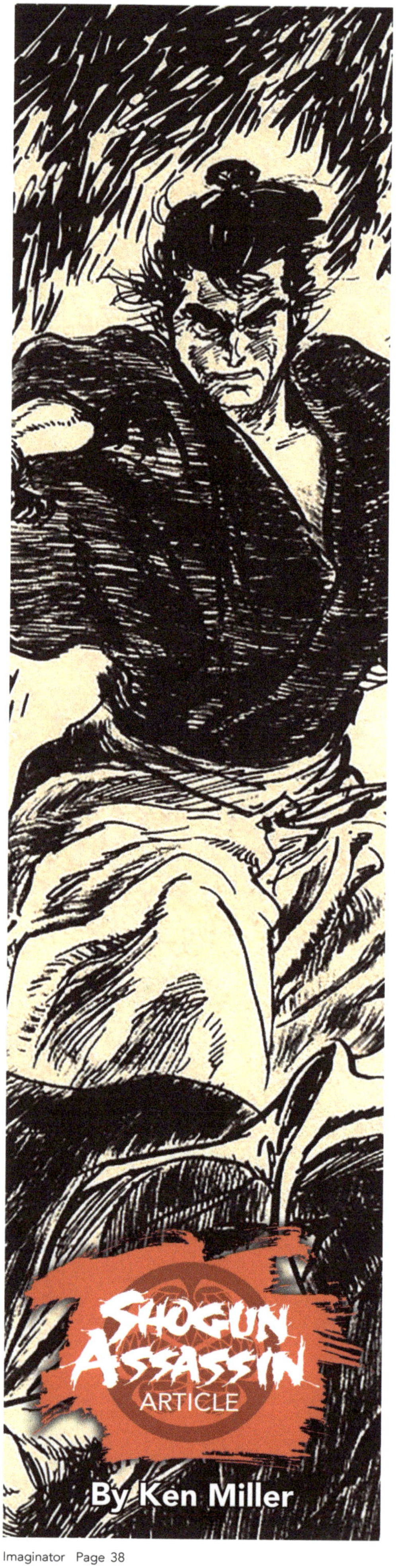

By Ken Miller

MAGNIFICENT MANGA

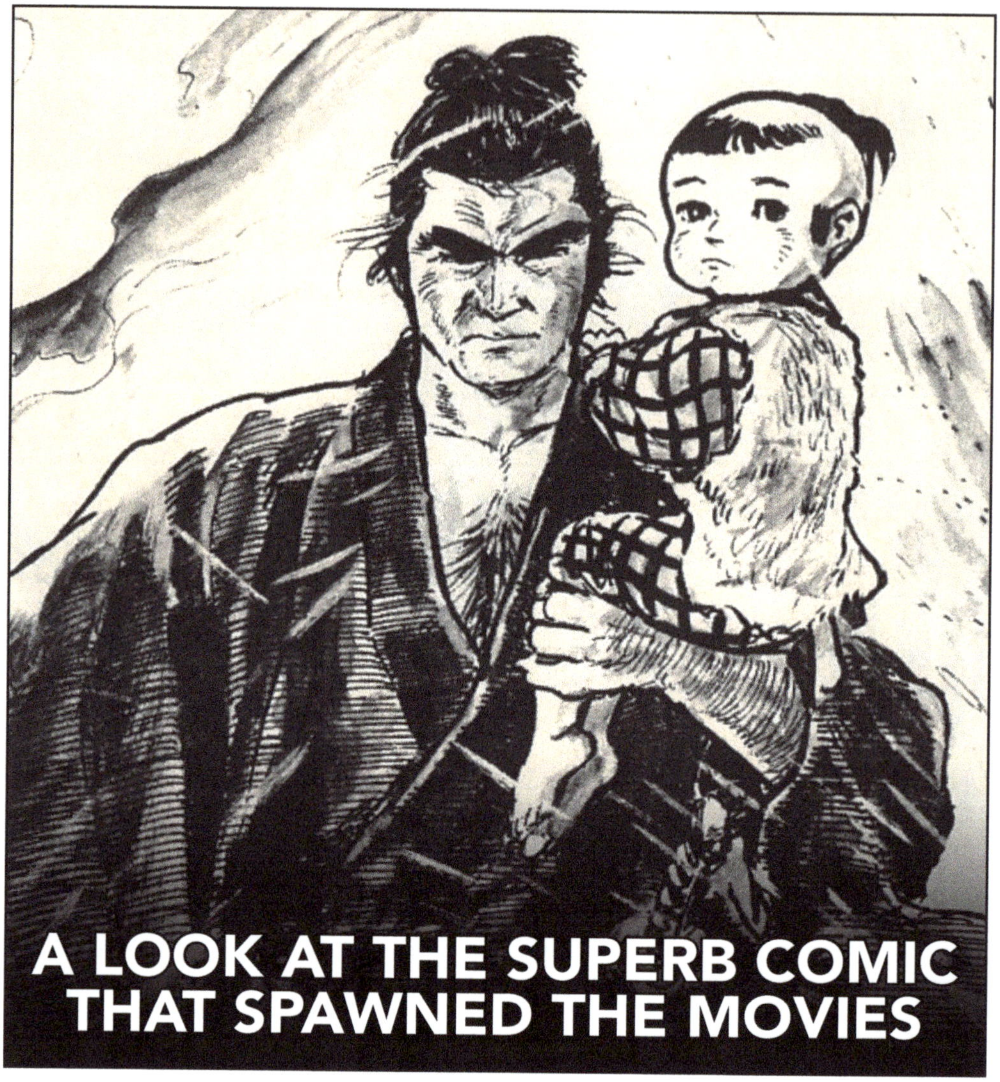

A LOOK AT THE SUPERB COMIC THAT SPAWNED THE MOVIES

The manga series *Lone Wolf and Cub* (known as *Kozure Ōkami* in Japan), created by writer Kazuo Koike and artist Goseki Kojima, was first published in 1970 and chronicled the story of Ogami Ittō, the Shogun's executioner, who is disgraced and framed by the supremely cunning villain Yagyu Retsudo of the Yagyū clan, forcing Ittō to take the path of the assassin after his wife is murdered and he refuses to commit seppuku. Bringing along his son, Daigorō, Ittō seeks revenge on the Yagyū clan and must tackle the many foes sent to kill him, whilst also taking on assassin-for-hire jobs, which he only undertakes after his employers are totally honest with Ittō, keeping no secrets from him.

Lone Wolf and Cub was originally published in the US in a translated English edition by First Comics, back in 1987, but the company unfortunately went bankrupt before all of the issues could be published.

I started reading the stories in 2000, when Dark Horse Comics began releasing their *Lone Wolf and Cub* trade paperbacks, which were similar in design to the volumes published in Japan. All the stories were released in 28 volumes over a two-year period, with cover art supplied by top comic artists Frank Miller (with Lynn Varley),

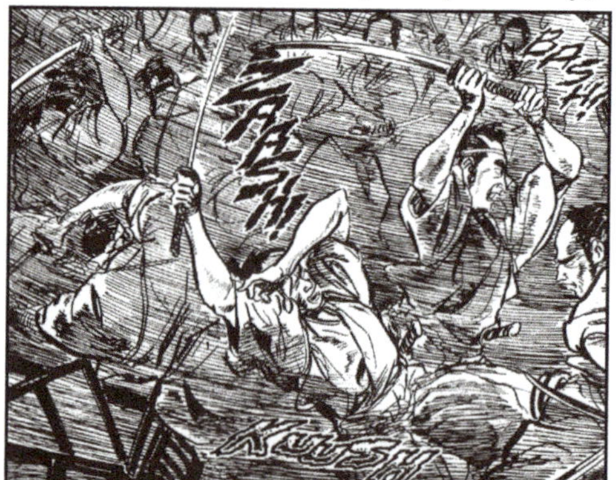

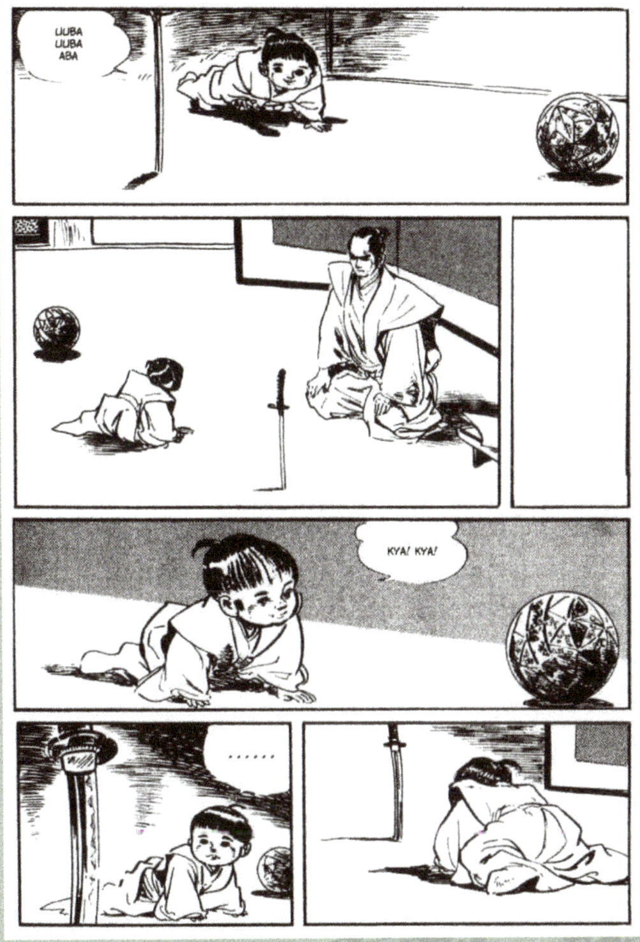

Here is the scene in which Ogami Ittō waits for his son Daigorō to choose between a ball and a sword, a decision that will change the course of his son's life forever, as depicted in the manga and in the film *Lone Wolf and Cub: Sword of Vengeance* (1972), footage that was also used in *Shogun Assassin* (1980)...

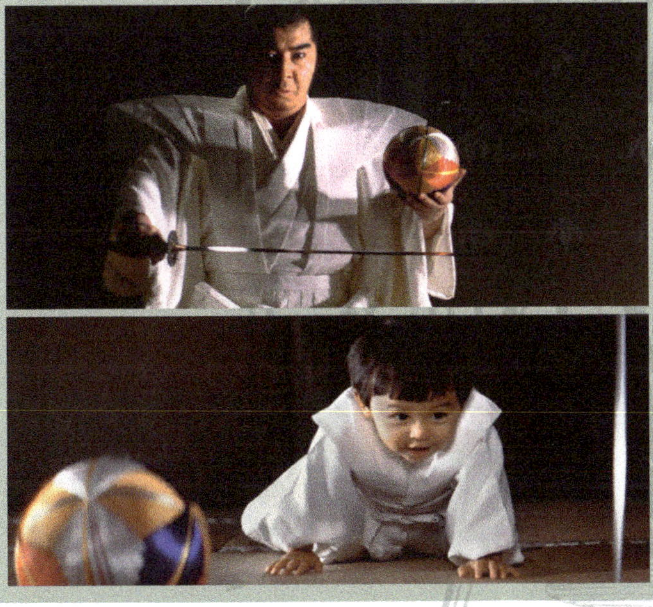

Matt Wagner, Guy Davis (with Vince Locke) and Bill Sienkiewicz (some of these cover illustrations were originally created for the First Comics series). The Dark Horse editions came with a glossary at the back to explain many of the Edo-era terms used in the stories. Dark Horse would later rerelease all these stories in a set of 12 larger format omnibus editions.

Kazuo Koike's plotting in this manga series is flawless. Stories are structured with precision, balancing tons of Tokugawa shogunate-era world-building detail, deft characterisation, and expertly-handled twists and reveals wonderfully. When I read the first story, *Son for Hire, Sword for Hire*, I was immediately sucked into this harsh world of skilled swordsmen, action, the internecine strife within feudal clans, and the unorthodox central relationship between Ogami Ittō and his son Daigorō. But what really sealed the deal and made me a *Lone Wolf and Cub* manga fan was the cool, unexpected turnabout in this story: Koike throws in a great twist as we realise that the clan warriors who've used a special 'hawk-wing eye attack' technique to hunt down and capture Ittō have actually been tricked! Ittō wanted to be caught all along and had even written a fake warning message to the clan, telling them that he was an assassin travelling with a small child, thus guaranteeing that he'd get identified, arrested, and taken to the clan's castle... so that he could kill his targets! This sort of writing is a constant in the manga, ensuring the stories are never as straightforward as they sometimes might seem at the outset of each wonderfully-formed yarn. Along with the twists, the tales are also prone to keep readers guessing as to whom Ittō is actually going to kill, and the means by which Lone Wolf goes about his tasks in the plots can also be surprising.

Koike populates the world of these stories with every kind of character: ronin, soldiers, peasants, thieves, samurai, lords, ladies, innkeepers, poisoners, priests, prostitutes, stage performers, elders, chieftains, monks, yakuza, riflemen, policemen, ninjas, crippled ninjas, archers, sleeper agents, and every other character-type to be found in Edo-period Japan. Some of these people are honourable, some are devious, some are pitiable, some are evil or murderous,

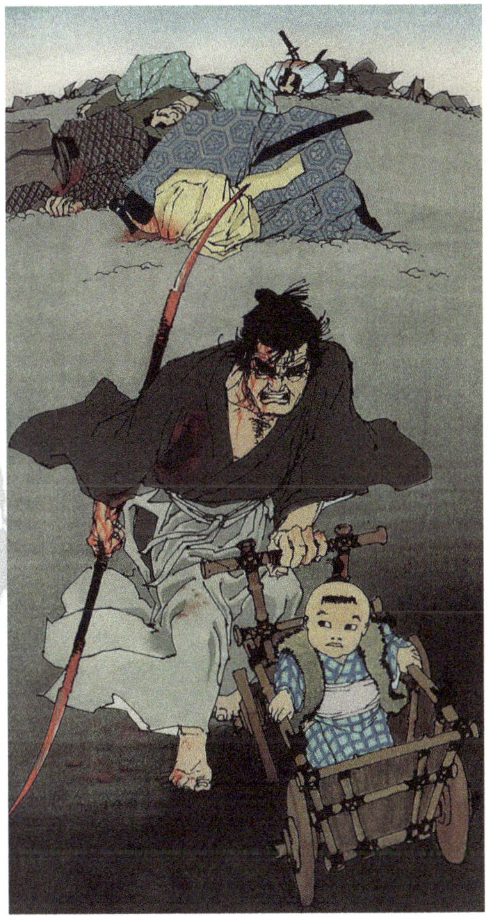

A cover illustration by Frank Miller and Lynn Varley

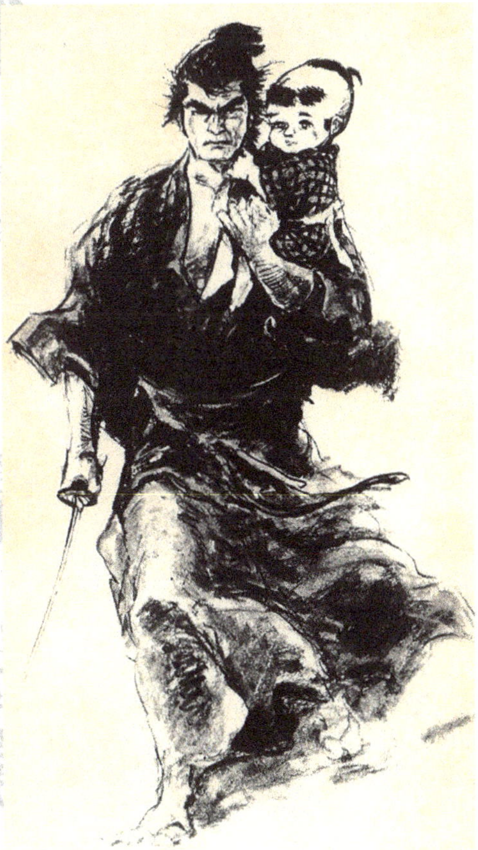

and others are degenerate grotesques. Kazuo Koike surrounds all these folks in a well-researched period milieu, working Japanese history into the narrative, whilst never allowing the detail to impede the flow of the plots, and his deft handling of the characters makes the bizarre and outlandish things that sometimes occur in the yarns seem believable.

The chapters are a mixture of standalone adventures and murder-for-hire missions, peppered with backstory flashbacks, and an overarching plotline involving Retsudo and his laser-focused need to take down Ittō. This story thread becomes more and more foregrounded as the series progresses. Towards the end of the saga, after a bounty is put on Ittō's head, pretty much the whole of Japan is gunning for him! But there's an ebb and flow to this grand tale too, and this is definitely part of its strength, because the stories aren't just nonstop tales of bloodbaths and killings: there are tales that are more intimate, there's character development, there's the critical look at the intricacies of feudal Japanese notions of honour and duty, and, of course, there's the central relationship between Lone Wolf and his Cub.

Perfectly complimenting Koike's writing is the wondrous art of Goseki Kojima. His b&w illustrations exude an incredibly cinematic visual storytelling style, and I'm

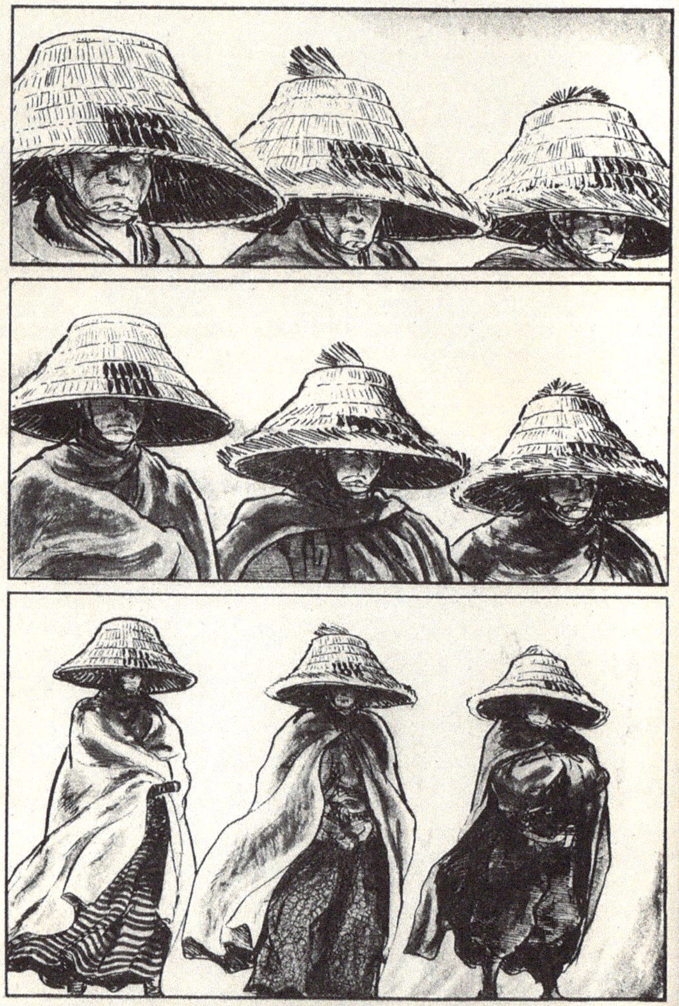

The Hidari Brothers, also known as The Bentenrai Brothers, as they appear in the manga (above), and how they look (below) in the film *Lone Wolf and Cub: Baby Cart at the River Styx* (1972), where they are referred to as the Gods of Death. They look very similar to their manga counterparts! Footage of them is used in *Shogun Assassin* (1980) too, where they are called the Masters of Death...

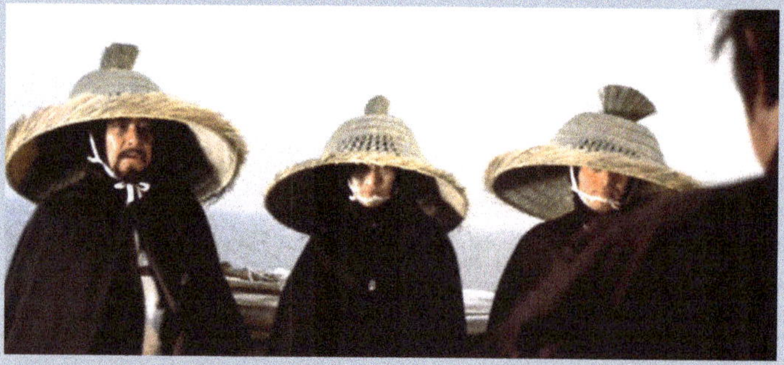

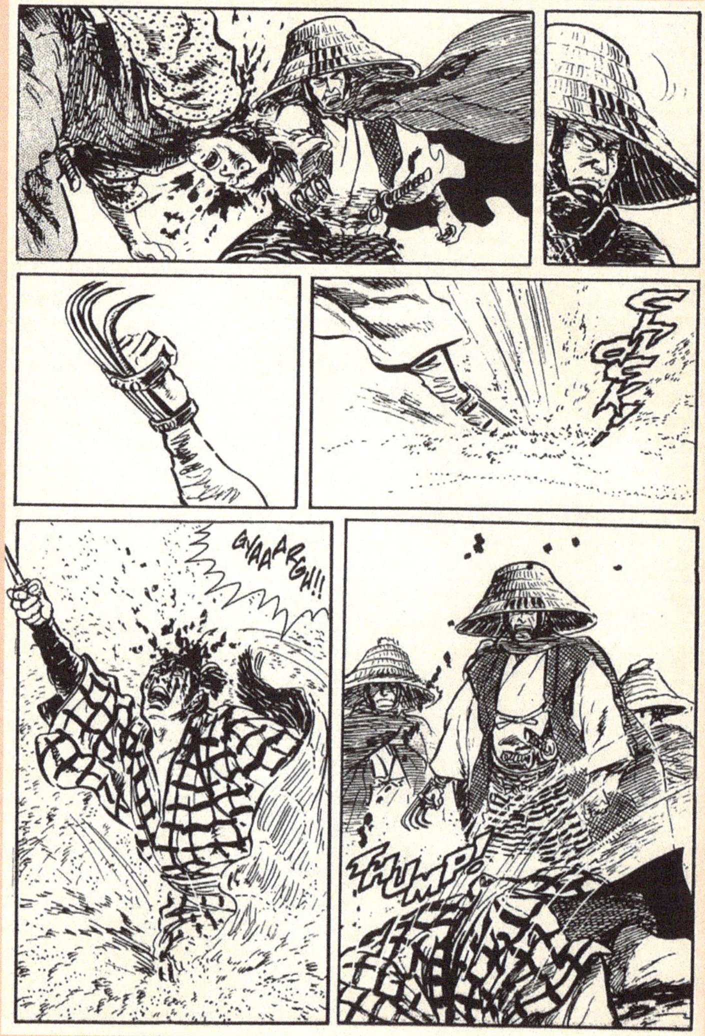

In the *Lone Wolf and Cub* manga, the lead Hidari Brother uses his metal claws to pull rebels from beneath the sand. The same thing happens in the movie *Lone Wolf and Cub: Baby Cart at the River Styx* (1972) and, of course, in *Shogun Assassin* (1980)...

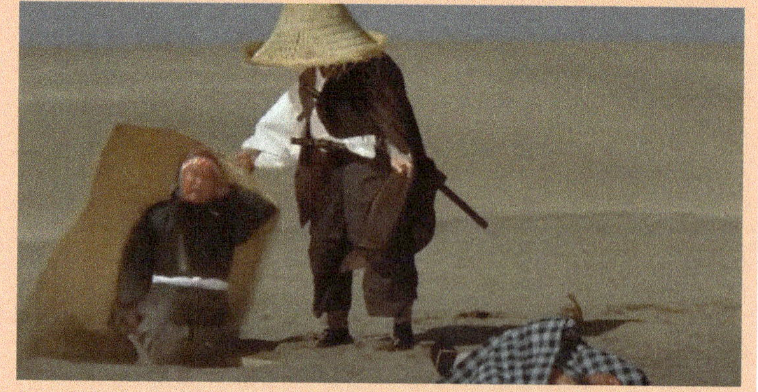

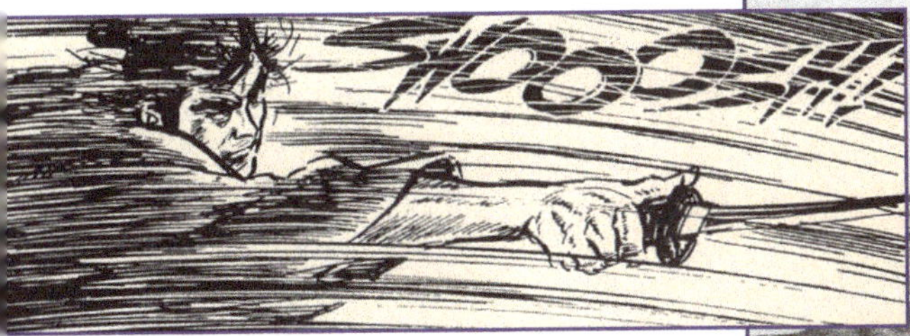

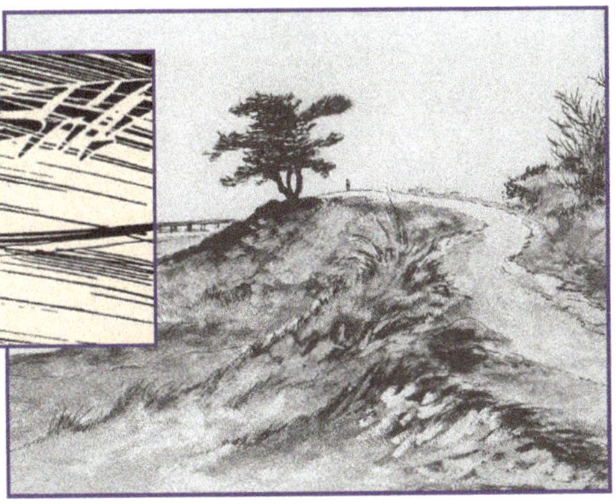

sure that many of these panels worked as ready-made storyboards when the *Lone Wolf and Cub* movies were produced.

Kojima manages to infuse a sense of the 'fog of war' into his fight sequences, using multiple speed lines to turn some of the action panels into a blur of motion, making the reader unsure of quite what is happening during the fights! Conversely, exquisitely-composed establishing shots

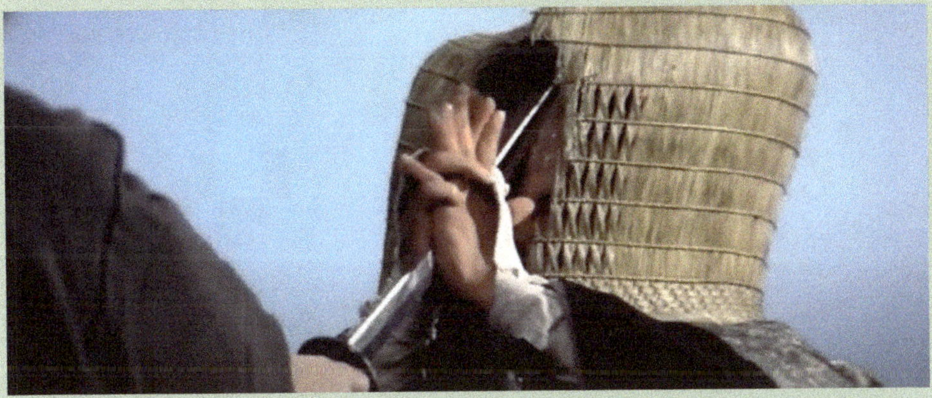

Various characters wear distinctive headgear in the *Lone Wolf and Cub* manga series and also in the *Lone Wolf and Cub* movies...

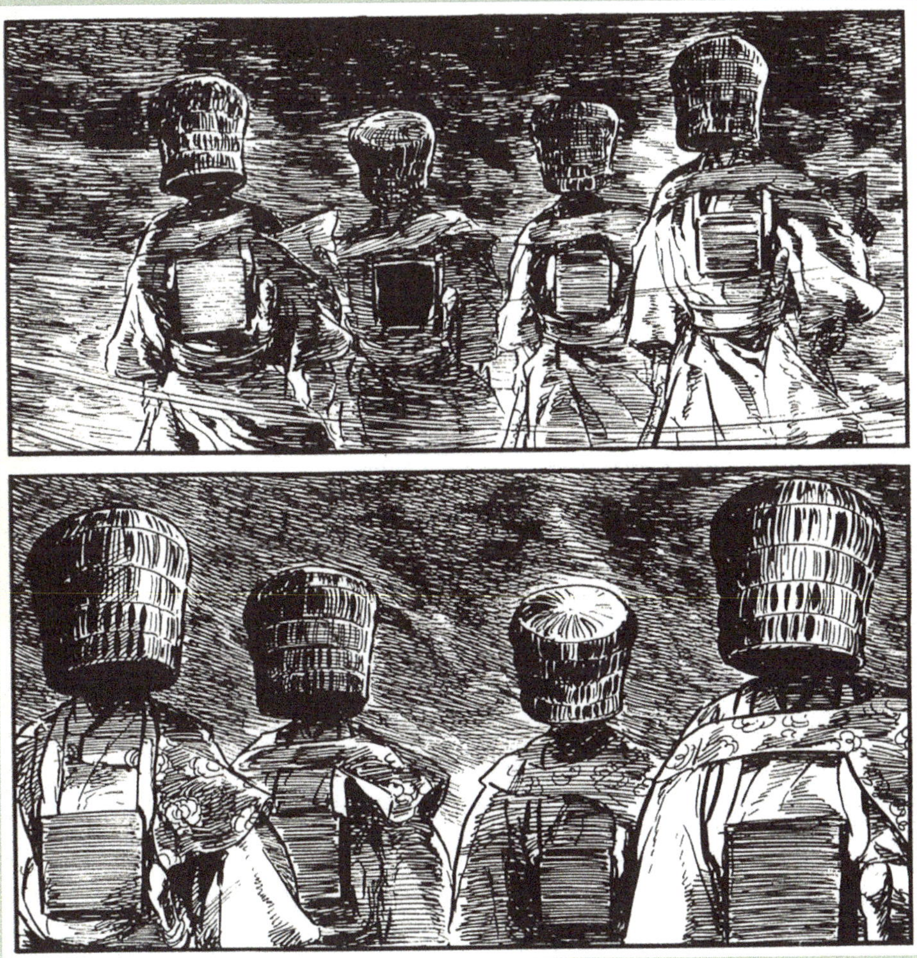

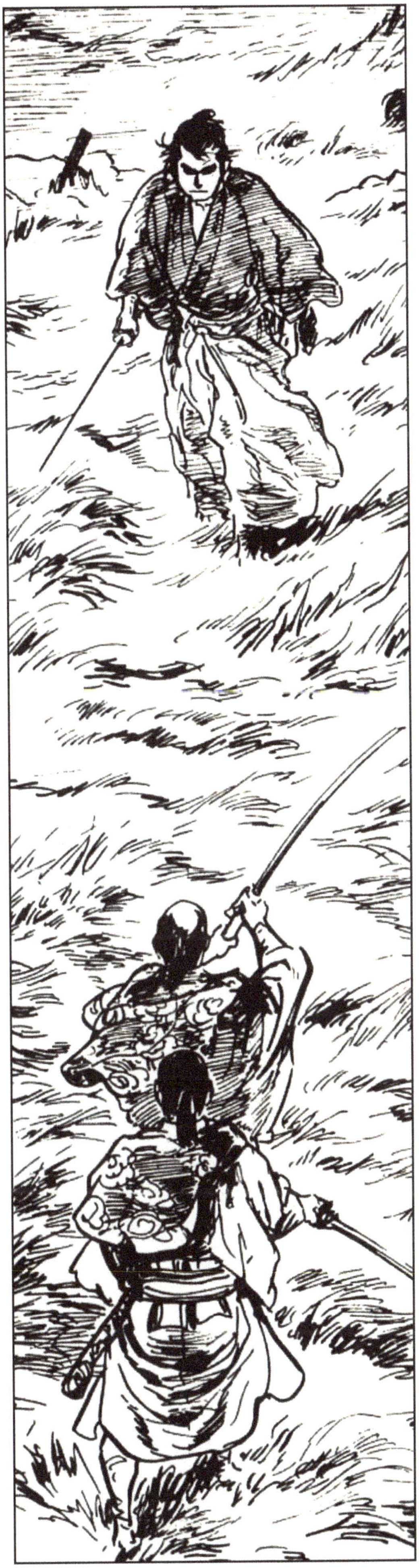

Swords are drawn...

of temples, tree-shrouded trails, forested valleys and other scenic delights not only set the scene for the stories, they also demand that the reader should slow down a little and pay full attention to the detail.

The effective use of wide-angle panels, which spread across two pages, adds to the dynamism of sequences. Pages of compelling, dialogue-free sequential art keep you glued to the story, such as when the Yagyū clan marches through a rain-swept landscape, or when a group of unspeaking 'nighthawk' prostitutes approach a remote shack that Lone Wolf and Cub are sleeping in.

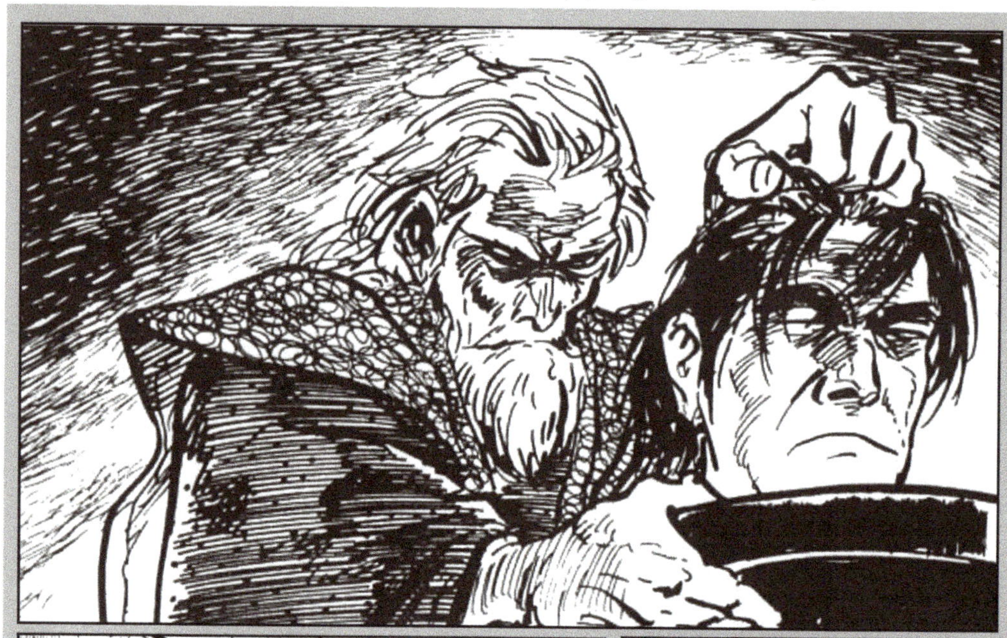

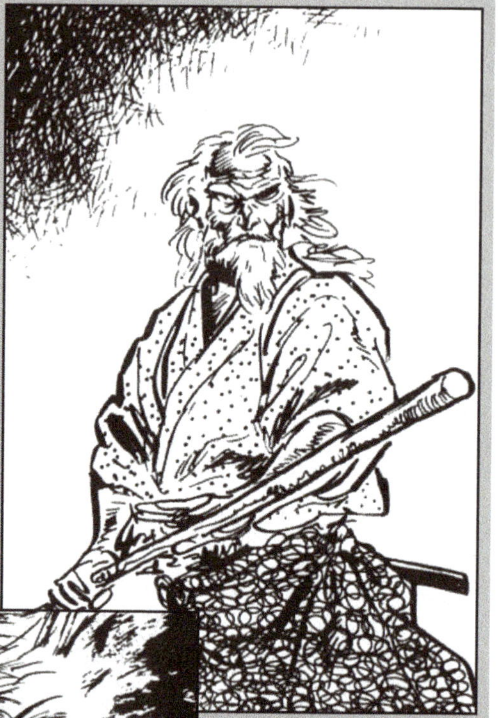

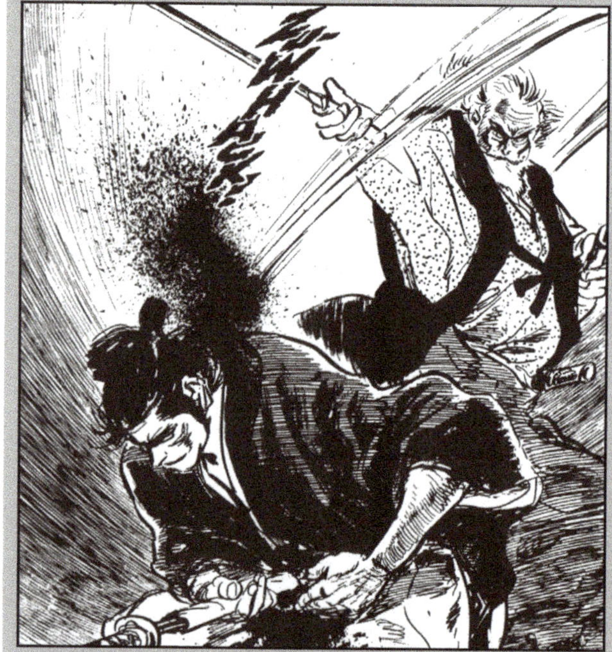

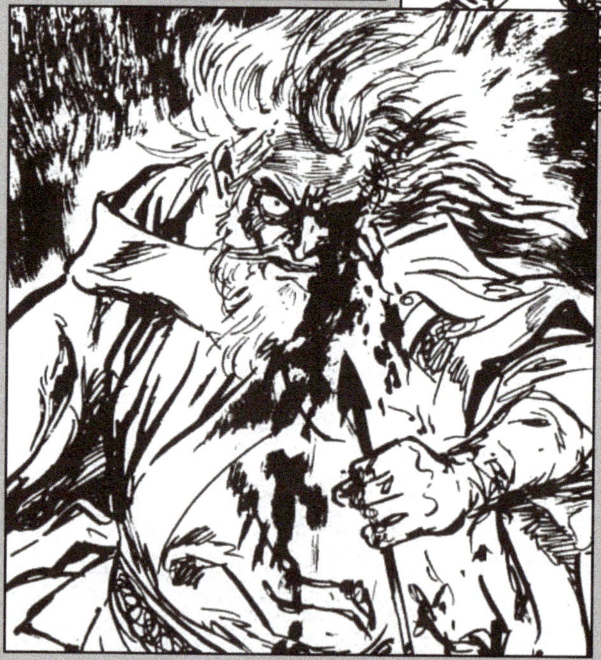

Yagyu Retsudo (above & left) as he is drawn in the *Lone Wolf and Cub* manga. This cunning, extremely ruthless and manipulative lead villain may have been an old man, but he was also a wily, tough fighter. In *Lone Wolf and Cub: Sword of Vengeance*, Yagyu Retsudo was played by Yūnosuke Itō (below). In the *Shogun Assassin* plot alterations his character was turned into the mad Shogun...

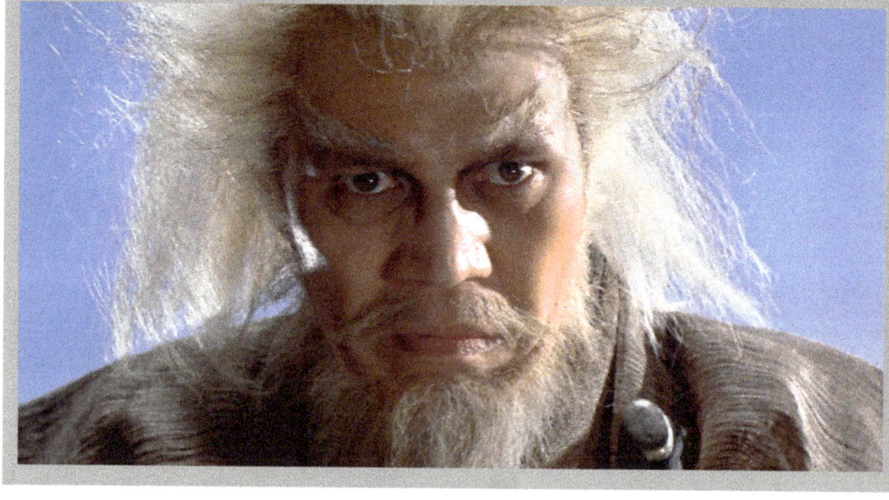

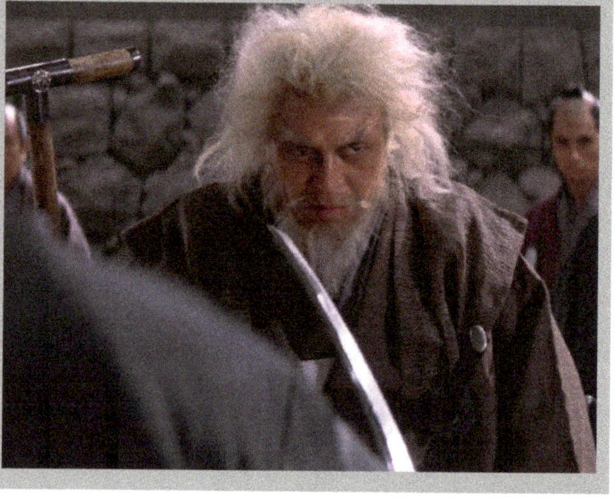

From the massive to the minuscule, panels with no figures in them are utilised to emanate a sense of mood and place, whether showing the close-up view of a stone road marker or the full page vista of a flock of birds flying across a cloudy dawn sky.

Kojima's art alternates between panels crammed with fine black line work, to others using greyscale washes, to panels that are a mixture of line work and areas of full black. All this b&w imagery makes *Lone Wolf and Cub* the distinctive manga classic that it is, and there's no doubt that adding colour to this artwork would ruin the special vibe of the saga.

Koike and Kojima's talents combined here to create one of the greatest ever examples of manga, which deserves all of the praise it has garnered over the years. It is a stunning tale that, through well-rendered words and pictures, exudes heaps of atmosphere, mixes meditations and violent action together, evokes a totally complete sense of place, and brings to life a plethora of memorable characters, especially the titular duo of father and son.

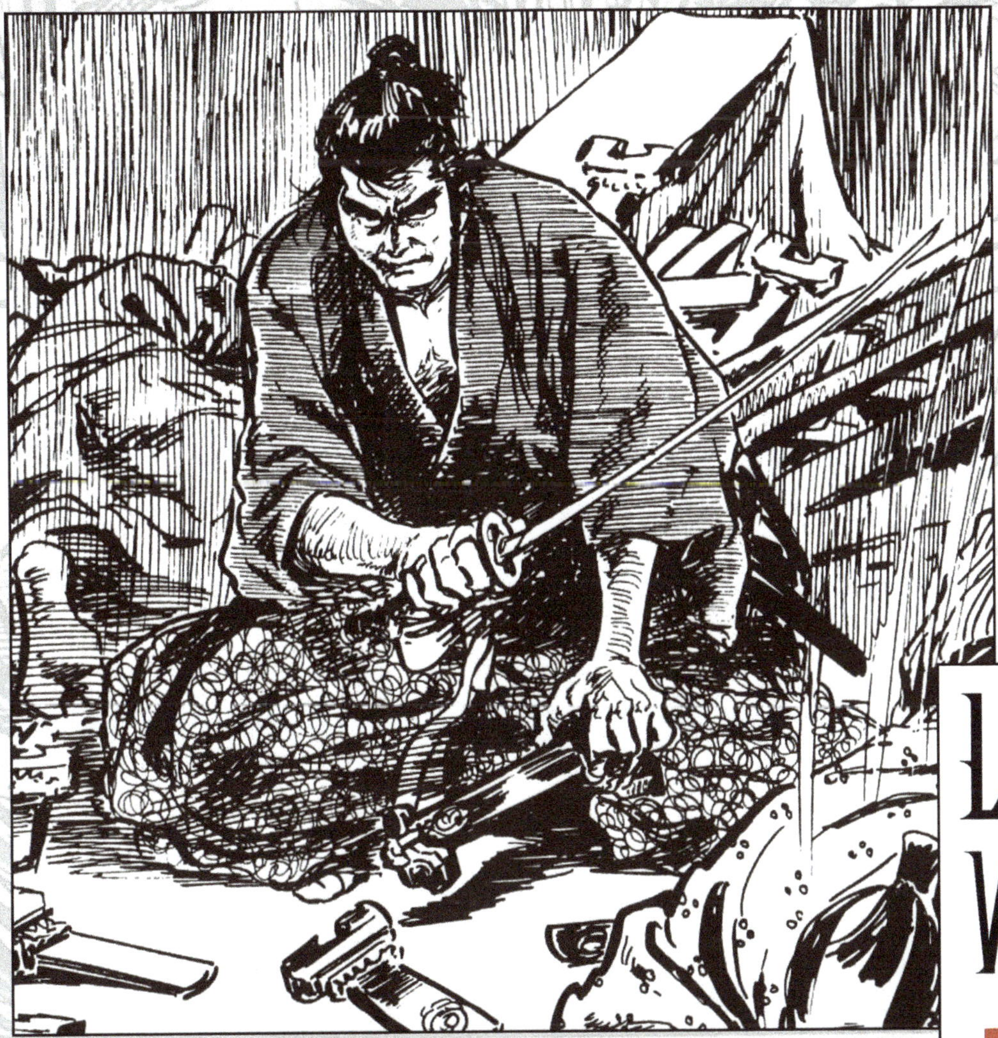

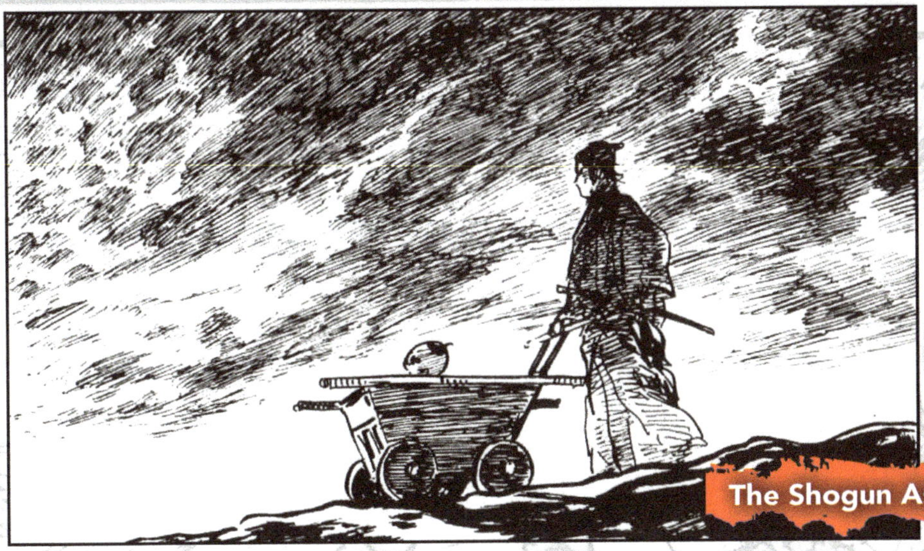

There was a follow-up manga series to *Lone Wolf and Cub*, called *Shin Kozure Ookami - Lone Wolf*, released in English as *New Lone Wolf and Cub* by Dark Horse Comics in 2014. It was written again by Kazuo Koike and drawn this time by Hideki Mori (Goseki Kojima had passed away in 2000). The 11 volume series focused on Daigorō and Tōgō Shigetada of the Satsuma clan, who is a skilled master of the Jigen-ryu sword style.

Dark Horse Comics also released *Samurai Executioner*, a manga written by Koike and drawn by Kojima, focusing on Yamada Asaemon, the man entrusted with testing the edge and quality of the Shogun's newly forged swords. Asaemon actually appears in the *Lone Wolf and Cub* crossover story *Decapitator Asaemon*, where he duels with Ogami Ittō. This tale is included in *Black Wind*, volume 5 of the Dark Horse *Lone Wolf and Cub* series.

If you're thinking of immersing yourself in this world for the first time, be sure to start with the original *Lone Wolf and Cub* series and plunge into an epic yarn that's full of compelling characters, dramatic fight scenes, and intriguing narratives, all of which is layered with a superbly evoked exploration of the customs, history, caste system, honorifics, and terminology of Edo-period Japan.

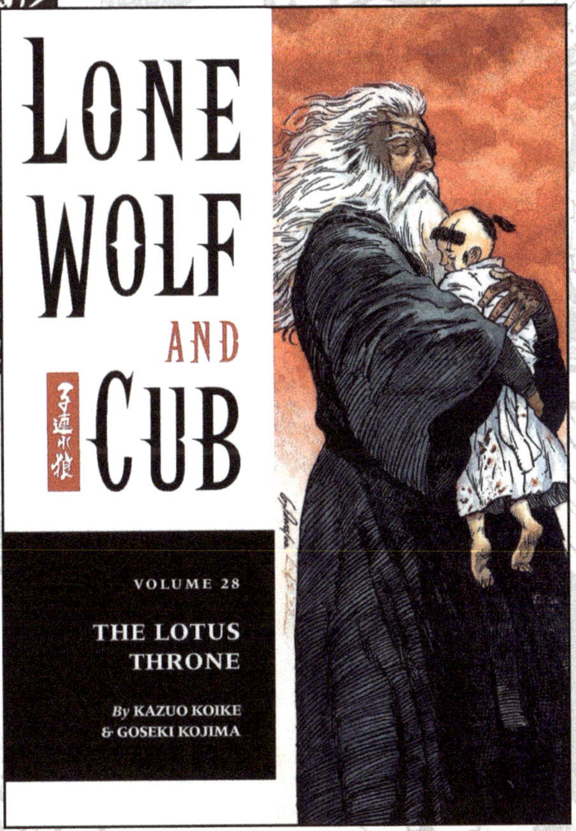

The Shogun Assassin Celebration continues on page 50

RADIOACTIVE REVIEWS

Here's a selection of reviews for films - old and new - that deal with such *Imaginator*-friendly subjects as monster sharks, jaded superheroes, Cthulhu, cannibals, mythical creatures... and gill-men! Woot!

MONSTER ISLAND (2024)

Starring Dean Fujioka, Callum Woodhouse
Written and directed by Mike Wiluan
Produced by Eric Khoo, James Khoo, Fumie Suzuki Lancaster, Ninin Musa, Fong Cheng Tan, Darryl Yeo, Freddie Yeo
Gorylah Pictures/Infinite Studios/SC Films International/ Tigon Pictures/Yaman Films/Zhao Wei Films

During World War II a Japanese soldier, Saito (Fujioka), and a British POW, Bronson (Woodhouse), find themselves stranded on an island after the ship they were being transported on is sunk. At first the two men are antagonistic towards each other, but Saito, who is himself a prisoner of the Japanese military due to his beliefs, finally teams-up with Bronson... so that they can defend themselves against a marauding gill-man.

Aka *Orang Ikan*, this Singapore/Indonesia/ Japan/United Kingdom production is a solid monster movie that comes across like a melding of *Hell in the Pacific* with *The Creature from the Black Lagoon*.

The story doesn't hold too many surprises, but attempts are made to provide the creature with its own motivations (its mate has been killed and it has an as-yet-unborn embryo in a cave to protect), which is a nice touch. The creature attacks are quite gory, and the practical monster suit looks bloody good.

This Orang Ikan costume, courtesy of Creature Designer Allan B. Holt, is what impressed me the most about the movie. Though the footage of the ship being attacked by warplanes at the start of the film was achieved using so-so CGI, the gill-man itself is brought to the screen via splendid practical effects. This is a sleek, muscled creature design that is a pleasure to look at. Niiiiiiice.

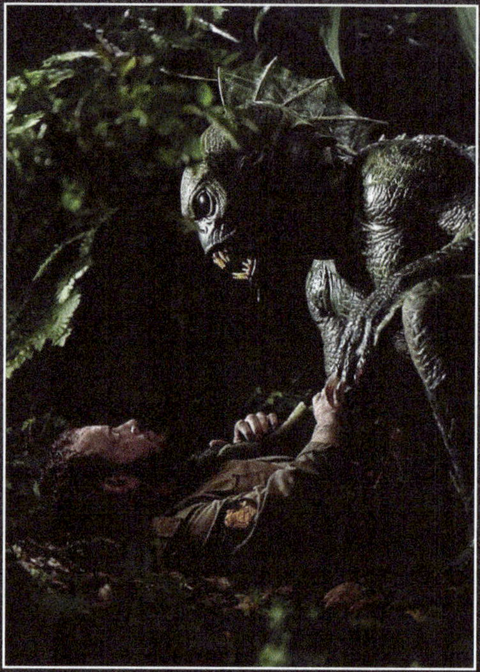

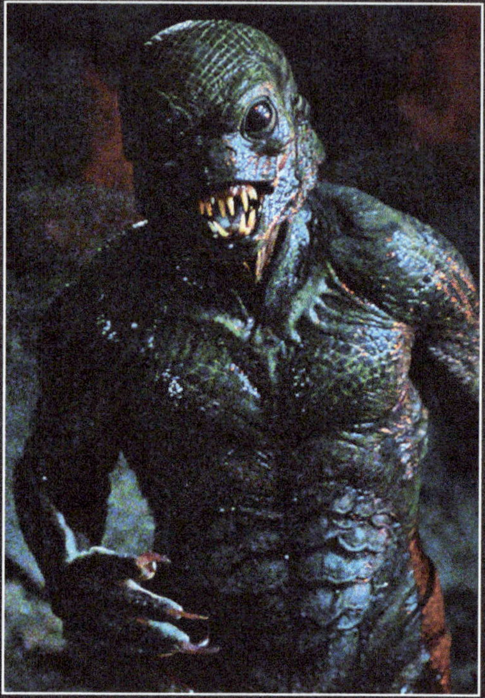

DEATH OF A UNICORN (2025)

Starring Jenna Ortega, Paul Rudd, Richard E. Grant, Will Poulter, Téa Leoni, Anthony Carrigan, Jessica Hynes, Sunita Mani
Written and directed by Alex Scharfman
Produced by Lars Knudsen, Tim Headington, Drew Houpt, Lucas Joaquin, Theresa Steele Page, Alex Scharfman
A24/Ley Line Entertainment/Square Peg/Secret Engine/Monoceros Media/The Royal Budapest Film Co

When Elliot Kintner (Rudd) is invited to spend the weekend at the palatial country retreat of his super-rich boss Odell Leopold and his family, Elliot decides to bring along his daughter Ridley (Ortega), who accuses him of including her on this trip purely so that he can look like a doting father. But, as he drives through the nature reserve surrounding the Leopold mansion, Elliot accidentally hits a strange wild animal... a small unicorn. This injured (soon to be dead) creature possesses special healing qualities, and soon the Leopolds are busy figuring out how to monetise the unicorn's body parts, especially its horn, but Ridley, who'd experienced visions after grasping the unicorn's horn, researches the legend surrounding the exotic beast and warns everyone that they could be in danger. The Leopolds and Elliot ignore Ridley's advice... and soon two large parent unicorns come calling...

Selling itself as a dark fantasy horror-comedy, *Death of a Unicorn* is actually not overtly funny, nor is it very horrific - it seems content to be a left-field, quirky tall tale that passes the time. The dialogue is okay, though not as witty as writer-director Alex Scharfman thinks it is, and Paul Rudd, usually effortlessly likeable in his roles, here plays a protagonist who is far too low key, obsequious and weak-willed for most of the film's running time. Will Poulter, as the dim bulb rich-kid Shepard Leopold, who finds out he can become smarter by snorting powdered unicorn horn up his nose, is the cast member who best grasps what acting style is required for the tone of this film, hence he's the only character you're likely to remember once the end credits start to roll.

The CGI is okay: not bad but not great either. The look of the unicorns is quite interesting, though, with the creatures portrayed not as slender and graceful mythical beasts, but as sharp-toothed, sturdily-built killer equines. These vengeful critters are willing and able to transfix victims on their horns, rip people in two, and tear out intestines with their teeth. Nasty!

Idiosyncratic films like this are usually criticised if their third act becomes too conventional and action-oriented, but *Death of a Unicorn*, for me, definitely gets more enjoyable and satisfying once it decides to treat us to a creatures-on-the-loose action-and-thrills finale.

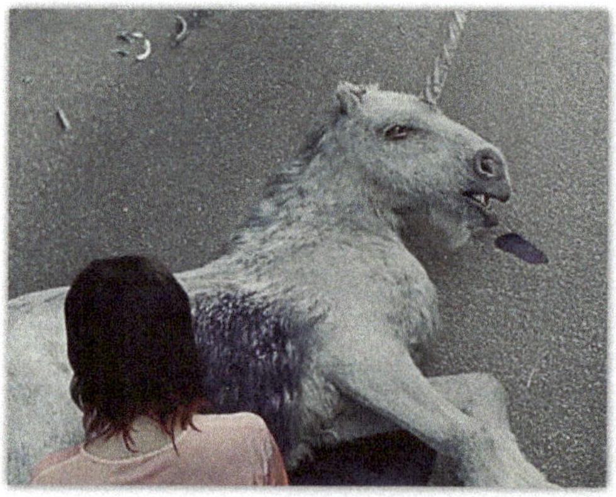

RIVER OF BLOOD (2024)

Starring Louis James, Sarah Alexandra Marks, Ella Starbuck, David Wayman, Joseph Millson, Tiffany Hannam-Daniels, Suwajchai Anubhat
Written by Tom Boyle
Directed by Howard J. Ford
Produced by Tom Boyle, Howard J. Ford, Rikke Ennis, Frederik Nelsson, Kim Pijselman
Latitude Films/REinvent Studios

Whilst they're on vacation in Southeast Asia, two young couples, Ajay and Maya & Ritchie and Jasmine, are taken on a jungle kayak trip by a river guide, but circumstances lead them into a fateful venture down a tributary... towards cannibal country.

With the cannibal survival horror movie sub-genre dominated by the likes of *Cannibal Holocaust* (1980) and *Cannibal Ferox* (1981) - productions infamous for their transgressively violent imagery - the makers of *River of Blood* wisely choose not to attempt to out-gore those aforementioned movies and, instead, they decide to develop a story with characters that viewers will become engaged with enough to want know if they manage to survive their ordeals.

After being introduced to the four main protagonists, it soon becomes evident that underlying tensions are ready to bubble up to the surface. Ritchie (David Wayman) has just sold his company and, now that he's flush with cash, he announces to the others that he's going to pick up the tab for this holiday. Though this is a generous offer, Ritchie is unable to prevent himself from looking like he's showing off. Ajay (Louis James), Ritchie's long-time buddy, becomes increasingly bitter, unhappy that he's dependant on his wife's father for his own job, and he's also resentful of Ritchie's success. Jasmine (Sarah Alexandra Marks), meanwhile, is having an affair with Ajay behind her husband Ritchie's back: she's hoping for more commitment from her lover, but Ajay wants to keep things casual. Maya (Ella Starbuck) is the most level-headed of the foursome, though it's clear that she's aware of her hubby Ajay's dalliance with Jasmine... but has decided not to confront Ajay about it.

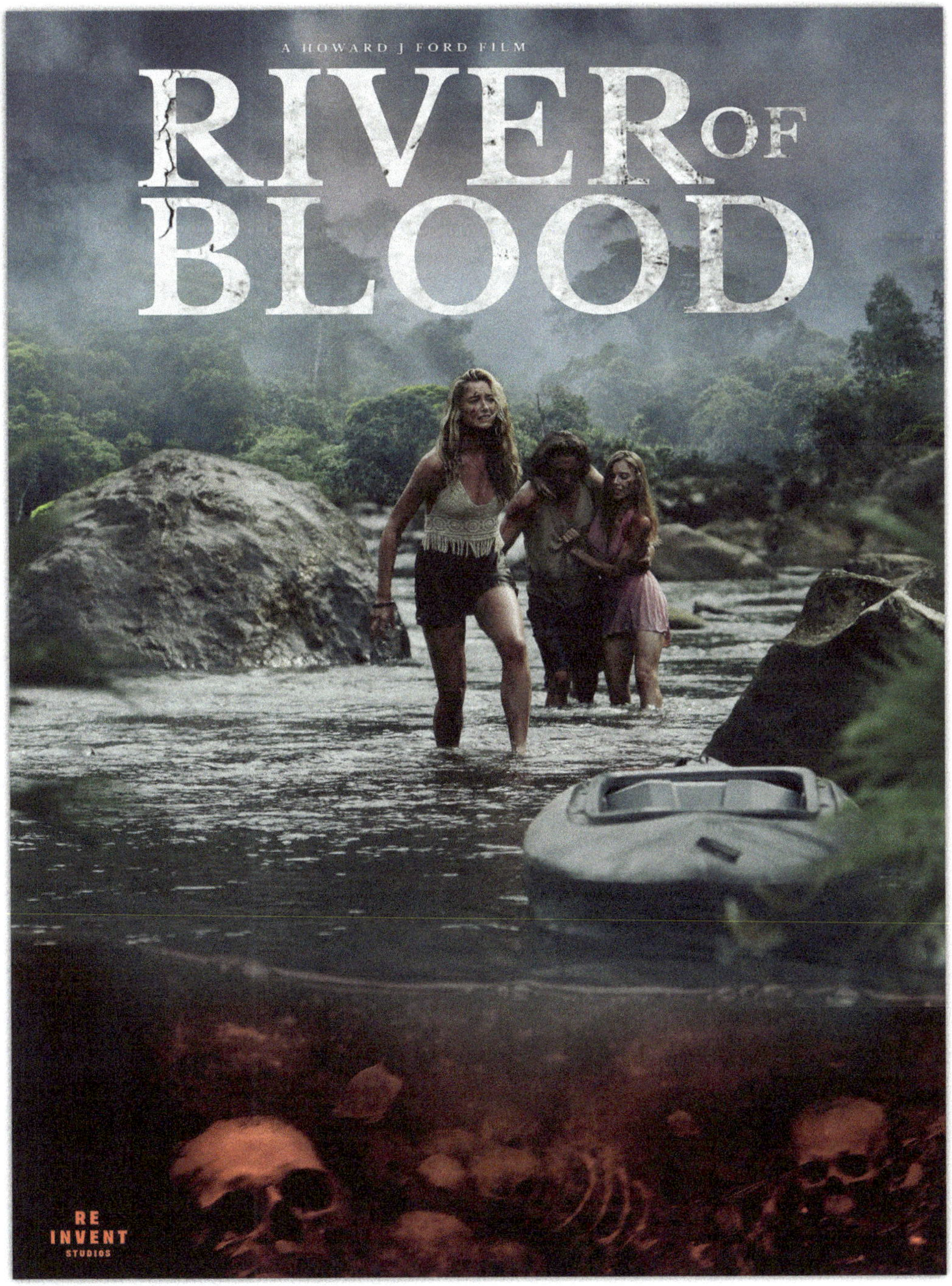

Once on their jungle river excursion, Ritchie finally gets wise to the fact that his friend is in a relationship with his wife, so he impulsively heads off in one of the kayaks, sealing everyone's fate by unknowingly rowing into ancient, protected land inhabited by the cannibals. The river guide, Nick (a solid performance from Joseph Millson), tries his best to spell out how dangerous it will be to go into this zone, explaining that the mysterious local tribe likes to wound its captives so that they're kept alive and fresh and unable to run away. Nick's warnings are brushed aside, however, as Jasmine, Ajay and Maya search for Ritchie.

River of Blood's crisp photography ensures the film always looks as attractive as its cast. Impressive locations include a cavern and various waterways. The cannibalistic natives, their faces decorated with pigments, also look interesting, with a buff lead cannibal, covered in white body paint, proving to be the most memorable of the tribe.

But it's the way director Howard J. Ford and writer Tom Boyle sketch-in enough petty little conflicts and tangled relationships between the couples that keeps you watching: you become interested in finding out what's going to happen to everyone, regardless of how gory or not the cannibal content of the film is. Don't get me wrong, there is some gore, including a heart being chomped on, a beheading, and scenes of impalement on wooden spikes (though I wasn't a fan of the use of digital blood in a couple of scenes) - but the splatter quota isn't the main focus of the film - it's the characters that matter most: you actually do want to see them survive their ordeal.

And the character who really kept me glued to the proceedings was Ajay. This guy has a big chip on his shoulder, he's fucking his best mate's wife, he drips bitterness from every pore, and at a pivotal moment he even leaves another main character to their fate...
...and yet, though Ajay is undoubtedly an A-grade asshole, Louis James manages to ensure you root for Ajay anyway! Whether it's where he's caked in mud sliding down a hillside, or endeavouring to save Maya and Jasmine, Ajay is an interesting protagonist to hang out with, and he even manages to become something of a stoic, driven, heroic figure by the film's end.
I enjoyed this flick!

LA HERENCIA VALDEMAR (2010)

LA HERENCIA VALDEMAR II: LA SOMBRA PROHIBIDA (2010)

Starring Daniele Liotti, Óscar Jaenada, Laia Marull, Silvia Abascal, Santi Prego, Francisco Maestre, Paul Naschy
Written and directed by José Luis Alemán
Produced by José Luis Alemán, Miguel Ángel González, Íñigo Marco
La Cruzada Entertainment

"Tarantulas from Innsmouth – eat them quickly!"

While he was alive August Derleth did his best to keep an eye on work that drew on Lovecraft. Since his death Lovecraft's mythos has expanded in a bewildering number of directions and been codified by admirers, reversing Lovecraft's original bid to create a suggestively incomplete body of myth that would avoid what he saw as the excessive formalisation of occultism in fiction. By now most of his inventions have left their original context far behind, and are available for any kind of use. Purists may want to tell themselves this before watching José Luis Alemán's extravagant epic.

The first part, *La herencia Valdemar*, aka *The Valdemar Legacy*, is classical in form and pace. Lusia (Silvia Abascal) is sent by the Immoberance agency to value the Valdemar mansion in Montenegro and its contents. Beset by manifestations – a face that appears at a window in a photograph, a figure visible only in a viewfinder, the monstrous guardian of the mansion - she's apparently rescued by the caretaker Santiago (Santi Prego) and his associate Dámaso (José Torrijo), only to vanish. Two of her colleagues are sent to find her, and Immoberance also employs private detective Tremel (Óscar Jaenada) in the search. He's joined by the president of the Valdemar Foundation, Nora (Ana Risueño), who proceeds to tell him the tale of the mansion. The flashback occupies an hour of the film.

It conflates Poe and Lovecraft. There it has the precedent of Corman's *Haunted Palace* (based on "Chuck Beaumont's rather good & faithful script" – August Derleth's words – The Haunted Village), but its borrowings from the authors are, shall we say, random. Lázaro Valdemar (Daniele Liotti) and his wife Leonor (Laia Marull) are fake psychics who attract the interest of Aleister Crowley (Francisco Maestre). Though the occultist is portrayed with some depth – he wants power, but not necessarily for evil, and he's a feminist without being condemned for it as Dennis Wheatley no doubt would have done – he's several decades older than Crowley would have been at the time. His motivation is intriguing - false séances inadvertently draw real manifestations – but why would he have needed to leave England at the height of Victorian spiritualism to find a practitioner? He performs the "Dunwich rite" (which has nothing at all to do with Lovecraft's Dunwich tale) at the mansion with (among others) Lizzie Borden and Bram Stoker, who is apparently in search of inspiration, and perhaps it's best to tell ourselves that we've entered an alternate universe. The entity they invoke escapes and arouses worms to reconstitute a corpse (presumably inspired by a motif in Lovecraft's "The Festival"). Leonor sacrifices herself, and at last the film remembers Lusia, apparently imprisoned in a room outside which Dámaso rolls up insect wings to smoke.

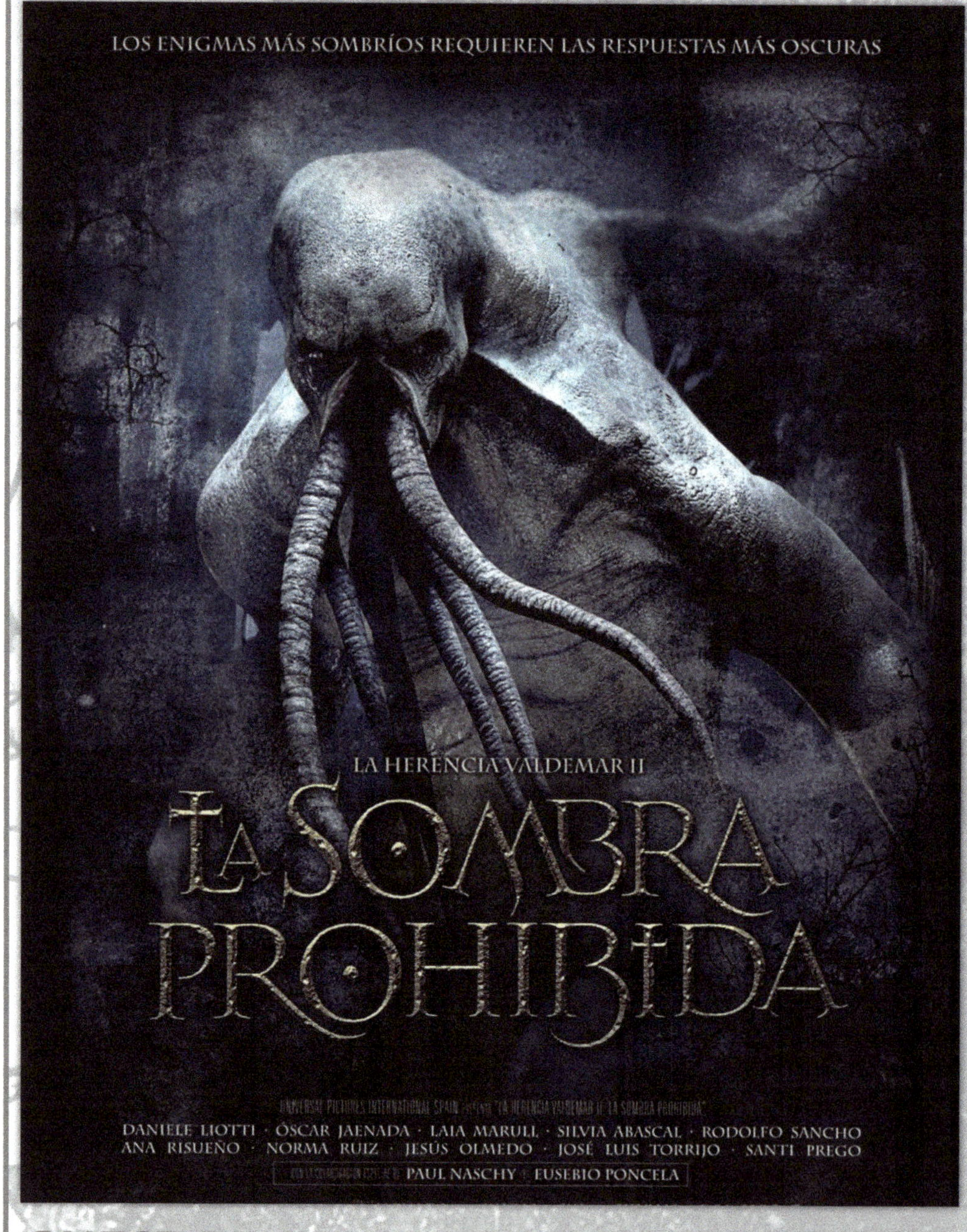

Six months pass – at least, they did before the second film, *La herencia Valdemar II: La sombra prohibida* (aka *The Valdemar Legacy II: The Forbidden Shadow*), was released in Spain. Perhaps the impatience of the audience has transmitted itself to the story, which sets off at a great pace - too fast, perhaps, to make much sense of Lusia's escape. She takes refuge in a gypsy caravan straight out of a Universal monster movie, an influence that may explain the increasingly overstuffed structure of the film. After all, Paul Naschy's roots were in the Universal monster bundles (specifically Frankenstein Meets the Wolfman), and Alemán's film is dedicated to his memory, not least because he plays the Valdemars' manservant Jervás. A quietly touching performance, it's one of his finest, and the narrative anchor of the film.

It needs one. Lovecraft (Luis Zahera) shows up on a bike, having apparently pursued Valdemar across Europe and Iran in the hope of beating him to a spectacularly pristine copy of the Necronomicon. (At least Pascal Laugier's *Incident in a Ghostland* provides a reason for him to show up in that film.) Santiago proves to be a cannibal who thinks the store mannequins in his room are people, all of which seems most Italian of him (in the filmic sense). The various searchers for Lusia turn out to have such a bewildering array of hidden motives and interlocking involvements that several genres appear to be wrestling for control of the narrative. The searchers attempt to escape beneath the mansion through caves equipped with that staple of fantasy cinema, the collapsing stone bridge, and plagued by the gymnastic zombie from the first film. Soon we learn that much of the plot has been a preparation for the "Cthulhu rite" (apparently the way to return the first film's demon to the abyss). The conspirators behind the whole setup are revealed, two of them for some reason known as Chamberlain and Sommelier. Another does indeed serve up the tarantulas I mentioned earlier, and might we think that intentional comedy has been added to the narrative cauldron? Certainly there's what can only be a gag about sacrificing a baby (I promise you I'm not being tasteless). Cthulhu has already been reduced to the status of an omen in the gypsy fortune-teller's teacup, and now – presumably objecting to the gag with the baby – he hops ponderously onstage, more like a kaiju (admittedly one conjured up by CGI) than Lovecraft's "mountain that walked". He's hardly had time to tromp on a worshipper and chuck a few more about before Valdemar puts in a request to the Necronomicon, which resembles a prop from an Arabian Nights tale (the kind of childhood reading that inspired Lovecraft to conceive it in the first place) rather than an even moderately forbidden tome. A demon that dwarfs Cthulhu yanks him back into the abyss, and the indulgent viewer may regard this as akin to Lovecraft's effect of topping his terrors with a glimpse of something even vaster. I fear it looks to me like a case of enfeebling his mythos by Christianising it, particularly since the scene is followed by the ethereal release of a flock of souls. The Necronomicon apparently has a self-destruct mechanism built in – perhaps this explains its rarity – but the film has one more genre to embrace: the conspiracy thriller. It seems a pity that it hints at this worldwide possibility but demotes Cthulhu to the status of just another monster.

The films each have a Spanish Blu-ray to themselves and their extras. The transfer of the second film is slightly brighter than that of the first. Extras include a documentary on the making of each film and a trailer for the first one ("inspired by the universe of H. P. Lovecraft", which is quite a claim under the circumstances). The second disc includes *The Man Who Saw Frankenstein Cry*, Ángel Agudo's fine account of Paul Naschy's life and career.

THUNDERBOLTS* (2025)

Starring Florence Pugh, Sebastian Stan, Julia Louis-Dreyfus, Lewis Pullman, David Harbour, Wyatt Russell, Olga Kurylenko
Written by Eric Pearson, Joanna Calo
Directed by Jake Schreier
Produced by Kevin Feige, David J. Grant, Allana Williams, Simona Paparelli Wolf
Marvel Studios

That's more like it. A good Marvel movie. Lots of heart, and a couple of scenes that really work emotionally. Florence Pugh gives a great performance and Harbour delivers the normal lines funny. Pullman looks just like his dad. This is a movie about past sins and being a fuck up and knowing that you are not a good person... but finding redemption through that sliver of good that's basically making you realise that you aren't a good person - leaning into that sliver of good and doing things that have a slim chance of success.

It's a movie about the light and darkness in all of us, and how sometimes the darkness just envelopes us. We become the darkness. People could help us, but they ignore us - we're the screw ups. The ones everyone avoids. And then one character is offered a helping hand - but it's really a con to use their darkness. They become the darkness. Figuratively and literally. And the darkness that was inside of them spreads...

The great thing about a movie where the characters hit rock bottom and struggle to find hope is that it's focused on the characters (in another battle where NYC needs a lot of construction workers afterwards to put the city back together). All of these characters are haunted by those past sins - and Pugh's character, Yelena Belova (Scarjo's "sister" and Harbour's "daughter" in *Black Widow*), was raised to be an assassin from childhood, and we see the wreckage of a life that comes from killing when you are a child. Yikes! Each of the characters are really battling the darkness within - and that's what gives this a lot of meaty drama. What makes it the best Marvel movie since *Endgame*.

If you missed the great Disney+ series *Falcon and the Winter Soldier*, the film brings you up to speed on the substitute Captain America - but I don't think you really need to remember Laurence Fishburne's daughter from *Ant-Man and the Wasp* - she's just another one of these third-string superheroes who aren't good guys. If you stay through the never-ending end credits, there's a set up for a *New Avengers* movie.

Watching this film again was just as great as the first time. So many big moments and great lines. And this time I tried to look at how the story was pushing these cranky, sad individuals together and then pulling them apart until they become a team... But I kept getting involved in the story. I love how their armour gets chipped away until they can all be honest with each other... and themselves. And the Pugh is just raw and amazing. Pullman is also great playing both sides of the same character. Harbour is great comic relief, but that scene with Pugh, where he gets serious, was great - and the idea of the goofy one making the serious speech works well because we don't expect it from him... so it seems more honest and real. It's his big character moment, too.

Small things: I like how Yelena blows up the lab in the beginning, but rescues the lab animal. They are all lab animals, after all. "What super serum did you get?"

I do wish the Valentina character had seemed more dangerous. I don't know if that's a casting thing, because Julia Louis-Dreyfus brings all of those *Seinfeld* memories with her, or her performance. Sometimes it's hard to figure out if it's me, or the material, or the performance. Maybe it needed a stronger demonstration of her evil up front? It's hard when you have an antagonist who sends people to do their dirty work. She is the true villain of the story. But maybe that's the point - it's that banality of evil - the bureaucrat who gives an evil order while complaining to her assistant about the coffee?

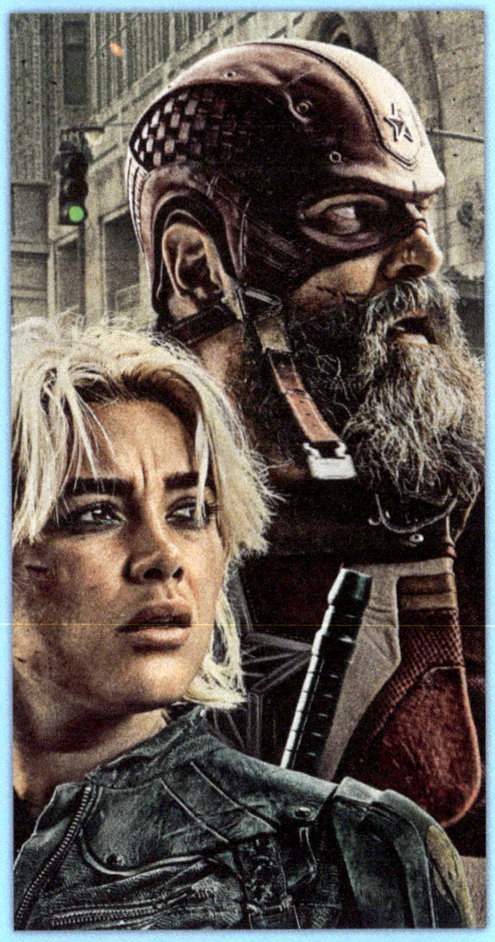

GUEST REVIEW BY WILLIAM MARTELL

THE LAST SACRIFICE (2024)

Starring Ronald Hutton, Tim Stanley, Jonathan Rigby, Geraldine Beskin
Written and directed by Rupert Russell
Produced by Sam Cryer, William Day Frank, Alexander McNeill
Intermission Film

Was the 1945 murder of Charles Walton, who was found on Meon Hill, near the Cotswolds village of Lower Quinton, with a pitchfork impaled through his face and a trouncing hook (also known as a billhook) embedded in his neck, the last ritual killing to take place in Britain?

This deliriously enjoyable documentary uses this unsolved murder, often rumoured to be linked to witchcraft, as the springboard from which it dives into a swirling conglomeration of subjects: true crime reporting, folk horror, social history, occult-flavoured news reports, the history of old pagan beliefs, horror movies, the resurgence of interest in witchcraft in Britain, and much more, all of which bleeds into one another to create a multifaceted, imaginative, sometimes salacious, engrossing, strange and quirky witch's brew of elements that keep you engrossed throughout.

Together with to-camera pieces courtesy of luminaries like historian Ronald Hutton, director Rupert Russell utilises loads of clips from horror films, TV documentary footage, and old stills, to tell his story, which posits the argument that the Charles Walton killing helped inspire a growing interest in witchcraft in the UK and the development of the folk horror genre, leading to the production of films like *The Wicker Man*.

The documentary looks at the way famed British police officer Robert Fabian tried but failed to solve the Walton case, it reveals how rumours were circulated claiming Walton was killed because he was breeding toads to kill nearby crops using witchcraft, and it discloses how the 1875 killing of a woman called Ann Tennant - accused of being a witch - mirrored the Walton murder: Tennant was transfixed by a pitchfork too, and this murder took place in a village very close to Lower Quinton!

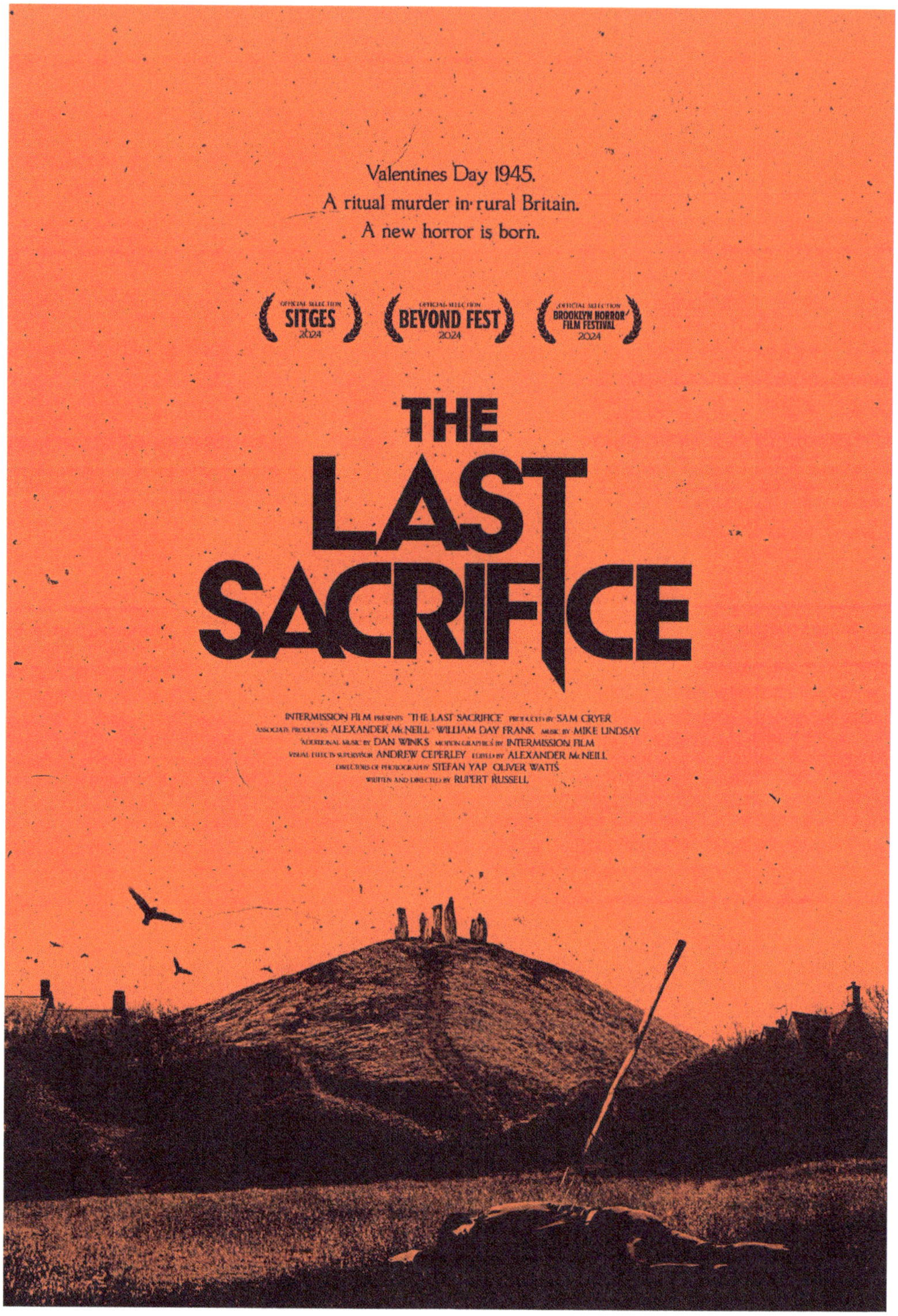

Russell lets his documentary stray from the central murder case thread, allowing it to shine a light on Britain's growing fascination with witchcraft and all-things occult-oriented back in the 60s and early 70s. The film looks at the various characters who embraced witchcraft and influenced others back in the day, and it highlights how horror movies influenced news reports of such things as the 'Highgate Vampire', and how this journalism itself influenced subsequent films, like *Dracula A.D. 1972*.

The plentiful film clips come from movies that include *Legend of the Witches* (1970), *Witchfinder General* (1968), *Twins of Evil* (1971), *The Wicker Man* (1973), *Secret Rites* (1971), *Virgin Witch* (1971), *Satan's Slave* (1976), *The Nude Vampire* (1970), *The Witches* (1966), *Eye of the Devil* (1966), *The Blood Beast Terror* (1968), *Plague of the Zombies* (1966), *The Blood on Satan's Claw* (1971), and television productions like the *Play for Today* episode *Robin Redbreast* (1970).

The Last Sacrifice zigzags around narratively, jumping down various arcane rabbit holes to explore such things as UK traditions and festivals (including the use of the hobbyhorse and horned dancers), a real-life exorcism - and even the BBC kids show *Teletubbies*(!) becomes enmeshed within the overarching tale. Add to this the way Russell makes use of copious amounts of horror movie clips to help illustrate the various voiceovers, and you might think that such a technique ran the risk of having a detrimental effect on the production. Far from it: this scattershot approach to the subject matter, with Russell following intriguing, winding paths to stories only tangentially connected to the Walton case, actually helps to infuse *The Last Sacrifice* with an idiosyncratic, sometimes manic, always engrossing vibe, which perfectly encapsulates how the UK's attitude to the occult can somehow be simultaneously eccentric, comical, and horrific.

Wonderful in so many ways!

MONSTER SHARK (1984)

Starring Michael Sopkiw, Valentine Monnier, Gianni Garko, William Berger, Iris Peynado, Lawrence Morgant, Cinzia de Ponti, Paul Branco
Written by Gianfranco Clerici, Vincenzo Mannino, Dardano Sacchetti, Hervé Piccini
Directed by Lamberto Bava
Produced by Mino Loy, Max Pécas
National Cinematografica/Nuova Dania Cinematografica/Filmes International/Les Films du Griffon

With victims getting chewed up by a large sea creature in the ocean just off the coast of Florida, a team of marine experts attempt to work out what exactly this huge fish-beast is, whilst also devising a way to capture the thing before the local cops find it first and kill it. But violent thugs working for a shadowy Mister Big are intent on scuppering all these plans...

This Italian-French coproduction, also known as *Devil Fish* and *Devouring Waves*, looks great, with an easy-on-the-eye cast, though it's a shame its plot (which supposedly needed 8 people to write it) tends to focus more on the murders and acts of sabotage perpetrated by the villain's main square-jawed henchman (played by Paul Branco), rather than give us more monster attack scenes, which is what we really want, right?

But, hey, I'm a sucker for Italian killer critter flicks like this and *Tentacles* (1977) and *The Great Alligator* (1979), so I have to give *Monster Shark* a thumbs up!

The enjoyably schlocky story sees the protags using recordings of the monster to trick it into thinking it's hearing the mating call of another of its kind. Meanwhile, the cops and the coastguard fill marine buoys with explosives, hoping to blow the beast to smithereens, but when it's revealed that the creature possesses unique cells capable of reproducing themselves individually, the race is on to get rid of the bomb-buoys before the beast explodes into a million fragments, all capable of becoming new killer beasties. It could be the end of the world!

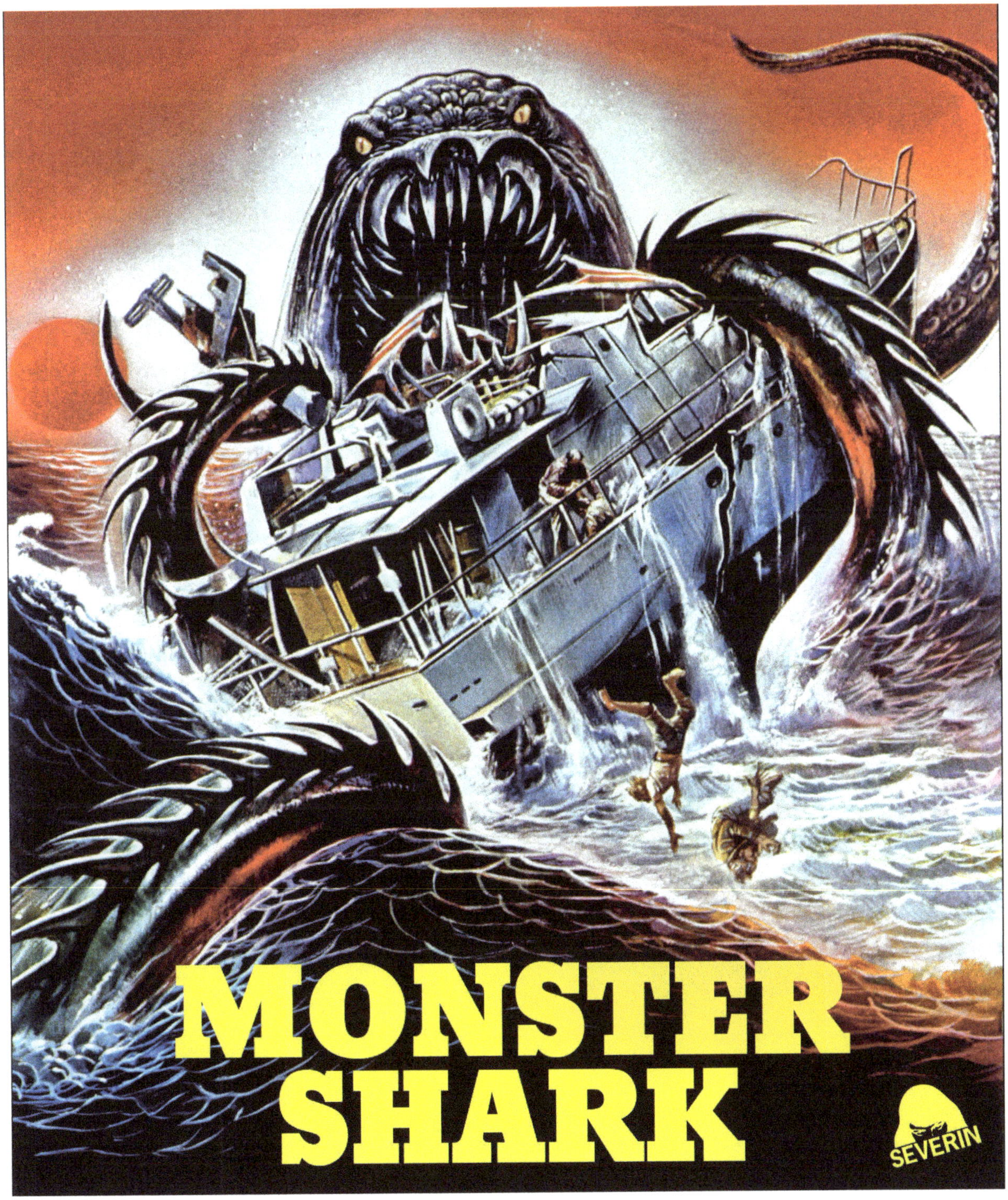

The monster shark itself is a funky, bizarre creation: it has the head of an extinct prehistoric fish from the Devonian period, known as Dunkleosteus, which is attached to the body of a octopus! Eat your heart out *Sharktopus*, this toothsome terror made it to the screen twenty six years before you did! The creature is pretty much just an enormous head with tentacles affixed behind it - and you do get some decent full-body shots of the tentacle-monster as it undulates through the water. We really did need this freaky fish on screen more often! Oh well. And just how the scientist-baddie (whose identity is cleverly obscured in the film) managed to breed such a monstrous mash-up is hard to fathom, as are his motivations for wanting to create such a mongrel-monster in the first place!

The movie's highlights include a sopping wet palaeontologist babe battling a tentacle with an axe, and the nighttime-set finale, where the big-headed brute sinks its teeth into a victim and bites off his head, just before we reach a suitably fiery ending involving fuel-filled water and flamethrowers. Hot stuff!

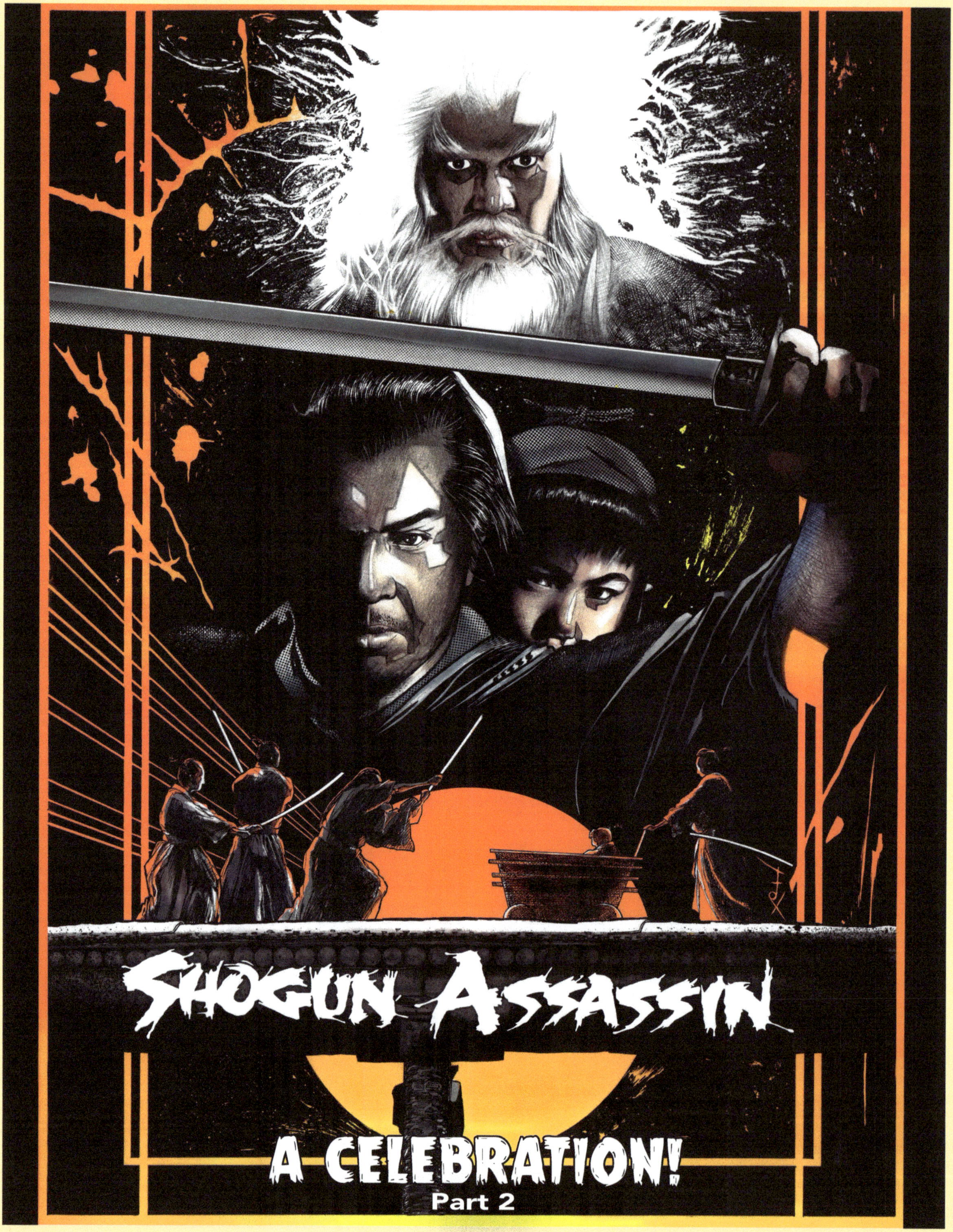
SHOGUN ASSASSIN
A CELEBRATION!
Part 2

"When I was little, my father was famous. He was the greatest samurai in the empire, and he was the Shogun's decapitator."

Voice of Daigorō

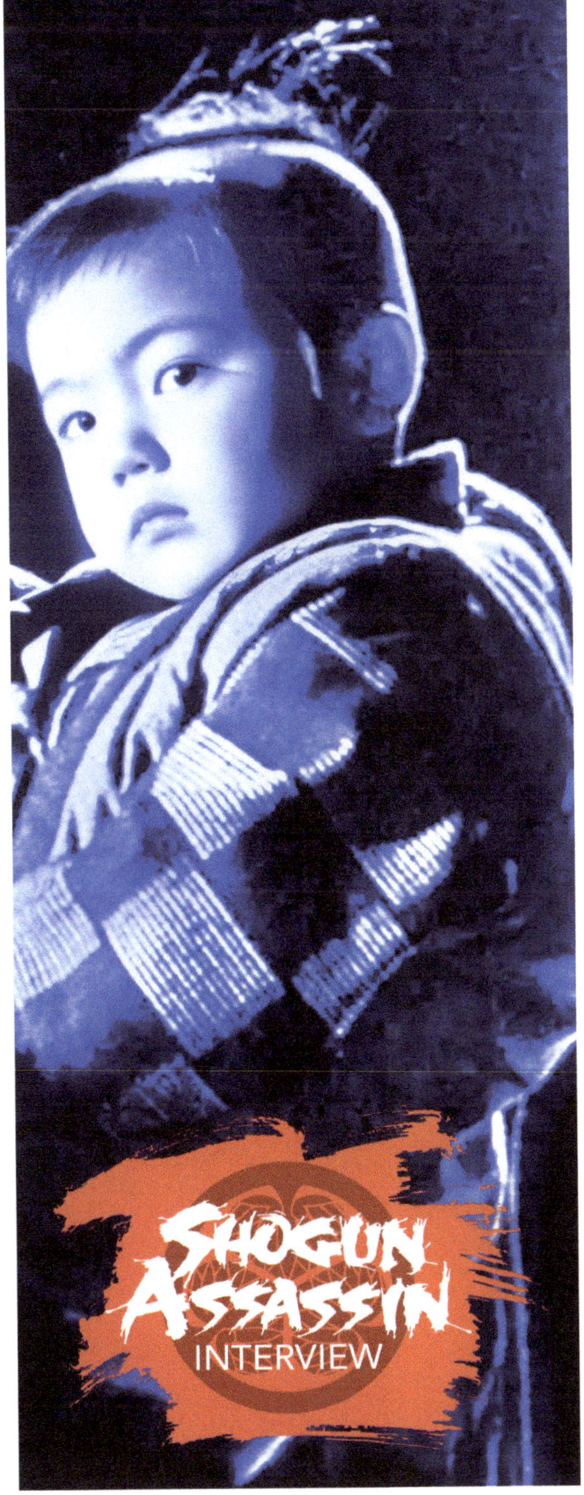

VOICE OF THE WOLF CUB

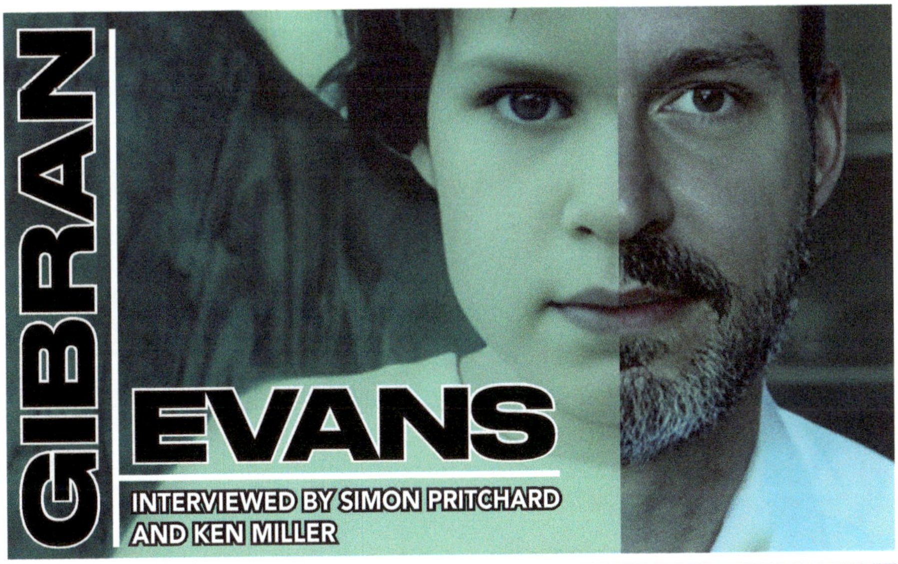

In *Shogun Assassin* the hero's young son, Daigorō, is the storyteller, his voiceover used to connect all the re-edited footage together, helping immeasurably with the overall flow of the tale. This decision to use Lone Wolf's Cub as the central narrator was a masterstroke, utilising the innocent-but-world-weary childish vocals of the boy to infuse the film with a truly distinctive tone. Daigorō was played by Akihiro Tomikawa, but it was an American youngster, **Gibran Evans**, who provided the Cub with his characteristic voice in *Shogun Assassin*...

How old were you when you did the voice work for Daigorō in *Shogun Assassin*?

I was 7 years old when the recording took place in 1980, living in Malibu at the time with my father, brother and two dogs.

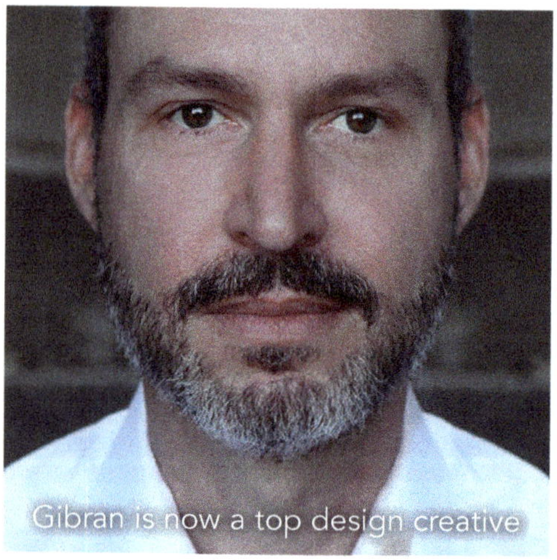

Gibran is now a top design creative

What was the background to you becoming involved in the project?

My father was creating the poster art along with the title logo for the film and was a close colleague and friends with the producer David Weisman and director Bobby Houston.

Did it take long to record the voice tracks?

The entire process took one afternoon at a sound studio next door to the old Hollywood Storage Company Building at 1025 Highland Avenue.

I have fond memories of the giant Bekins Storage sign painted on the building's side, during those years of being shuttled around Hollywood while my father worked.

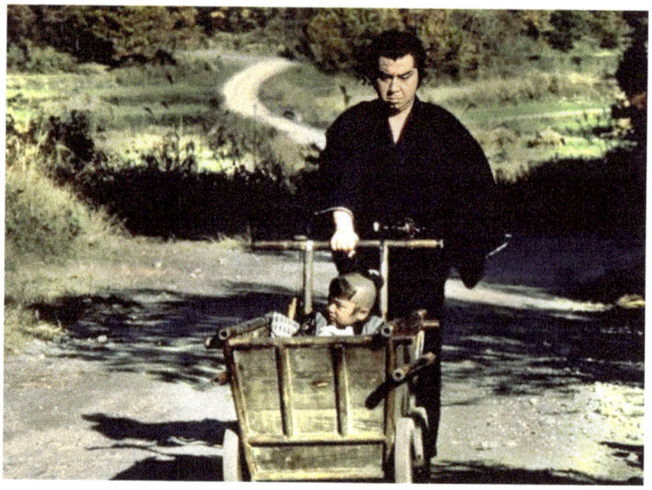

Did you have any influence or were there any changes to the script once you started to record it?

I had no direct influence, I was 7 and barely understood what the context was of anything I was recording.

However, I do recall some alternate takes due to getting tongue twisted by some lines that were too long or too

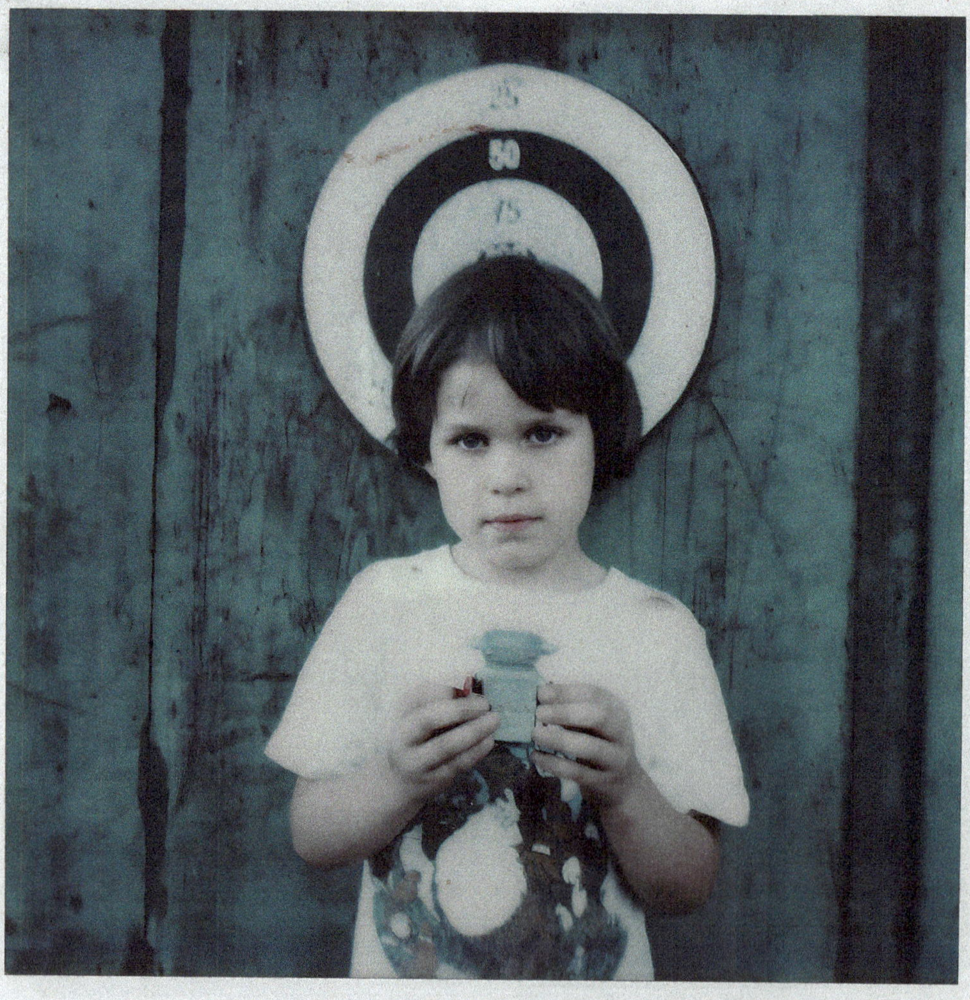

A Polaroid shot of Gibran from when he was a youngster...

"Then, one night, the Shogun sent his ninja spies to our house. They were supposed to kill my father, but they didn't. That was the night everything changed, forever. That was when my father left his samurai life and became a demon..."

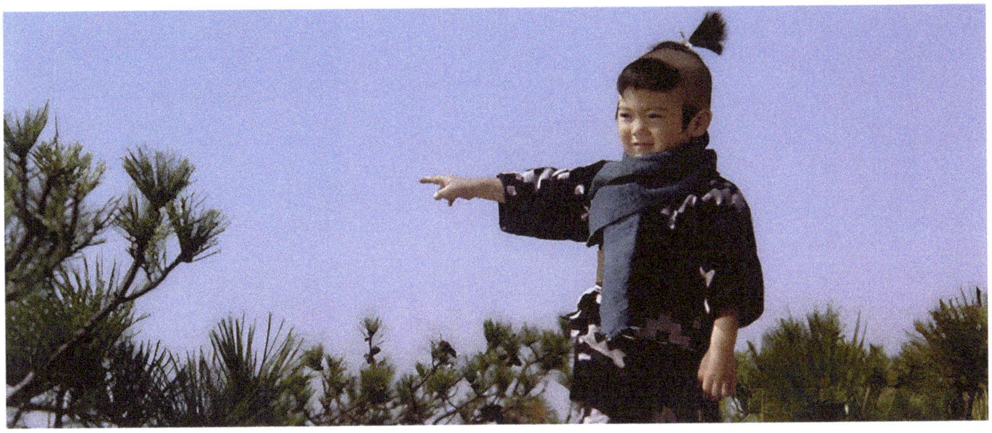

complex, which forced them to adjust on my behalf.

Were you shown footage from this movie when you were dubbing it? It's very violent and bloody!

I was not shown the footage prior or during the recording but did see it shortly after release when I was 8. The violence was almost fantasy-like and the film so culturally obscure that it didn't really frighten me.

The only violence that really stuck with me was the guy hiding under the sand getting clawed on the top of the head - it looked painful and lasted a while, whilst many other incidents were quick and precise. The guy getting all of his limbs sliced off for sport/demonstration by the Supreme Ninja seemed a bit mean-spirited and I also found that a little distressing.

Shogun Assassin was a US movie created by editing together footage from the Japanese films *Lone Wolf and Cub: Sword of Vengeance* (1972) and *Lone Wolf and Cub: Baby Cart at the River Styx* (1972), with a new soundtrack and dubbed English voices added. But *Shogun Assassin*

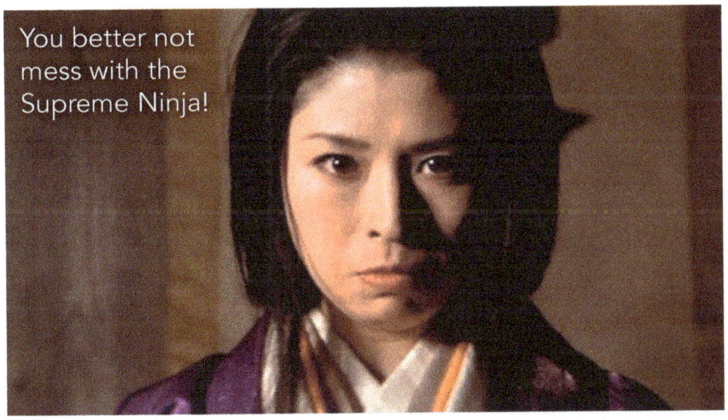

You better not mess with the Supreme Ninja!

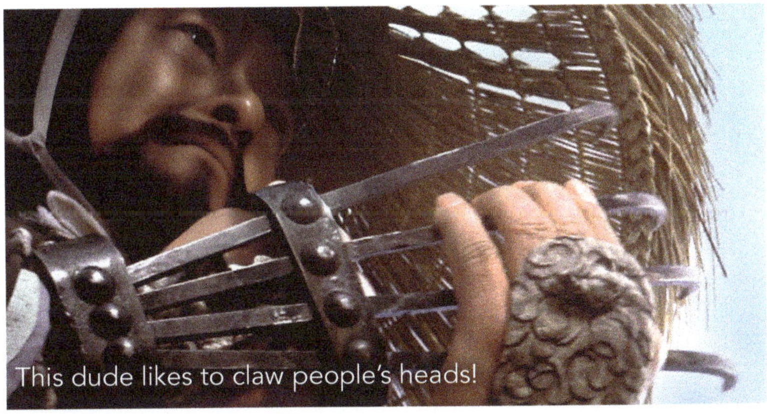

This dude likes to claw people's heads!

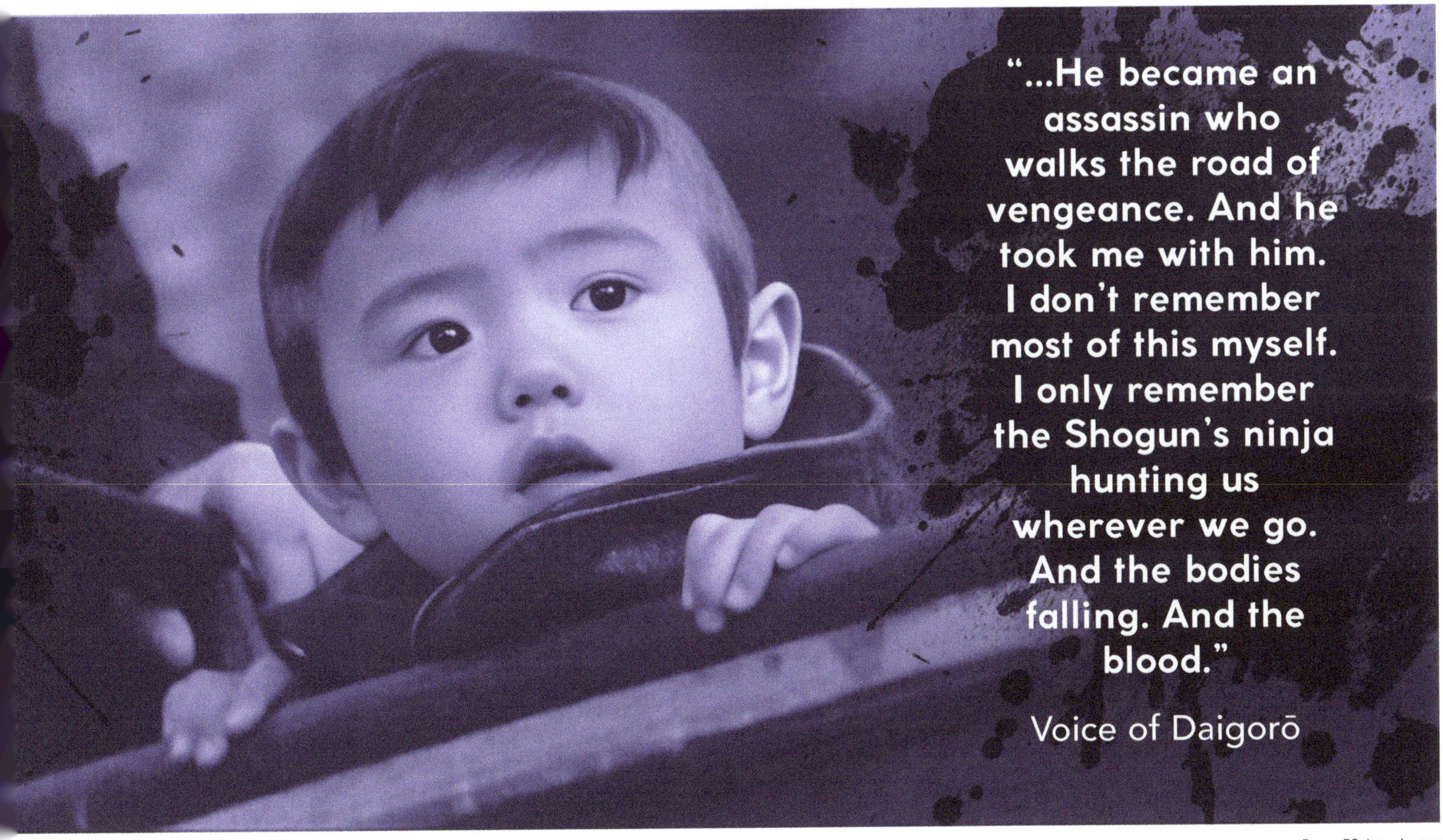

transcended its origins to become a well-liked movie in its own right. What do you think has helped it to become such a long-lasting cult favourite?

As far as I know there wasn't a lot of this kind of cinema available in the US unless you knew where to look. In retrospect, even as early as 10 years later, the music, my voice, the premise of the father & child, the quite elegant directing, the editing and voiceover/writing turned it into a unique, well crafted film by any standards, and it had no choice but to become a timeless classic.

You provided an audio commentary for *Shogun Assassin* on the Eureka Entertainment Blu-ray release. What was this like to revisit the film in such depth and what memories did this bring back?

In 2010 I had gotten the request via my father by way of David Weisman. I was terrified and very nervous at the prospect of being recorded for something I hadn't thought about since *Liquid Swords* was released in 1995, 15 years earlier, and 15 years prior to that when I recorded it. I didn't really feel like I had much to contribute - David was the main point on that interview, and I felt a bit more of a decorative appearance. However, a woman named Carmen who worked at the studio doing the recording, seemed to be oddly excited about my presence, and it turned out she was a huge fan. I was shocked to meet anyone this excited about me or my childhood voice, and it was only shortly after I learned that GZA was still performing *Liquid Swords* and thousands of people were reciting my voice at concerts.

“When we're on a mission, I keep count of how many ninja my father kills. He says not to keep count, only to pray for their souls. But if I don't keep count, I don't know how many souls to pray for. So I keep count. So far it's three hundred and forty-two.”

Voice of Daigorō

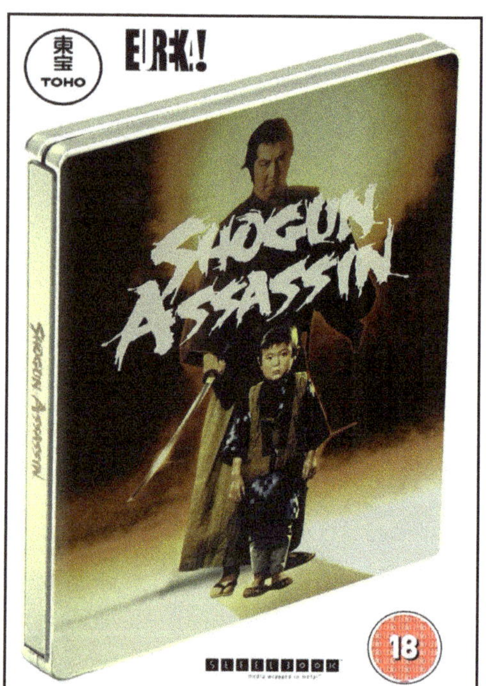

What are your favourite scenes from the film?

The whole sequence of the Supreme Ninja and her minions with their three-tiered attack on the road: I thought it was cool how they hid knives in their radishes, and Daigorō got to use his spring-loaded front blade, and got his ponytail sliced off by a flying hat.

What do you remember about the time *Shogun Assassin* was originally released?

Not much really, I think I saw it on VHS at home for the first time under the context of... 'here is that thing you did'.

Your voiceover narration is a central, memorable component of the film's appeal. How did you create the tone in your voice that exudes that famous 'sombre/innocent finality'?

I was a quiet kid, spending a lot of time in nature, I was generally polite and soft spoken. I think the music really helps the tone, but this is pretty

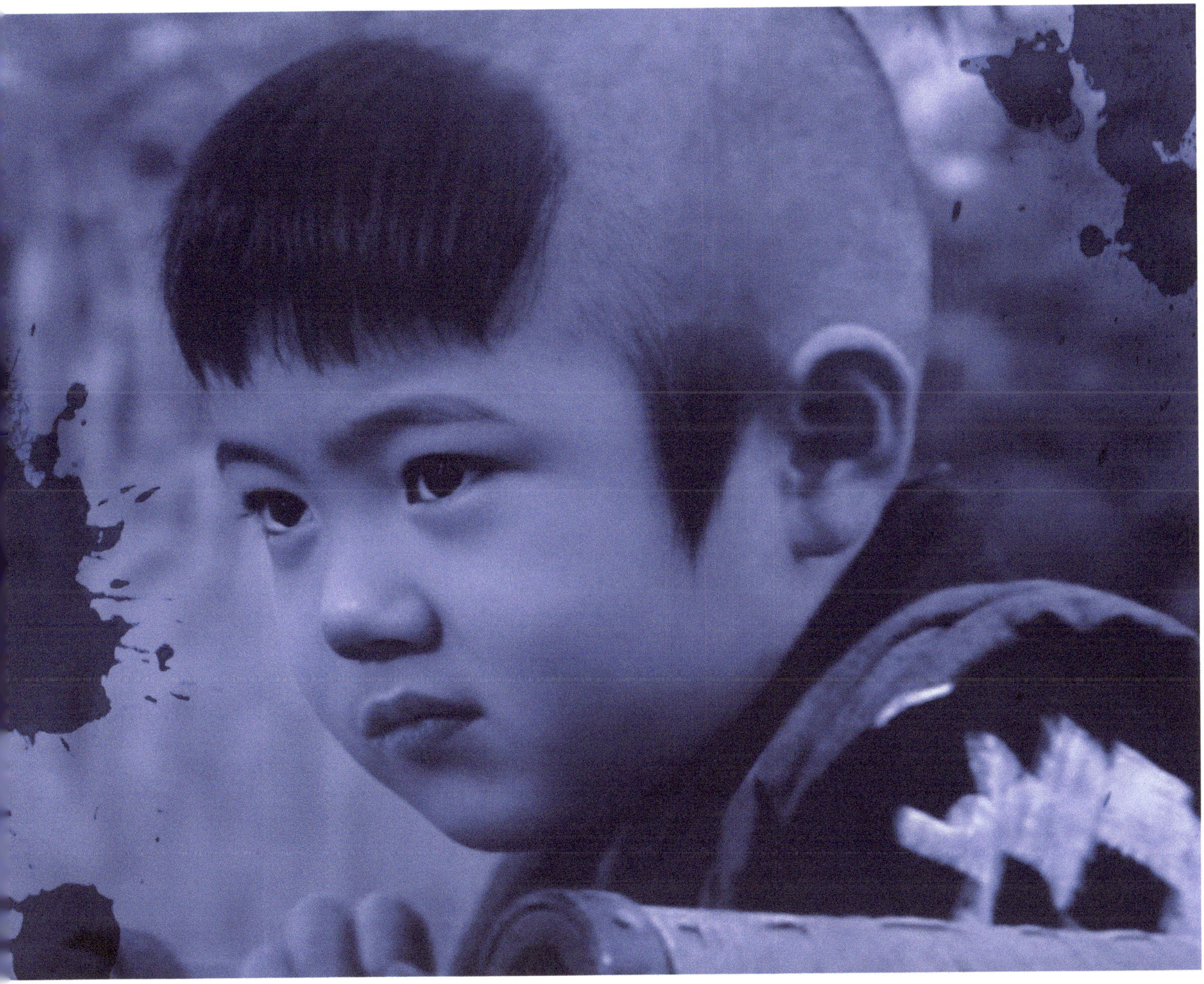

much how I sounded without much effort at the time.
The lines were spoken to me first, which I believe led to a slow, thoughtful recitation/presentation on my part, which comes out. The only major direction I recall was whenever the word 'Shogun' came up, that I should try to say it with a deeper voice and hold the 'O' for emphasis, neither of which I feel I really achieved, but I was making a mindful effort at the time.

Shogun Assassin became a cult film and was included on the British Board of Classification's original "banned" list of films. Copies were seized and the film was prosecuted for obscenity, but the prosecution failed. It was not until the late 90s that the film was released uncut in the UK. Were you aware of the film's popularity and infamy worldwide after its release? What do you think about this?

I knew it was a cult classic but wasn't aware it was banned or seized till I got my hands on a DVD in the early 2000s that said 'Banned Since 1983' on the cover.
I think I was always about a decade behind knowing how popular this film and my voice had become. It's a bit shocking any movie gets banned, and in the case of *Shogun Assassin* seems like an overreaction.

You did the voice work for *Shogun Assassin*, but never did anything similar in movies afterwards. Were

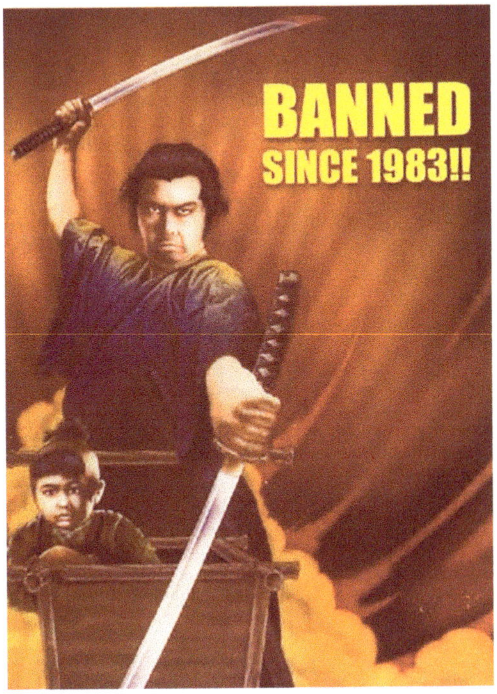

you ever interested in getting more involved in the movie industry as a performer?

I was thrown into another film in 1984 called *Bad Manners* as an extra along with my brother, also directed by Bobby Houston. I was not inclined to perform; this was more spearheaded by my father who as I recall was a bit too busy to be running me and my brother around for this kind of work in the centre of his career as a commercial illustrator.

Shogun Assassin has been sampled many times, including by GZA from The Wu-Tang Clan. It must be cool to hear your voice used in albums like *Liquid Swords*?!

Yeah, it's pretty cool and has definitely got me a bit of cred over the years, a few friends on social media and my first official autograph request, which led me to *Eastern Heroes*. At the time *Liquid Swords* was released, it was very weird for my voice to seemingly come out of nowhere and most people looked at me in disbelief when I told them it was me.

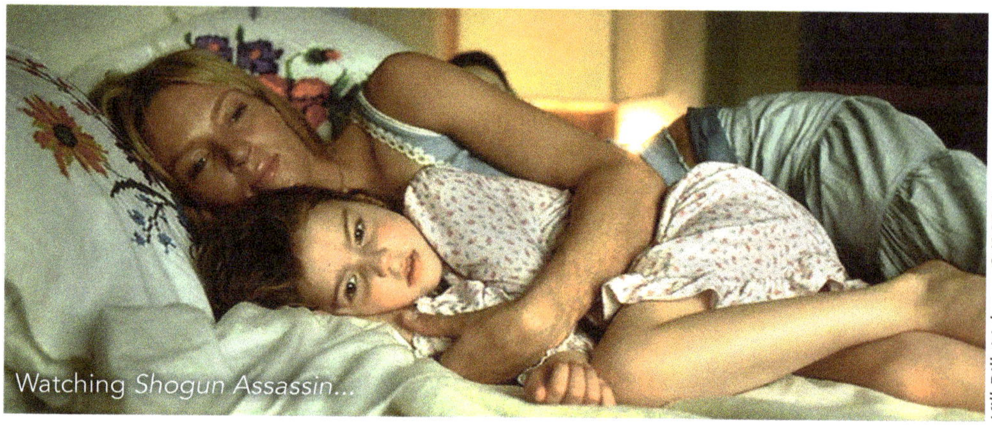
Watching *Shogun Assassin*...

Kill Bill: Volume 2 (2004)

I remember being in the theatre with my son when they played the bit in *Kill Bill 2* and I got all teary-eyed with a warm feeling in my stomach.

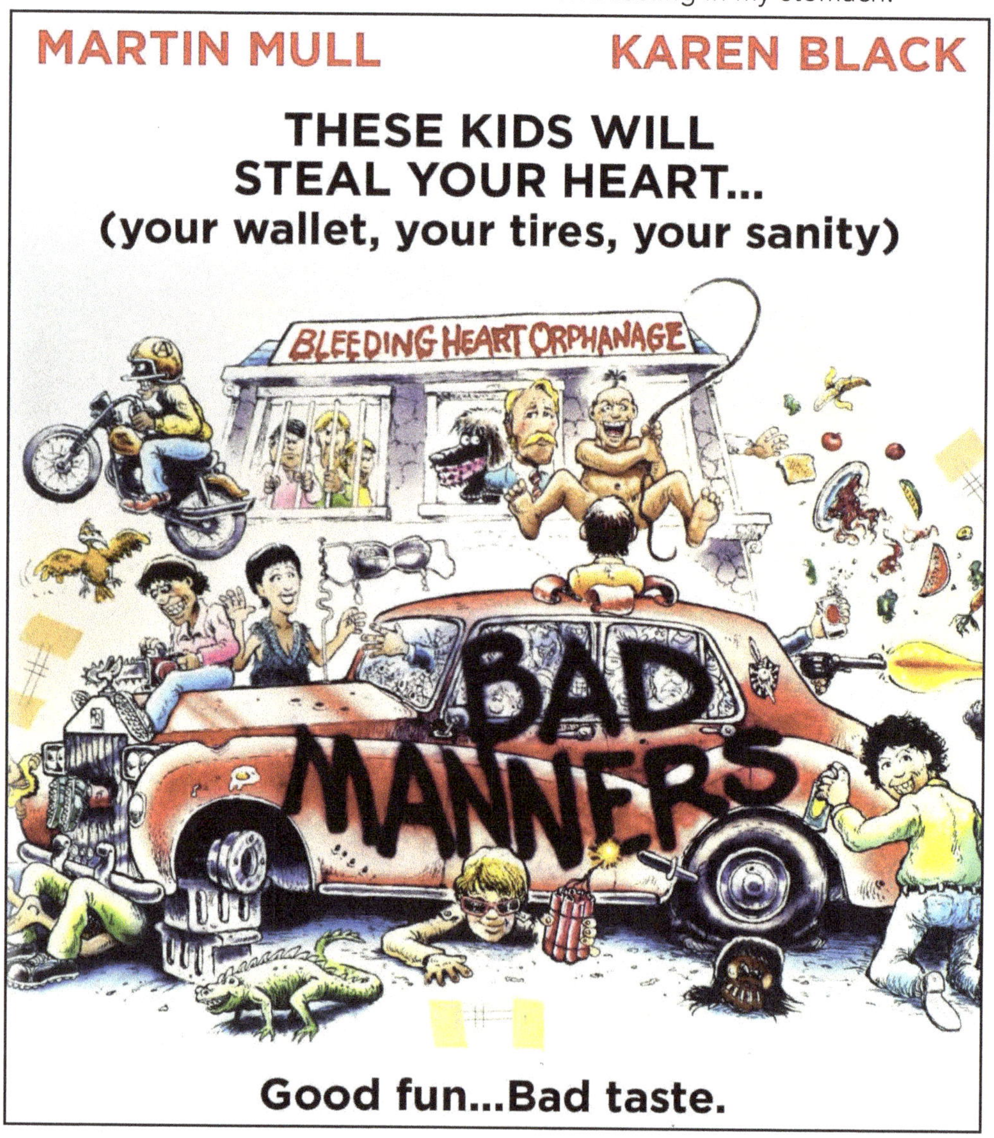

You've been part of your father's TAZ collective and you are a senior creative at the Division 13 Design Group, a creative team that designs & produces posters, websites/social media, games, live events, mailers, digital stickers, video promos, and other branded activations for the entertainment industry. What posters and other movie-related branded activations that you've worked on are you most pleased with?

The large series of TAZ posters from the 90s were a blast and the ever so popular *Ill Communication* album packaging was pretty fun. I'd say I've

"I guess I wish it was different."

"But a wish is only a wish."

Voice of Daigorō

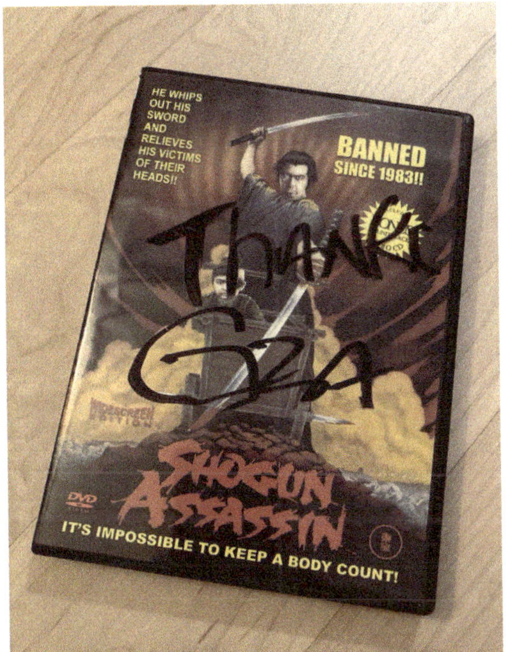

Gibran's DVD - signed by GZA!

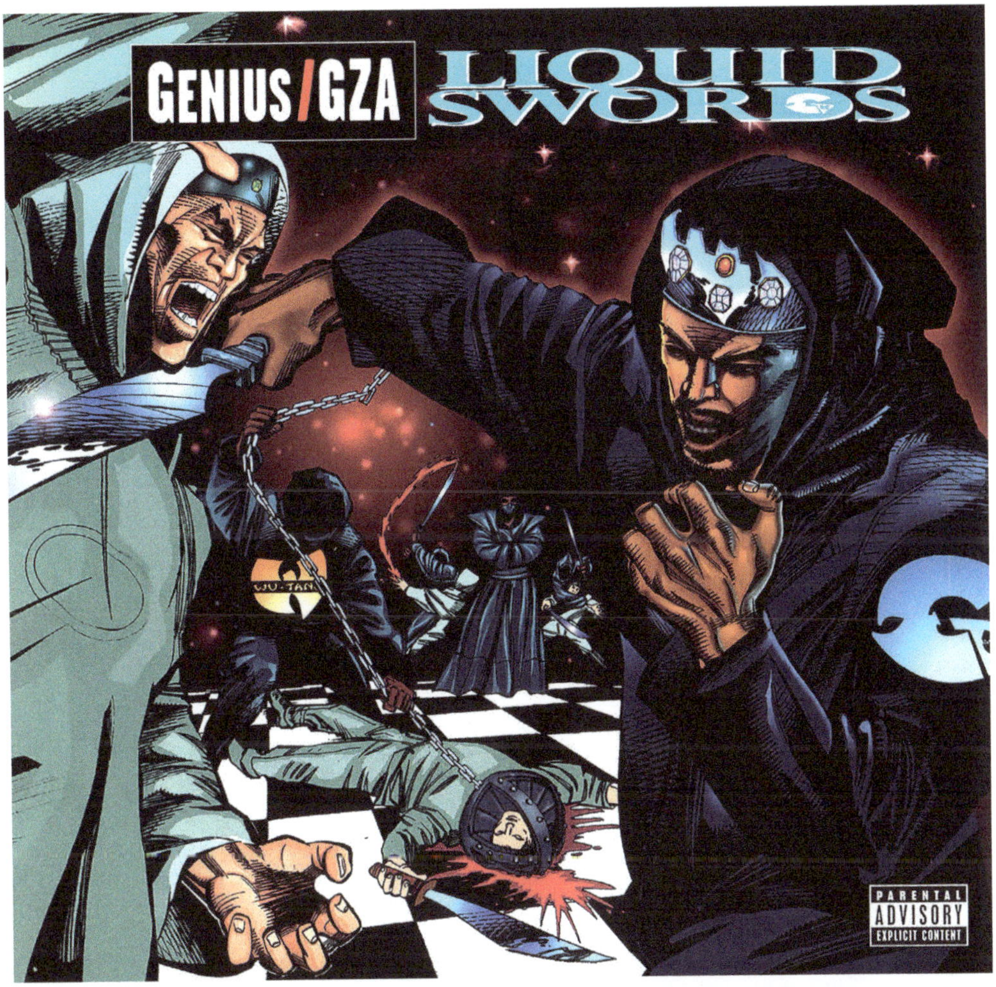

worked on about 400+ major film productions over the last 25-30 years.

Favourite websites I worked on from way back were for *The Big Lebowski*, *The Ring*, and a pile of DreamWorks animation sites such as *Sinbad*, *Madagascar*, *Shark Tale*, *Kung Fu*

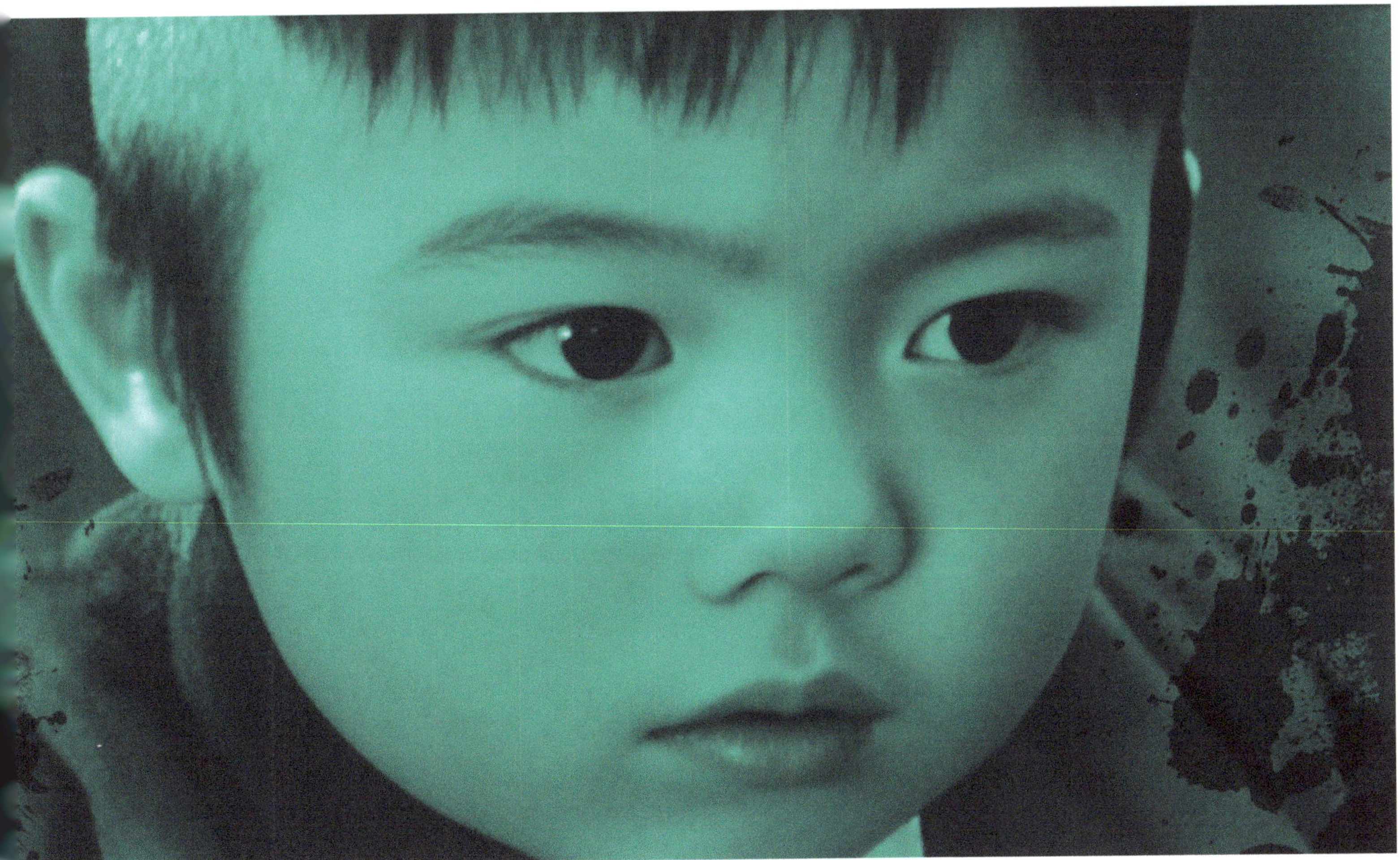

Panda, *Monsters vs. Aliens*, *Shrek 3* & *Shrek 4*, etc... These days things have moved more into ad banners, social media content and mobile games.

Things I'm most proud of usually come with a love of the property, or creative direction, that promotes a deep inspiration, and brings great satisfaction to their executions.

Recent hits were *Gran Turismo*, *Dumb Money*, *Napoleon*, *Thanksgiving*, *65*, and some series work for *Outlander*, *Better Call Saul*, *Cobra Kai*, along with catalogue work doing a huge set of 4K Ultra HD Steel book animated pack shots.

What are your plans for the future and is there any chance fans will ever see you at a Comic Con?

The future regarding little Daigorō... I've been dancing around the idea of directing and animating an interpretive short to run over 'The Legend Of Lone Wolf' (track 1 from the *Shogun Assassin* film score), which I recently obtained permission to monetise. I love animation, however, to solo something of that scope in my spare time will likely take the better part of a year. Regarding Comic Con, not likely, public appearances aren't really for me.

Thank you for all your time, Gibran. Is there anything else you would like to add, maybe another memory related to your recording session for *Shogun Assassin*?

During the initial casting call to sample children's voices, they had me sit on a table to reach the mic, and I recall the sound tech getting annoyed at how fidgety I was, swinging my legs back and forth making unnecessary noise. It was my understanding they voice-tested at least a couple hundred options. During the actual recording they put me in a lounge chair and put a pillow under my legs and one under each

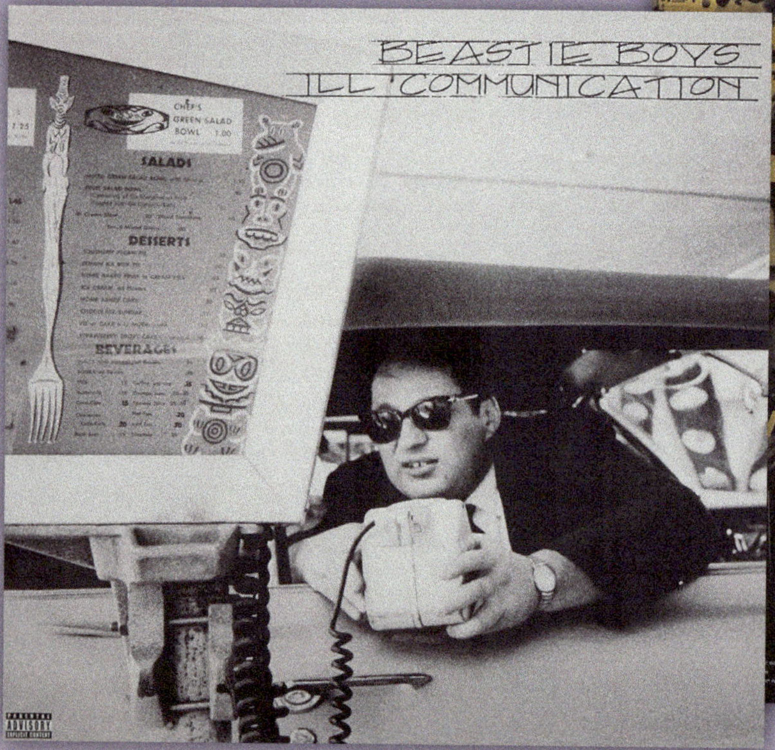

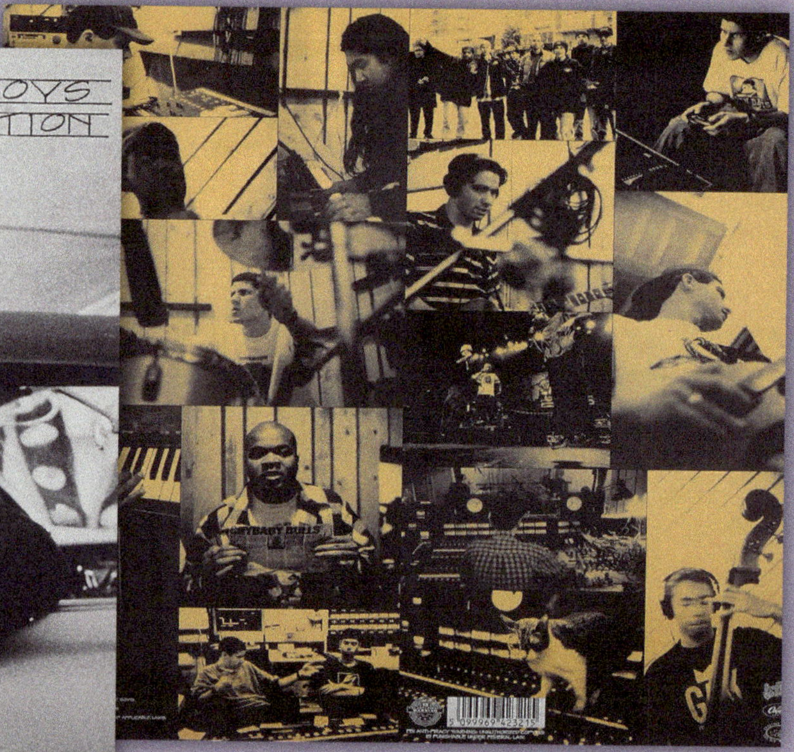

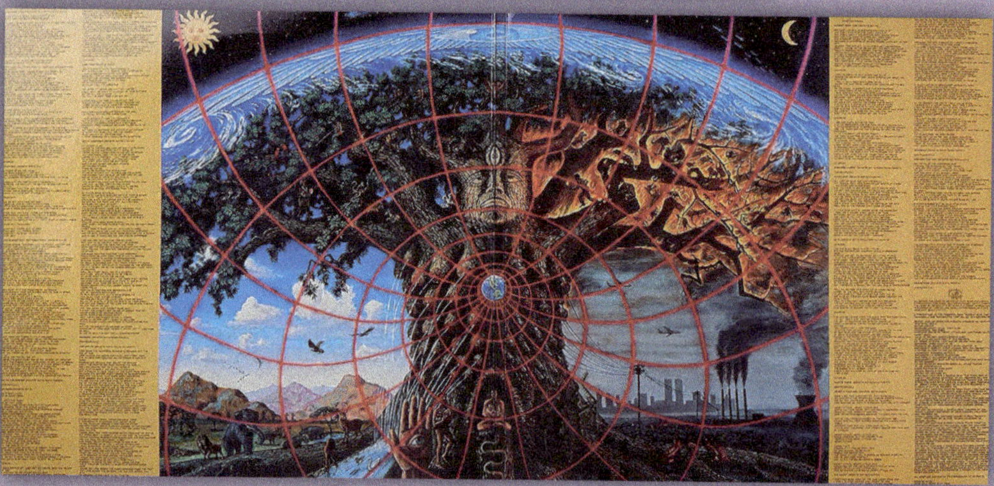

ILL COMMUNICATION
BEASTIE BOYS

Gibran collaborated with Adam Yauch to create all the album's packaging. The b&w photograph chosen for the front cover was taken by Magnum photographer Bruce Davidson in 1964 at a Los Angeles drive-in diner. The painting 'Gaia' by Alex Grey was featured in the album's spread. Gibran got his father Jim to draw each letter of the special typeface used for this album, then he scanned them, cleaned it all up in Illustrator, and assembled everything in the font editor Fontographer.

arm to keep me from making noise. The negotiated price for my recording was 200 dollars and as many Famous Amos cookies and all the Coca-Cola I wanted.

One more thing: I went to a concert nearby in January 2023 for a performance of *Liquid Swords* along with a meet & greet ticket for GZA, where I obtained a lovely photo and a signed DVD... The expression on his face when I told him who I was reminded me of all those people with looks of disbelief. His manager, on the other hand, seemed very excited.

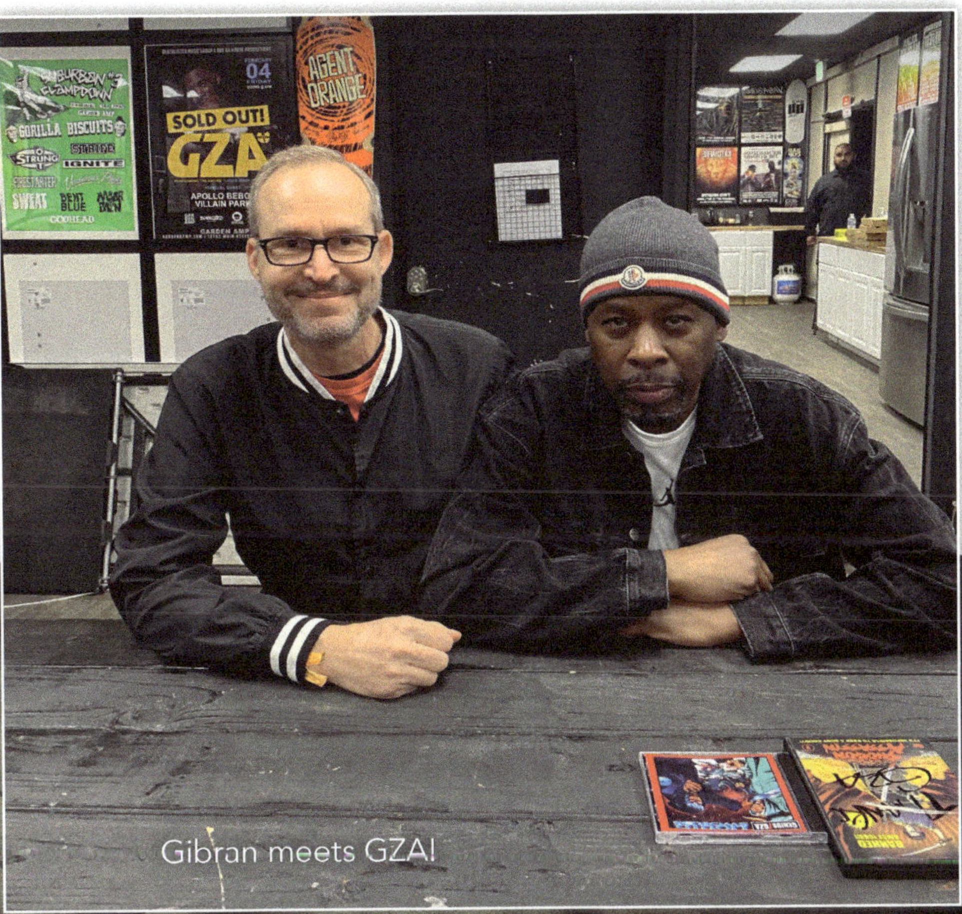

Gibran meets GZA!

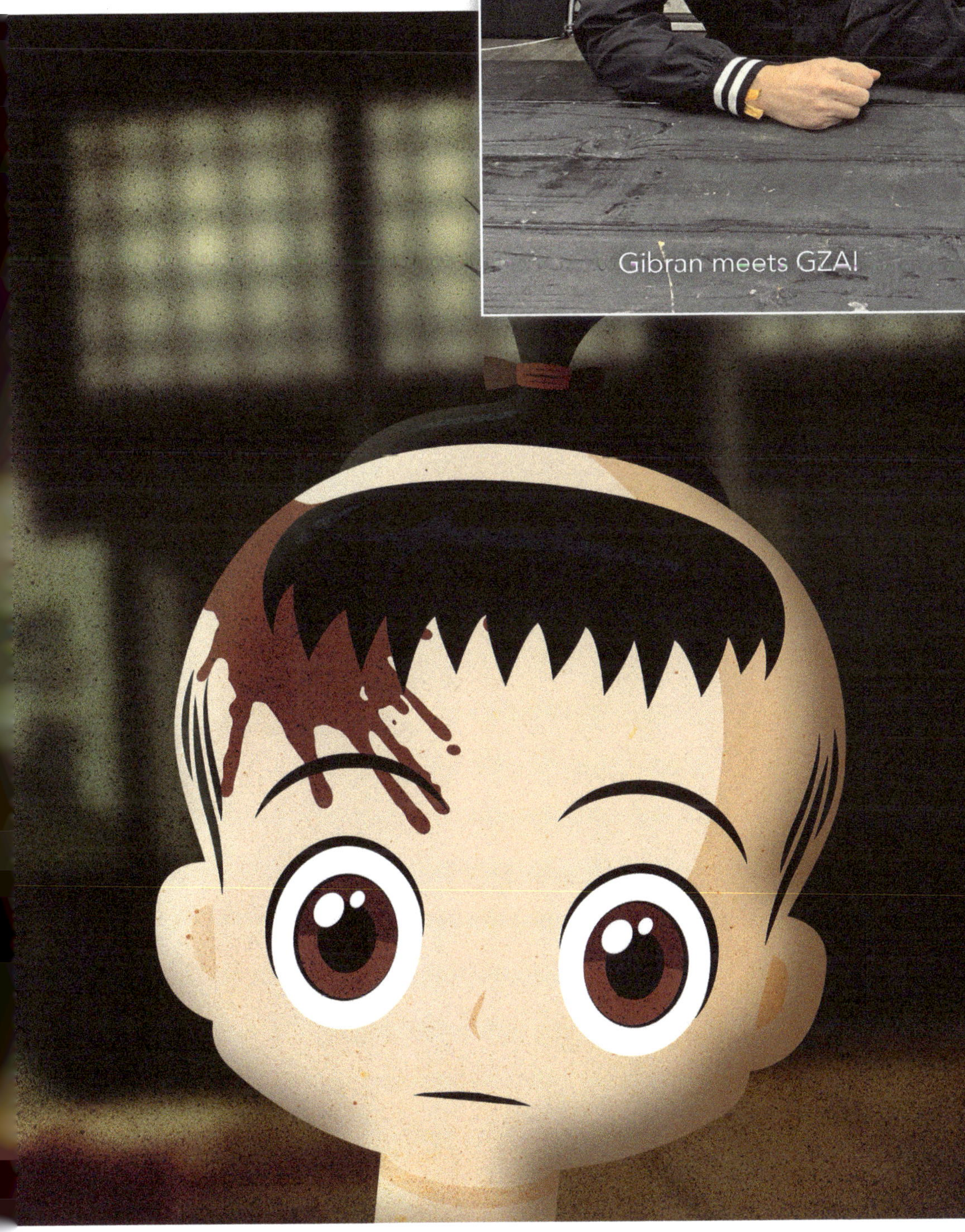

AN ANIMATED DAIGORŌ

This is Gibran's initial character design concept for Daigorō, showing how he would look in the animated short he is planning to make!

Gibran intends to do the concepts and storyboards by hand, the design in Illustrator & Photoshop, and all the animation in After Effects.

MASTER OF POSTERS

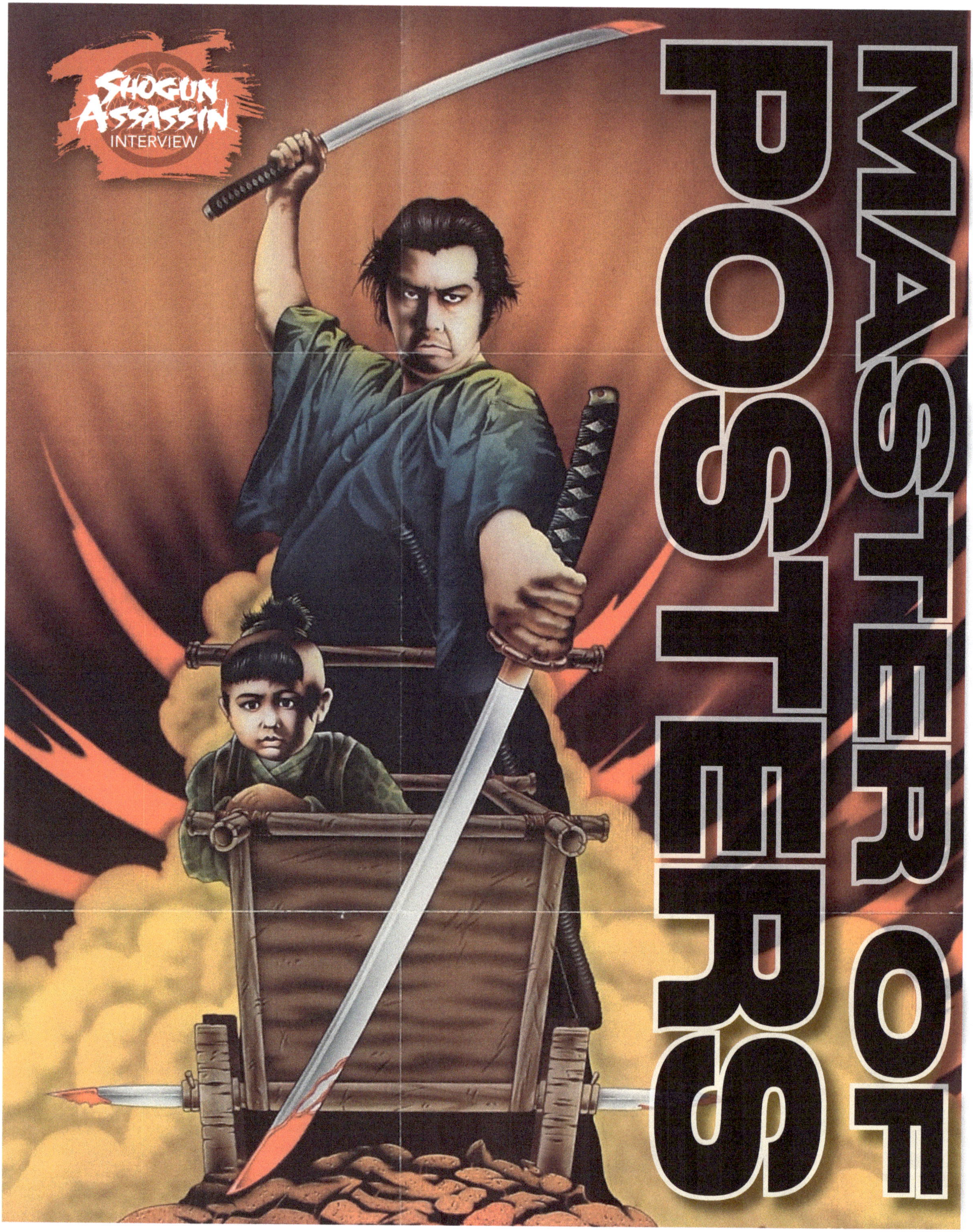

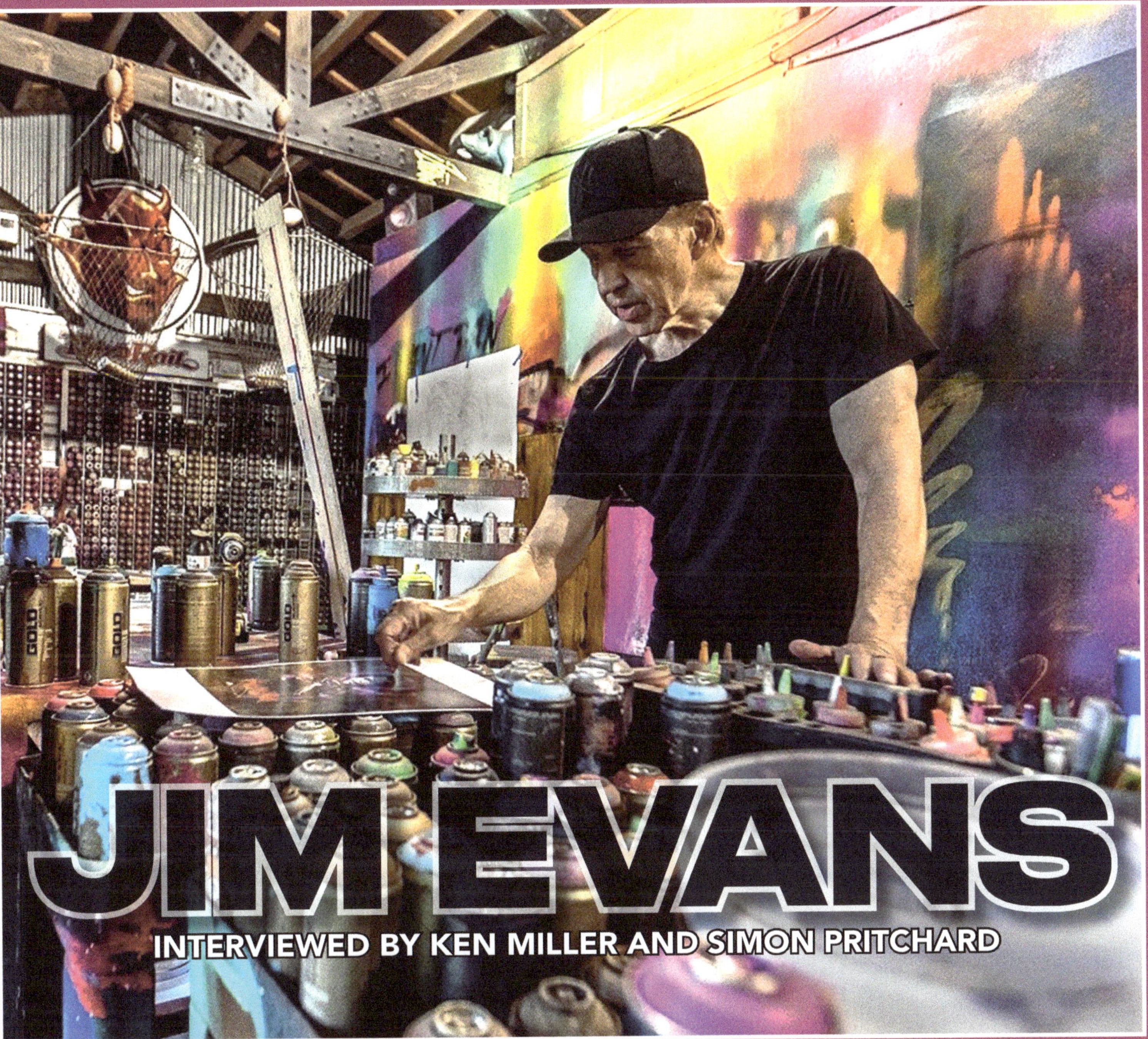

JIM EVANS

INTERVIEWED BY KEN MILLER AND SIMON PRITCHARD

Jim Evans, aka **TAZ**, is a creative renaissance man within the world of commercial art: he has been an Underground Comix artist, a surfing magazine illustrator, a creator of gig posters, record sleeves and rock ephemera for major bands. He has produced many movie posters too, has displayed work at exhibitions, and is the founder of the TAZ collective. Jim was one of the main members of the creative team that brought *Shogun Assassin* into the world, painting the awesome poster and contributing to the film from the outset of the project, influencing all aspects of the graphics and production, helping to develop what ultimately evolved into an iconic piece of pop culture. Here Jim talks about his art, about working on *Shogun Assassin*, describes how he went about painting the legendary poster, and he also reveals an exclusive snippet of information regarding a link between *Shogun Assassin* and a certain Arnold Schwarzenegger movie... ➔

Early in your career you worked as an artist on Underground Comix, on titles like *Yellow Dog*, *Illuminations* and *Slow Death Funnies*. What was it like back then, working within such a heady, countercultural environment?

It was an amazing time to be a young artist. With underground publications in every major city having huge readerships, an artist could gain instant recognition.
This often led to getting a shot at being included in comix like *Yellow Dog*, etc. and eventually getting your own title. Doing covers was always cool, because you got to work in full colour.

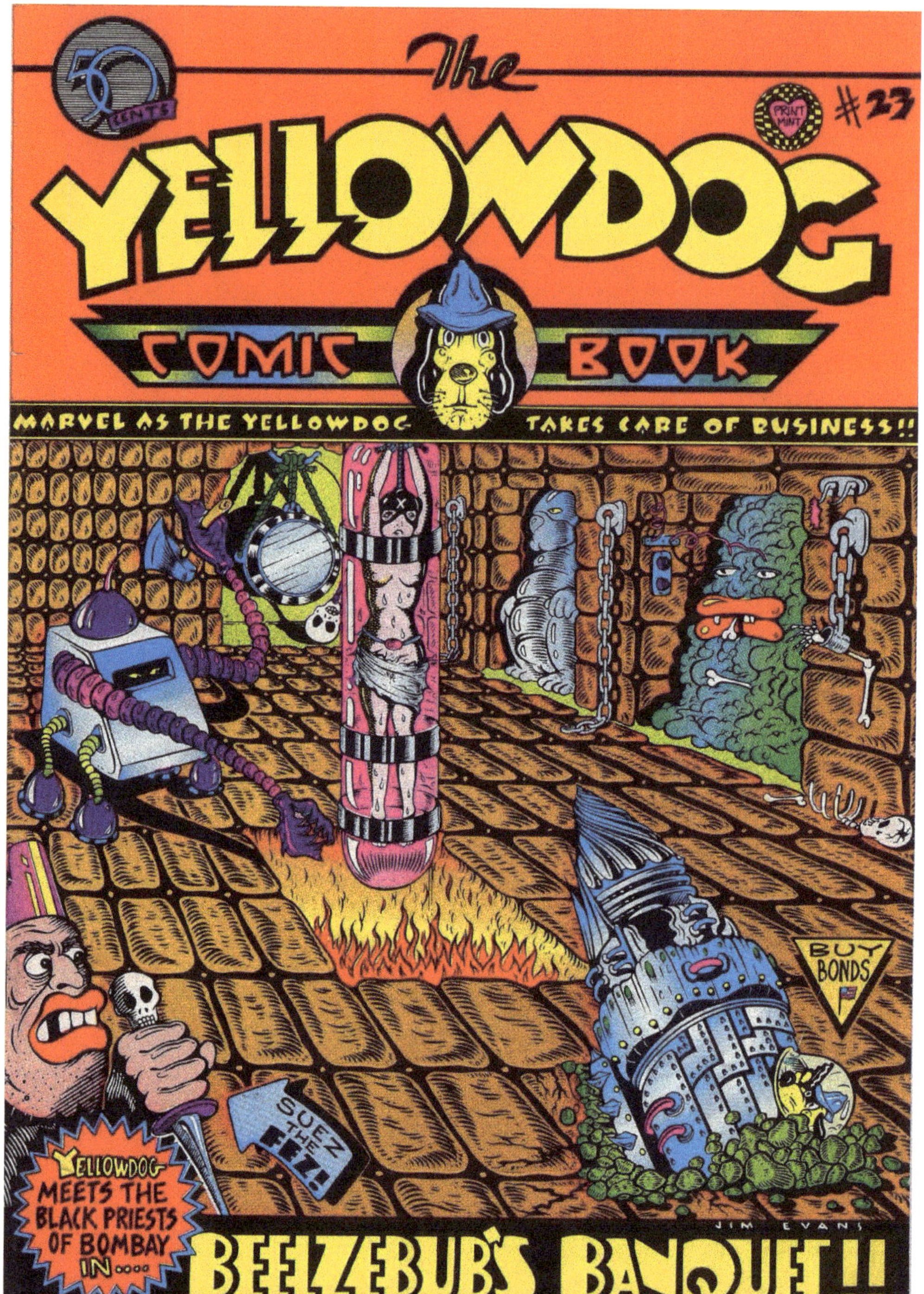

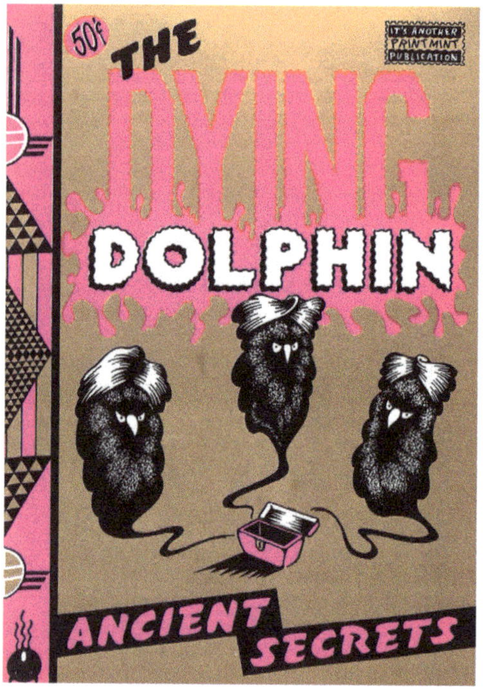

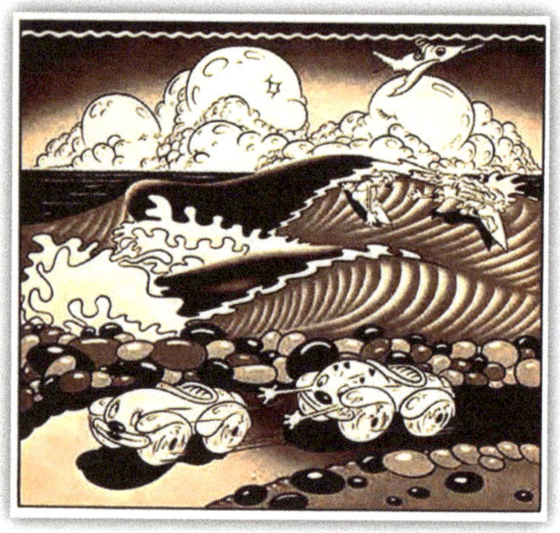

Did you meet-up with other renowned Underground Comix creators at the time, folks such as Robert Crumb, Gilbert Shelton and Richard Corben?

I did meet all of them, except for Richard Corben. I was close friends with Rick Griffin and Robert Williams and did cartoon jam-session collaborations with both of them. Rick, along with Ron Cobb, was key to kick-starting my career, and got me introductions to major publishers like the Print Mint. Rick, myself, Robert Williams, S. Clay Wilson, and Robert Crumb all contributed to *Tales From The Tube*, a comic that was published by *Surfer Magazine*, then later expanded and republished by the Print Mint.

You moved to Hawaii, where you contributed to surfing mags and you illustrated surfing posters. Did you move to Hawaii specifically because you were a surfer and such a big surfing fan?

I planned to move my family to Australia and live a more off-the-grid lifestyle. Being an obsessed surfer, I wanted to take some time in Hawaii and try my hand at giant waves on the North Shore of Oahu. I started getting lots of work in Hawaii and realised I'd disappear in Australia,

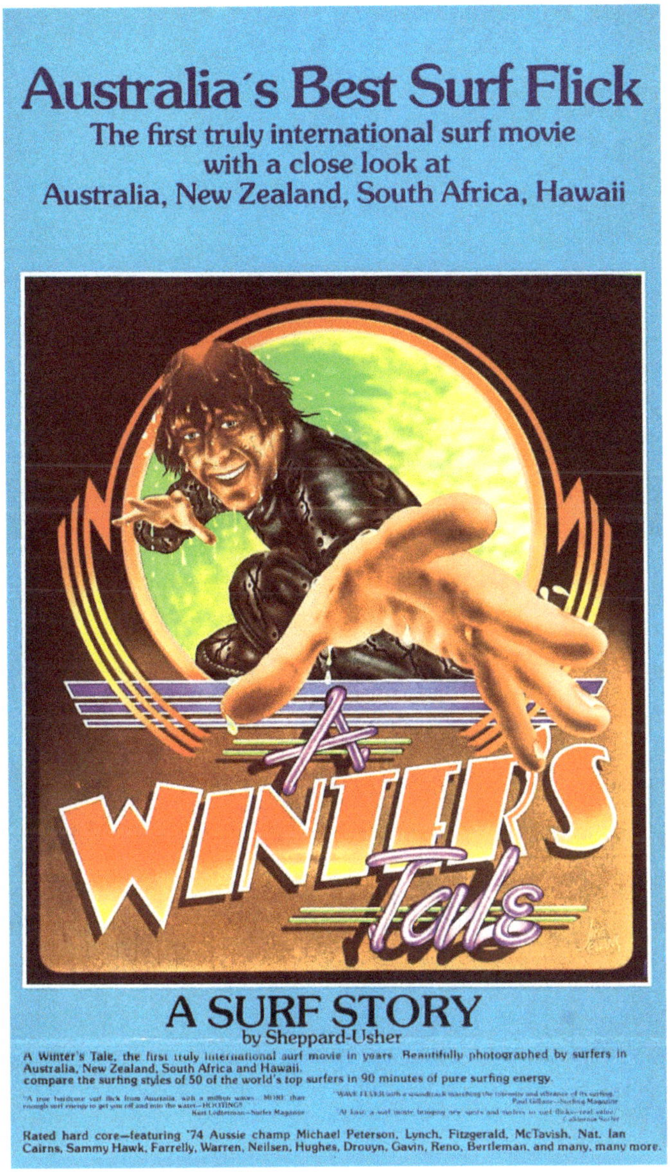

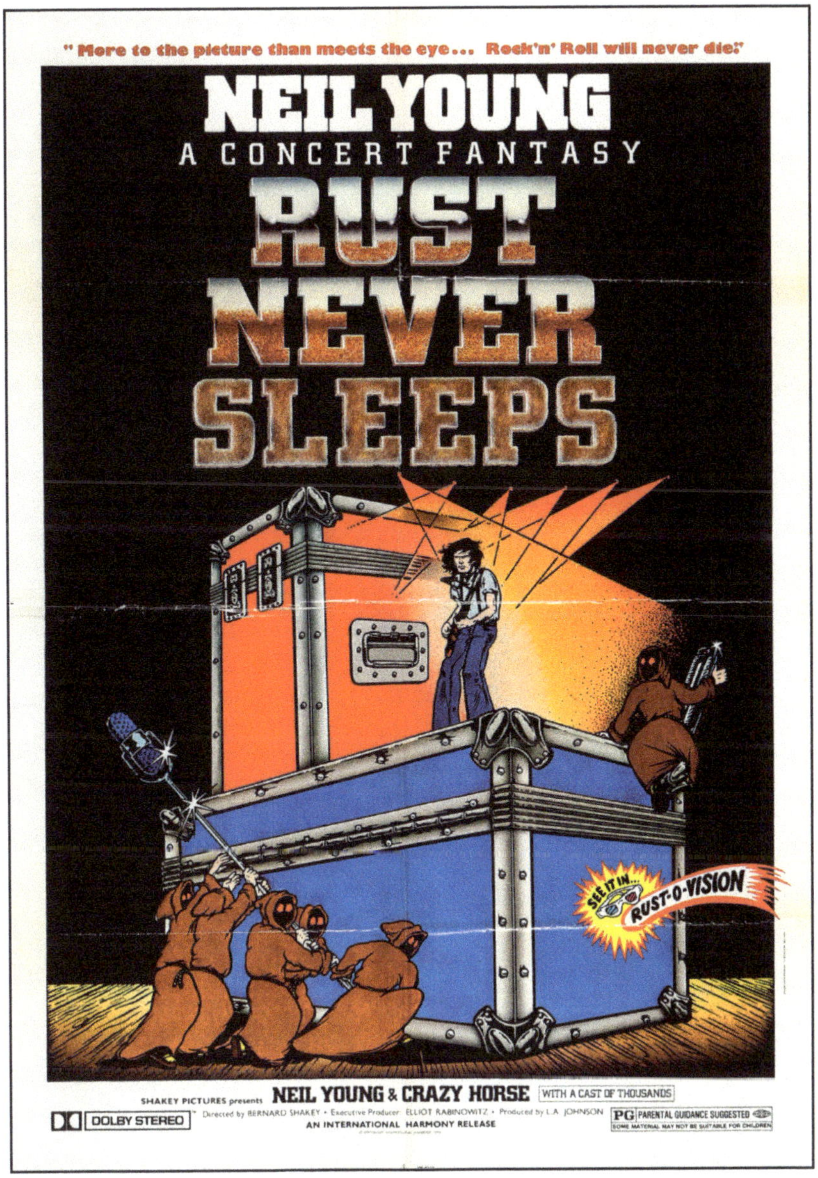

so came back to the mainland after a few years and started getting big album covers, film posters, and a lot of advertising work. My off-the-grid plan did not work out.

You returned to mainland America and did a lot of album sleeve work, for bands including The Beach Boys and Chicago, plus skateboarding magazine illustrations. Was your move from Comix, to surf mags, to album art and skateboard mags always an intentional decision, or did the shift into these different creative areas happen organically?

The shift happened organically; the jobs just kept getting bigger.

Fortunately, I was not an artist who was tied to any medium or movement. For me, the comics were an entry level thing, a way to showcase my ideas and techniques. I had a ton of ideas, and pretty much embraced every new challenge. The album covers and magazine illustrations also entailed more collaboration, and the responsibility to visualise something that was not generated by me, like a band's music and the band's need for a unique and iconic image that represented how they saw themselves.

You started creating movie poster illustrations for films such as *20th Century Oz* and *Rust Never Sleeps*, and you were also a storyboard artist. What movies did you produce storyboards for?

Yes, I did a lot of film posters, and I still do them now for films like

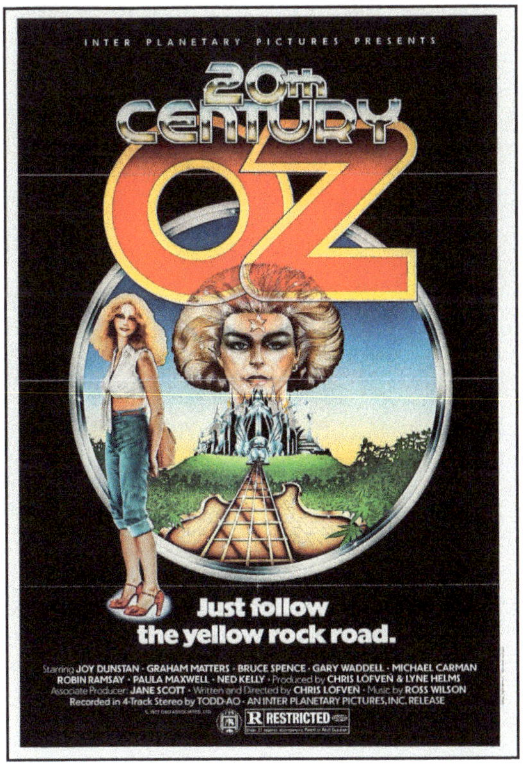

Zombieland 2, *Jumanji*, *Jigsaw*, etc. I did the storyboards for a film titled *Bad Manners*, and another titled *Strangers Kiss*.

My son Gibran, the voice of Daigorō in *Shogun Assassin*, also appears in *Bad Manners*, along with his brother Tagore. Some of the same production team was involved, and the director Robert Houston was the co-director of *Shogun Assassin*. He later went on the win an Academy Award for a documentary film.

How did you become involved with the *Shogun Assassin* project?

I did a lot of genre film posters for the producer, David Weisman, and one day he said that he wanted to create some sort of ultimate Samurai film for domestic US consumption. He asked me what my favourite Samurai film was and I told him a series titled *Lone Wolf and Cub* aka *Baby Cart* was next level cool – that is how it began.

I took him to see an episode at a theatre in Little Tokyo and he agreed immediately that this was the one. David spoke fluent Japanese, and was able to get on the phone and kick the project into gear very quickly.

How was it decided to release a mix between the first two Japanese *Baby Cart* movies rather than just re-releasing them as original 'stand alone' versions?

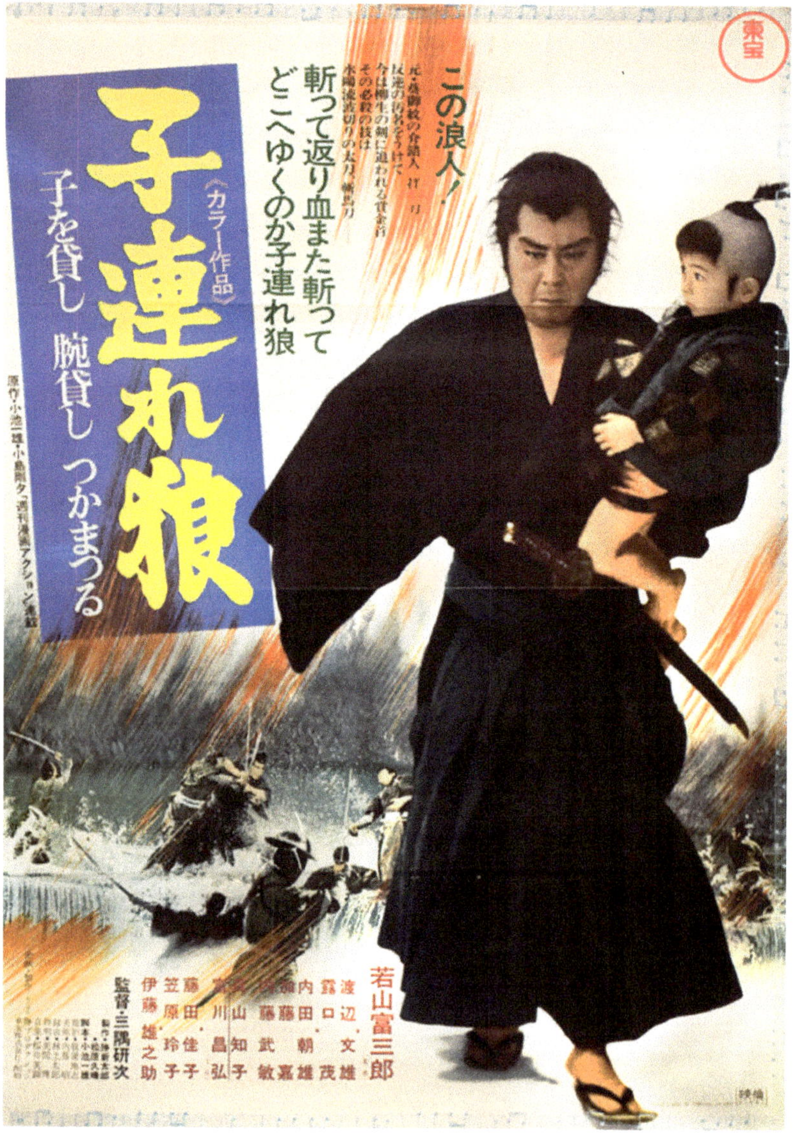

Japanese B2 poster for *Lone Wolf and Cub: Sword of Vengeance* (1972)

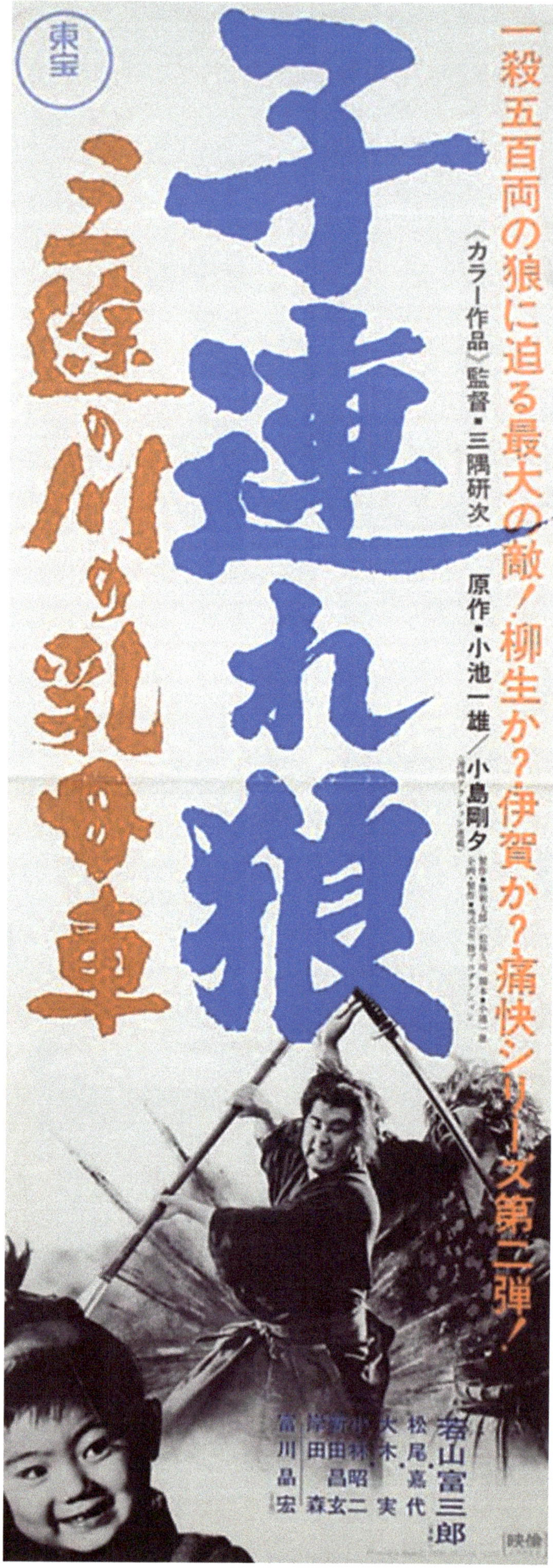

Japanese insert poster for *Lone Wolf and Cub: Baby Cart at the River Styx* (1972): Jim already knew about these Baby Cart movies and encouraged producer David Weisman to purchase the rights...

They wanted to redo it completely, and the first two episodes provided the best way to do that.

The team behind it had talented scriptwriters and some seasoned filmmakers. They wanted to showcase the genesis of Ogami Ittō's journey, and why he had taken his young son on such a merciless path of vengeance. Now the original *Shogun Assassin*, if released, would likely become the first part of a trilogy.

Do you remember anything about when or how the decision was made to take the first twelve minutes of *Sword of Vengeance* and use the majority of *Baby Cart at the River Styx* to create the film?

I think once the decision was made to give the child a voice and make him the narrator, all the thoughts about what footage to use was based on that. The first two episodes fit the bill, and the idea was to use the child's voice as a poetic counterpoint to the brutal violence.

The voice of Daigorō has become the most memorable part of *Shogun Assassin*, and the iconic juxtaposition of the sword or the ball is a classic meme.

There may have been rights issues at play as to how much footage could be used, and I remember endless discussions and negotiations about that.

I have read that it was actually you who suggested to producer David Weisman that he should buy the rights to the *Lone Wolf* movies?

That is true, once we watched it together, I told him this was the one to get, especially since no one outside of Japanese audiences or a

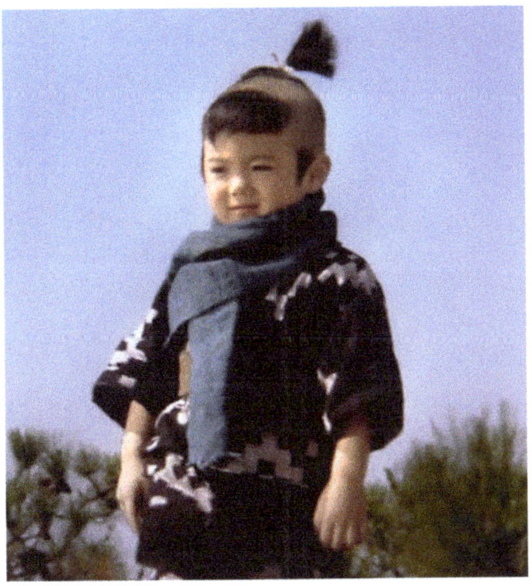

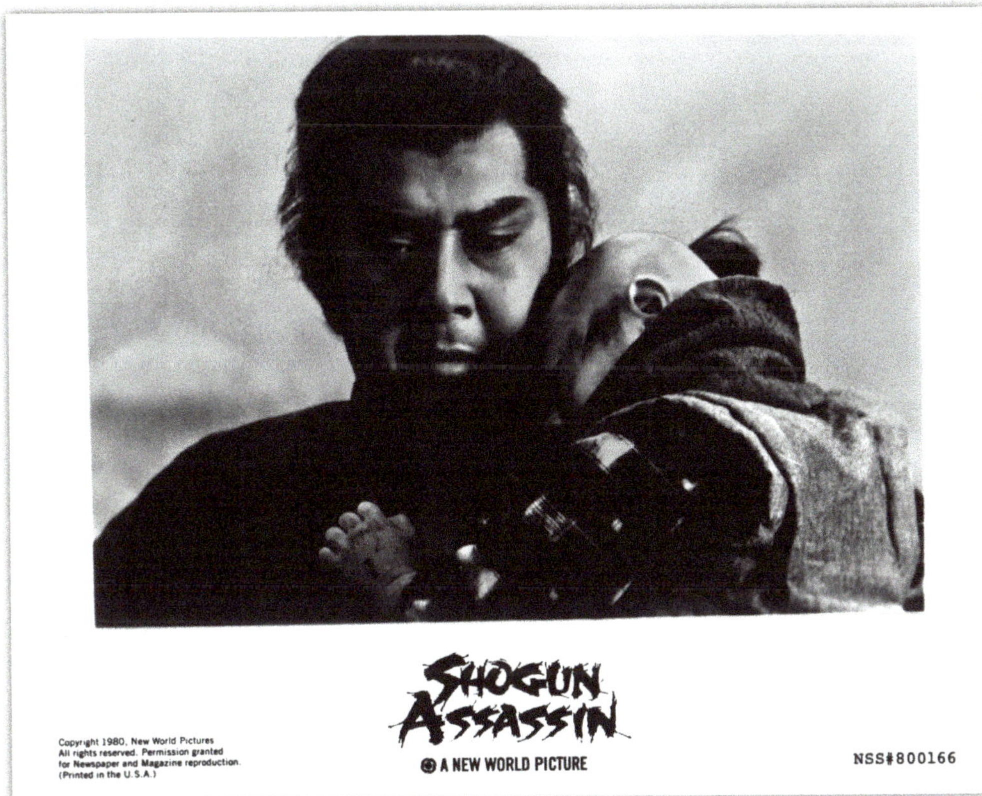

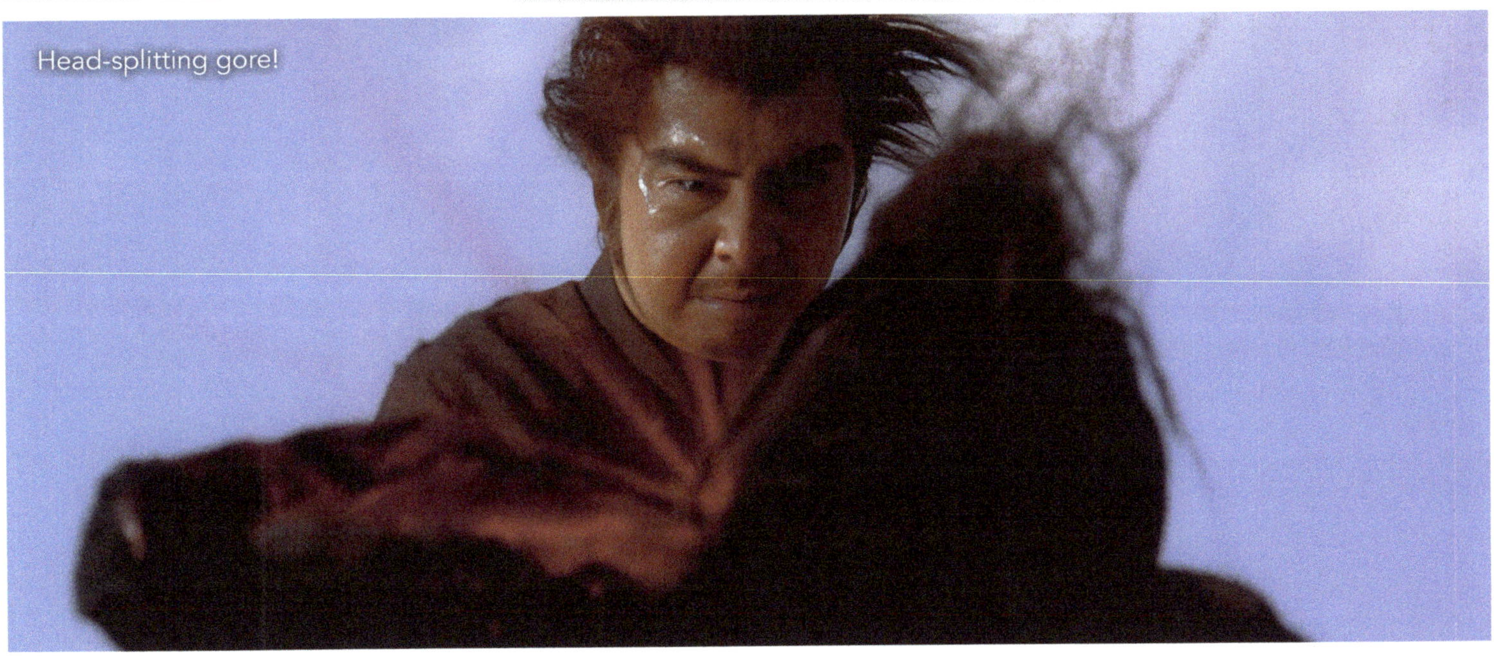
Head-splitting gore!

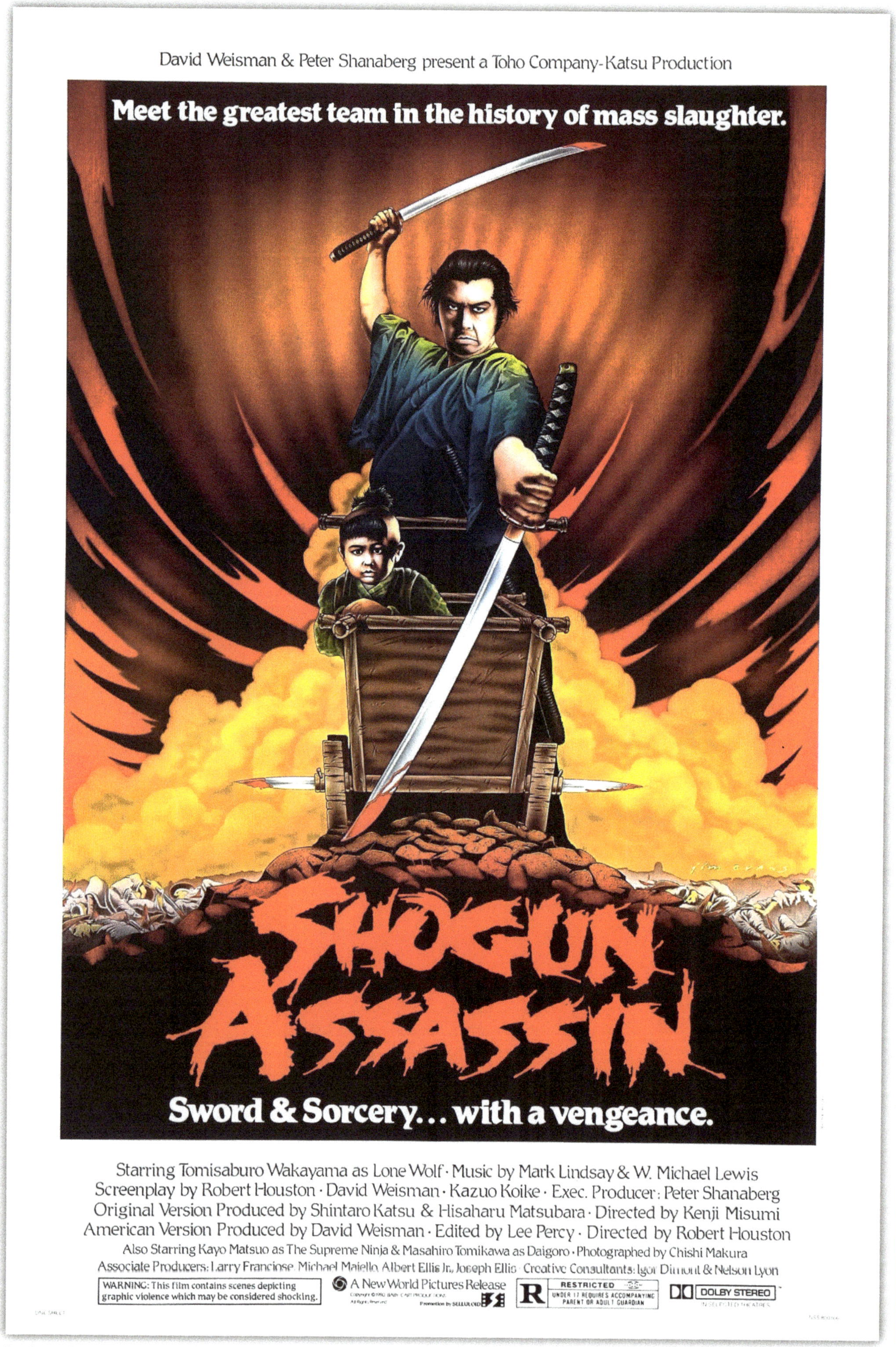

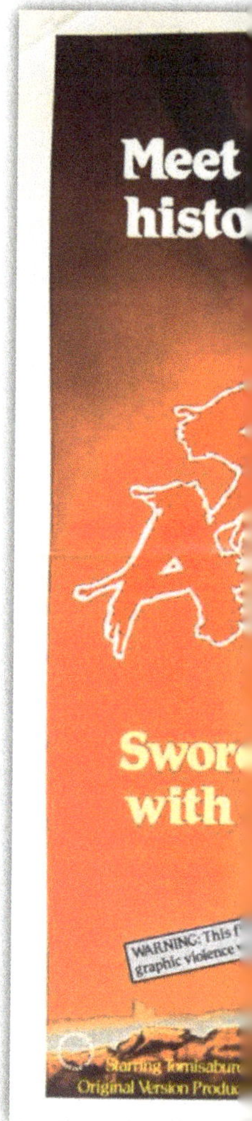

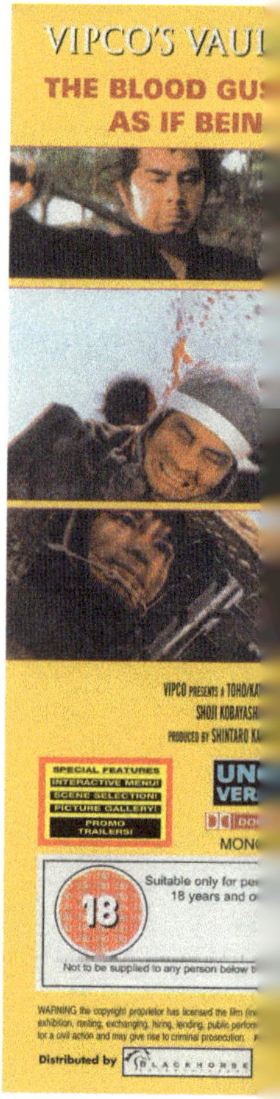

Jim's astounding US poster for Shogun Assassin (1980)

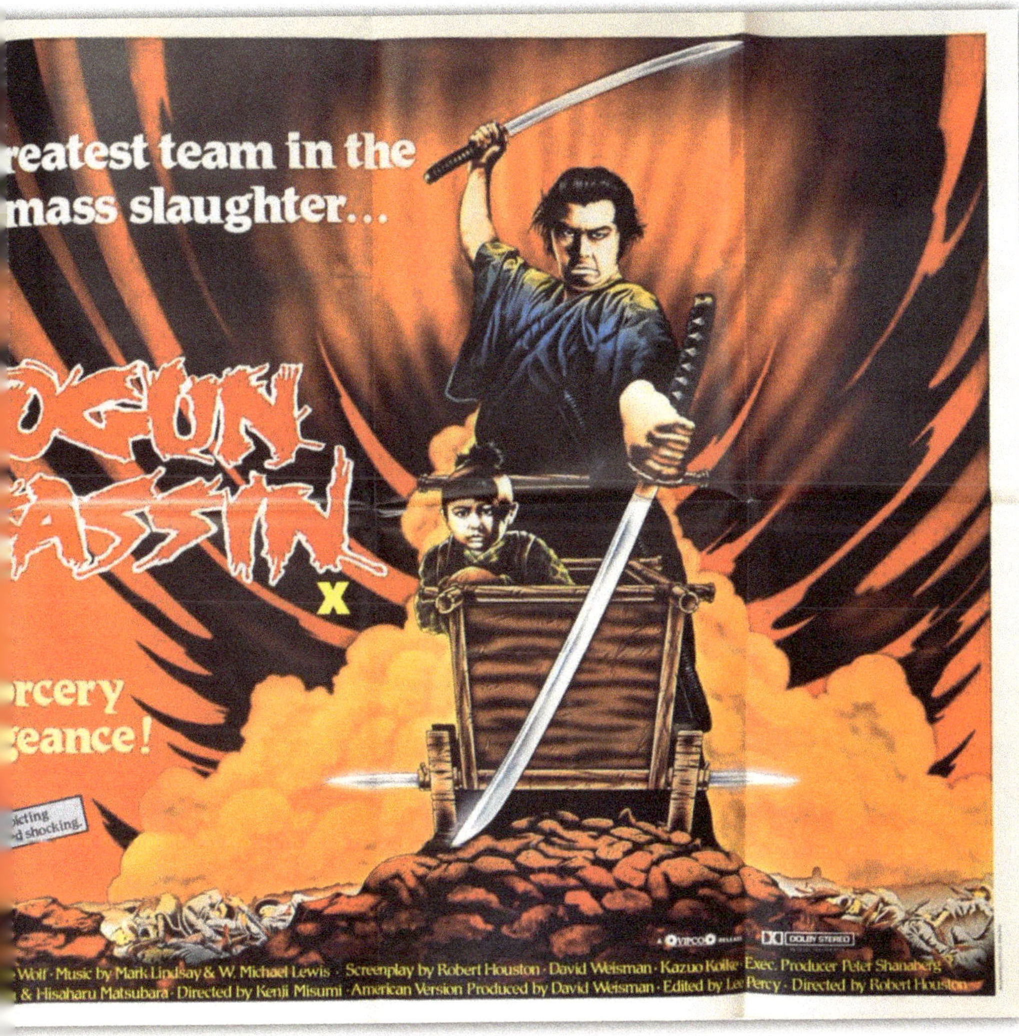

Jim's artwork is used for the UK quad poster for *Shogun Assassin* (1980)

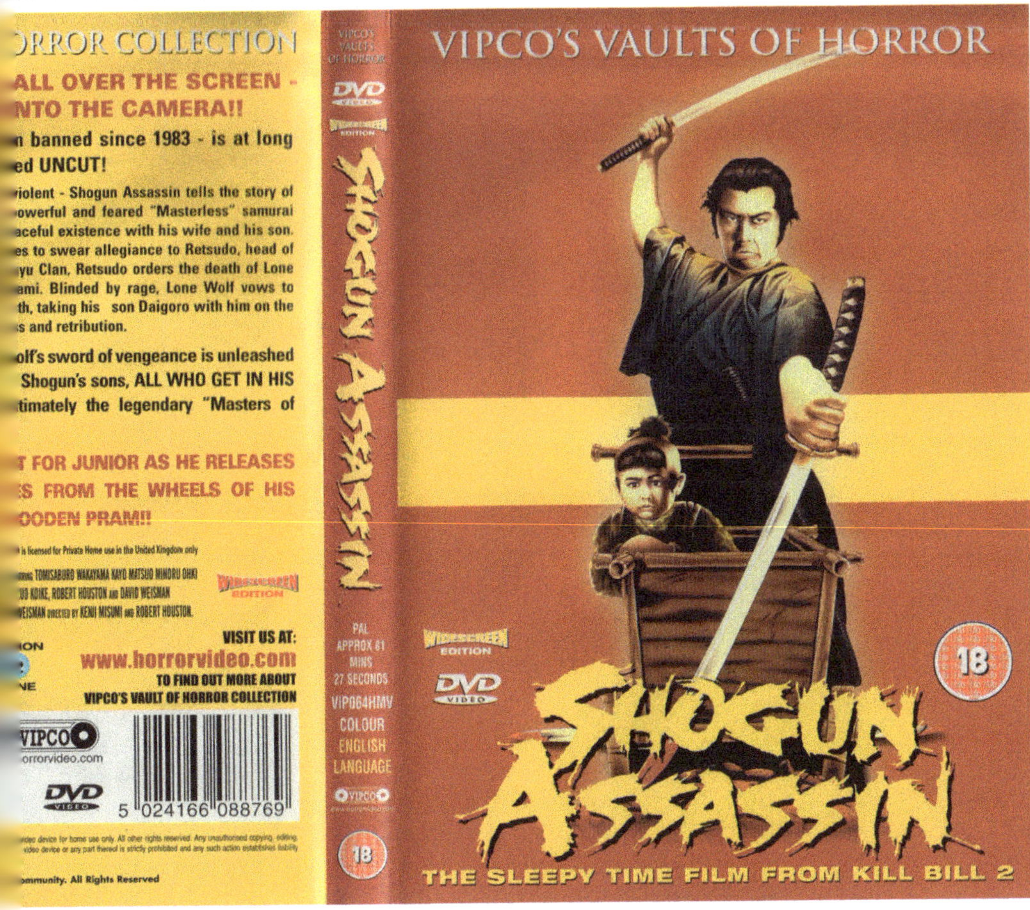

Just the main figures from Jim's painting are used on this later Vipco rerelease DVD cover

few obsessives like me, had any clue it existed. Truthfully, I saw it as a revisionist western.

Your son Gibran provided the voice of Daigorō. Did you suggest to the producers that Gibran might be a good choice to provide the voice for Lone Wolf's child? His clear, quite sweet-sounding voice is certainly one of the most iconic elements of *Shogun Assassin!*

I was in a meeting with David and Bobby, and they were depressed that they had seemed to have exhausted every young actor voice they could find, with no luck. I told them I had a son with a tiny child voice, and they asked me to bring him in. They did a test and proclaimed immediately that they had their Daigorō.

Your artwork for the *Shogun Assassin* poster is iconic. How long did it take you to produce the illustration?

That illustration took about 3 weeks and ran right up against the print deadline. The army of dead ninjas in the background were done in a final all-night session at David's house, and we drove to the printer while the paint was still drying. An interesting bit of trivia is that Gary Panter, who was designing the *Pee-Wee's Playhouse* production, and had done the poster for Pee Wee, had also done a *Shogun Assassin* poster, but it was never used. Had I not finished on time, it would have been the one sheet instead.

What inspired the final image? And what art media did you use?

I really wanted it to look epic, so the background needed an apocalyptic feel, like a cathedral of blood. I wanted to try to bring Ittō's rhythmic double sword style to life and include his dead-eyed glower.

From a visual standpoint I wanted to show the danger of the baby cart, but at the same time make it look rickety, with Daigorō being the calm child, relaxed, but deadly.

Everything in the composition draws the eye to the two faces, standing at a bloody pinnacle in triumph, with a world of death behind them, their weapons tipped in blood. I used a combination of Dr. Martin dyes and acrylics painted with an airbrush, all the finish and detail work was done with colored pencils and tiny brushes. It was painted on illustration board.

Did you experiment with other layouts/compositions for the *Shogun Assassin* poster design?

No, with this one I sketched it out, David and Bobby loved it. I finished out the drawing, transferred it to illustration board, and painted it to finish without stopping or making any changes. The image in my mind was exactly what you see on the poster.

You also did the titles that appear in *Shogun Assassin*. What other stuff did you do for this movie?

I did the bloody logo that appears on the poster and in the title animation and got a friend of mine who was an Aikido instructor to create the sword slicing sound effects for the film by cutting through watermelons. Beyond that I just worked with David and Bobby on the editing and getting that epic soundtrack created by Mark Lindsay finished.

Logo designed by Jim

Have you considered re-releasing any of the original artwork that was created for *Shogun Assassin*?

I have considered releasing it in some kind of limited edition boxed set with detailed notes. It will likely happen, just haven't figured out what I want to do yet – maybe in conjunction with the release of a book or something.

Shogun Assassin has remained a cult favourite: it appeared as the 'sleepy time film' in Quentin Tarantino's *Kill Bill: Vol 2* (2004) and has been sampled in hip-hop music. GZA's *Liquid Swords* album (which boasts the talents of all the Wu-Tang Clan members) has samples from the film interspersed throughout it, which adds immeasurably to the tone and overall enjoyment of the album. You must be pleased that *Shogun Assassin*, which you helped bring into the world, has continued to have currency within popular culture?

My goal in choosing a career in commercial art over fine art was to create memorable cultural signposts. I felt that if I was successful, the world would be influenced by the images, and include them as part of an ongoing pop dialogue. With *Shogun Assassin*, my personal obsession with Samurai films and Asian martial arts films helped launch a project that resonated in ways that I could never have anticipated. Being part of the creative team from inception to finish, I was able to influence all aspects of the graphics and production and collaborate in developing what has become an iconic pop culture milestone.

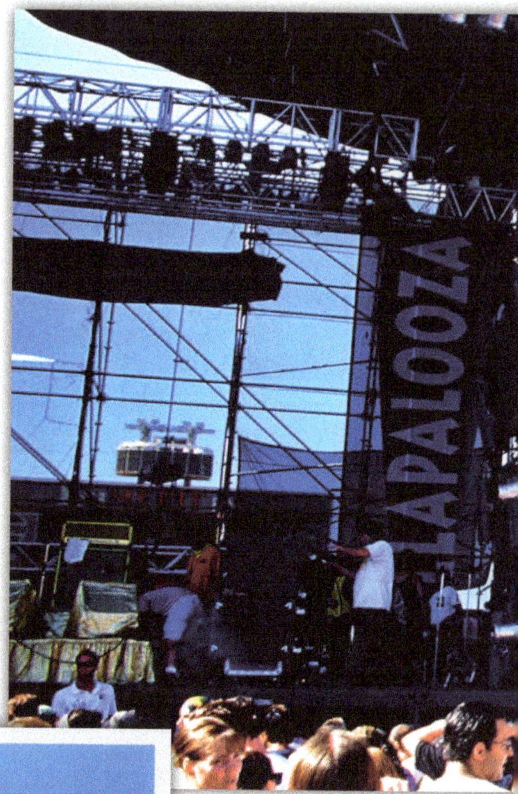

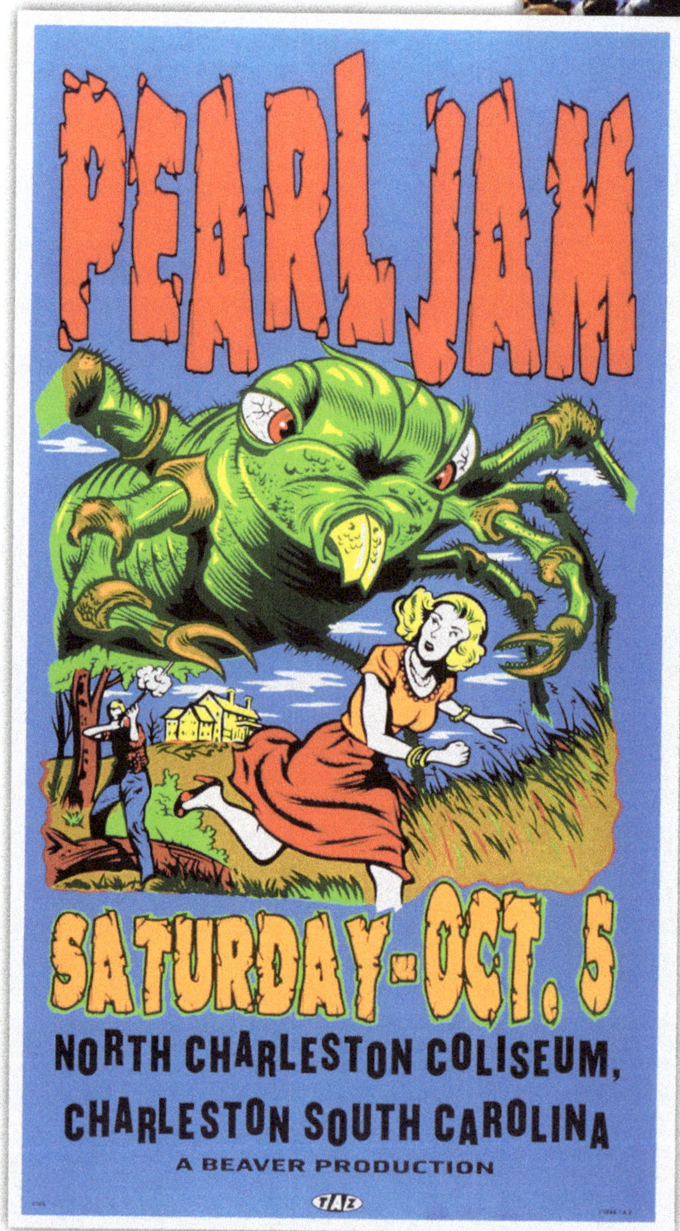

You started producing work under the moniker TAZ, and founded the TAZ collective. Many, many music posters have been designed and produced for leading bands and performers like Pearl Jam, Beck, Nirvana, Rage Against The Machine, Beastie Boys, Metallica, Foo Fighters, U2, Oasis, Porno For Pyros, Green Day and so on, plus

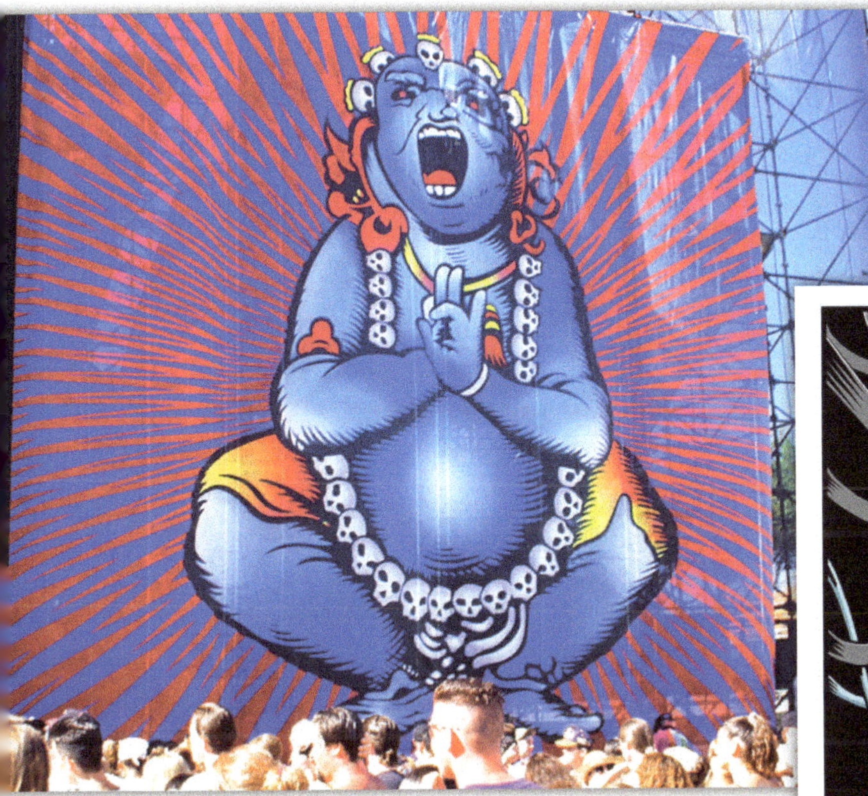

TAZ's art has appeared at many rock concerts and festivals

movie posters for the likes of *Jigsaw* and *Zombieland Double Tap*. Did you feel that there was more creative freedom for you as TAZ, rather than continuing simply as Jim Evans?

Yes, it allows me much greater freedom to experiment, rather than

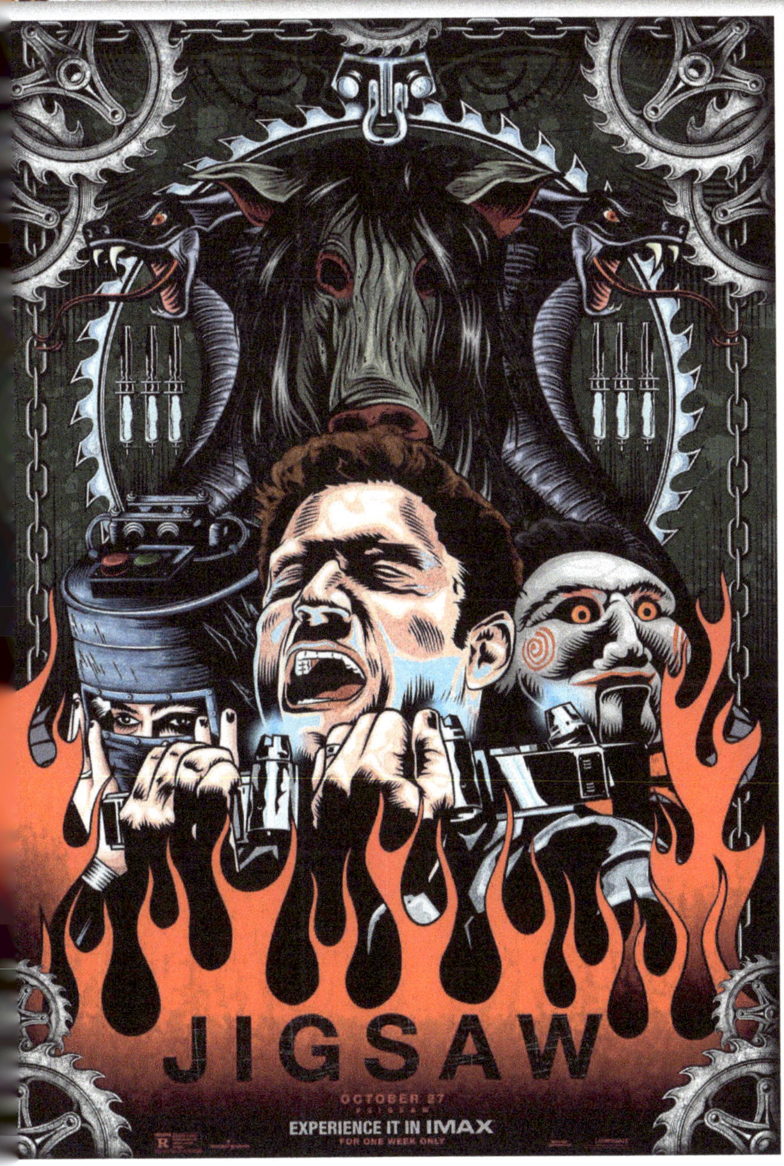

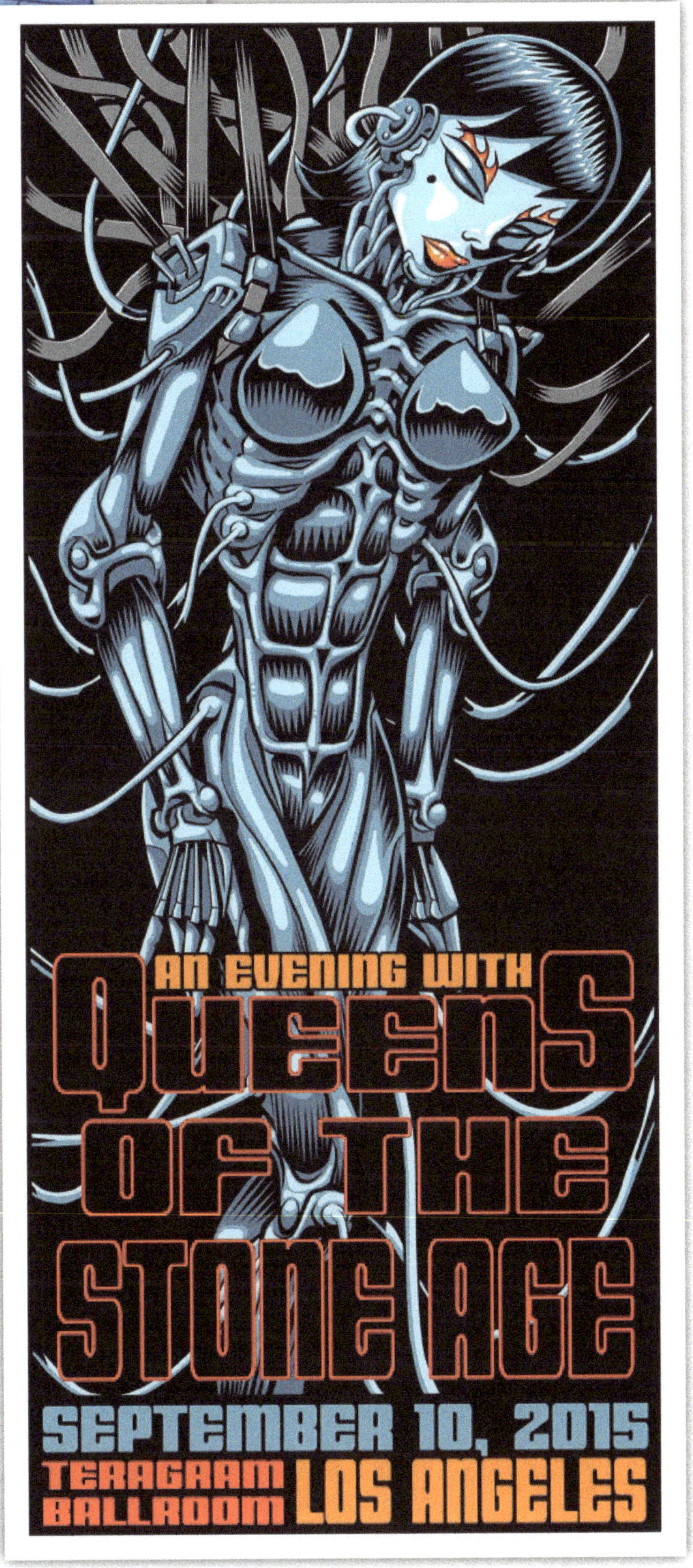

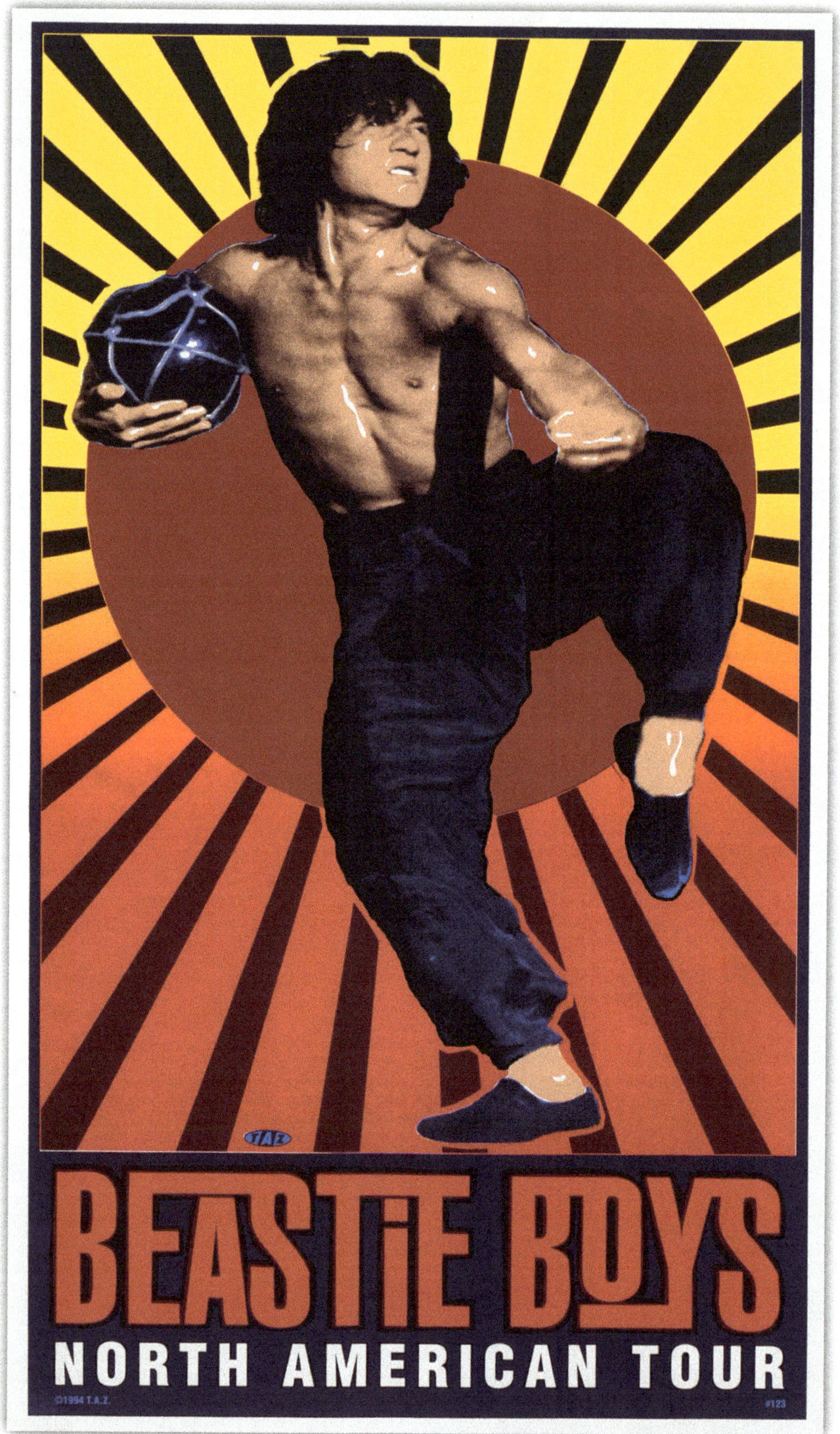

being tied to my own identity and the need to try and skew my output to just what Jim Evans does. TAZ was originally created to engage a new approach to doing rock posters, freely collaborating with other members of the team, and allowing them to make irreversible (by me) creative decisions. This immediately led to a more eclectic output, with aesthetically greater impact. Now it has taken on a life of its own, and sometimes leads me to new places in ways that limiting myself to being Jim Evans never would.

Jackie Chan is featured in a North American tour poster you did for the Beastie Boys. Have you seen and do you like Jackie Chan films, or were you just interested in using that specific image of Jackie Chan in that particular poster design?

I love Jackie Chan, as do the Beastie Boys. Together our favourite Jackie film was *Drunken Master*, thus that image was chosen. At the time, I was also working on the promotional

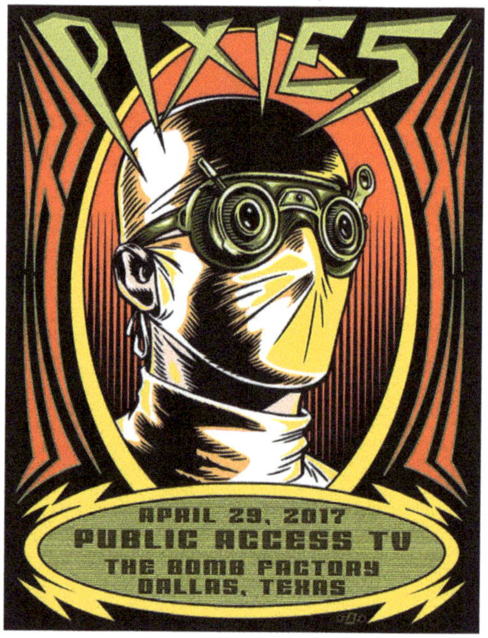

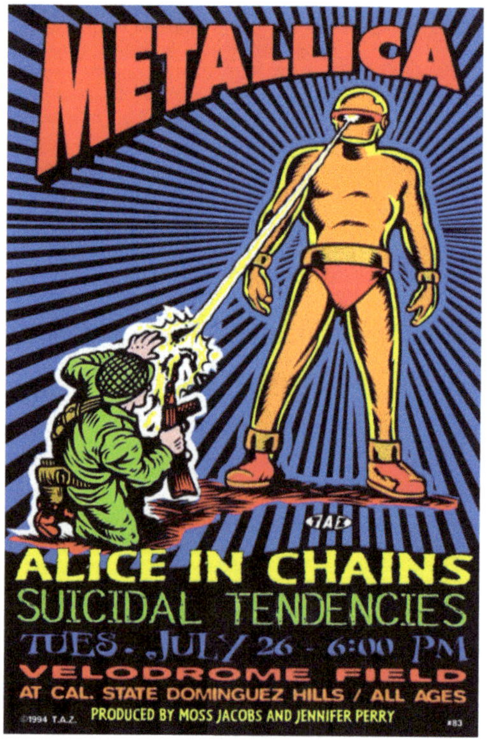

materials for *Rumble in The Bronx*, and my wife Nancy and I got to meet Jackie Chan – a very charming man.

Did you create any tour posters for Nirvana?

I did not create a full tour poster for Nirvana, though they were included in shows that I did posters for. I had them headlining Lollapalooza 1994, but, of course, that never happened, so it got changed to The Smashing Pumpkins.

Most posters came from requests by managers, the band members themselves, or concert promoters like Goldenvoice.

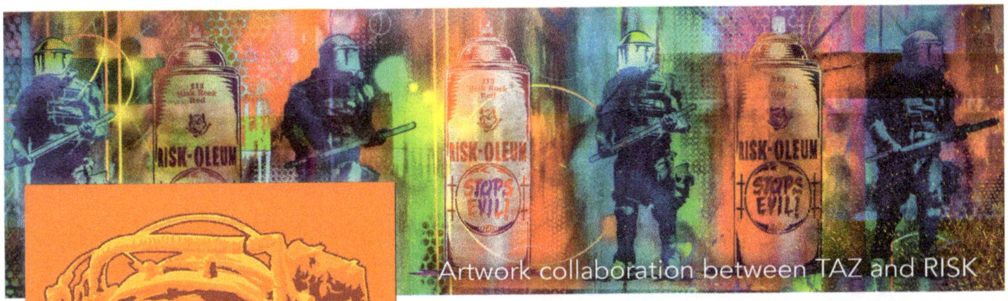

Artwork collaboration between TAZ and RISK

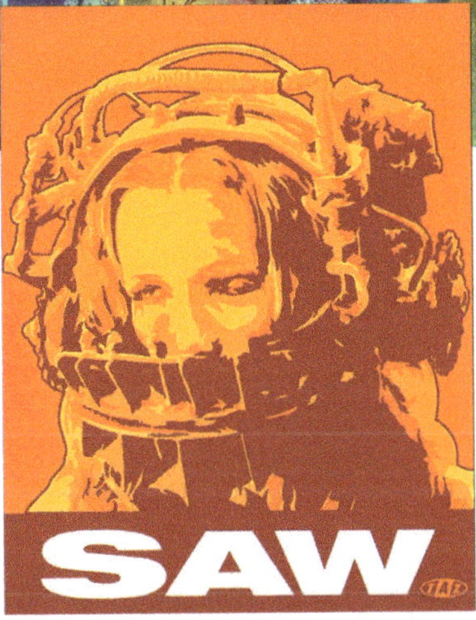

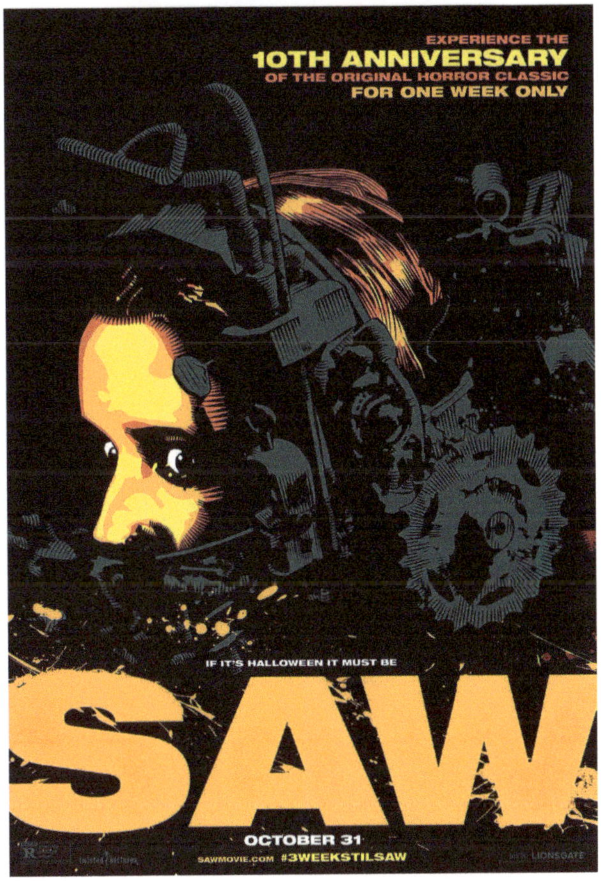

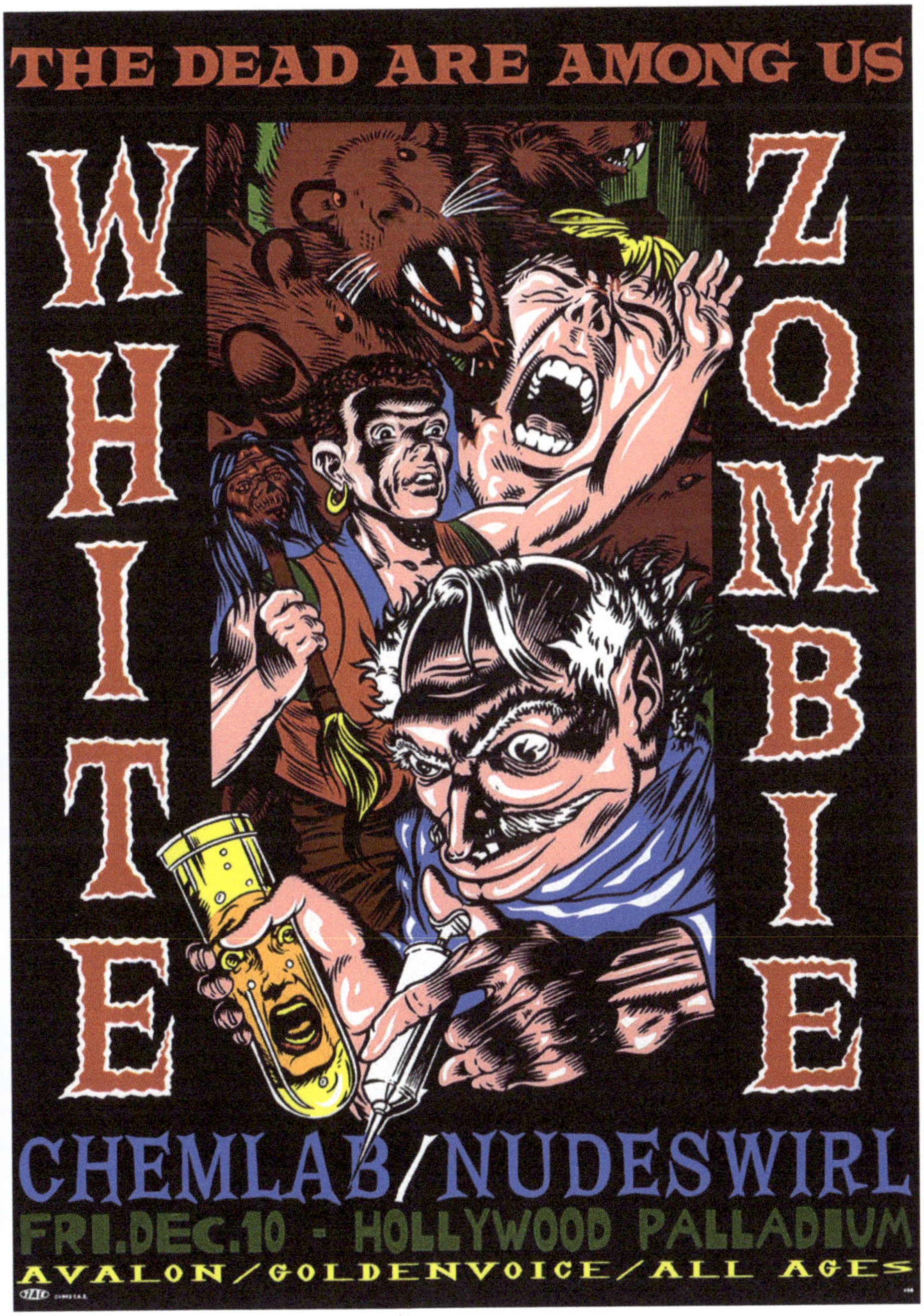

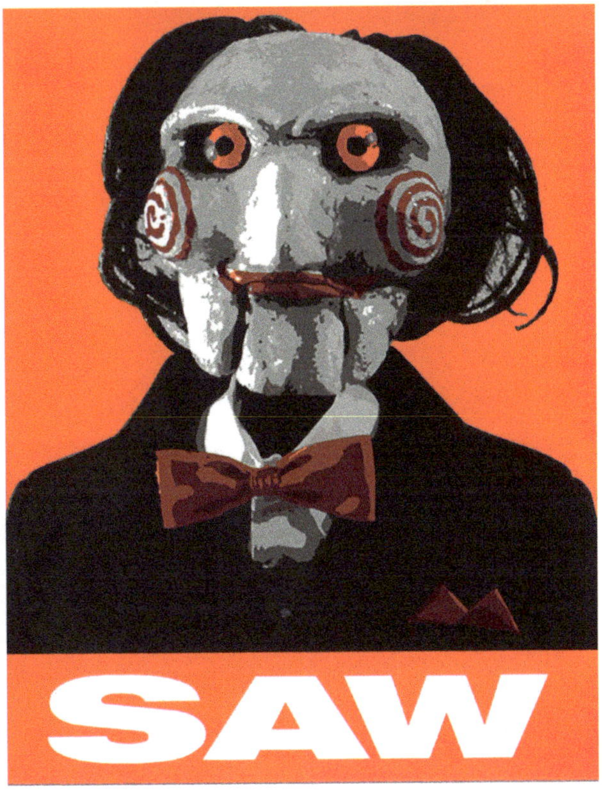

Nowadays do you use computers to produce your art, or do you still physically create your illustrations?

I still do all my initial sketches and drawings by hand, as I still love to draw. The difference now is that I transfer all the drawings to the computer and use Adobe Illustrator & Photoshop for the final deliverable. It allows far more flexibility for change and fine-tuning.

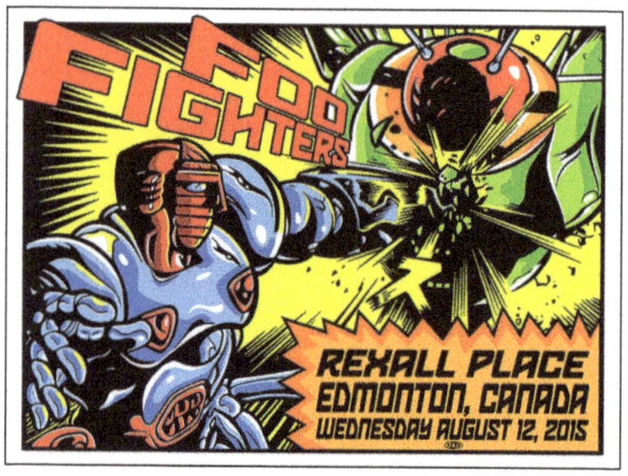

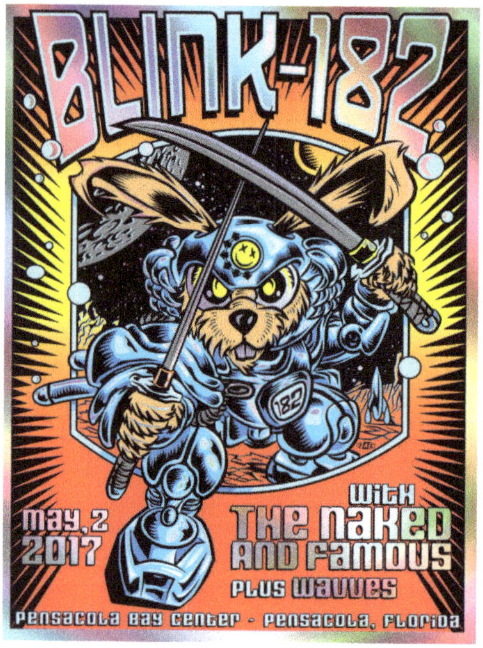

Quentin Tarantino's *Once Upon A Time In Hollywood* (2019) famously recreated the LA/Hollywood milieu of the late 60s, drenching the big production in the pop culture of the time. You must've loved it when Sony Pictures commissioned you to deliver a series of portrait posters as part of the film's promotion. How did you come up with the final look for these posters?

I actually worked in Westwood during the Manson period, and was having breakfast with artist Ron Cobb at a restaurant only a few miles from the house when the news broke, so I understood the milieu quite well and was excited about getting that job. Tarantino wanted something that looked vaguely retro without being retro, and he wanted the image to tell a little story so they could be animated and easily translate to world-wide use for promotion. I chose two artists that were hot in 1969, Warhol and Rauschenberg, and combined their techniques and color usage along with my current graffiti influenced approach to fashion a unique set of portraits. The

The Legend of the Yokai

When *Teenage Mutant Ninja Turtles* (2014) was released, production house Paramount Pictures created an online exhibition, called 'The Legend of the Yokai', which showed work by international artists that explored 'the secret origins of the Ninja Turtles'. The Legend of the Yokai story was based on a folkloric tale of four Kappa (referred to as 'ancient turtle warriors') who vowed to protect a village from an evil warlord and an army of monsters. The show featured creative from 30 artists, including a very dynamic piece of work courtesy of Jim...

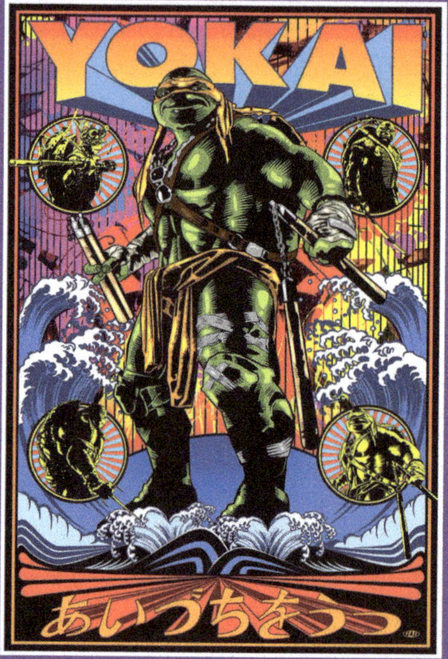

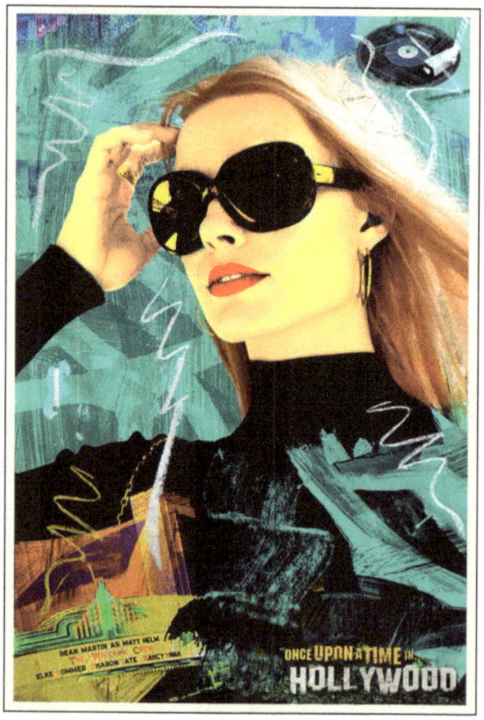

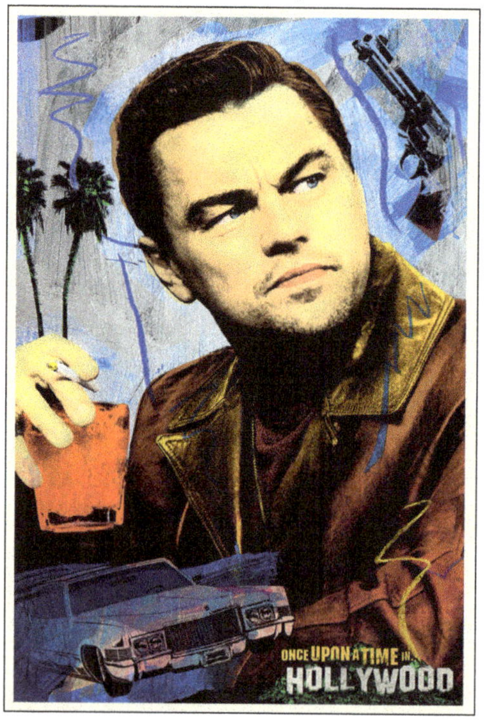

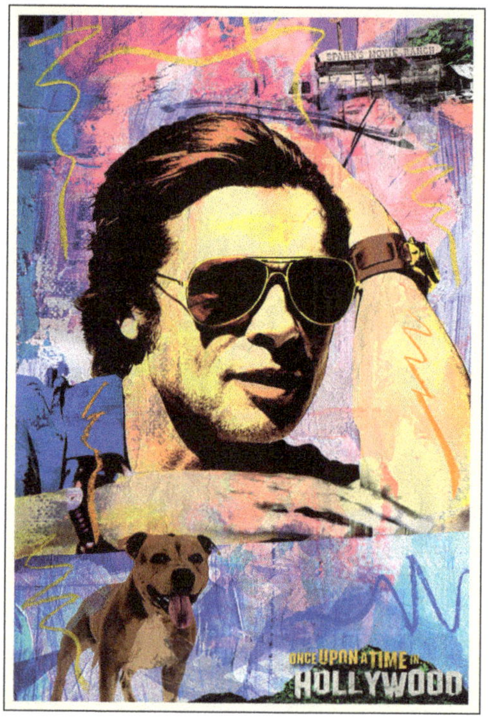

originals of the limited editions were given to the filmmakers, the stars, the production team, and the Sony marketing folks.

What are your plans for the future?

I'll likely be having a big art show at some point this year, and in addition to my usual poster commissions, various art projects, and limited-edition releases, I have some original properties I am developing with a team at CAA. One of these is titled *Sim Warriors*, and it involves a group of street savvy future-tech kids that operate in a not-so-distant future where simulation theory is a fact. I've created original art, characters, and intersecting parallel worlds where they battle an AI-based adversary. Their foe is a next level up civilisation engaged in programming a multiverse of overlapping realities. It will likely initially be released as a book.

Thank you for all your time. Is there anything else you would like to add?

Yes, here is my exclusive...

...that I do not believe has been revealed before concerning *Shogun Assassin*... At the time I was working on *Shogun Assassin*, I was also working on a body building poster with David Weisman that involved Arnold Schwarzenegger, who I had also met while working on a documentary with him. *Shogun Assassin* was almost done, and Arnold heard about it. He had just gotten the job to play *Conan the Barbarian*, that also included a surfing friend of mine, Gerry Lopez. Arnold asked if he could see a rough cut of *Shogun* to get some ideas for how to handle a big sword properly and add some cool Asian action to his approach. A screening was set up, and we all attended with Arnold. After the screening, Arnold was effusive with praise for what he had seen. When leaving the screening, Arnold, myself, and Gibran climbed into the elevator, Gibran looked up at Arnold and said "hi", Arnold looked down, pressed his hand on Gibran's head and said...
"Oh, so you are Daigorō!"

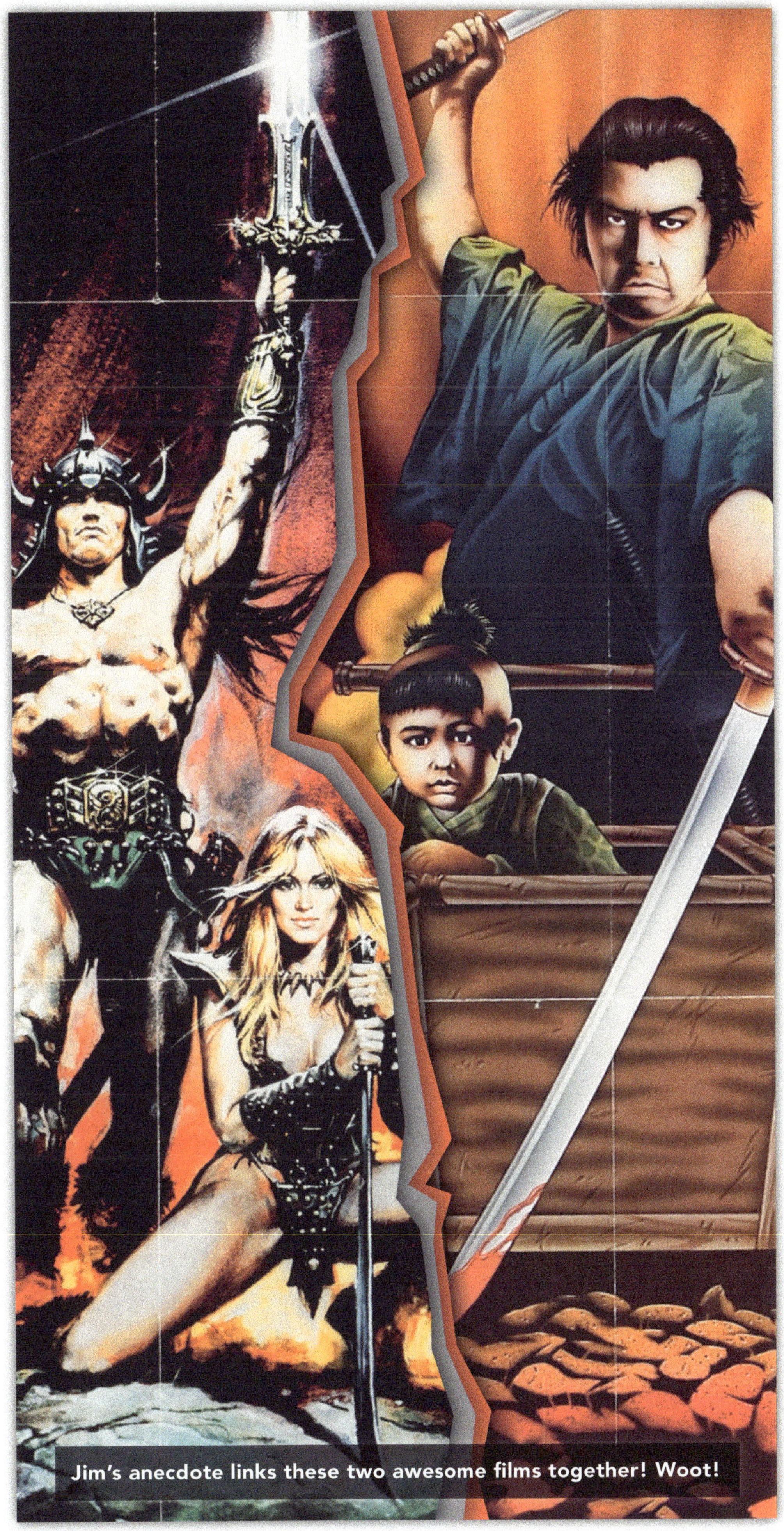
Jim's anecdote links these two awesome films together! Woot!

LIGHTNING DISCS OF DEATH!

Johnny Burnett

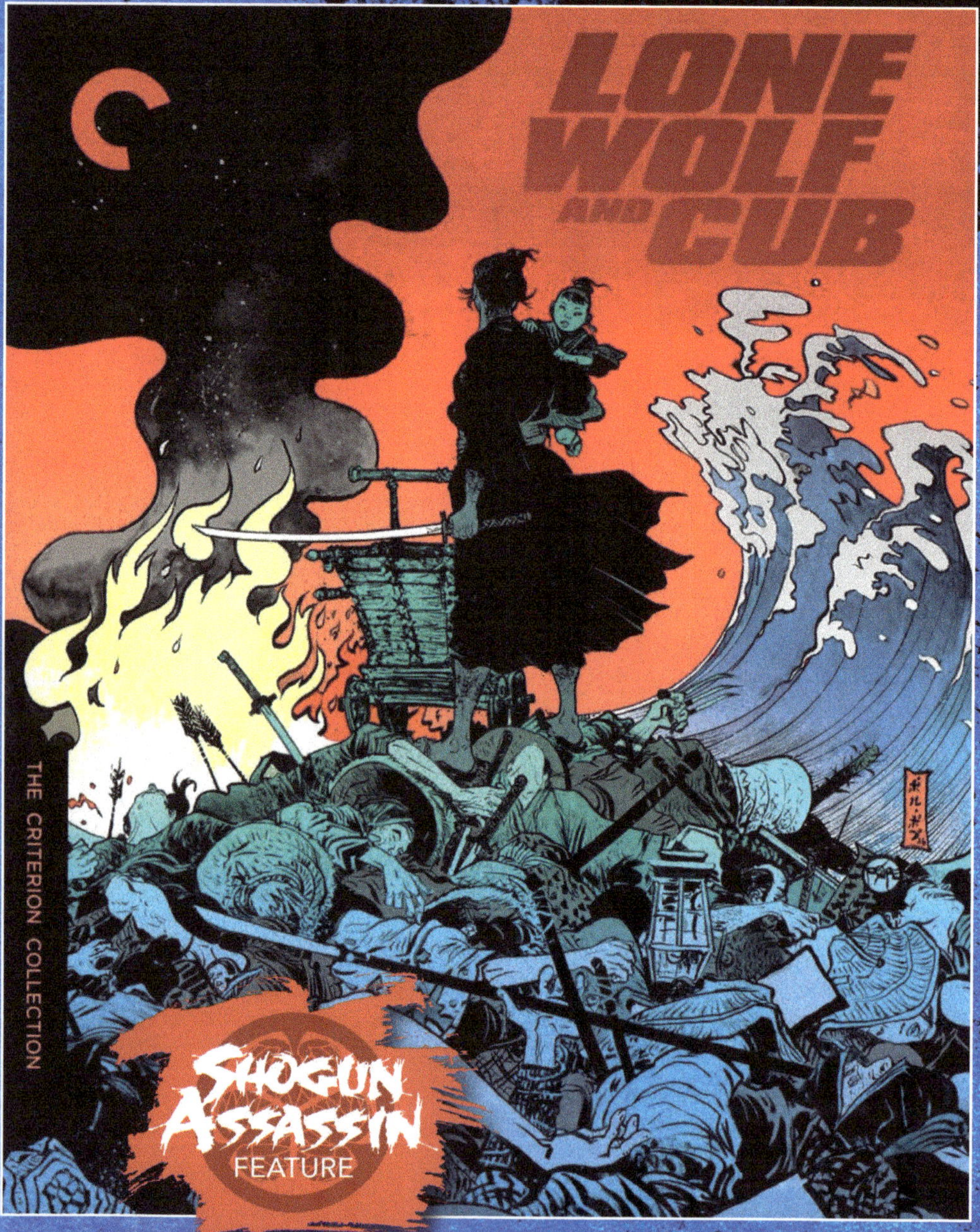

Lone Wolf and Cub Criterion Collection

Of all the incredible examples of Japanese cinema that have found their way to the West over the years, few films have had such an interesting and controversial journey as the awesome *Shogun Assassin*.

Unjustly restricted from sale amid the awful 'Video Nasties' period overseen by the UK Board of Film Classification, the film broke free in the 90s to arrive uncut and in all it's glory, finally reaching us in Blu-ray format.

As mentioned elsewhere in this issue, *Shogun Assassin* rather skilfully combines two films from the exceptional *Lone Wolf and Cub* series into one movie, taking some initial elements from *Sword of Vengeance* and combining them alongside most of *Baby Cart at the River Styx*, adding the greatest voice-over in cinematic history to create a new film that is arguably more famous than the source movies it was so lovingly assembled from.

Thus was produced a new work of popular art...

Join me now on the road to hell, as I take a look at the various options you currently have available to you on shiny Blu-ray disc (or DVD, if that's your bag still) to own this slice of absolute chanbara heaven and, in a few cases, all the other movies from the series which gave birth to it.

Strap yourselves into the baby cart, get comfortable... and let's begin...

Lone Wolf and Cub
Criterion Collection
Region A Blu-ray (US)
Region B Blu-ray (UK)
Region 1 DVD (US Only)

Let's just cut to the chase and put the very best up front, in pole position: *The Lone Wolf and Cub* boxset from Criterion is one of the few samurai/chanbara releases from the label to be available in both the US and the UK. It remains THE absolute best restoration of the full series of all six movies in the series, and also includes the *Shogun Assassin* cut, so really it's a seven film set, all lovingly presented with gorgeous cover art and some really great extra features. If you only pick up one release from this list, make it this one. Hell, if you only pick up one single title from Criterion, make it this one. It's easily in my top five of their best releases of all time.

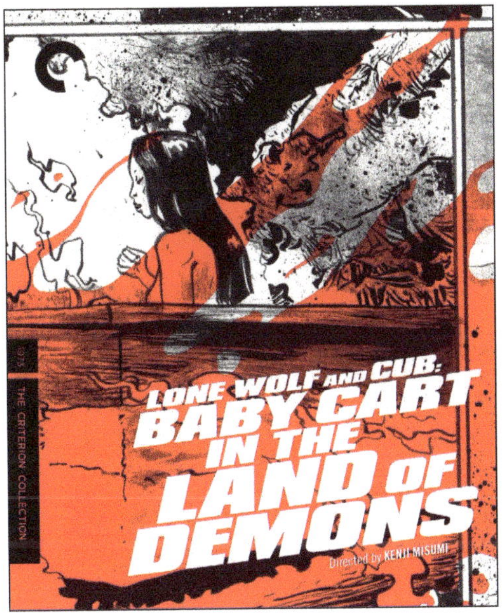

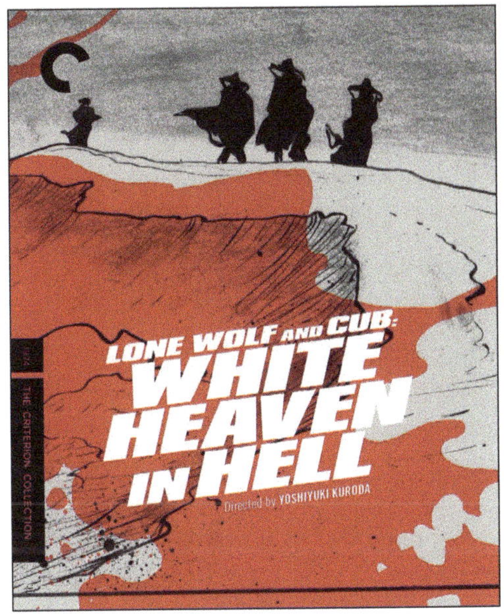

We get all six films lovingly presented from brand new 2K restorations, all featuring the original Japanese mono soundtracks as well as a new HD transfer of *Shogun Assassin*, the best it's ever looked anywhere imho.

Just look at these goodies...

> A newly-filmed (at the time) interview with Kazuo Koike, who is the original writer of the *Lone Wolf and Cub* manga series and was also the screenwriter on five of the *Lone Wolf and Cub* films.

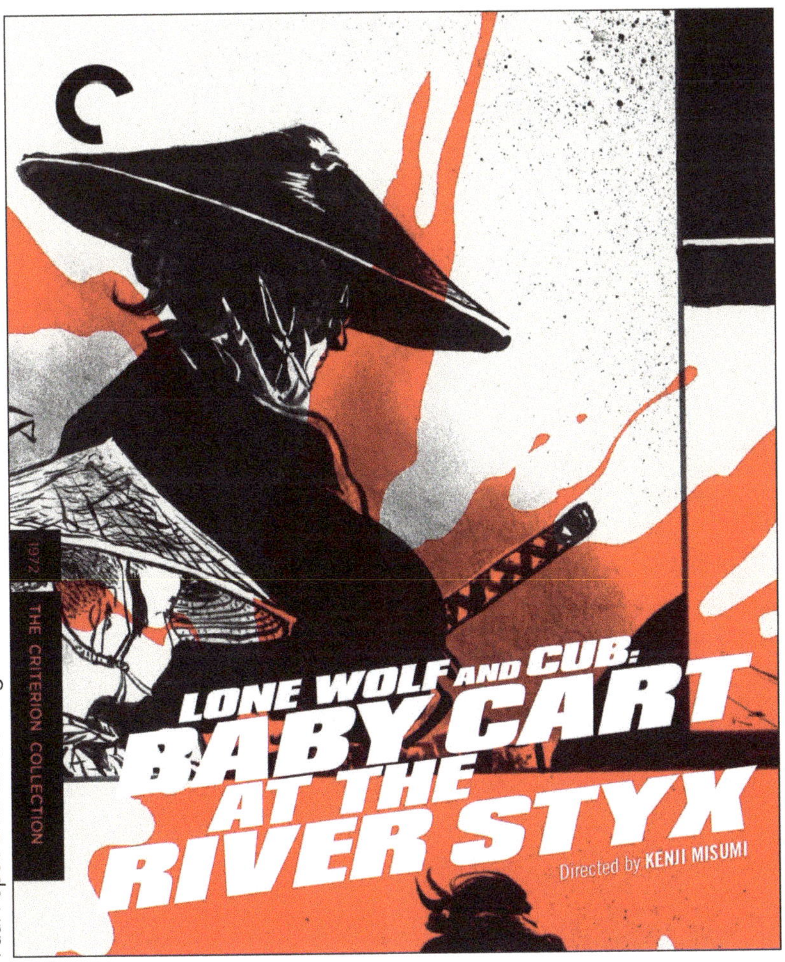

Paul Pope's art is used throughout the *Lone Wolf and Cub* Criterion Collection assets

> A cool 2005 documentary, called *Lame d'un père, l'âme d'un sabre*, about the making of the series.

> An interview with Sensei Yoshimitsu Katsuse, who talks about and demonstrates the real 'Suio-ryu' sword techniques that inspired the ones depicted in the manga and the movies.

> An interview with biographer Kazuma Nozawa. He discusses Kenji Misumi, director of four of the original six films (and is a favourite Japanese film-maker of mine.)

> A wonderful silent 1939 documentary that details the making of samurai swords. This doc comes with an optional new ambient score by Ryan Francis.

> All the original trailers for all six movies.

> A gorgeous booklet that features film synopses and an essay by Japanese writer Patrick Macias. The stunning cover and booklet art is by renowned American comic book artist Paul Pope (who drew and wrote the comic mini-series *Batman: Year 100*).

To be blunt, if you pick any other release over this, you're choosing to pick up the ball and will join your mother in death, but if you pick this release, you're really, truly choosing the sword and can willingly join us all on the road to hell! It's absolutely flawless.

Available on DVD and Blu-ray in the USA and on Blu-ray here in the UK. These crop up fairly often on the secondhand market too, though why some folks choose to sell the set on is really beyond me. If you have the boxset already, make sure to check for the hidden physical 'easter egg' hidden inside the spine of the outer box: it's a fold-out blueprint of the baby cart. A one-off for Criterion who, to my knowledge, have never done anything like this on any other release.

Sublime: 10/10!

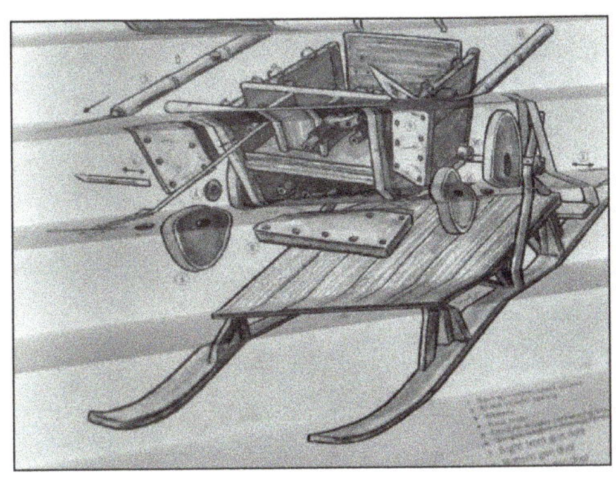

The baby cart blueprint!

Shogun Assassin
Eureka Entertainment
Region B Blu-ray (Region 2 DVD)
Out of Print

Maybe you couldn't care less about seeing *Shogun Assassin* in it's original form, maybe you're one of those curious souls who refuses to 'read a movie' and won't watch anything subtitled. You just want the recut, reassembled Western version of the material because you're a full-blooded *Shogun Assassin*-only kinda person (though if this is you, you're missing out on what is truly an amazing series of movies!) If the above describes you, then fear not my dear reader, as Eureka have you covered, or rather they did, because this is now out of print.

Eureka released two editions of *Shogun Assassin* as a standalone title: one version was a combo pack which contained both DVD and Blu-ray copies of the 1980 classic in a fancy steelbook, the other version was a Blu-ray-only edition. The extra features are very different compared to the Criterion release, and to some they will be of much more interest than the more Japanese-focused Criterion set. Here we get two commentary tracks, one with Ric Meyers and Steve Watson, which is ok, and is more of an amiable chat than an informative experience. The second track, though, is an absolute delight, as we have the producer of the US film version, David Weisman, joined by the original US poster artist, Jim Evans, and his son Gibran, who is the English voice of Daigorō. This track is so fantastic it's worth double-dipping on this release, even if you already have the stellar Criterion version.
As if that wasn't enough of a draw on its own, there is also a fantastic video interview with Samuel L. Jackson, speaking about his love for Japanese Cinema and for samurai movies in particular. This was filmed in 2009, when Jackson was firmly entrenched working on his *Afro Samurai* series. It's about 13 minutes long and is pretty good fun.
Eureka also opted to include all six of the original trailers for the *Lone Wolf and Cub* movies, as well as the original theatrical trailer for *Shogun Assassin*.

As previously mentioned, this is now out of print, but comes around quite often in the UK on the second hand market. Expect to pay about £20 for the standalone Blu-ray and £30-£40 for the steelbook. CEX is a good starting point for both.

Back in 2009 Eureka did also put out the original *Lone Wolf and Cub* series in full in a DVD boxset, along with an extra disc that housed *Shogun Assassin*. This set tends to sell for so much money these days that I wouldn't recommend tracking it down. The discs are all bare bones in terms of extras, and the quality of the transfers is nowhere near as good as later Blu-ray restorations. This will cost you far more than the formidable Criterion Blu-ray set (or it's DVD counterpart) by a long shot.

7.5/10 for the Blu-ray release
6/10 for the old DVD set (and that would be 5/10 if the movies weren't all so great!)

Shogun Assassin 5 Movie Collection
AnimEigo
Region A Blu-ray (US Only)

This is essentially the same *Shogun Assassin* cut and extras found on the Eureka Blu-ray release, but with the other 4 movies in the series (if we're counting *Shogun Assassin* as the first two) to create a five movie boxset. These 4 movies go by their alternate US titles, which is a bit confusing, but they are essentially the same movies, just with different names and they ONLY come with English audio tracks. This set

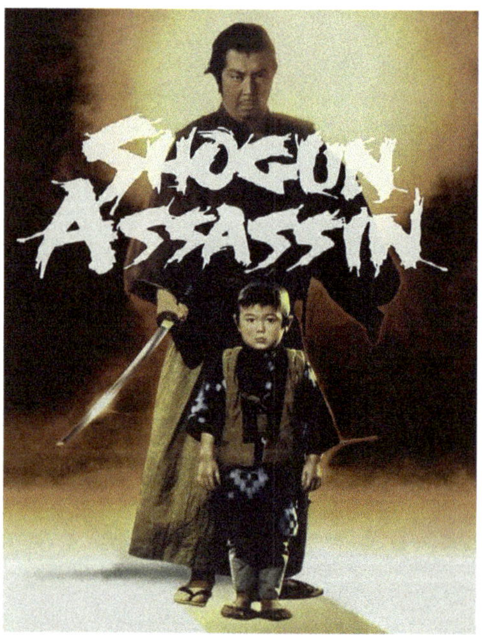

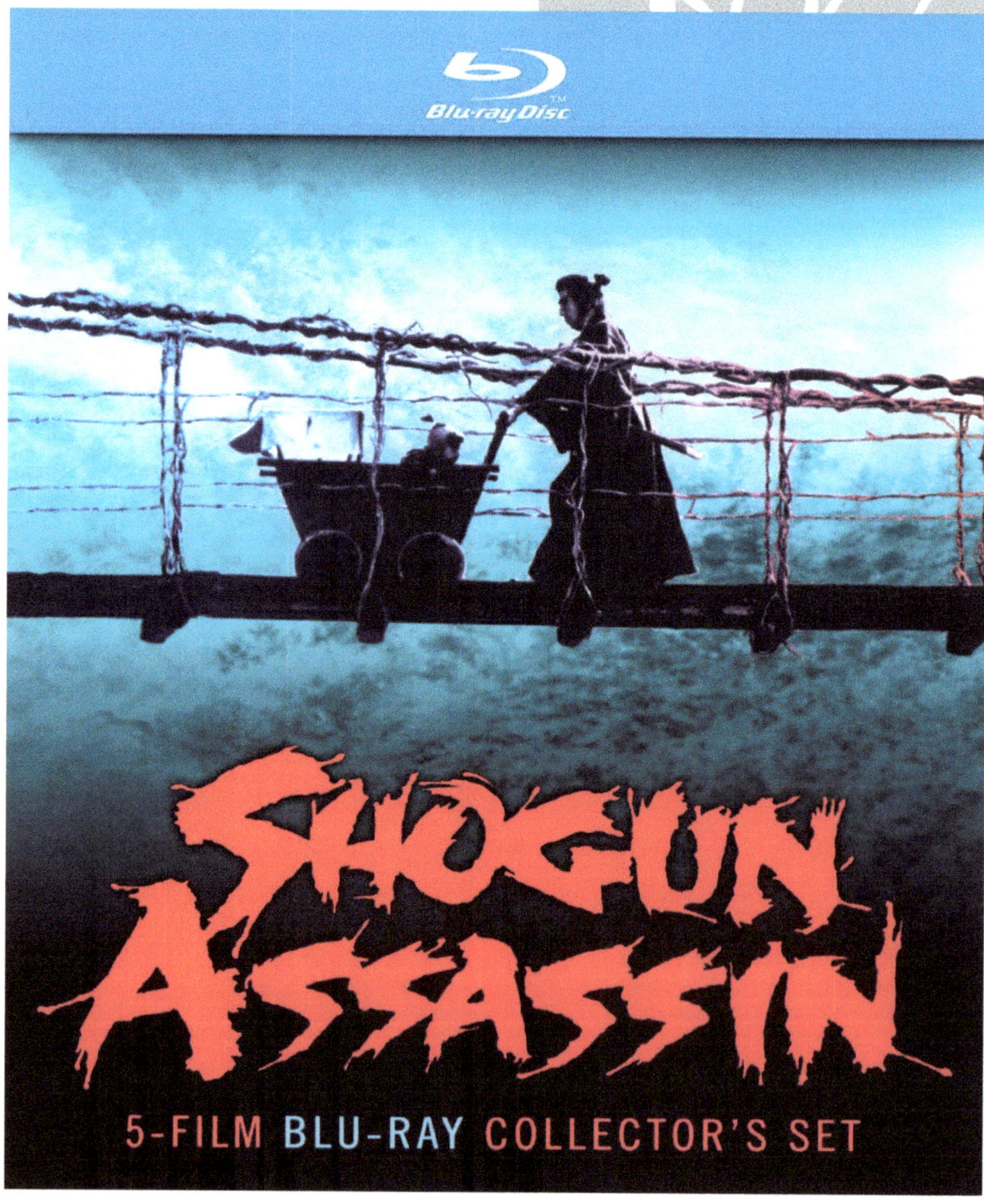

actually predates the Criterion release, as it came out in 2012. If you're expecting the same type of care and nuance in the audio dubs which was afforded *Shogun Assassin*, you will be sorely disappointed. I put this collection on the list for the sake of completion, but I can't in good conscience recommend the set to anyone other than those strange folks who flat out refuse to watch a movie with subtitles (which, if this is you, have a bloody word with yourself, mate: you're missing out on a whole lot of truly incredible cinema from around the world! Your brain is entirely capable of watching an image AND reading subtitles at the same time, I assure you!)

The set is, to my knowledge, still available stateside, though you'll obviously need a multi-region player to view the discs in the UK: they're all region A locked.

5/10 - Watching the English dubs of the rest of the series is a painful experience!

Shogun Assassin remains a curious anomaly where the recut, re-dubbed compilation of the first two movies stands as an entirely satisfying film experience in it's own right, and that voice-over has such a massive part to play in that.
It's really quite sad to watch the rest of the movies in English without it.

Lone Wolf and Cub (Book)
Arrow Video
163 Pages

Tom Mes wrote this in-depth, stunning examination of the *Lone Wolf and Cub* series for Arrow Video back in 2018. It's still in print and often available for just £5 in the Arrow sales, which seems to happen every few months. It's a truly wonderful book, my favourite of Tom Mes's many publications examining various periods and key figures in Japanese and Asian cinema.

It provides a amazing overview of the whole series, the stars and filmmakers behind the movies, the original manga source material, as well as all the various tributes, references and spin-offs that have come about over the years. The book gives a wonderful overview of not just the time period when the films themselves are set, but also the historical landscape of Japanese cinema at the time when the movies were made. Tom Mes is a legend, highly knowledgeable and a far, far better writer than my clumsy efforts here to praise him can convey. Highly, highly recommended.

Oh, and also worth mentioning: the beautiful cover art for the book is by the insanely talented Kung Fu Bob O'Brien.

The Bounty Hunter Trilogy
Radiance Films
Region Free Blu-ray (UK & US)
Releasing March 2024

Lastly, for those who fall in love with lead actor Tomisaburo Wakayama (really, how could you not?!) and are keen to see more movies where he takes the lead role, Radiance Films released a boxset of the 3 Bounty Hunter movies he created just before he went on to make the *Lone Wolf And Cub* series.
These movies - *Killer's Mission* (1969), *The Fort of Death* (1969) and *Eight Men to Kill* (1972) - are all hella good fun. They're very James Bond inspired, with great soundtracks.

I've opted not to include the old, out of print DVD boxset of the full series that Eureka put out in the UK, or any of the other individual releases (on DVD or VHS) of the original *Lone Wolf and Cub* standalone movies, because that's a deep rabbit hole that will prove frustrating to jump into, as many of these can be very hard to track down and, anyway, are of most interest only to the real die-hard, gotta-catch-them-all collectors.

The *Lone Wolf and Cub* films look better than they ever have before on Blu-ray disc, are easily available stateside and here in the UK, and the glorious Criterion set remains permanently placed within my top five physical media releases of all time. It's a stunning boxset for a truly exceptional series of movies.

We can only hope that in the near future we also get a decent Blu-ray release of all five of the *Wicked Priest* series of movies, which Wakayama also headlined. They're as different from the *Lone Wolf and Cub* movies as his brother's bonkers *Hanzo The Razor* films are to Katsu's more well known *Zatoichi* series of films.

Whilst we're talking Zatoichi, it's worth also noting that Wakayama appeared in a couple of those films too, playing the brother of Zatoichi, alongside his real life brother, in the second feature, *The Tale of Zatoichi Continues* - and he returned to play an entirely unrelated character in the sixth feature, *Zatoichi and the Chest of Gold*. Criterion's *Zatoichi* boxset is a masterpiece of a release, but that's one for a different issue, if we ever get to turn our attention to Katsu's blind masseuse/master swordsman someday...

Thanks for joining me for this quick walk through Ogami Ittō's journey on Blu-ray. For more movie reviews, physical media unboxings, *Imaginator* magazine showcases and much more Asian Cinema chat, you can find me still walking the path to hell over on YouTube...

www.youtube.com/thefanaticaldragon

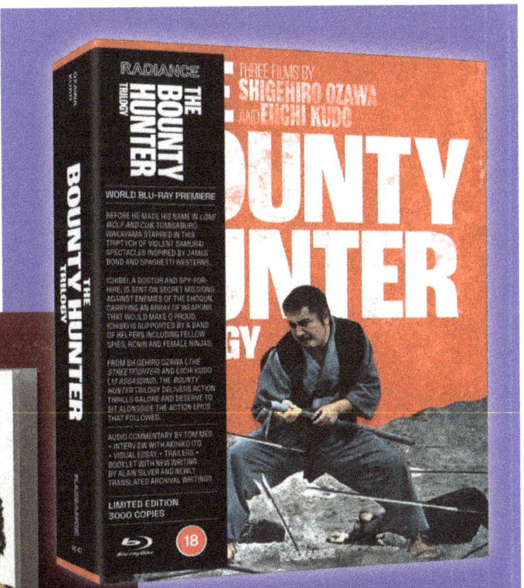

He's not playing Ogami Ittō here, but Tomisaburo Wakayama is definitely always worth watching!

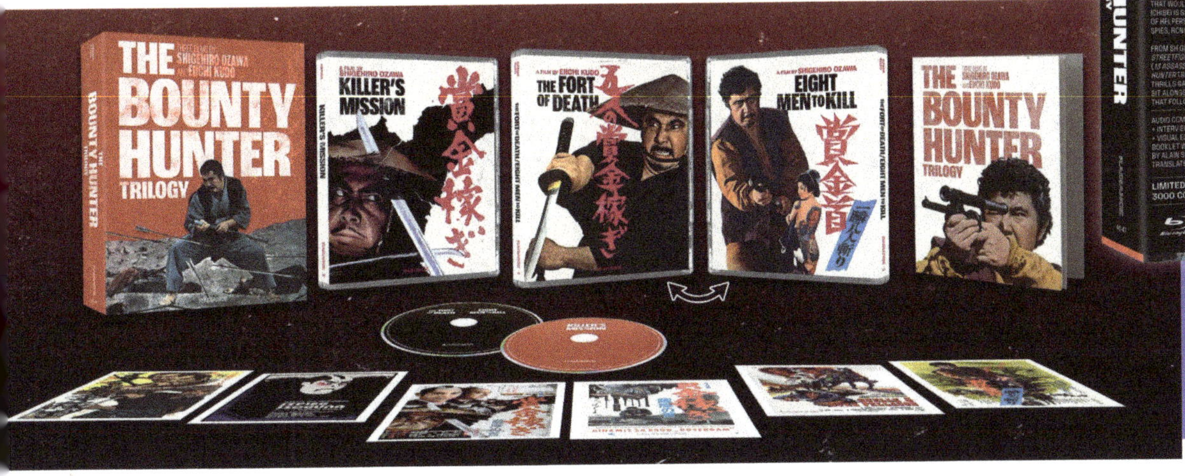

LIGHT AND SHADOW

The graphic storytelling of Russell Fox

Listen, people, **Ken Miller** is an unapologetic cheerleader for the exquisite illustrations produced by comic book artist **Russell Fox**. Whenever he gets an excuse to enthuse about this guy's work, well, Ken jumps at the chance - because this will hopefully mean more people will discover Russell's work and then the world will become a better place. Ken claims that this is a scientific fact!

Imaginator #8 was a Folk Horror Special Edition and it included a preview of Russell's in-progress folk horror graphic novel *A VVitch. Imaginator* #9 included an update feature, where Russell shared some new *A VVitch* artwork. And now this issue of *Imaginator* just so happens to include the *Shogun Assassin* art that Russell originally produced for *Film Frenzy* magazine... thus giving Ken an excuse to wax lyrical about Russell's illustrative take on the *Lone Wolf and Cub* characters. Plus - Ken has decided to share here even more of Mr. Fox's creations for us to scrutinise! Enjoy...

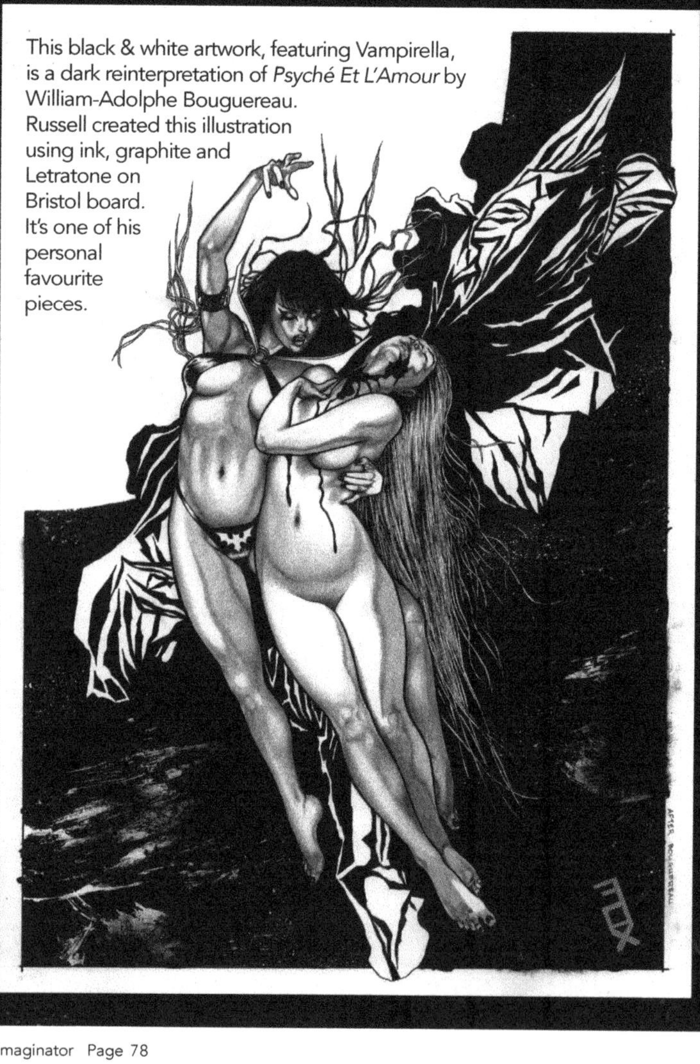

This black & white artwork, featuring Vampirella, is a dark reinterpretation of *Psyché Et L'Amour* by William-Adolphe Bouguereau. Russell created this illustration using ink, graphite and Letratone on Bristol board. It's one of his personal favourite pieces.

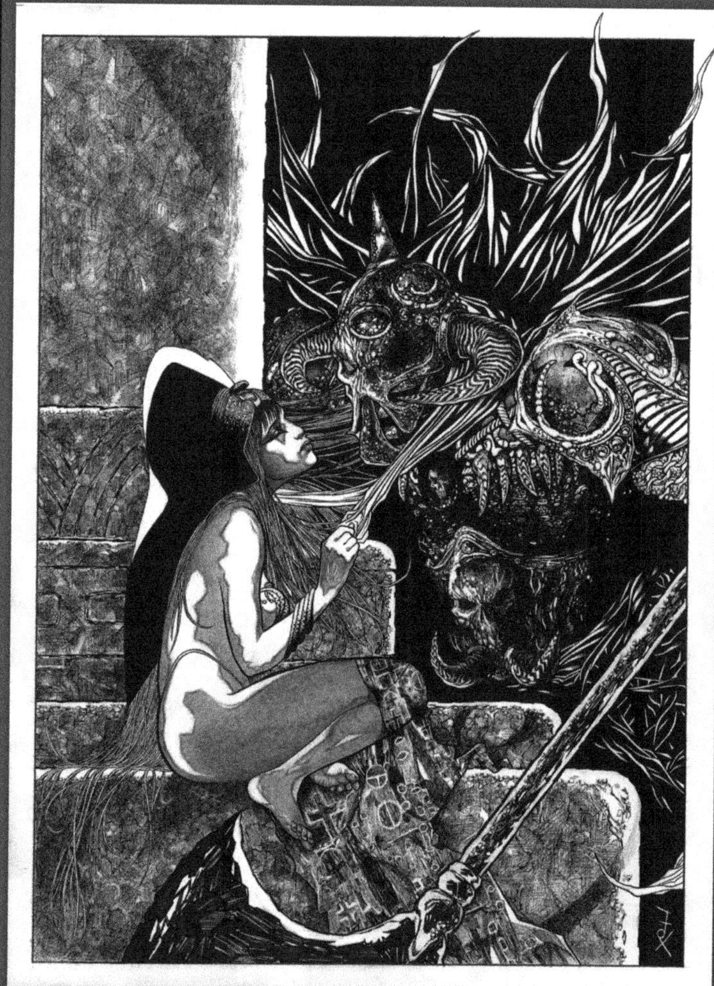

This beauty was inspired by two Frazetta works (*Egyptian Queen* and *Death Dealer*), plus *La Belle Dame Sans Mercy* by J W Waterhouse, with a little added design inspiration from Gustav Klimt. This was originally intended to be a cover for the *Death Dealer* comic book series published by Opus.

This awesome pin-up art appeared in issue 131 of *Blade of the Immortal* from Dark Horse.

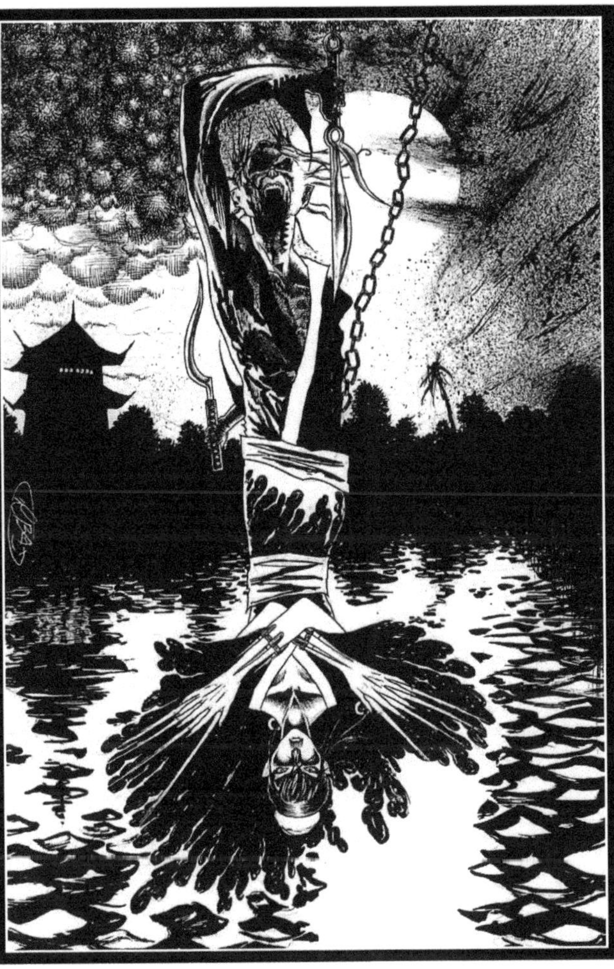

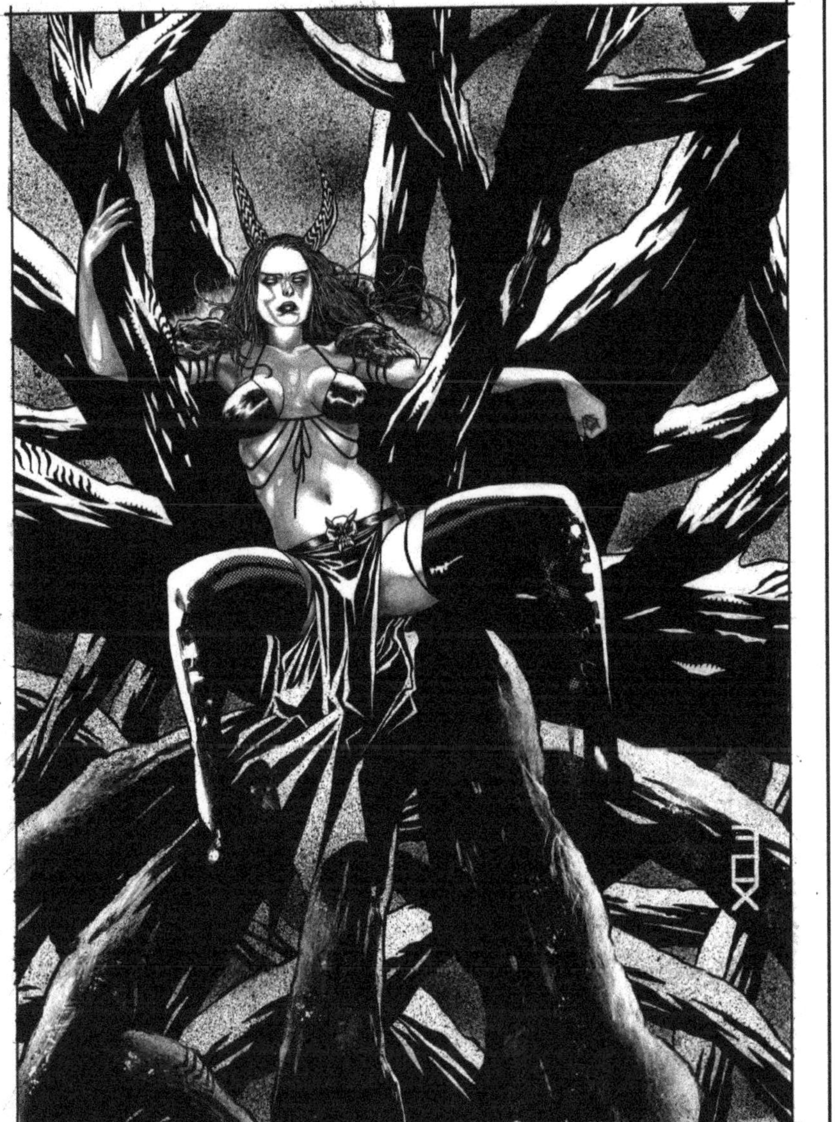

Black & white cover art for *Purgatori* issue 2 (2021), published by Dynamite Entertainment. Art is a mix of ink, graphite and Letratone on Bristol board.

Detail from a panel from *The Crannog of the Black Loch* story that will be featured in Russell's folk horror anthology graphic novel: *A VVitch*.

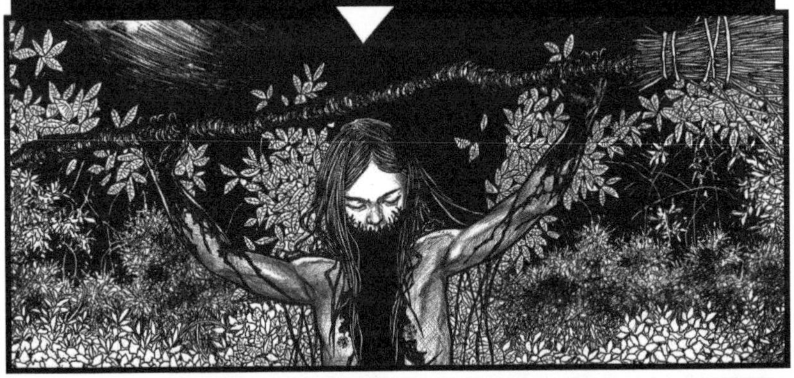

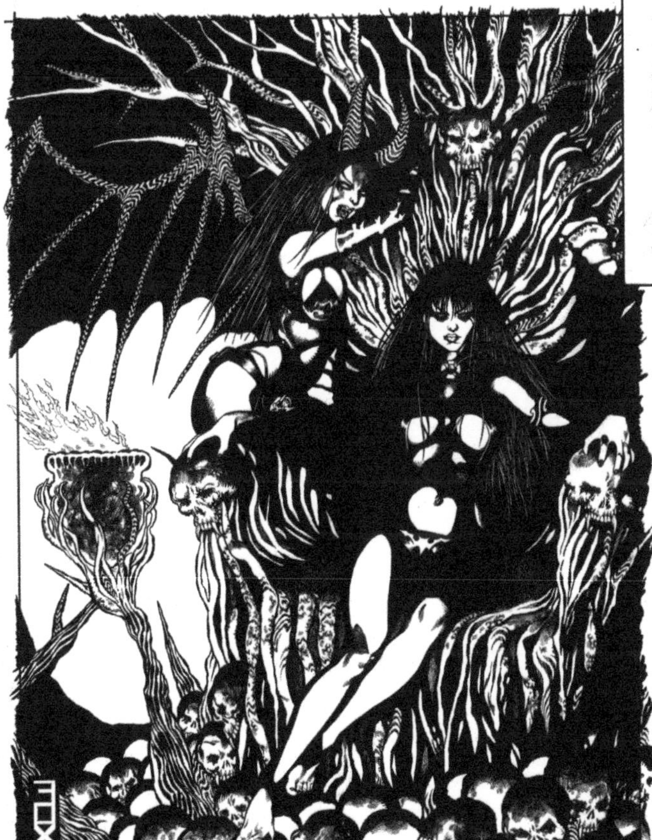

Russell's black & white cover art for *Vampirella vs Purgatori* issue 3 (2021), which was published by Dynamite Entertainment. Russell applied additional ink work after publication. Drawn in ink on A3 Bristol board.

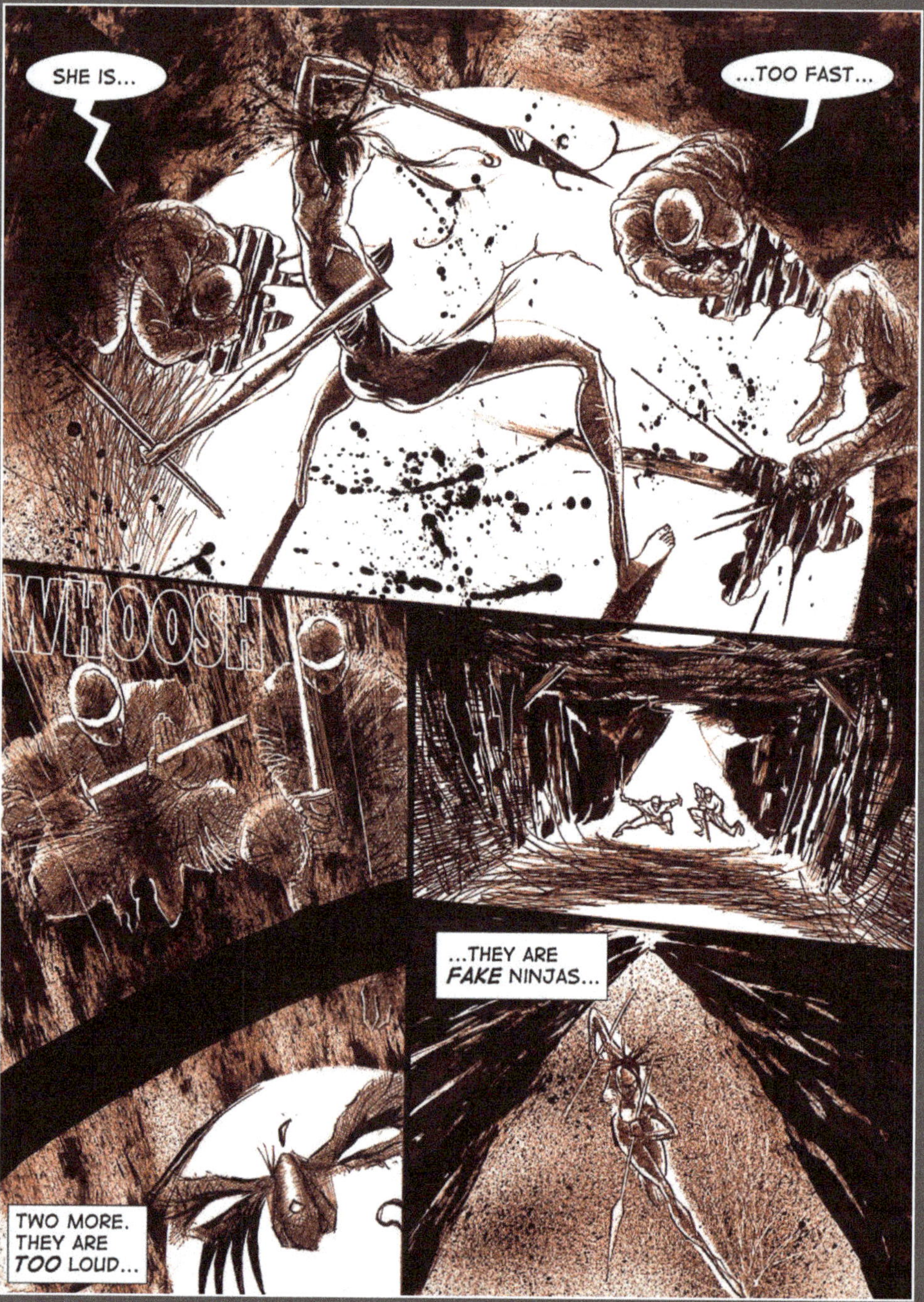

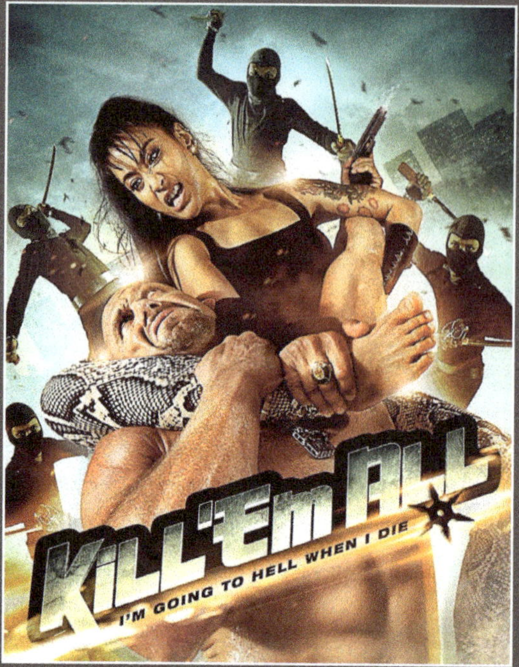

Russell drew several pages of dynamic comic art to illustrate an action sequence featured in the spec script for a proposed movie called *Kill 'Em All*. These pages of comic art, which showed the weapon-wielding lead female protagonist battling ninja opponents, were used by one of the producers to help sell-in the action project to Epic Pictures Group.

And it worked!

Epic Pictures liked the idea of this film, and they financed the production, which was shot by director Raimund Huber in Thailand. It was released in 2012.

Kill 'Em All starred the great Gordon Liu (*The 36th Chamber of Shaolin, Legendary Weapons of China, Kill Bill*) and the equally great Joe Lewis (*Jaguar Lives!, Force: Five*). This low budget film, punching way above its weight, also boasts mobs of ninjas, masked maniacs, assassins, explosions, and LOTS and LOTS of exciting martial arts fighting!

Details from two panels that occur near the end of the *A Witch* anthology story *The Crannog of the Black Loch*. Intestines will get spilled...

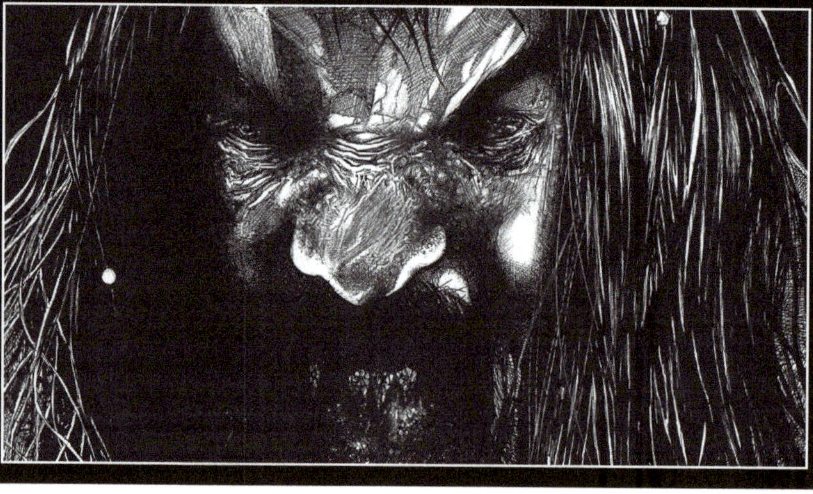

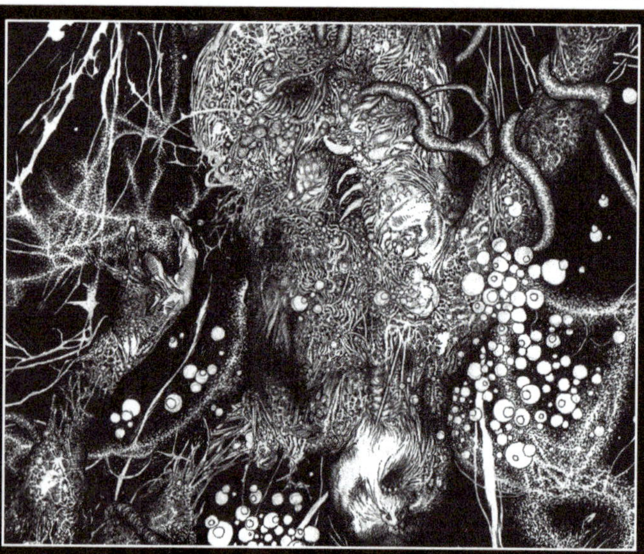

Okay, the reason another version of Russell's amazing *Shogun Assassin* pic is being included here is because it looks sublime in black and white! It is wonderful how this drawing brilliantly encompasses both the vibes of the film AND the original b&w manga series.

***Imaginator* has asked Russell to explain a little about the process he used to create his amazing colour illustration on page 50.**

Over to you, Mr. Fox...

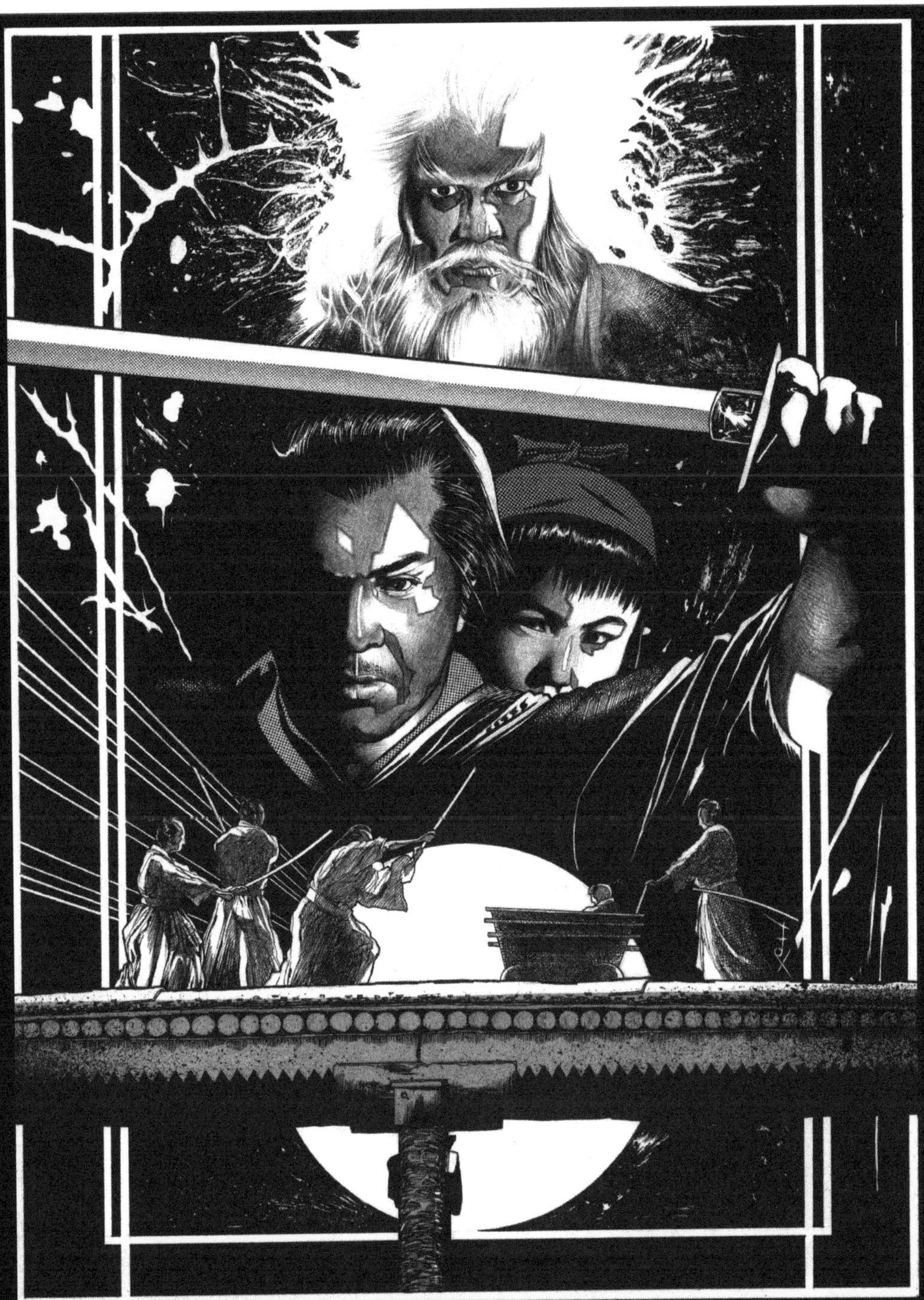

Hello, my name's Russell Fox and I'm the artist + writer of forthcoming horror anthology graphic novel *A VVitch*, and artist of the full colour *Shogun Assassin* illustration on page 50.

As a fan of Kazuo Koike and Goseki Kojima's classic manga *Lone Wolf & Cub*, as well as the six classic "Babycart" films, I was thrilled when asked to produce the *Shogun Assassin* illustration that first appeared in the *Eastern Heroes Film Frenzy* Shogun Assassin Special Edition magazine.

My aim was to make an 80s film poster-style piece, which I created traditionally - ink + graphite on Bristol board - before adding minimal colour digitally. I wanted to keep the colour primarily muted and earthy, and then added some garish, almost-neon, borders to contrast and reinforce that of-the-era look. I also picked up some old Letratone transfer dot shading online, which also lent towards a slightly retro effect with the art.

While the main figures of Ogami Itto (Tomisaburo Wakayama), Daigorō (Akihiro Tomikawa) and Yagyu Retsudo (Yūnosuke Ito) are based on the actor's likenesses of the characters, the smaller figures on the bridge pay homage to Kojima's work from the manga.

Retsudo looms large over the composition as he does throughout the story's narrative, kept at bay by Itto's blade. The colours of the border bleed into the bridge confrontation, representing not only the duel at dawn portrayed here but also the blood and hellfire of the River Styx. Plus, it just looks cool.

Goseki Kojima's groundbreaking work on *Lone Wolf & Cub* has long been an influence on my own work. A master of his craft, able to generate drama with the merest hint of an expression or pose, or with the subtle rendering of rolling, moody storm clouds, to accentuate both important foreground moments and seemingly unimportant background details alike. Kazuo Koike's rich, unhurried scripts gave Kojima's art plenty of room to breathe, and eschewed the typical BANG-BANG-BANG momentum of western comic books. Again, something I've taken to heart in my own work.

Some of Russell's previous published work includes the Judge Anderson story *Baby Talk* - this was originally featured in the *Judge Dredd Mega Special* in 1992 and then was reprinted as one of the stories included in the *Judge Anderson: The Psi Files Volume 04* trade paperback. Russell drew *The Paranormals* - a supernatural horror/crime noir comic book written by Diallo Jackson, *Humans vs Zombies* - a promo comic that was released with the movie of the same name when it came out on DVD, he produced the illustrations (coloured by Robert Nugent) for the animated comic music video for the (now disbanded) group Dead By Midnight, and Russell has illustrated cover art for *Deathgasm* - a comic book published by OPUS comics.

Currently Russell is continuing to focus on his creator-owned folk horror anthology graphic novel project: *A VVitch*. The finished volume will contain three stories, and Russell is, as we speak, working on the third tale, titled *They Wailed The Mourning*. The other two yarns, *Noche de la Bruja* and *The Crannog of the Black Loch*, are completed.

Everyone at *Imaginator* is eager to see the finished *A VVitch* graphic novel. It is sure to be a starkly beautiful & brooding b&w folk horror extravaganza!

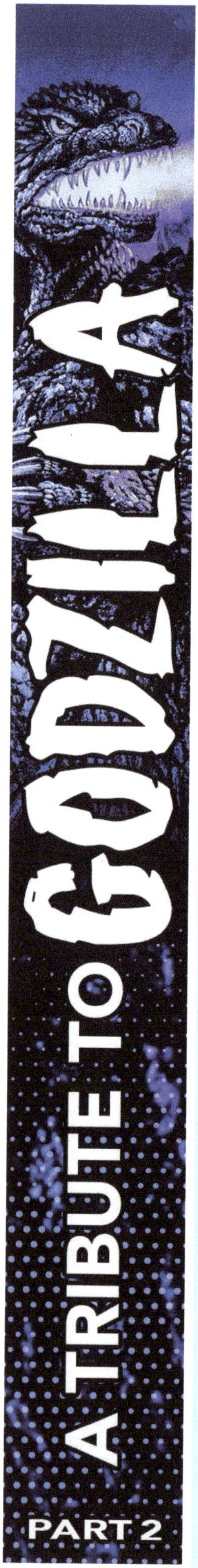

RUSSELL SHAW PRAISES...

GODZILLA MINUS ONE

Versatile, energetic and intuitive actor **Russell Shaw**, who was interviewed in issue 8 of *Imaginator*, where he talked about playing a time-travelling, demon-seeking spellcaster in the period horror film *Witch* (2024), has credits that include *Adventure Boyz* (2019), *The Lockdown Hauntings* (2021), and *Escape* (2023) - and some of his upcoming releases are: the cool-sounding genre productions *Jitters* and *Bone Keeper*.

Russell was greatly impressed by ***Godzilla Minus One*** (2023). He tells us now what he likes so much about it...

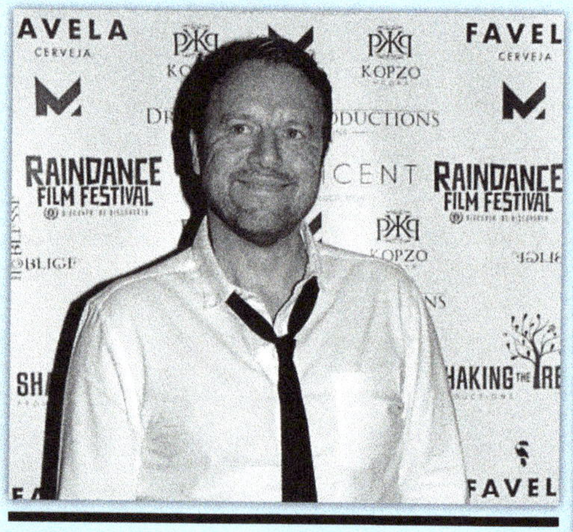

This movie had bags of soul. Out of all the Godzilla films, *Godzilla Minus One* completely hooked me. Unlike some of its predecessors, namely the US productions, it didn't rely on big-name stars or a massive budget - instead, it returned to its Japanese roots with a gripping story and outstanding performances.

The first reveal of the monster was unforgettable - I'd seen the trailer, but nothing compared to that moment on screen. I only wish I'd experienced it in the cinema; I can't remember the last time I felt so excited about a film's release. What struck me most was that this wasn't the usual "Godzilla destroys everything" storyline - it carried both heart and menace in equal measure. Naoki Satô's score was exceptional, beautifully heightening the tension and atmosphere.

A truly impressive film - I'll definitely be watching it again. Huge congratulations to everyone involved.

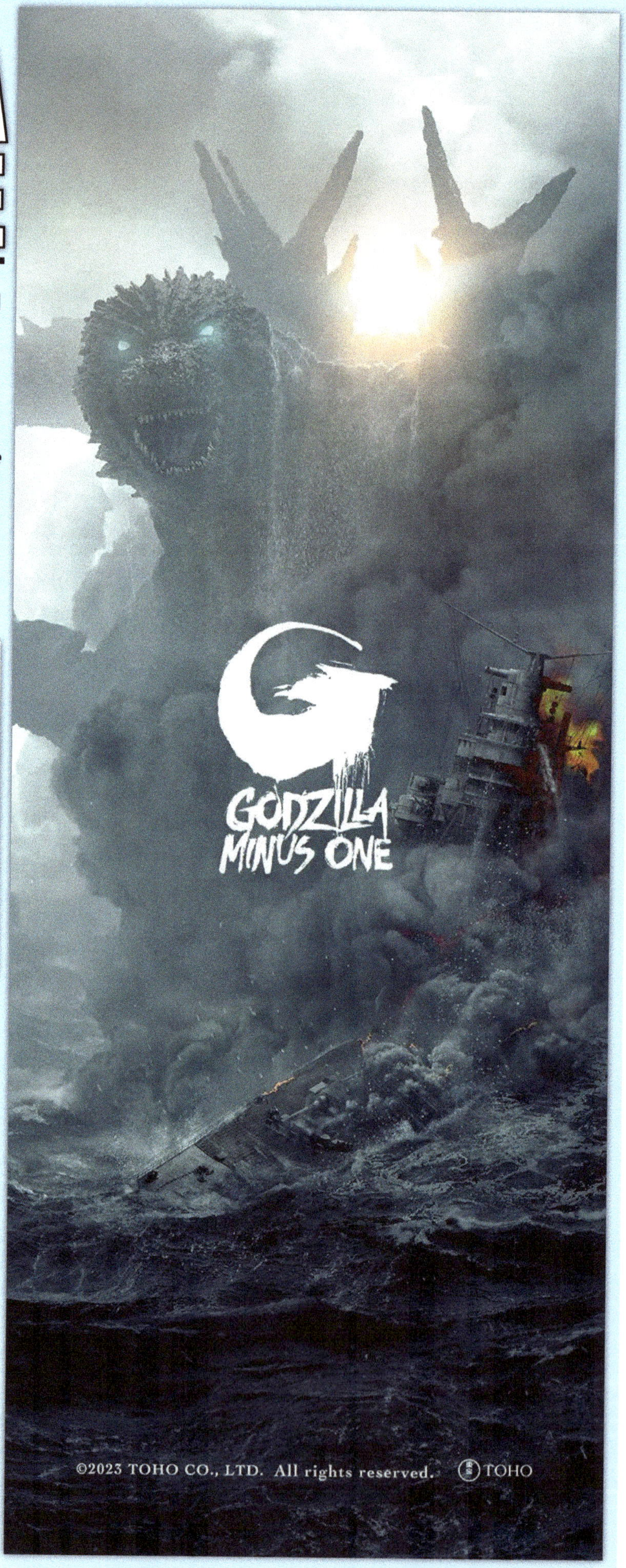

JOE CASTRO PRAISES...

GODZILLA VS. THE SMOG MONSTER

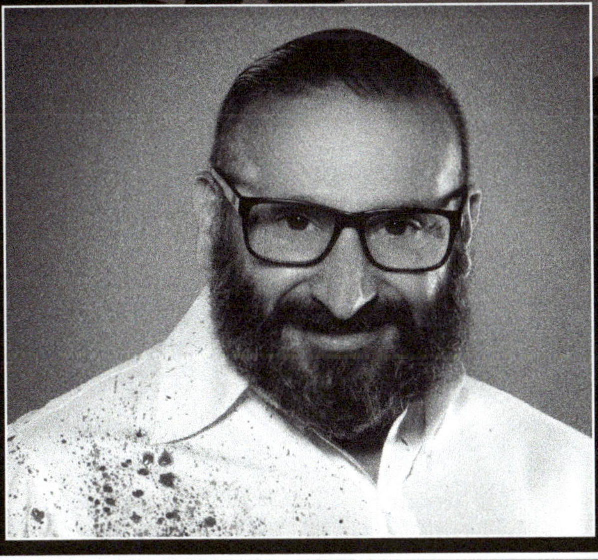

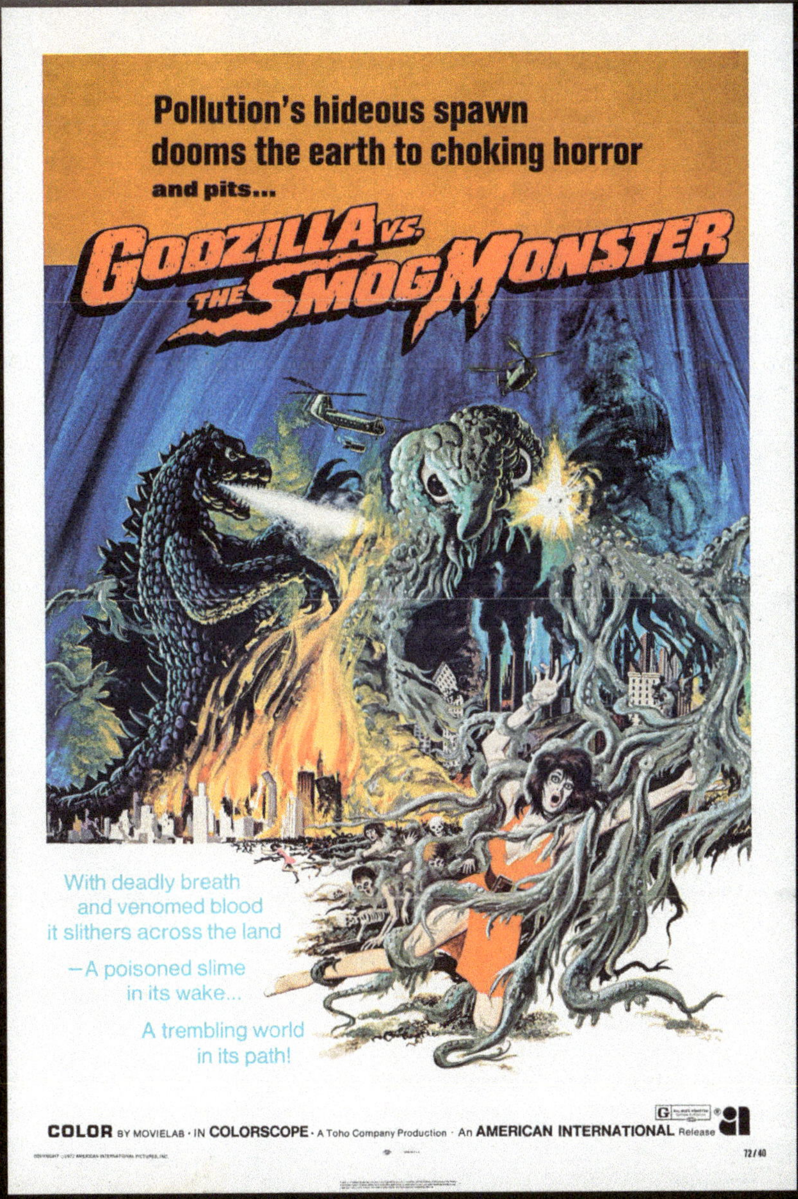

Joe Castro is a special effects artist who has created numerous great-looking practical (often very splattery) FX gems for many low budget horror and exploitation underground genre films, including *Blood Feast 2: All U Can Eat* (2002), *Bonehill Road* (2017), *Big Freaking Rat* (2020), *Clowning* (2022), *Pig Killer* (2022), *The Beast Comes at Midnight* (2023), *H. P. Lovecraft's the Old Ones* (2024), and *Infernal* (2025).

Joe often writes and directs the films he provides the special effects for, most notably the *Terror Toons* series of films, plus releases such as *The Jackhammer Massacre* (2004) and *The Summer of Massacre* (2012).

Joe reveals what key inspiration motivated him to become a practical movie effects artist: yes... it was all because of a Godzilla movie! Read on...

When I was seven years old, my father sat me in front of the television and said, "Watch this son. You will love it." My father was always my biggest supporter and he knew that I liked dragons and dinosaurs. This would be the first time I would ever watch a movie on my own. It was a Saturday afternoon. It was 1 PM and the creature feature was coming on TV...

The movie was... **Godzilla vs. the Smog Monster** (1971), aka Godzilla vs. Hedorah.

When the movie was over, I knew that I wanted to create special effects for movies. I asked my dad how did they make the monsters like that? So we watched the end credits roll up together - and he showed me where it said 'special effects' in the credits - and he said, "Son, that's the special effects - that's how they make the monsters."

And so began my adventures in filmmaking and special effects... all because of Godzilla.

MARK DUFFIELD PRAISES...

MONSTERS FROM AN UNKNOWN PLANET

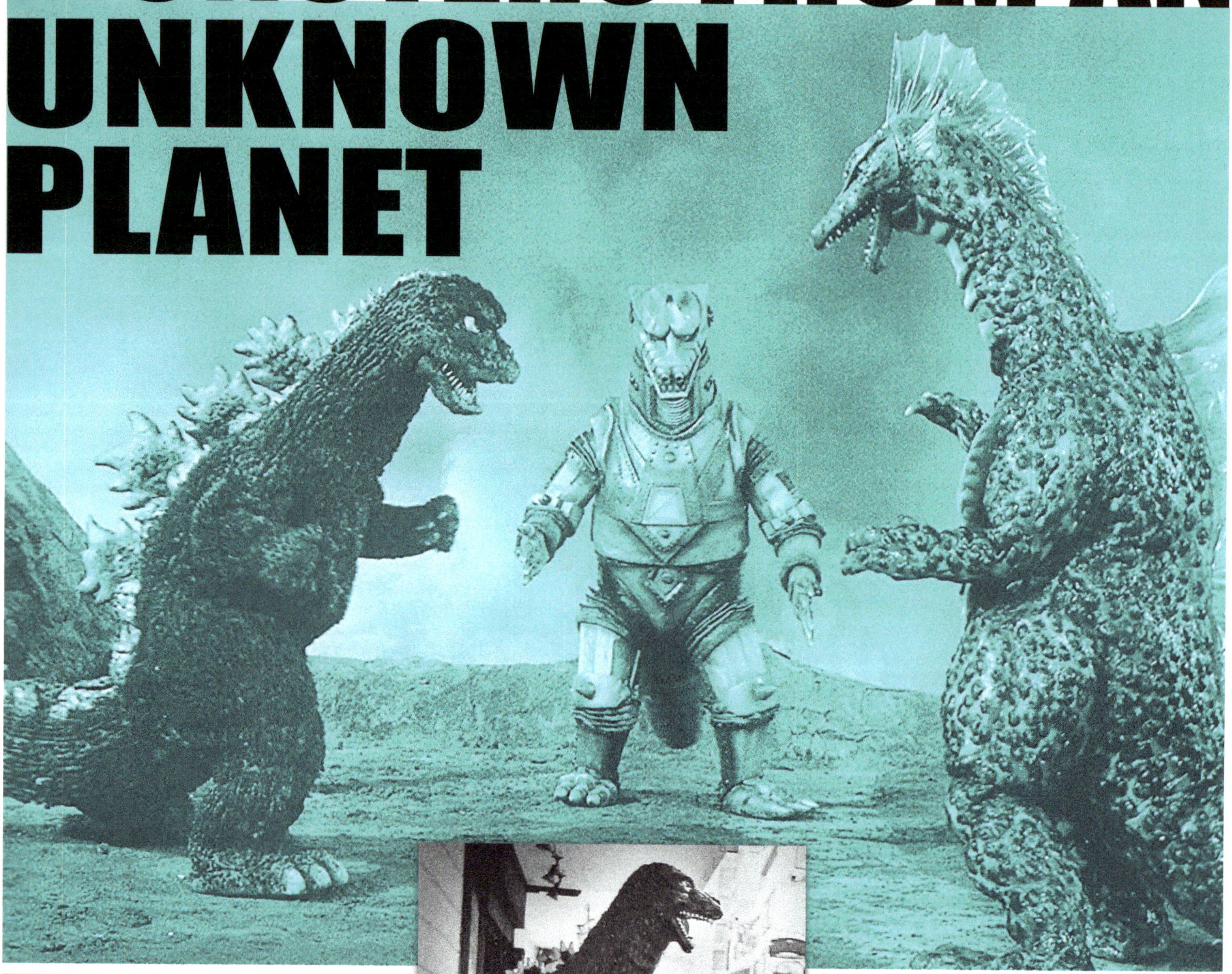

Talented director **Mark Duffield** was a cinematographer on feature films including *Butterfly Man* (2002) before going on to write, direct and act as cinematographer on the enjoyable Thai-based supernatural movie *Ghost of Mae Nak* (2005). He also wrote, directed, produced, edited, art directed and did the cinematography for the fine Victorian-set Gothic horror film *Demon* (2012).

Ken Miller asks Mark about the time he went with his friend Steve to the cinema, back in the 1970s, to see ***Monsters from an Unknown Planet***, aka ***Terror of Mechagodzilla***...

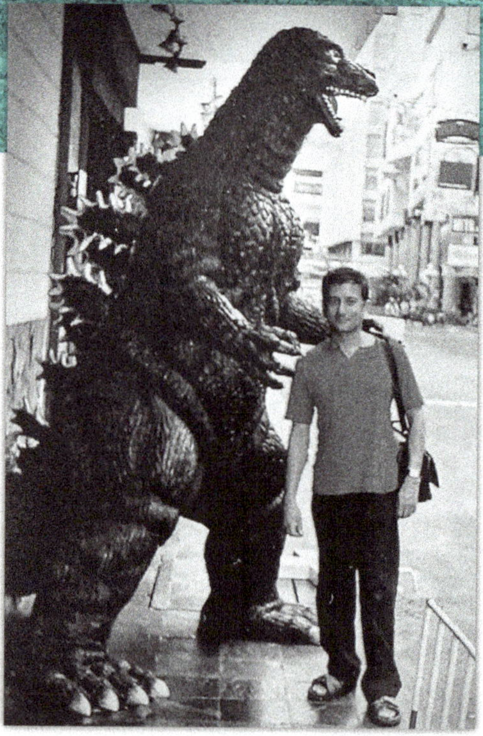

You saw *Monsters from an Unknown Planet* when it was originally released in UK cinemas back in the 70s. Was this the first Godzilla film you'd ever seen?

Yes, *Monsters from an Unknown Planet* was the first Godzilla film I saw at the cinema. My closest friend Steve was a massive Godzilla fan, so we both went to see the film. What struck me was the opening credits that went straight into the Godzilla vs Mechagodzilla fight action and with freeze frames for the credits. It was very cinematic; it was very Spaghetti Western. And then to add to it was the great music - which I didn't realise back then, but it was the original theme. It's a great piece of music equivalent to the *Jaws*, *Star Wars* or *Indiana Jones* themes. I cheered in the cinema when I heard it playing in the excellent *Godzilla Minus One*. The other aspect I remember of the beginning of the film, especially when the drama took place, was it was like the 1960's James Bond films in its style. Plus, the Japanese characters and locations made it different. And it was filmed in 2:40-1 cinemascope, which gave it the BIG movie look.

I was trying to figure out why it was called *Monsters from an Unknown Planet* (June 1976 UK cinema release) and not have Godzilla in the title. It may be to do with playing off the success of John Dark's *The Land that Time Forgot* (1974) and *At the Earth's Core* (August 1976 cinema release) and to promote it as a giant monster movie rather than a Godzilla film, since the awareness of Godzilla may have been limited in the UK.

My early memories of discovering Godzilla was through Forrest J Ackerman's *Famous Monsters* magazine, which often featured some great Godzilla images. No. 114 (March 1975) was a 100-page special issue featuring ALL OF JAPAN'S MONSTERS! But it was still all a bit of a mystery back then. There was no Blu-ray, DVDs, internet or social media to freely watch or research these films (or any other film). Sometimes you would just see one striking image printed that would create a lot of mystery and intrigue - that's all you had to go on for a good few years before the arrival of other magazines - *Starlog, Starburst, Cinefantastique* - and official VHS tape releases. But, there was the amazing 1972 Aurora "glow in the dark" Godzilla model kit (1/6000 scale) - approximately 10 inches tall. My friend Steve had both "glow in the dark" and normal versions that we both marvelled at.

I was also aware of the Godzilla Super 8mm films that were available back then. These were 12 minute edits of the film that you could project at home. But at the time I was keen to get all the *Planet of the Apes* films and some of the Hammer films - I bought *Revenge of Frankenstein* (in colour), *Frankenstein Must Be Destroyed* and *Taste the Blood of Dracula* (both black & white) that were available (which I still have).

This movie was the last Godzilla film made during the Showa era. It's a fun, kid-friendly flick that includes, of course, the heroic Godzilla, plus the dino-like, aquatic kaiju Titanosaurus, some ape-aliens, and the return of Mechagodzilla (who'd first appeared in *Godzilla vs. Mechagodzilla*, aka *Godzilla vs. Bionic Monster*): what was *Monsters from an Unknown Planet* like to see on the big screen?

I didn't see it as a 'kids' film back then. It still looked cool. And the tone is very adult. It's filmed as a serious movie with 'credible' acting and most of the cast, from what I remember, are adults. The film looked spectacular back then. The only comparison we had was *Doctor Who* - especially the men-in-monster suits. And the model work of the cities was on a grander scale to what *Thunderbirds* or even *Captain Scarlet and the Mysterons* did. Plus, in the cinema, there was the amplified sound. I was very impressed by the music and all the loud sound effects. TV still had that mono 'radio' type sound in the 70s and was still 4:3 square format. Godzilla was in cinemascope and loud!

You liked the film so much you asked the cinema for the poster, which you still own, I believe. The UK poster includes the line: 'From a black hole... they came to conquer Earth...!' This impactful poster features Godzilla, Mechagodzilla, Titanosaurus, UFOs, a whirlwind, and various explosions! Did you ever have the poster stuck up on your wall?

Back then, I discovered that if I went to the cinema on a Thursday night and waited outside for when they did the poster change-over, you could ask the 'poster-guy' for the poster. They always obliged. I wasn't even a teenager then, but I would get on the bus at around 9pm to go into town and catch the poster-guy doing the display case change over at the cinema. My growing passion for films, especially horror and giant monsters, outweighed the risks.
And yes, the poster was on my bedroom

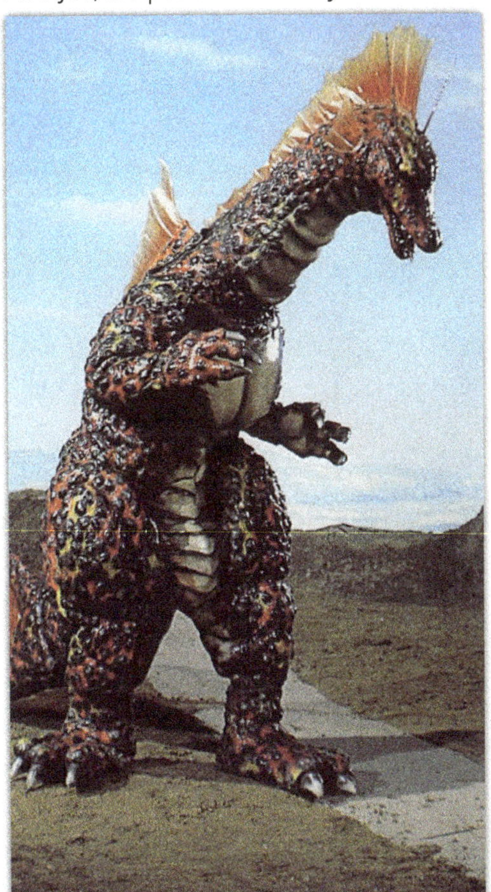

wall for a while. There was a regular turnaround as I collected several posters back then - *Planet of the Apes* films especially. Luckily, I was good at handling and looking after them - and I still have them. *Young Frankenstein* was my first quad poster I got from the cinema, which involved my first late night bus trip into town and back.

Though suitmation monsters are not to everyone's taste, Toho's pantheon of kaiju are still well loved by hordes of fans around the world. What do you think are the elements that make these tokusatsu monster movies so perennially popular?

I would say the tokusatsu monster movies have a tangible feel about them. We know it's a man-in-a-suit but at the same time there's something believable about it - maybe because it's all done for real as floor effects. And there's always an appeal about the model work - and then you add on the destruction aspect.
Alien (1979) had a man-in-a-suit, but it still holds up brilliantly.
Perhaps the man-in-a-suit costume taps also into our psyche of wanting to dress up and transform?

Finally, picture this: you need to extol the virtues of *Monsters from an Unknown Planet* to a suitmation film newbie. Go..!

I'd say, if you want to see a Godzilla versus giant monsters movie in the classic man-in-a-suit sense, then check out *Monsters from an Unknown Planet*. See it for what it is and the time it was made at. They are well made films, filmed in true cinemascope, with credible 'genre' acting - and the stories hold up - after all, it is science fiction. As far as I know, there are 15 Showa Godzilla films for you to explore and go on an intriguing journey featuring giant monsters. If you get a chance, see them on a BIG screen - they have a certain surreal quality about them that makes them unique.

A final bit of trivia, about 10 years ago Paul Mason, a Hollywood producer, contacted me about remaking my Thai film *Ghost of Mae Nak* (the photo of me with Godzilla is in Bangkok when I was researching for locations). Anyway, what I discovered was that Paul had written, along with Bruce Howard, the English translation for *King Kong vs. Godzilla* (1963).

Now, when I think of Godzilla, I automatically think of my friend Steve Whittaker, who was a massive Showa Godzilla and giant monsters fan, and he got me interested too. He collected a variety of Japanese monster models, had several original film posters and most of the DVD/Blu-ray films. Sadly, he passed away suddenly in December 2023, which is why I responded to this article as a tribute to Steve.

THE MISSING MONSTER FROM GODZILLA VS. KONG

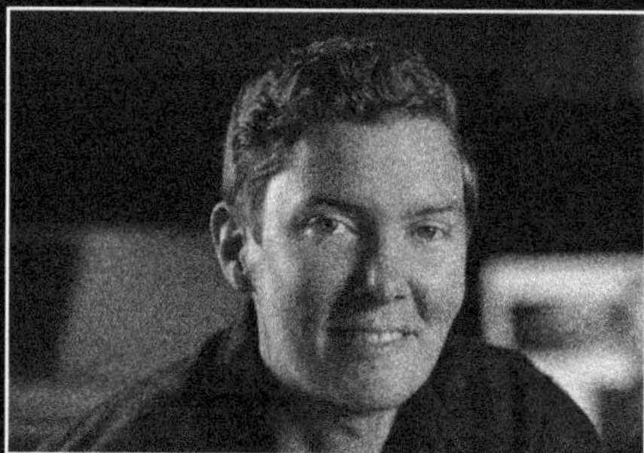

Imaginator's Creature Feature Special Edition included an enjoyable interview with the extraordinarily talented Hollywood concept designer Ken Barthelmey, who spoke about a huge creature he conceptualised whilst working on *Godzilla vs. Kong*. This monstrous beast was called Shimidah, and it didn't make it into the final film! So **Ken Miller** chats with **Ken Barthelmey** again, to discover more details about the kaiju-critter known as Shimidah...

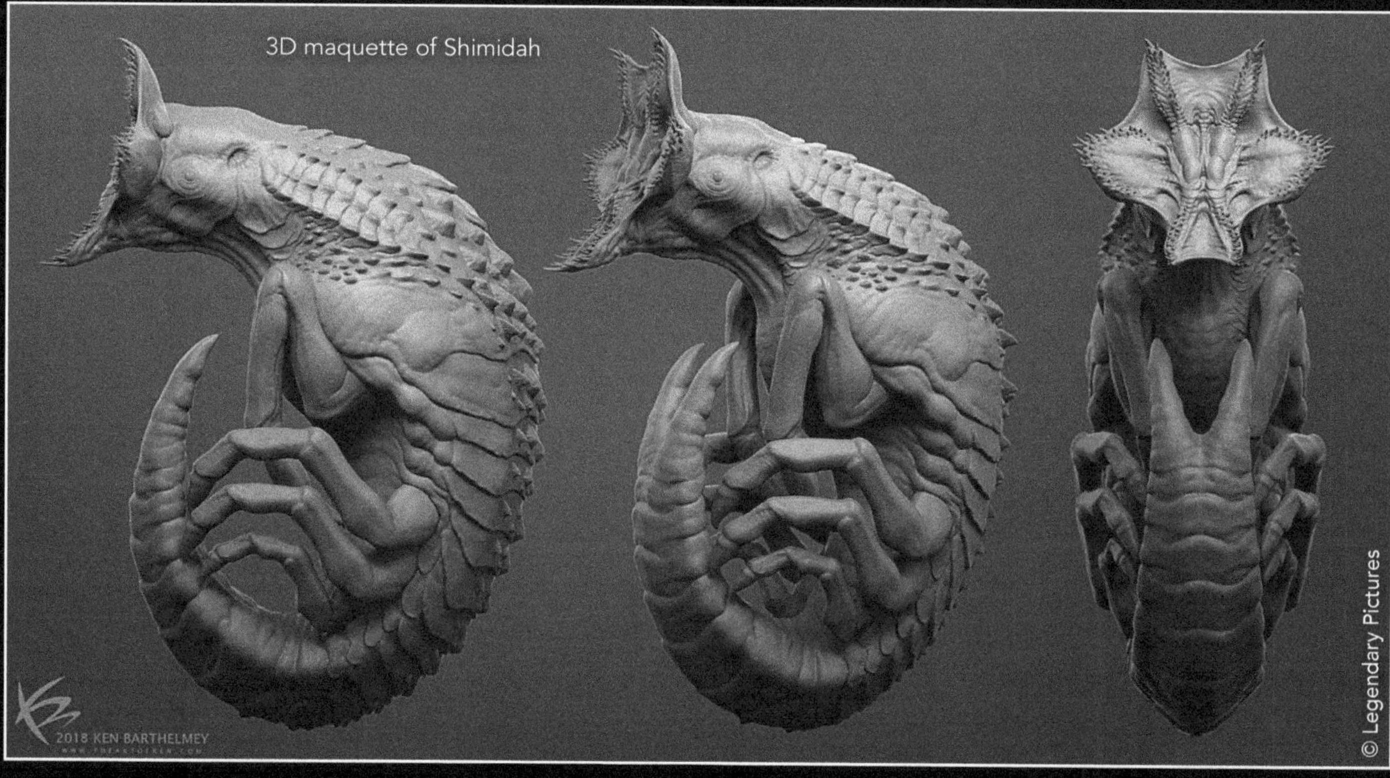

3D maquette of Shimidah

Was Shimidah the first creature you were asked to design when you joined the *Godzilla vs. Kong* production?

I was part of a design team at Amalgamated Dynamics, Inc., which included Bryan Wynia, Justice Joseph and later Xander Smith. Each of us was assigned one creature to design. Shimidah was assigned to me. Although Shimidah didn't end up in the film, ironically, it was the first design that got approved by the director, so I got to work on an additional design that we later called "Rock Critter". This creature had no official name, so we just referred to it that way. Later, artist Xander Smith came on board and did a 3d model based on my designs. The Rock Critters had a brief moment in the film, and were later reused in the Apple TV series *Monarch: Legacy of Monsters*.

You did various Shimidah designs in which you explored creating different types of clawed arms for the monster. I really like the big, almost flipper-like clawed arms you gave Shimidah in Version 2 of the design. So I'd like to know which of the different clawed arm

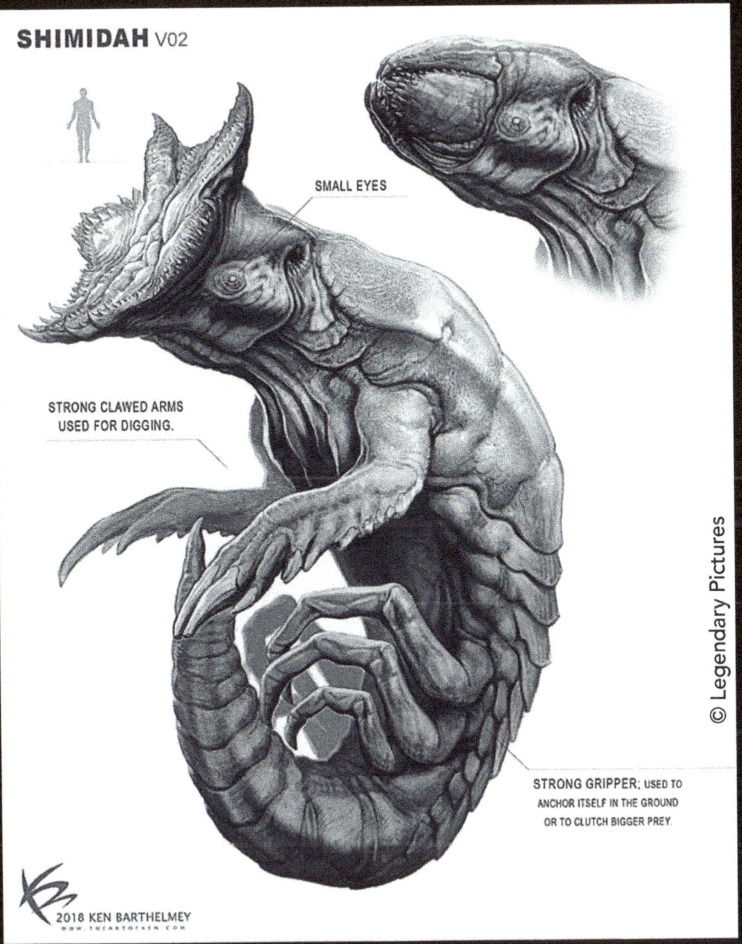

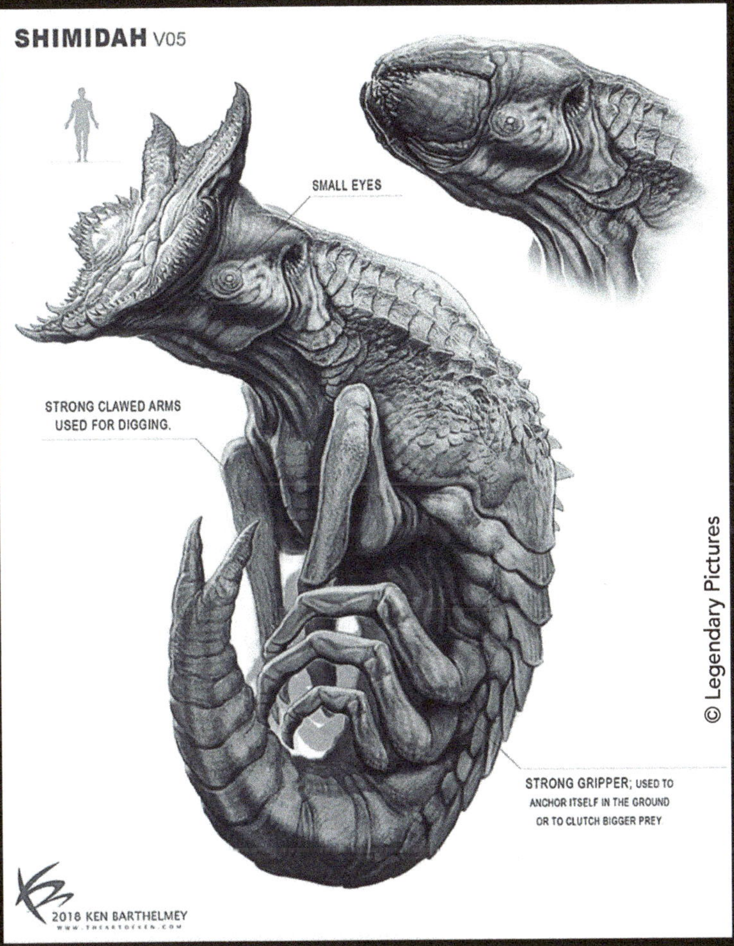

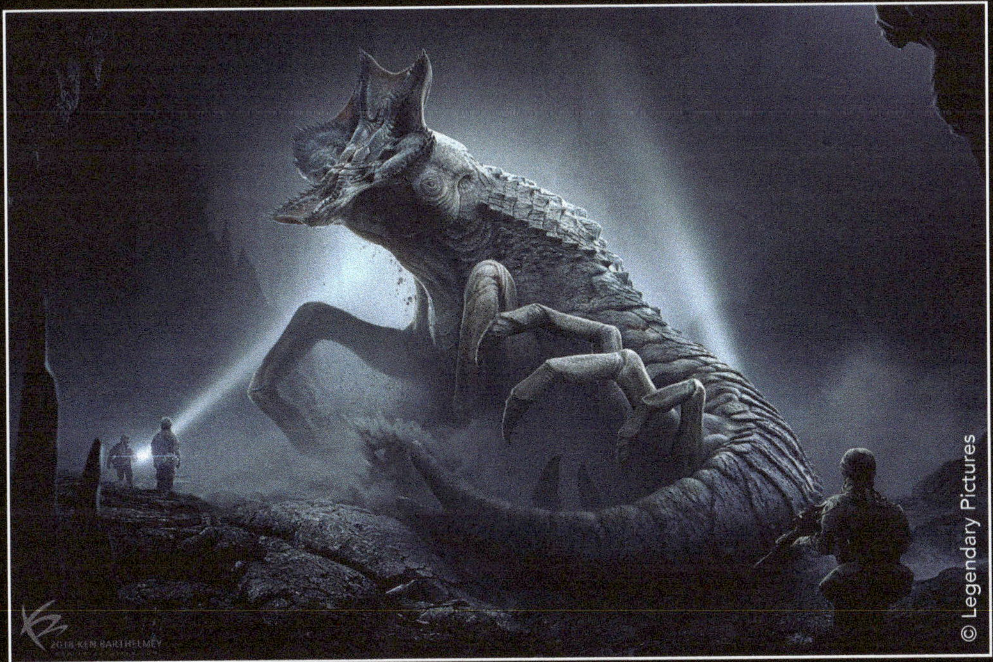

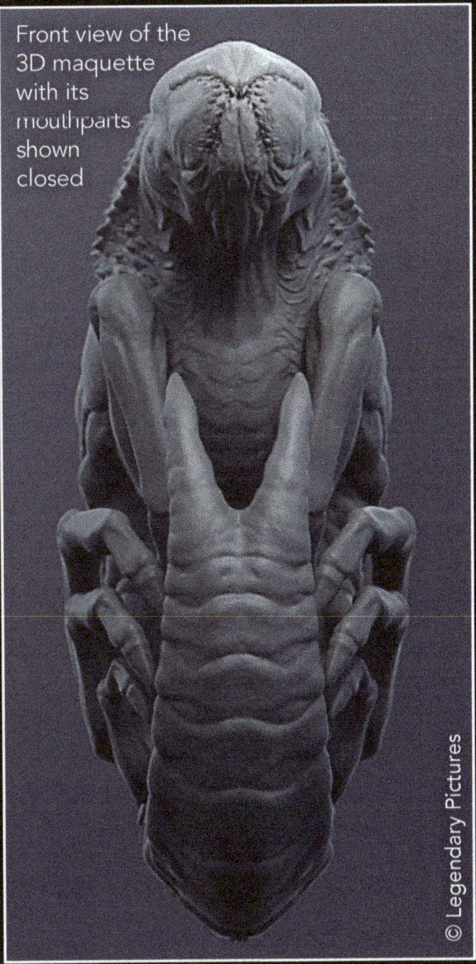

Front view of the 3D maquette with its mouthparts shown closed

versions did you personally like the most?

I actually like the final one (version 5) the most. I think it's also the most functional.

I always imagined Shimidah to be in a larval stage, living underground until it's fully developed. It uses its big arms for digging and clinging onto larger prey, like insects. These were my personal thoughts while designing the creature.

You did a series of illustrations showing how Shimidah lies in wait underground and then lunges upwards to devour its prey. Was Shimidah's stealthy method of attack agreed upon early in the design process?

Yes, that was the only description we received from production. Shimidah was described as a large creature, partially submerged in sand. It moves and rises out of the sand in reaction to something, then settles back in. Because there wasn't much information about the creature, I had a lot of creative freedom in developing the design and backstory.

We were also instructed to make each design cohesive by using texture elements similar to those of Godzilla.

How long did it take to create the 3D maquette of Shimidah?

The 3D maquette took me a couple of days. Since I had already finished the 2D design, the 3D process was relatively fast. I also didn't texture the model, instead, I used different render passes and I overpainted everything in Photoshop.

Shimidah's huge face peels open wide when it is ready to eat its victims: did you have to produce many versions of the mouthparts before director Adam Wingard approved the final design?

I only created a few different versions of the arms, texture and eye position, but the mouth remained the same.

At the very beginning, I started with three rough sketches of very different versions of Shimidah. Two looked reptilian and the other resembled a shrimp. Director Adam Wingard responded well to the shrimp design, so I developed a more detailed version of it.

Okay, I'd like to talk to you about the fact that Shimidah wasn't included in *Godzilla vs. Kong*...
When you design a creature as bizarrely beautiful as Shimidah, but then discover that it isn't going to be used in the finished film, do you get very frustrated?

I definitely would have loved to see Shimidah on the big screen. I was a bit disappointed, but it's quite common in big film productions for designs not to be used, so I never take it personally. Often, designs are created while the script is still being written, often just for inspiration, so you can never be sure what will make it into the final film. I had a lot of fun designing it and, who knows, maybe they'll still use Shimidah in another film. Fingers crossed!

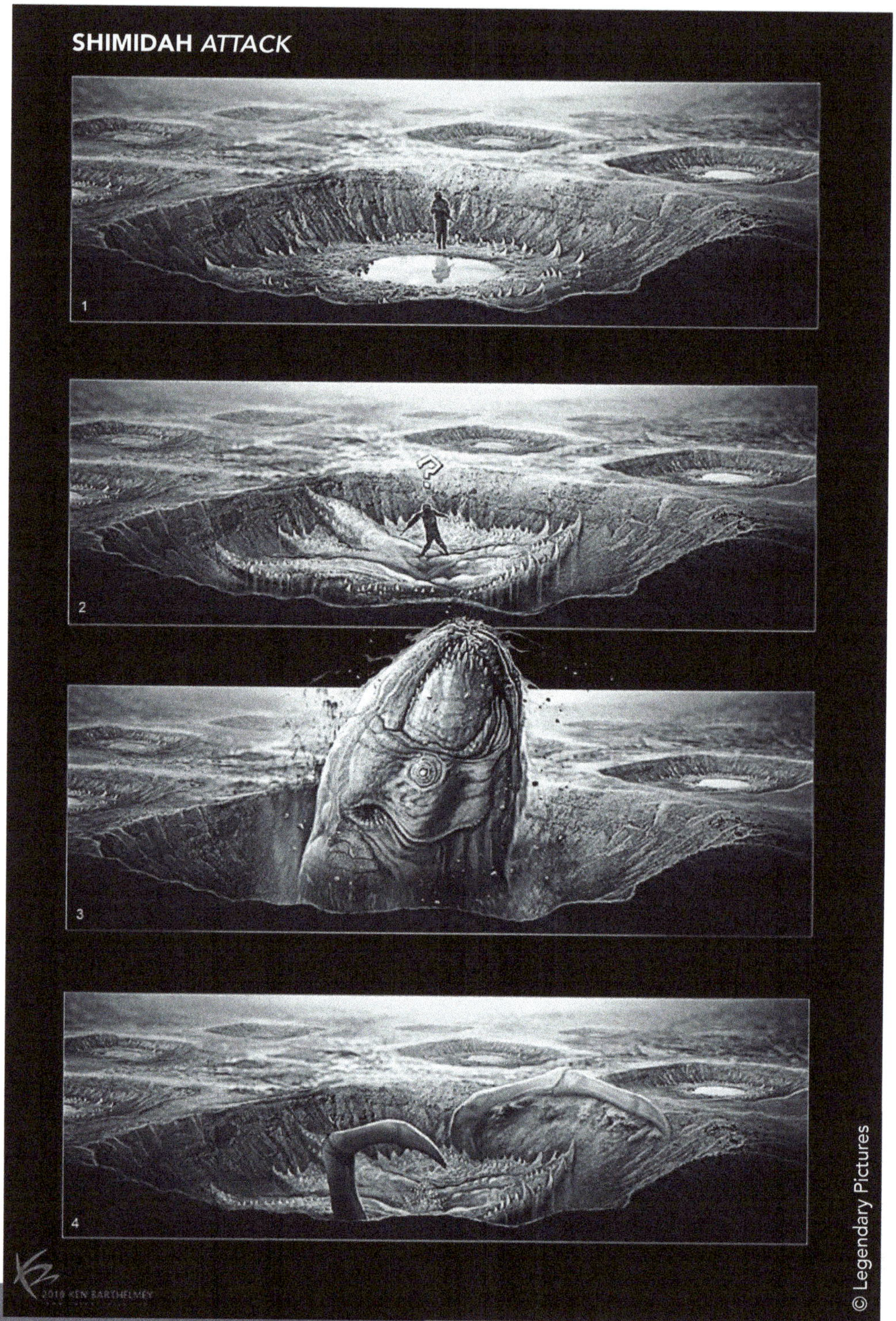

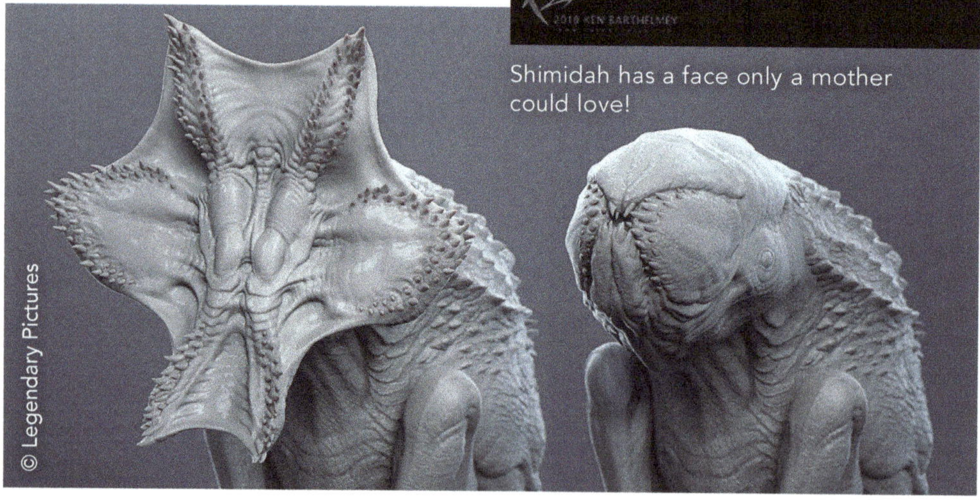

Shimidah has a face only a mother could love!

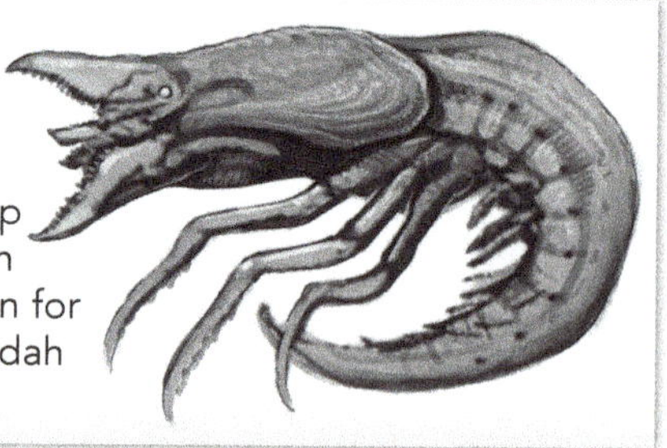

The shrimp sketch design for Shimidah

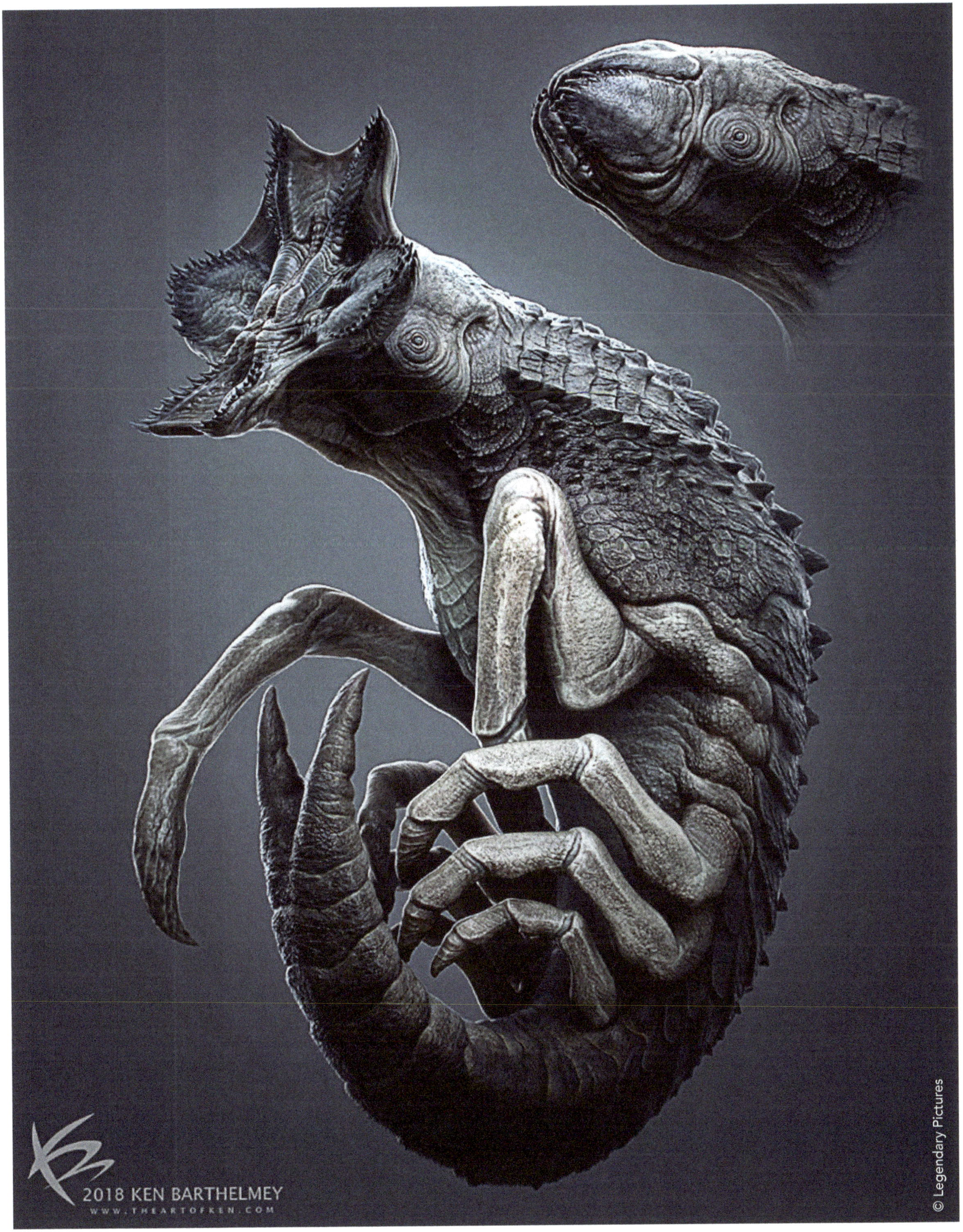
2018 KEN BARTHELMEY
WWW.THEARTOFKEN.COM
© Legendary Pictures

GODZILLA

POSTER GALLERY

Noriyoshi Ohrai illustrations

curated by Ken Miller

On the following pages are displayed a truly heavenly selection of Godzilla movie posters illustrated by the late, great, uber-gifted Japanese artist **Noriyoshi Ohrai**, who produced amazing artworks for science fiction movies, books and games, from the late 1960s up until the early 2000s. He is most famous for the stunning illustrations he created for Heisei and Millennium era Godzilla movie posters, the international poster for *The Empire Strikes Back*, and artwork for the *Metal Gear Solid* series of video games. Many of the Godzilla illustrations he did were for advance Godzilla movie posters.

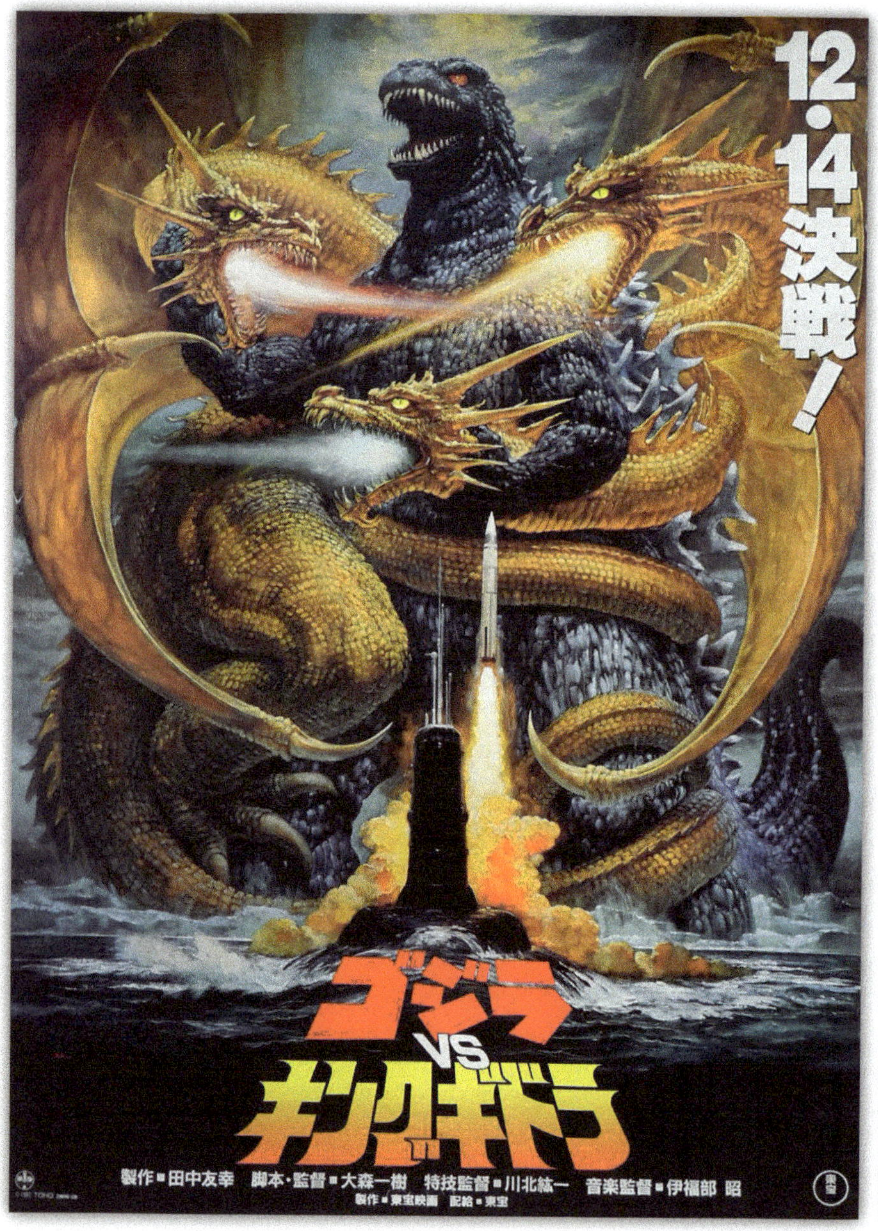

Godzilla vs. King Ghidorah (1991) Just look at this advance poster illustration by Noriyoshi Ohrai: Godzilla being constricted by his nemesis, the three-headed King Ghidorah! A nuclear submarine firing a big-ass missile at the behemoths! Godzilla stoically standing his ground, roaring like the king of the monsters he so definitely is!

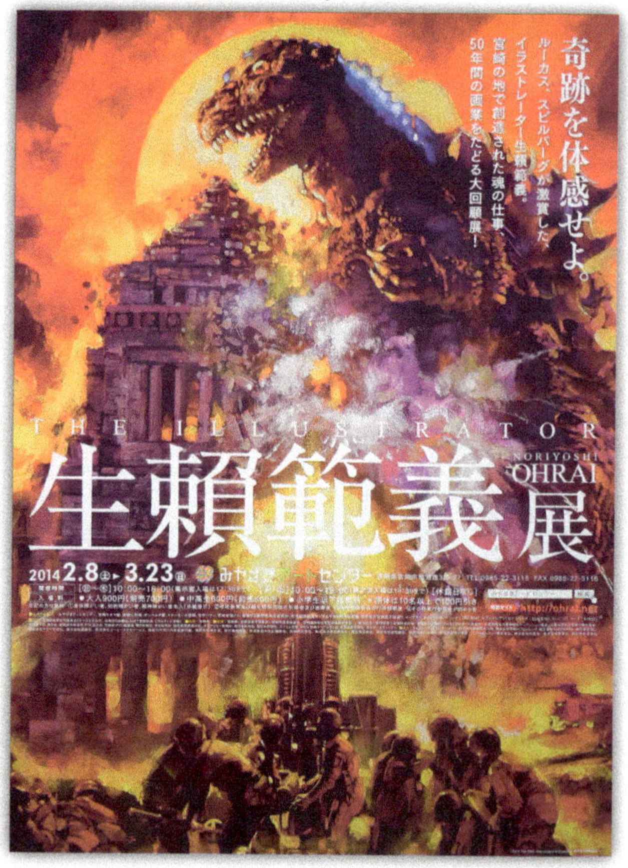

Miyazaki Art Center Poster (2014) A B2 poster used to advertise a Noriyoshi Ohrai exhibition that featured almost all of Ohrai's original art for movie posters, book covers, video games, plus editorial work, biology text books and more.

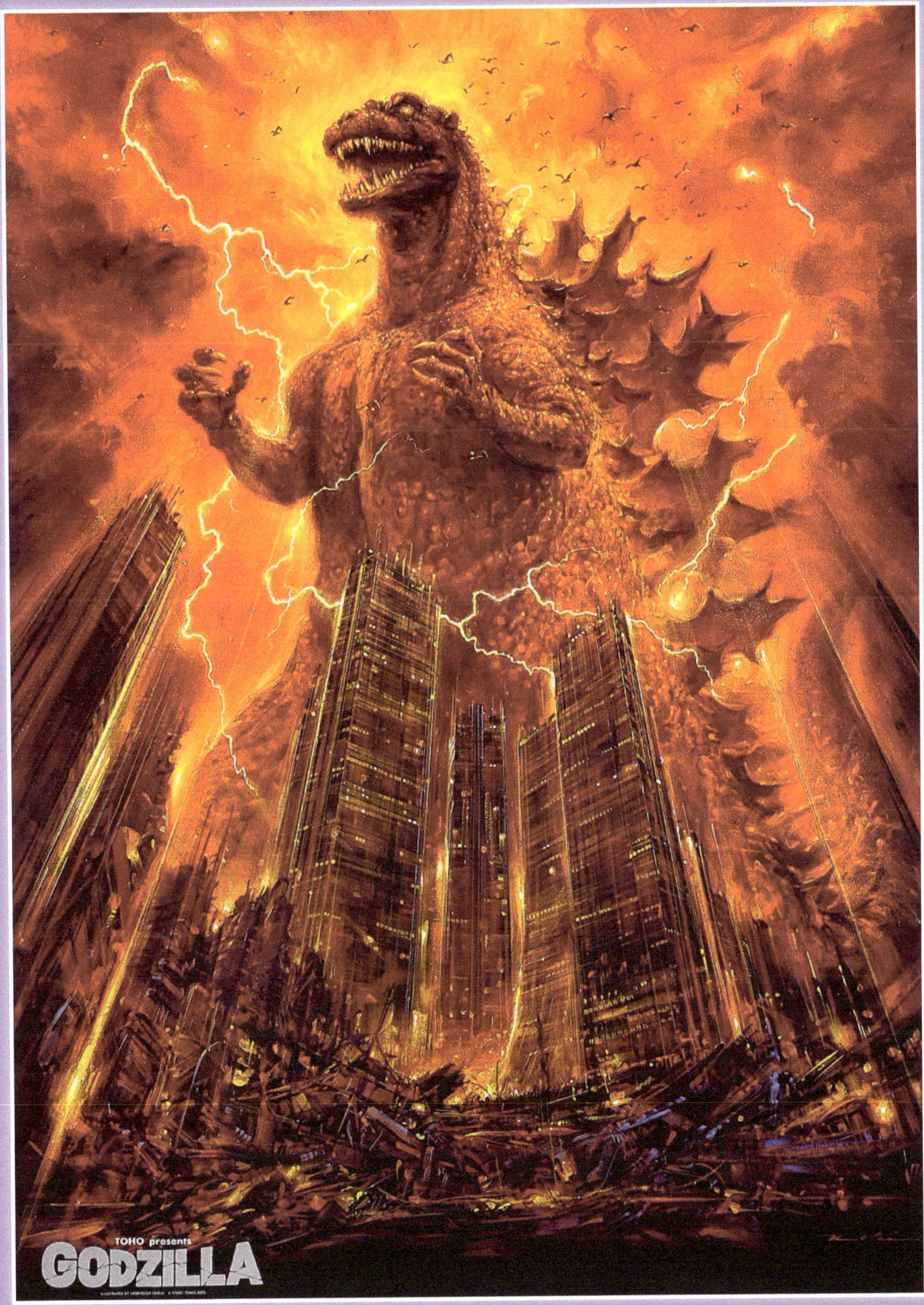

***The Return of Godzilla* (1984)** What a beauty! Noriyoshi created this simply sensational illustration for the advance poster for the first of the Heisei era Godzilla movies. So, so dynamic!

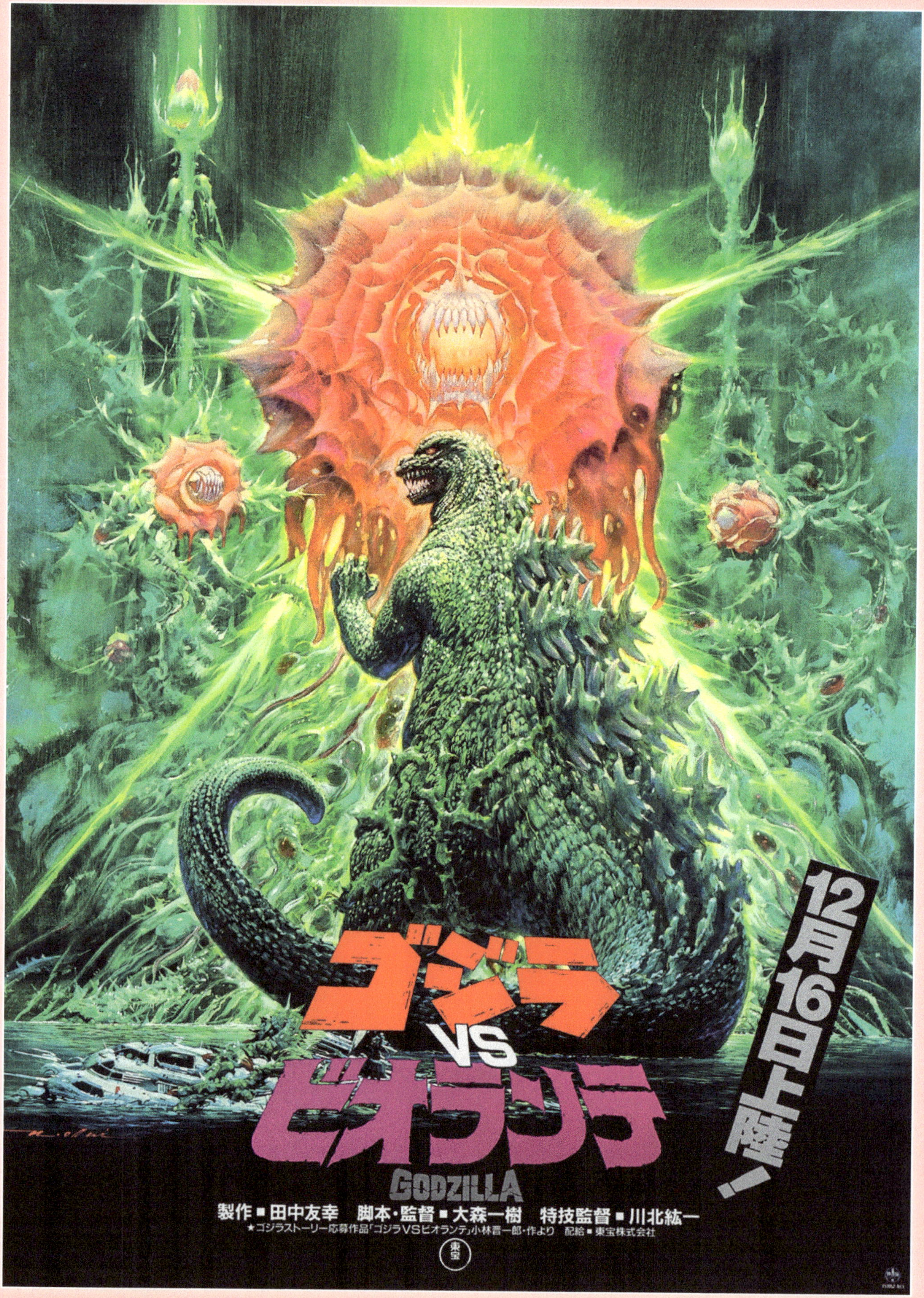

Godzilla vs. Biollante (1989) What I love about this stunningly-painted advance poster is that Noriyoshi makes sure this works as a well-detailed depiction of the creatures, whilst also ensuring it is a very well-structured composition.

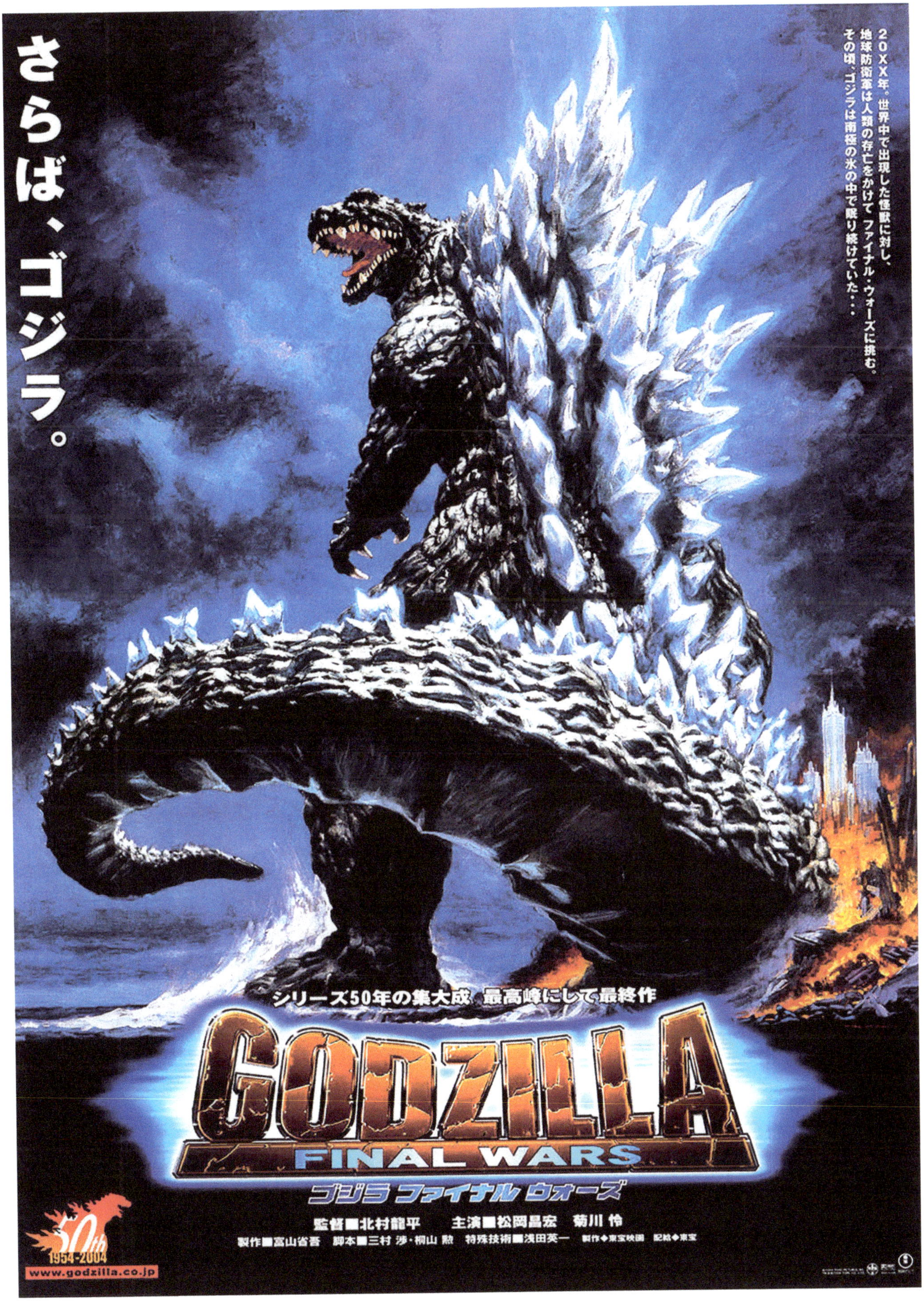

Godzilla: Final Wars (1995) Wow - this is such an eye-catching advance poster, boasting a truly dynamic rendering of the King of the Monsters in a pose that shows off his magnificent back plates. What a handsome beast!

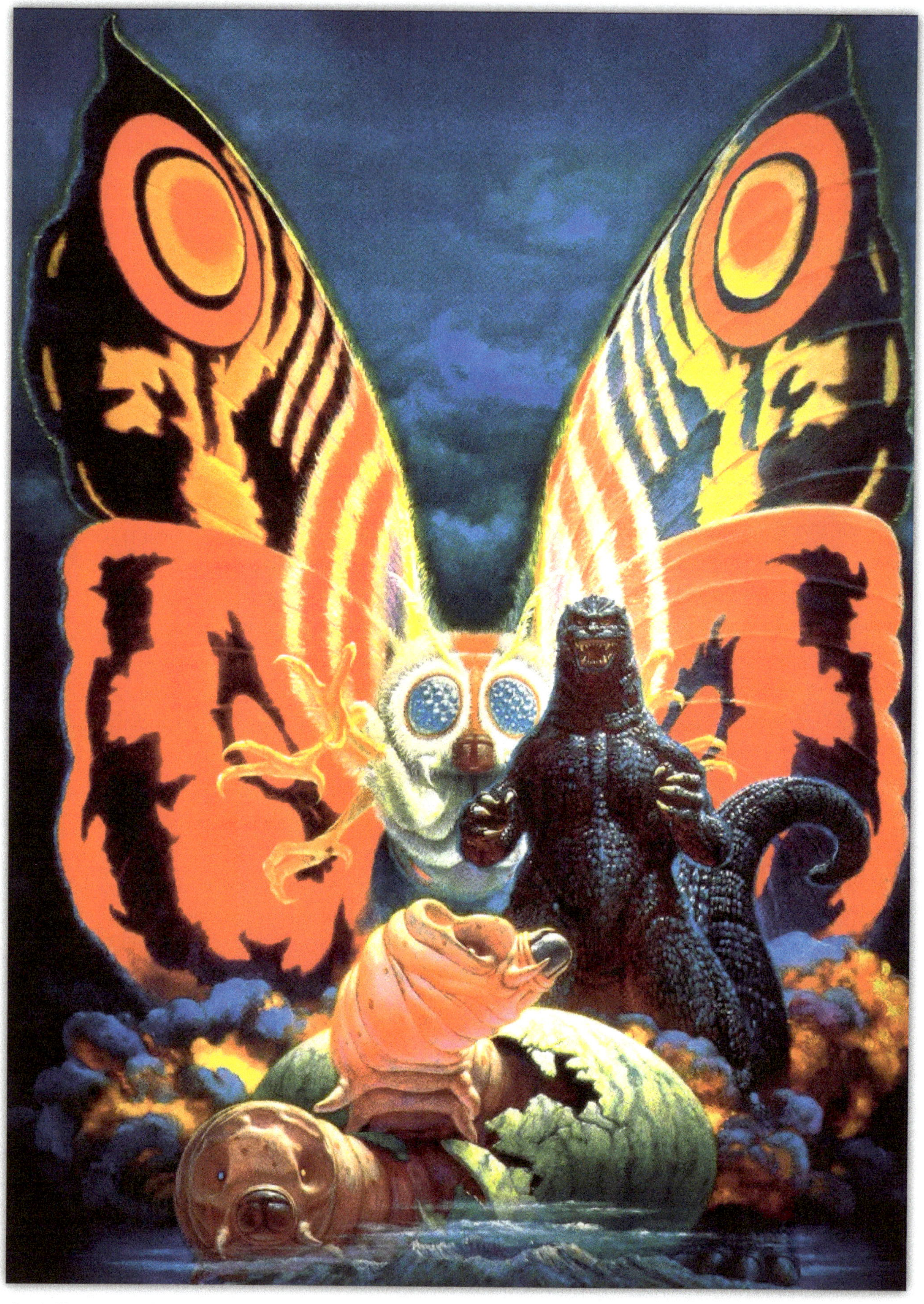

***Godzilla vs. Mothra* (1992)** This is Noriyoshi's dazzling painting for the fourth Godzilla film in the Heisei series, shown here without the poster typography. The decision to highlight the size of Mothra's wings helps to make this illo stand out.

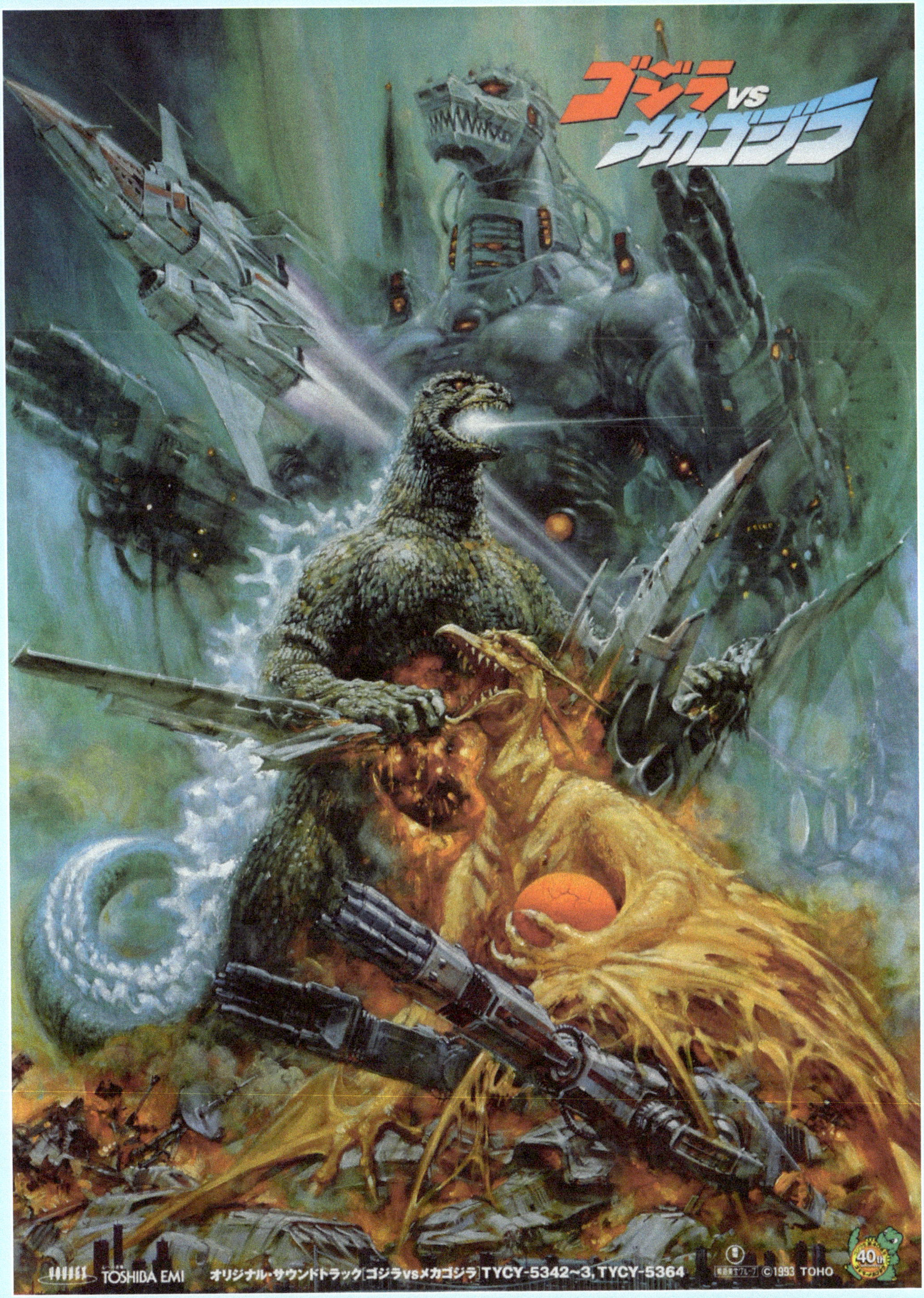

Godzilla vs. Mechagodzilla II (1993) A marvellous mix of monsters and mecha! The titanic Mechagodzilla towers above Rodan and Godzilla in this Noriyoshi Ohrai illustration for the advance poster.

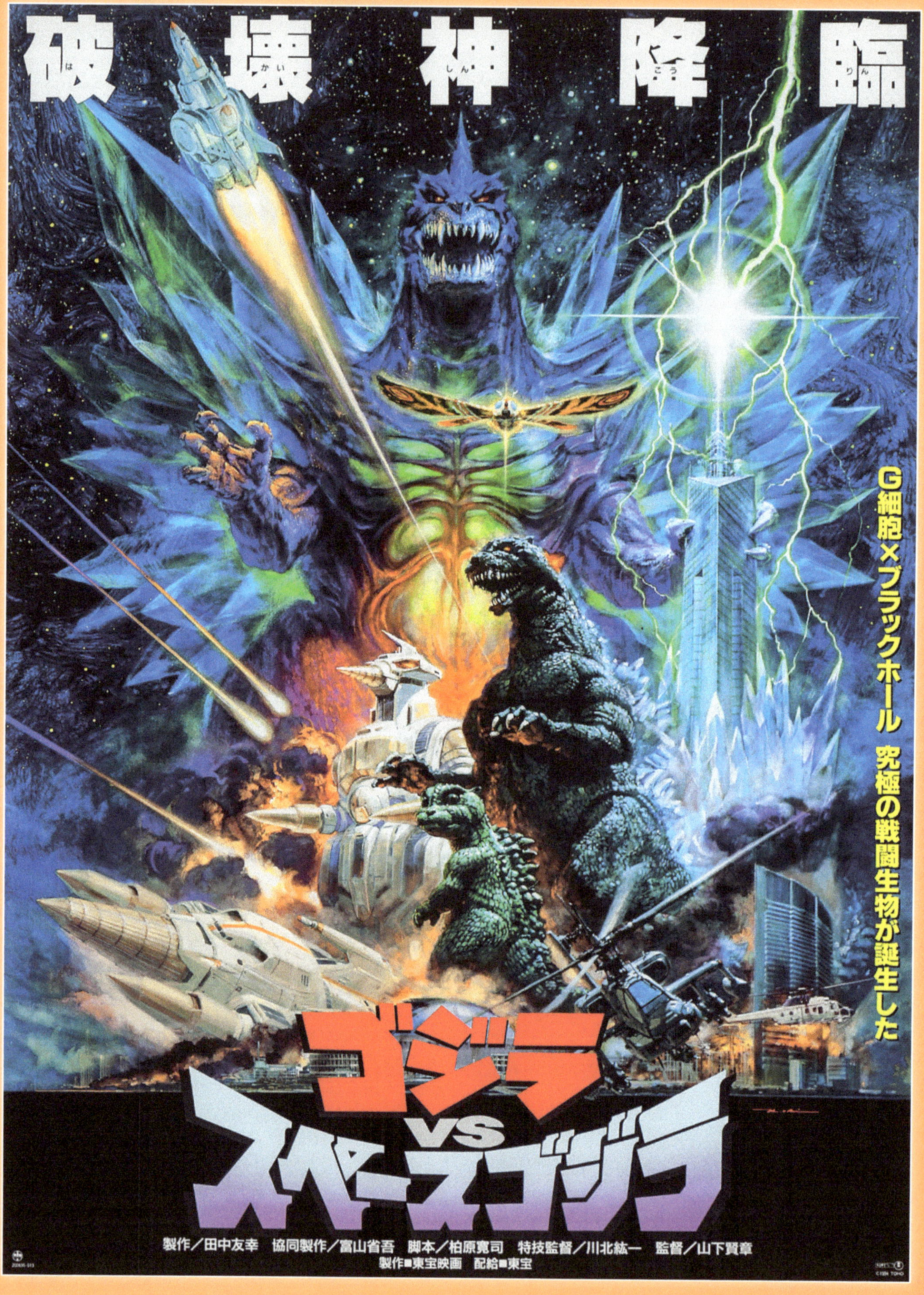

***Godzilla vs. SpaceGodzilla* (1994)** This colourful, scrumptious illustration has SpaceGodzilla looming majestically and menacingly upwards at the back of the composition. Honestly, this painting is so tasty it's good enough to eat!

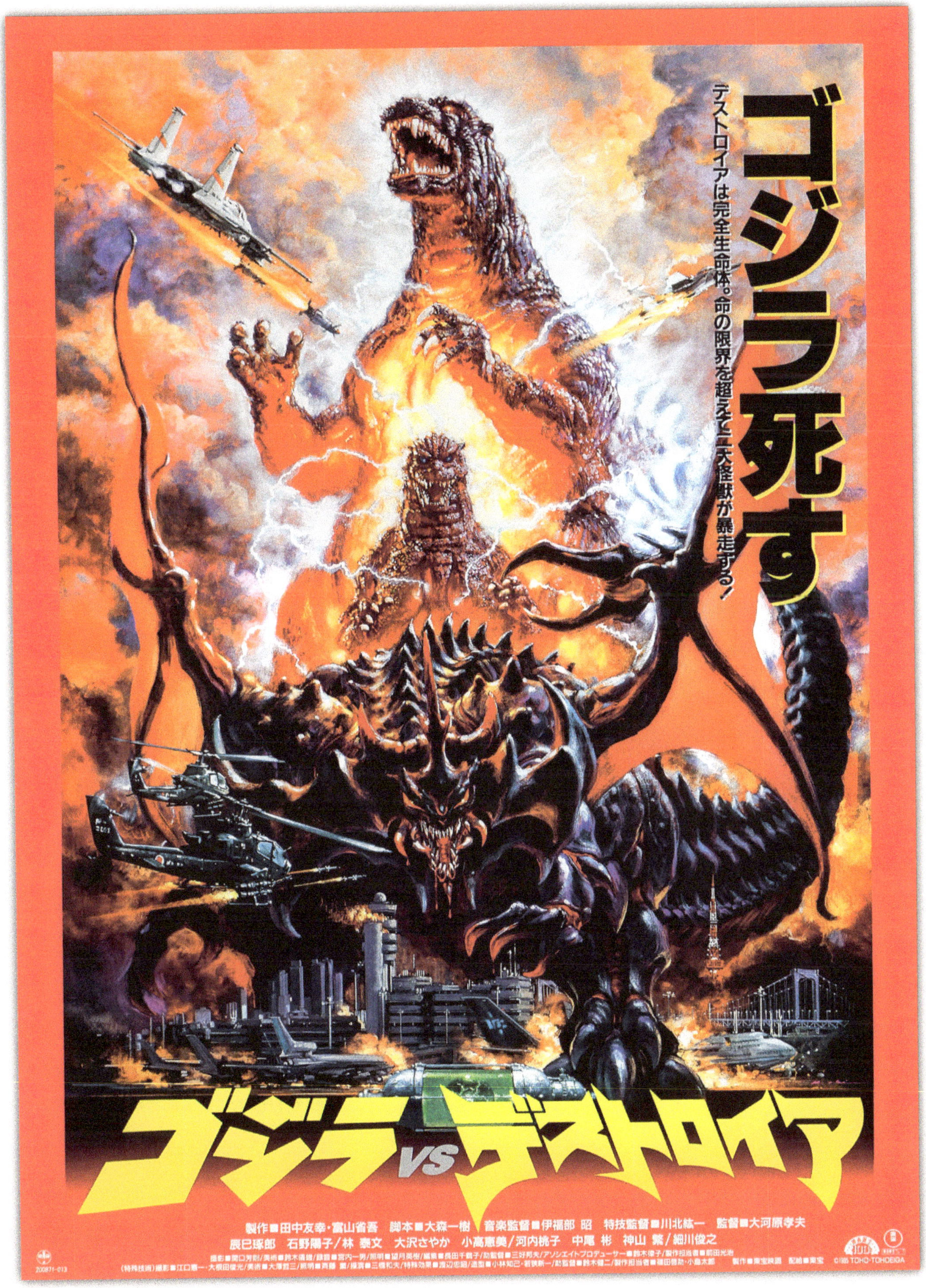

Godzilla vs. Destoroyah (1995) Noriyoshi makes sure that the image of the terminally overheating 'burning Godzilla' is centred in the painting, with Godzilla Junior positioned in front of him, hinting at what happens during the film's finale.

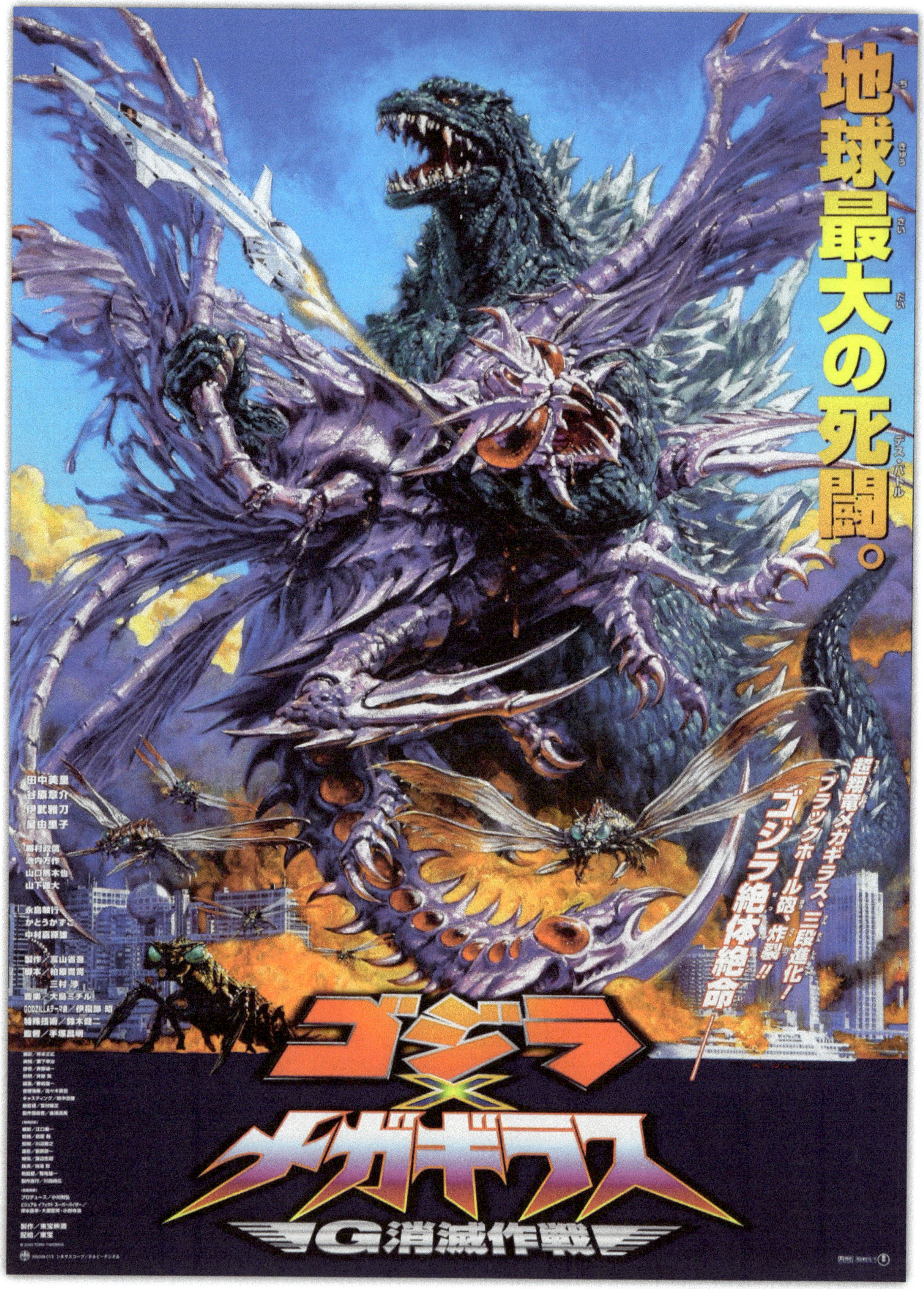

***Godzilla vs. Megaguirus* (2000)** Another stunner from Noriyoshi, who captures the look of Godzilla's Millennium era facial features superbly. Red-eyed Megaguirus looks stonkingly amazing here too!

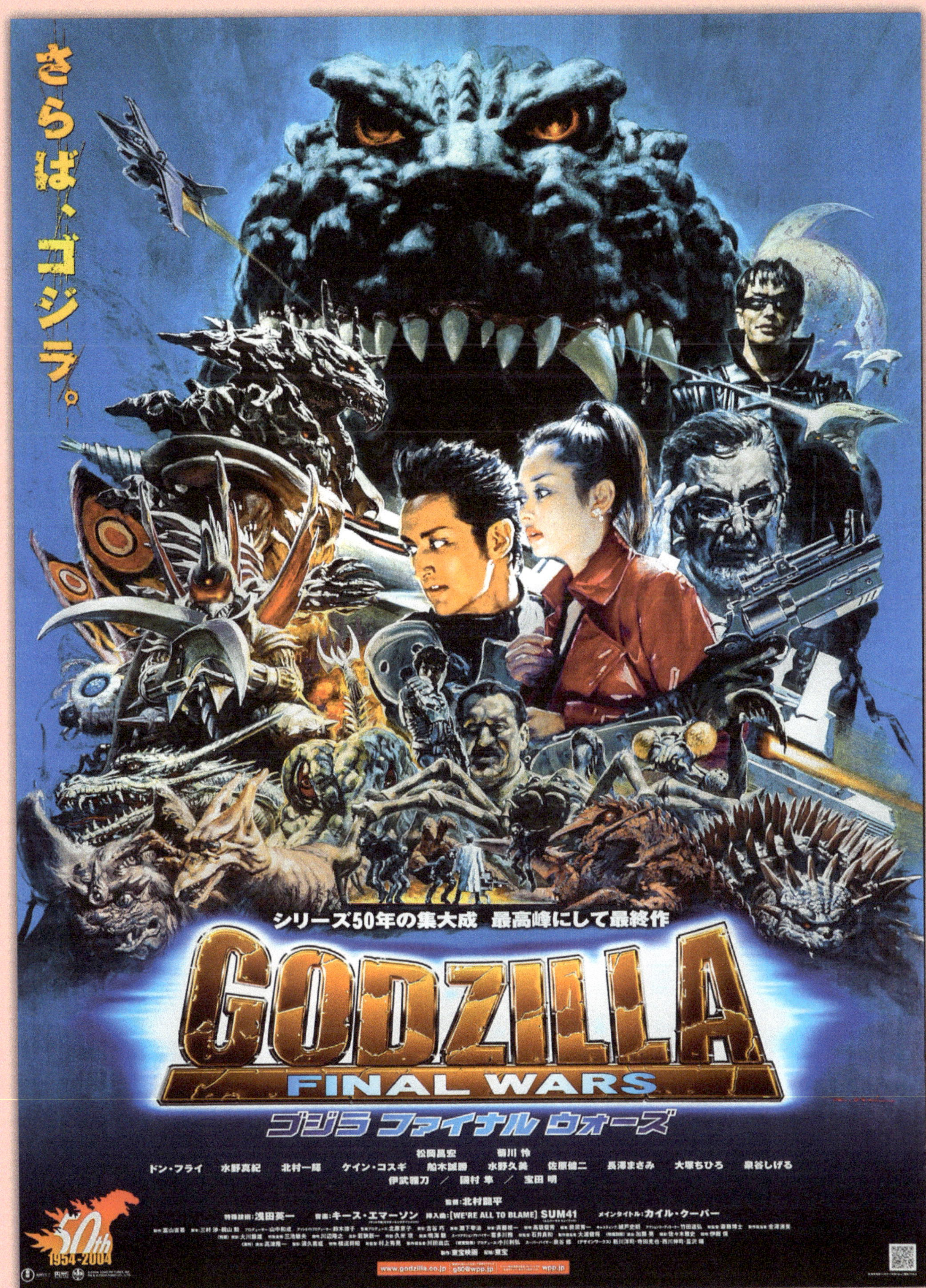

Godzilla: Final Wars (1995) This mad, mad movie is crammed with tons of monsters, plus lots of human and alien characters, so Noriyoshi does his best to include as many of the creatures and people within this montage as he can.

ULTRA HD HAVOC!

The best way to see Godzilla stomp on cities is to watch it all on 4K and Blu-ray!

By Johnny Burnett aka The Fanatical Dragon

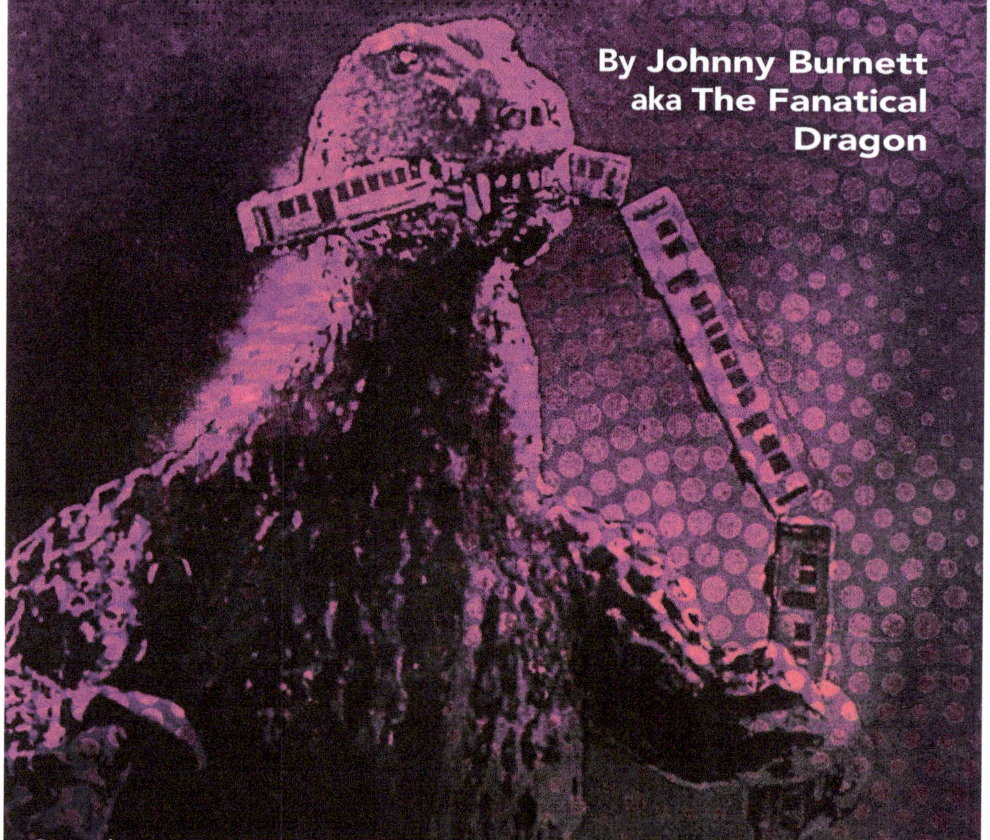

Given his incredible popularity and enduring legacy, it should come as no surprise that Godzilla has always had a sizeable presence on physical media for pretty much the entire time we've had the means to enjoy movies in the comfort of our own homes. There were countless VHS editions of the Showa (1954–1975) and Heisei (1984–1995) era movies released in the late 80s and 90s and the advent of DVD in the early 00s actually saw Gojira most often ONLY being released out into the wild on DVD disc for much of the Millennium era (1999–2004).

The Reiwa Era ((2016–present) has run concurrently with the advent of Blu-ray and in turn the 4K UHD format, which is starting to really grow in popularity these past few years as more and more people turn away from the oversaturated rash of overpriced, advert-fuelled streaming services with an ever-changing roster of available/unavailable titles, opting instead to start building up movie collections themselves at home…

This special issue of *Imaginator* offers me a great chance to do a quick round-up of the best of the various releases of Godzilla's movies on 4K (of which there aren't that many titles thus far) and on Blu-ray (which almost ALL the rest are available on) and give you all a guide to which versions of your favourite titles to look out for. I'm not going to spend much time talking about the movies themselves, I'm just focusing on the different 4K and Blu-rays already available or in the works, and what each release offers…

Set your PayPal/Klarna accounts and debit cards to standby…

…and prepare yourselves for the Mecha4K invasion!

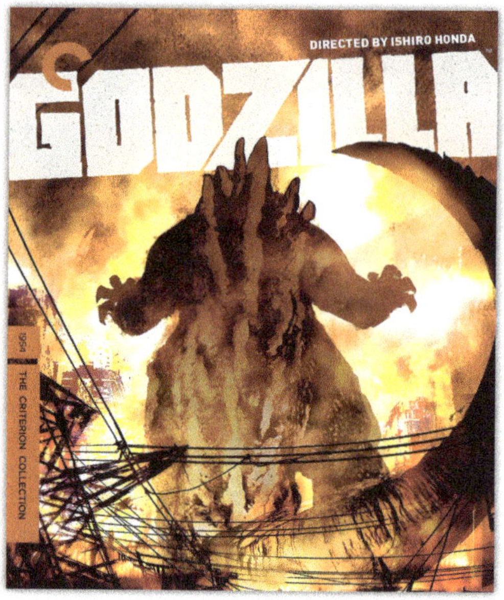

Godzilla (1954)
Criterion Collection
4K Digipack and Blu-ray Only Editions
Available in UK (Region B) & USA (Region A)

If you only buy one single release from this list, make it this one, Criterion's gorgeous Digipack edition of the original 1954 film: the movie that kicked off one of the most incredible cinematic legacies of all time. Criterion recently gave this a 4K overhaul with a new restoration and finally made the set available in the UK for the first time. This is an incredible edition of the first (and arguably best) of all the Godzilla films.
It also offers up a really great selection of extra features (sadly not repeated by Criterion for the other Showa era films to the same degree). The set comes in a beautifully packaged Digipack case with a pop-up Godzilla inside the case, a well written booklet, and the new 4K restoration of the film has it looking better than it has since its original cinema release back in the 1950's… Absolutely essential!

The extensive extras list on the 4K (and Blu-ray only set) are as follows:
A brand new 4K digital restoration, with uncompressed monaural soundtrack / One 4K UHD disc of the film and one Blu-ray with the film and special features / High-definition digital restoration of *Godzilla, King of the Monsters*, Terry Morse's 1956 reworking of the original, with uncompressed monaural soundtrack / Audio commentary for both movies by film historian David Kalat / Interviews with actors Akira Takarada and Haruo Nakajima and special effects technicians Yoshio Irie and Eizo Kaimai / Interview with legendary Godzilla score composer Akira Ifukube / Featurette detailing *Godzilla*'s photographic effects, introduced by special effects director Koichi Kawakita and special FX photographer Motoyoshi Tomioka / Interview with Japanese-film critic Tadao Sato / *The Unluckiest Dragon*, an illustrated audio essay featuring historian Greg Pflugfelder,

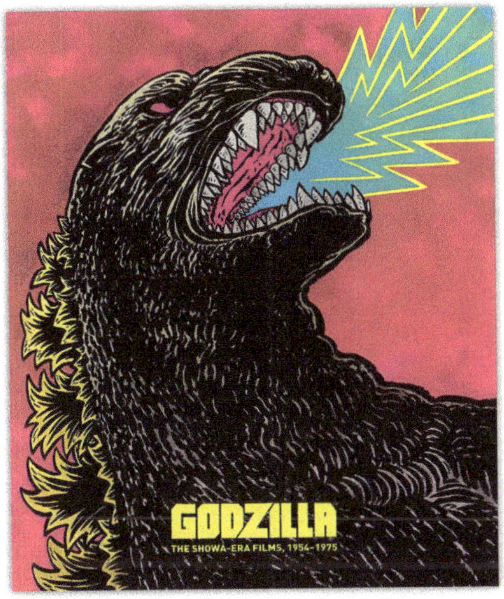

describing the tragic fate of the fishing vessel Daigo Fukuryū Maru, a real-life event that inspired *Godzilla* / Trailers and a printed booklet with an essay by critic J. Hoberman.

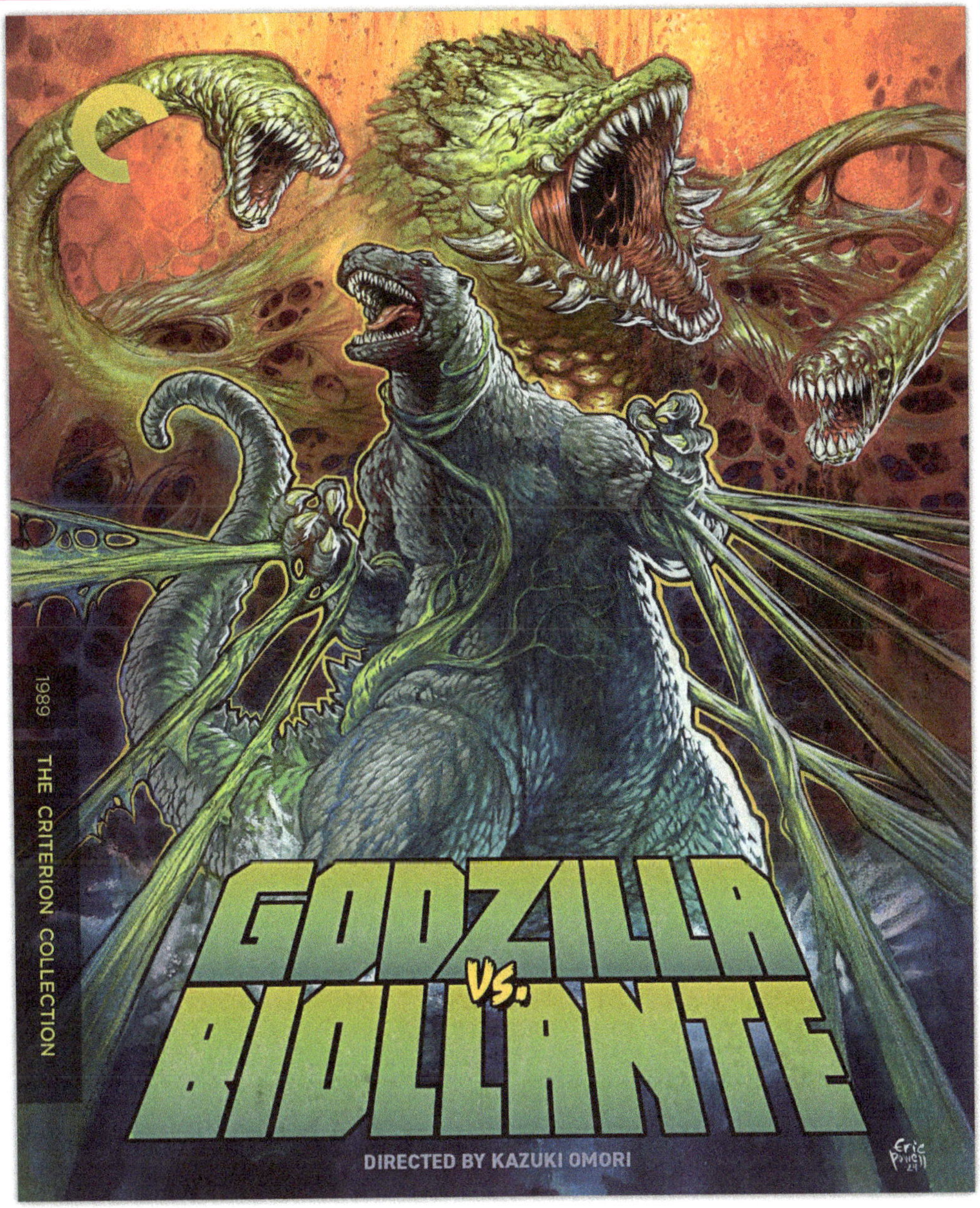

Godzilla - The Showa Era Films 1954 - 1975
Criterion Collection
Oversize Book Style Blu-ray Boxset
Available in UK (Region B) & USA (Region A)

Most Criterion collectors (myself included) have a real love/hate relationship with the company's mammoth Showa era collection boxset, not for the films themselves or the transfers: they look great and present all the Godzilla films most of us grew up on, fell in love with, and take great joy in revisiting. No, the issue came from the decision to put the 8 Blu-ray discs into a gargantuan sized book format which requires Kaiju-sized shelving to be able to store it properly. It's easily damaged both externally and internally. Most buyers report scratching the discs just getting them in and out of the box to view. Many of those who own this set have downloaded custom covers and put the discs into standard-sized boxes to make the whole experience much less troublesome. The weird format of the packaging aside, it's a mostly excellent collection of all 15 Godzilla films from the Showa era, all presented in HD, often from new remasters and with a smattering of extras. Movie-wise, you get HD versions of: *Godzilla* (1954) - with all the same extras as on the standalone version of the original movie (but no 4K disc) / *Godzilla Raids Again* (1955) / *King Kong vs Godzilla* (1963) / *Mothra vs Godzilla* (1964) / *Ghidorah, the Three Headed Monster* (1964) / *Invasion of the Astro-Monsters* (1965) / *Ebirah, Horror of the Deep* (1966) / *Son Of Godzilla* (1967) / *Destroy All Monsters* (1968) / *All Monsters Attack* (1969) / *Godzilla vs Hedorah* (1971) / *Godzilla vs Gigan* (1972) / *Godzilla vs Megalon* (1973) / *Godzilla vs Mechagodzilla* (1974) / *Terror of Mechagodzilla* (1975).

Extras aren't quite as good as one would hope given the high cost of the set (£130-£150) and the amount of movies on it, but what we do get is all high quality and well presented: International English-language dub tracks for *Invasion of the Astro-Monsters / Son of Godzilla / Destroy All Monsters / Godzilla vs Megalon / Godzilla vs Mechagodzilla / Terror of Mechagodzilla* / Directors Guild of Japan interview with director Ishiro Honda, conducted by director Yoshimitsu Banno in 1990 / Featurette detailing Godzilla's photographic effects / *Toho Unused Special Effects Complete Collection*: a 1986 documentary featuring archival making-of footage, scenes deleted from films including *Destroy All Monsters*, *King Kong vs Godzilla*, and *Mothra vs Godzilla*; and interviews with Honda, producer Tomoyuki Tanaka, special effects director Teruyoshi Nakano, and others / A new interview with filmmaker Alex Cox about his admiration for the Showa era Godzilla films / New and archival interviews with cast and crew members, including actors Bin Furuya, Tsugutoshi Komada, Haruo Nakajima, and Akira Takarada; composer Akira Ifukube; and effects technicians Yoshio Irie and Eizo Kaimai / Interview with critic Tadao Satō from 2011 / Illustrated audio essay from 2011 about the real-life tragedy that inspired *Godzilla* - and trailers - all housed in a lavishly illustrated deluxe hardcover book featuring an essay by cinema historian Steve Ryfle, notes on the films by cinema historian Ed Godziszewski, and new illustrations by Arthur Adams, Sophie Campbell, Becky Cloonan, Jorge Coelho, Geof Darrow, Simon Gane, Robert Goodin, Benjamin Marra, Monarobot, Takashi Okazaki, Angela Rizza, Yuko Shimizu, Bill Sienkiewicz, Katsuya Terada, Ronald Wimberly, and Chris Wisnia.

Godzilla vs Biollante
Criterion Collection
4K/Blu-ray Combo and Blu-ray Only Editions
Available in UK (Region B) & USA (Region A)

The only other Godzilla movie currently

available from Criterion outside of the Showa era movies is 1989's *Godzilla vs Biollante* - one of the better Heisei era entries and it's arrival on 4K and Blu-ray disc back in March of this year is hopefully a sign that Janus Films / Criterion have secured the rights for more of the 80s and 90s films and have plans to give them all the 4K makeover. For now, though, this is a solid release: a brand new 4K restoration has the movie looking better than it has before on any of the previous physical media releases - and likely better than most cinema screenings in the 90s!

Extras-wise we get a new audio commentary from film historian Samm Deighan / A making-of program from 1993 featuring director Kazuki Ōmori and special effects director Koichi Kawakita, among others / Short documentary from 1993 about the Biollante and Super X2 vehicle concepts / Deleted special effects / TV spots and trailers and a printed booklet with an essay by science-fiction and horror film expert Jim Cirronella. All in all, a great first outing for the Heisei era on Criterion - and hopefully a sign of more to follow!

Shin Godzilla

Coming to 4K late 2025 (USA) from Shout Factory
Available in 4K Boxset now (Japan) - Toho
Available on Blu-ray / DVD (UK) - Manga Entertainment

Later this year, Hideaki Anno's 2016 movie *Shin Godzilla* is getting a 4K cinema release in the USA (and hopefully the UK). This return-to-origins film really helped to open the door for *Minus One* to step through. And in turn, *Shin Godzilla* was also recently given the minus colour treatment in Japan after the success of Minus One/ Minus Colour. Just as I was finishing up this article, godzilla.com just announced a new Deluxe 4 Disc 4K/Blu-ray combo boxset of *Shin Godzilla* coming in October of this year.

That will include not only the new 4K restoration but also the Minus Colour version of the movie (which they are calling ORTHOchromatic), as well as a full disc of extra features containing over 3 hours of behind the scenes footage, VFX breakdowns and interviews. The entire set, including all extras, will also have English subtitles. This is pretty huge news! Absolutely the most exciting new Godzilla related release this year, but for now, available in the US only. We can only hope that Scottish label All the Anime pick up the *Shin Godzilla* set for a UK release, as they did previously with the *Minus One* Deluxe Version. Time will tell.

If you're not interested in all the bells and whistles, Shout Factory will also be releasing a regular box version of just the

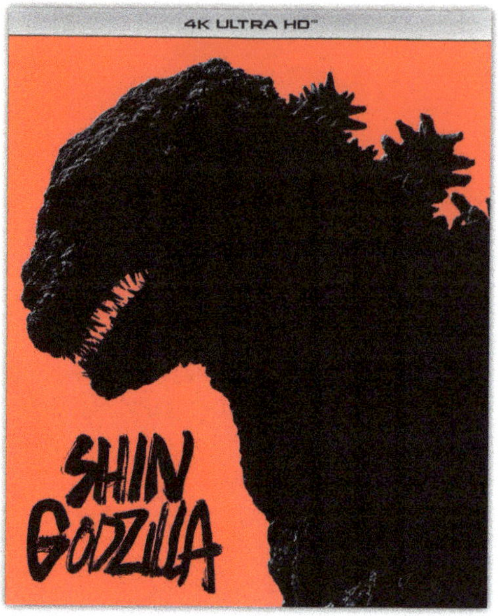

4K disc on it's own, and there is also a 3-Disc Wallmart exclusive 4K steelbook due in October, which will contain the extras disc, but no ORTHOchromatic version.

Having previously owned the Japanese Deluxe version, I can report that the extras disc is extremely comprehensive, though utterly impenetrable to a non-Japanese speaker.

So having this gorgeous boxset ported over to an English-friendly release AND adding 4K and the B/W version of the movie is great news indeed. The Deluxe set is priced at $55, but only available via godzilla.com - and they don't ship outside of the USA.

Godzilla Minus One

4K/Blu-ray Combo and Blu-ray Only Editions
Available in UK (Region B) & USA (Region A)
All the Anime (UK)
Toho (USA)

Takashi Yamazaki's *Godzilla Minus One* breathed an atomic breath of new life into the franchise when it hit cinemas in 2023, building momentum and steam like a juggernaut and even managing to win the first Academy Award ever for a Godzilla movie. A strong argument could be made that it's the best movie of the entire franchise to date, and I would suggest it's ultimately a close two-monster race between the original 1954 movie and *Minus One* for the prize...

Given *Minus One*'s incredible success worldwide it's no surprise that there are a stack of different releases of the movie. Most of the standard Blu-ray editions are near-identical to each other and all mostly bare-bones, which is to say, devoid of any extras to speak of. But there are a few collectors/deluxe editions. The Deluxe sets are all basically clones of the original Japanese 4K and Blu-ray Deluxe boxsets made available in the UK and US with the addition of English subtitles. These Deluxe sets all also include the Minus Colour version of the movie as well as a wealth of

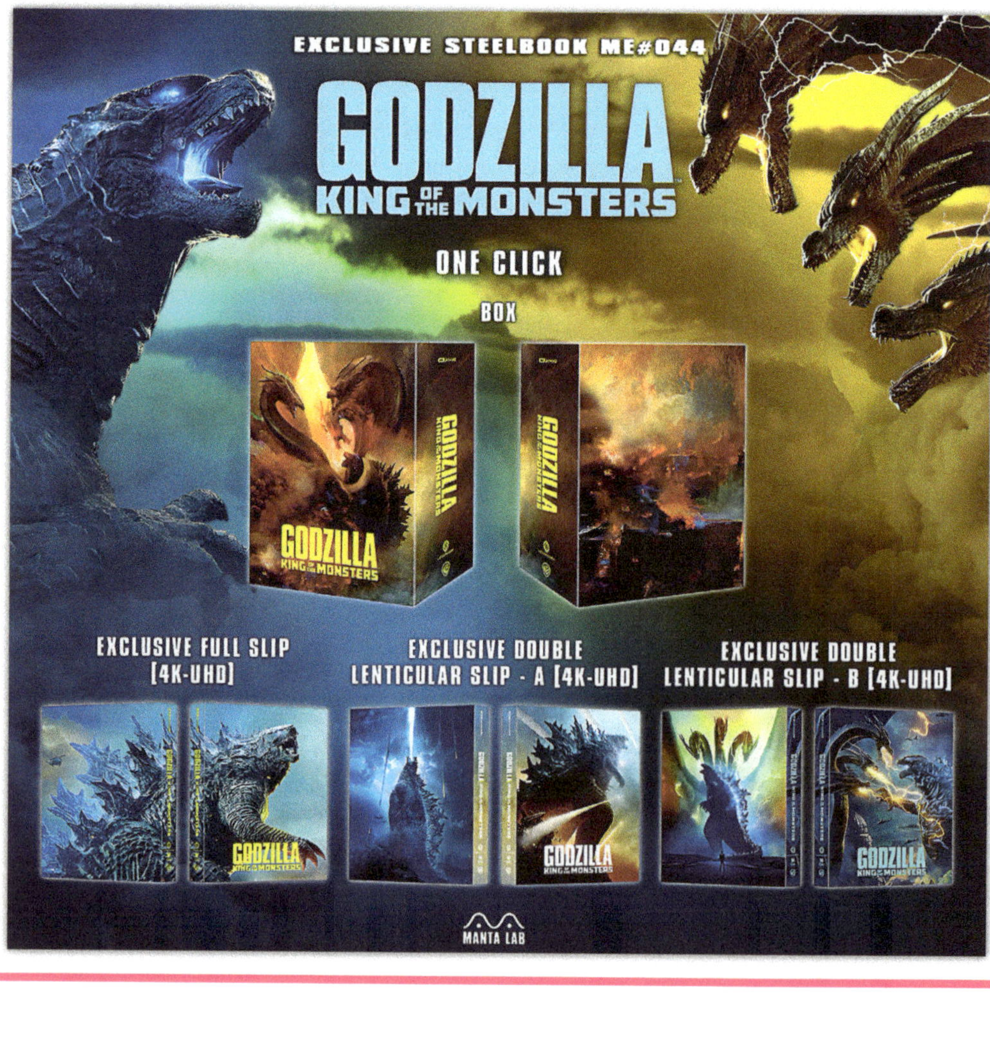

behind the scenes material, VFX breakdowns and interviews with the tiny team responsible for this truly epic movie. The only real difference between the UK and US sets is the overall physical size: the UK edition from All the Anime is standard

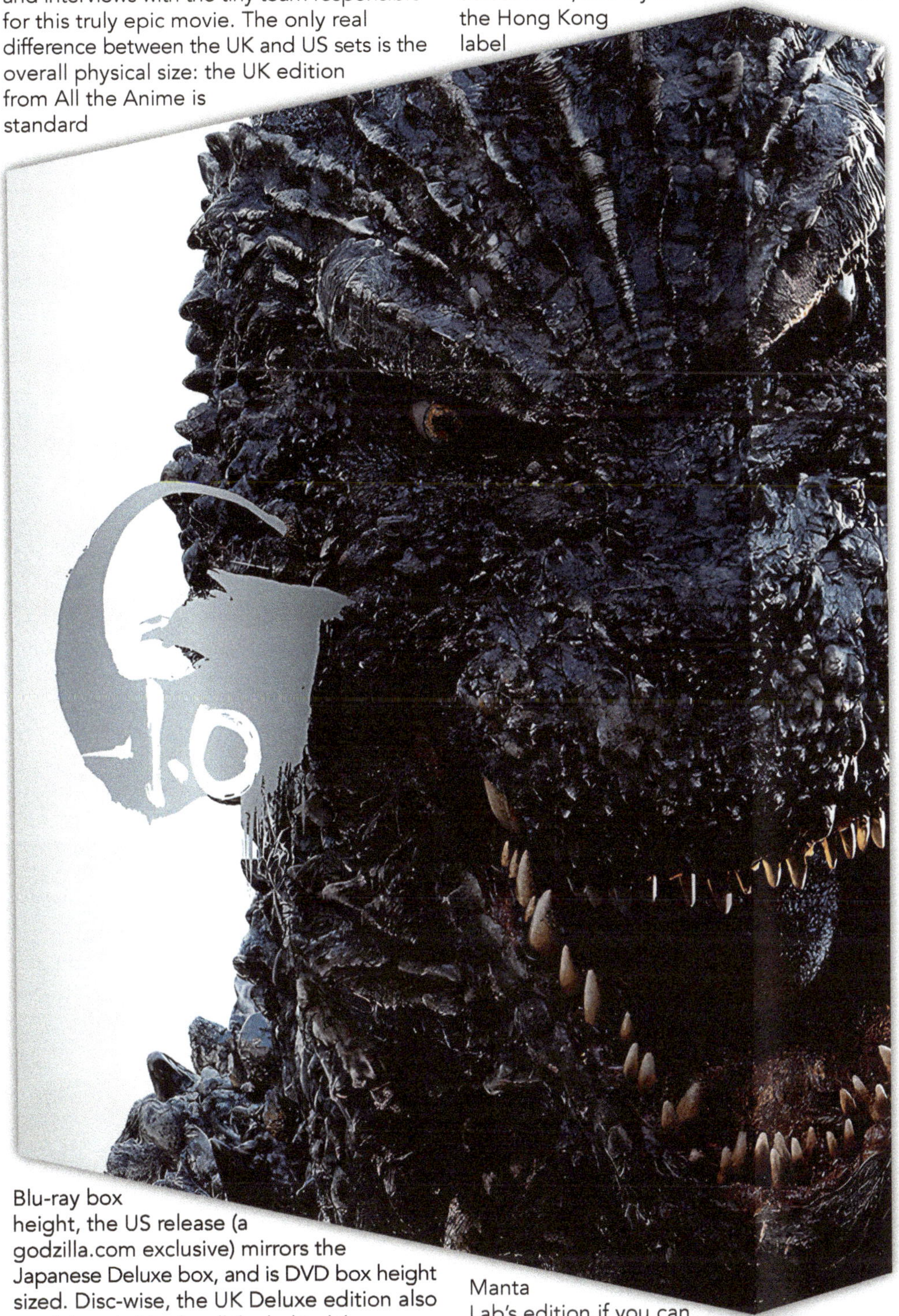

Blu-ray box height, the US release (a godzilla.com exclusive) mirrors the Japanese Deluxe box, and is DVD box height sized. Disc-wise, the UK Deluxe edition also provides subtitles for all the behind the scenes footage and other extras. The US Edition only includes English subs for the main feature.

Godzilla 2014

4K/Blu-ray Steelbook
Manta Lab
Region Free

The best (imho) of the US-produced Godzilla movies to date, Gareth Edwards' 2014 movie holds up more and more favourably each year, as things continue to go from bad to worse in each subsequent Warner Brothers MonsterVerse movie. There are a bunch of different versions of Edwards' film across DVD, Blu-ray and 4K: I'd recommend the Hong Kong label Manta Lab's edition if you can find it at a reasonable price. It comes with both 4K and Blu-ray discs held in a steelbook, housed in a full slip case along with a bunch of printed extras. All the on-disc special features from the standard UK and US Blu-ray release are also ported over. There are three different cover options for the full slip case, or for those with extremely deep pockets, you can buy a 'one click' edition which gives you all three variations of the release housed together in a larger rigid box with alternate artwork on the One Click box. The Manta Lab releases are extremely expensive items, whether bought as a single 4K Steelbook release (£75-£100), and even more so when going for the One Click set (£250-£350).

Another solid option for the 2014 movie is HMV's Cine Edition, which still offers the film on 4K and in a full slip case as well as a bunch of posters and art cards. The on-disc extras between the two different versions mentioned here are exactly the same, so it just comes down to which packaging you prefer and what price you want to spend...

Godzilla - King of the Monsters

4K/Blu-ray Steelbook
Manta Lab
Region Free

Whilst director Gareth Edwards didn't return to direct *King of the Monsters*, some of his original cast did, and the tone and style he set carries over nicely into the sequel. Composer Bear McCreary also does a great job of channelling Akira Ifukube's original score. For me, this is the point I stopped at with the US releases in terms of appreciation. Once Kong got involved everything became the 'King Kong show', with Godzilla reduced down to essentially just a glorified cameo in the MonsterVerse movies that followed.

Manta Lab are set to release *King of the Monsters* in September of this year, again, in three different variations of full slip case artwork and an option for a One Click. If you don't want to go down the boutique route, or if you don't mind (or even actually enjoy) the Kong side of things, there is also a UK MonsterVerse boxset which came out just prior to *Godzilla x Kong: The New Empire* and assembles the 2014 film, *King of the Monsters*, *Skull Island*, and *Godzilla vs Kong*, each on 4K/Blu-ray steelbooks, all housed in a metal case - it sold out quite quickly but comes around lots on eBay and in CEX for a pretty good price (around £50).

The Rest of the Heisei & Reiwa Era

All the rest of the Japanese Heisei and Reiwa era films have been released by Sony

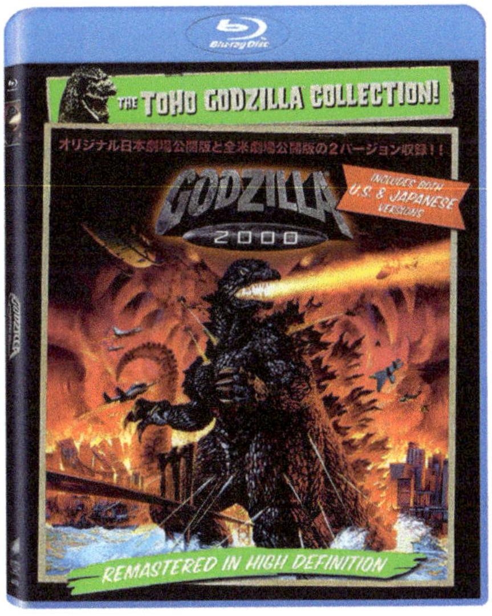

onto Blu-ray. These are all mostly 1080p HD masters and look pretty good, all things considered. Many of these films never received cinema screenings outside of Japan, so they tend not to be as well known even to fans as the more widely televised and screened Showa Era movies. All of the releases are bare-bones, with no real extra features - just a trailer or two. These are all US only releases, available in 2-Movie Blu-ray Packs from Sony (USA)

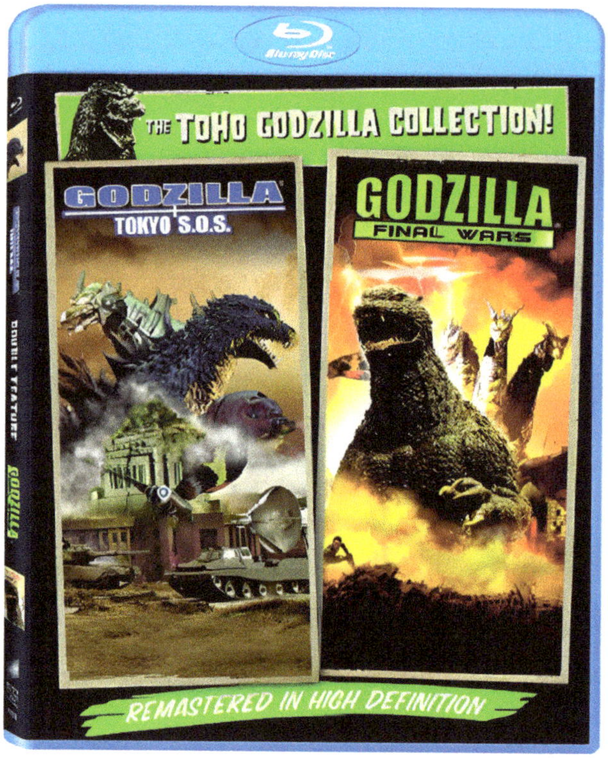

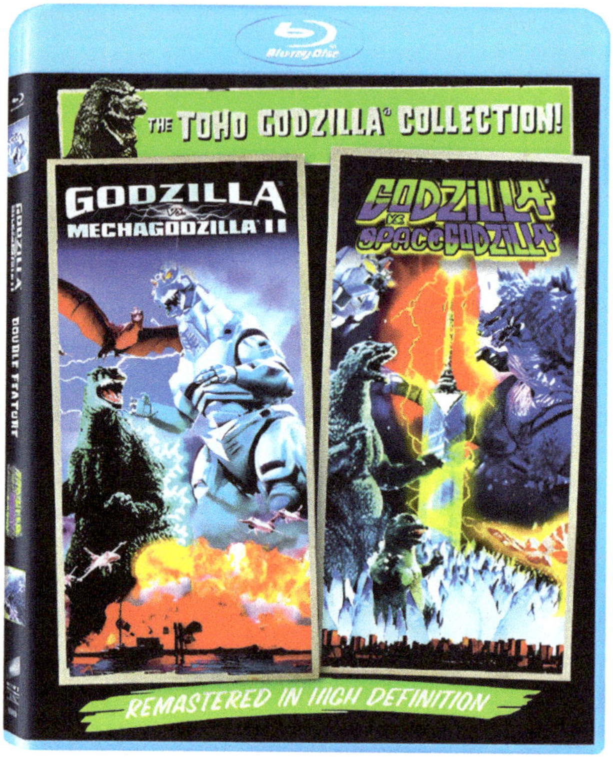

Pack A - *Godzilla Vs Mechagodzilla / Godzilla, Mothra, and King Ghidorah: Giant Monsters All-Out Attack.*
Pack B - *Godzilla vs Destoroyah / Godzilla vs Megaguirus.*
Pack C - *Godzilla 2000* Blu-ray
Pack D - *Godzilla: Final Wars / Godzilla: Tokyo S.O.S.*
Pack E - *Godzilla vs Mechagodzilla II / Godzilla vs SpaceGodzilla.*

Godzilla: Planet of the Monsters / City on the Edge of Battle / The Planet Eater

The three feature length animated Godzilla films produced in recent years have only been released onto physical media in their native Japan. Netflix secured the worldwide rights to the films, so for the time being they are only available to view on Netflix, though there are a boat-load of Chinese bootleg discs floating around eBay. But if you really want the sets for your shelf, the Japanese collectors editions of the three features are beautiful. But, as with all Japanese Blu-rays and DVDs, they have no English subs: time to start those Japanese lessons on Duolingo!

And finally: those that (some of us) shall NOT really speak of....

Godzilla (1998), Godzilla vs Kong, Godzilla x Kong: The New Empire

If you're a real completist, or a sadistic maniac who loves to make your eyeballs suffer, the 1998 American *Godzilla*, produced by Dean Devlin and Roland Emmerich, does also have a 4K release in the USA and a regular Blu-ray in the UK, with a smattering of extras on both versions.

The more recent Kong-centric MonsterVerse movies have, for me, really dropped the ball, and given just how magnificent a movie *Godzilla Minus One* is, they really pale in comparison. Both *Godzilla vs Kong* and *Godzilla x Kong: The New Empire* have premium releases from Manta Lab (as does *Kong: Skull Island)* but I had limited space for this breakdown and opted not to highlight them too much.

The upcoming *Godzilla x Kong: Supernova* is slated to be released in 2027, but by that time there is a very good chance that Takashi Yamazaki will have made his *Minus One* sequel and that's where all our hopes and attention should be focused on!

If you want to know more, you can find me over on YouTube offering up physical media news and updates, unboxing new 4K and Blu-ray releases, and reviewing movies and Blu-rays at:

www.youtube.com/thefanaticaldragon

And for the time being, that's all, folks!

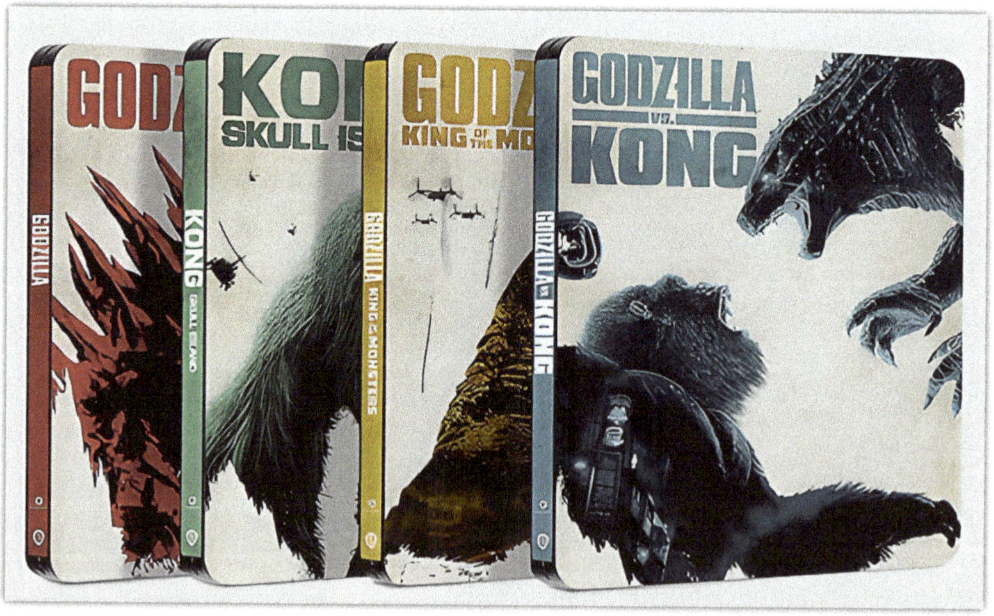

NEXT ISSUE: ACTION MOVIES! STOP-MOTION MOVIES! HORROR MOVIES! ALL KINDS OF MOVIES!

www.ingramcontent.com/pod-product-compliance
Ingram Content Group UK Ltd.
Pitfield, Milton Keynes, MK11 3LW, UK
UKHW062001290726
14090UKWH00021B/1319